Quick Reference to Clinical Dietetics

Lucinda K. Lysen, RD/LD, RN, BSN
Registered Dietitian In Private Practice
Stuart, Florida

AN ASPEN PUBLICATION®
Aspen Publishers, Inc.
Gaithersburg, Maryland
1997

Library of Congress Cataloging-in-Publication Data

Quick reference to clinical dietetics / [edited by] Lucinda K. Lysen
p.   cm.
Includes bibliographical references and index.
ISBN 0-8342-0629-3
1. Dietetics—Handbooks, manuals, etc. 2. Diet therapy—
Handbooks, manuals, etc. I. Lysen, Lucinda K.
[DNLM: 1. Dietetics—handbooks. WB 39 Q5 1997]
RM217.2.Q53 1997
615.8′54—dc21
DNLM/DLC
for Library of Congress
96-50455
CIP

Aspen Publishers, Inc., grants permission for photocopying for limited personal or internal use. This consent does not extend to other kinds of copying, such as copying for general distribution, for advertising or promotional purposes, for creating new collective works, or for resale. For information, address Aspen Publishers, Inc., Permissions Department, 200 Orchard Ridge Drive, Suite 200, Gaithersburg, Maryland 20878.

Orders: (800) 638-8437
Customer Service: (800) 234-1660

About Aspen Publishers • For more than 35 years, Aspen has been a leading profes-sional publisher in a variety of disciplines. Aspen's vast information resources are avail-able in both print and electronic formats. We are committed to providing the highest quality information available in the most appropriate format for our customers. Visit Aspen's Internet site for more information resources, directories, articles, and a search-able version of Aspen's full catalog, including the most recent publications: **http:// www.aspenpub.com**
Aspen Publishers, Inc. • The hallmark of quality in publishing
Member of the worldwide Wolters Kluwer group

Aspen Publishers, Inc., is not affiliated with the American Society of Parenteral and Enteral Nutrition.

The authors have made every effort to ensure the accuracy of the information herein. However, appropriate information sources should be consulted, especially for new or unfamiliar proce-dures. It is the responsibility of every practitioner to evaluate the appropriateness of a particular opinion in the context of actual clinical situations and with due considerations to new develop-ments. Authors, editors, and the publisher cannot be held responsible for any typographical or other errors founds in this book.

Editorial Resources: Gregory M. Balas
Library of Congress Catalog Card Number: 96-50455
ISBN: 0-8342-0629-3

Printed in the United States of America

1   2   3   4   5

This book was written
in memory of my beloved,
Jerry R. Kramer, M.D.,
who made a lifetime
of contributions to medicine
and nutrition in just a
few brief years.

Born June 27, 1951–Died January 15, 1994

Table of Contents

Contributors

Stacey J. Bell, DSc, RD
Instructor in Surgery
Harvard Medical School
Research Dietitian
Surgical Metabolism Laboratory
Beth Israel Deaconess Medical Center
Boston, Massachusetts

Lucille Beseler, MS, RD, CS, LD
Board Certified Specialist in Pediatric Nutrition
Private Practice dedicated to Infants, Children,
    and Adolescents
Margate, Florida

Chris Biesemeier, MS, RD, LD
Clinical Nutrition Manager
Nutrition Services
Saint Luke's Hospital
Kansas City, Missouri

Bruce R. Bistrian, MD, PhD
Professor of Medicine
Harvard Medical School
Chief, Clinical Nutrition
Beth Israel Deaconess Medical Center
Boston, Massachusetts

George L. Blackburn, MD, PhD
Chief, Section of Surgical Nutrition
Department of Surgery
Beth Israel Deaconess Medical Center,
    West Campus
Boston, Massachusetts

Abby S. Bloch, PhD, RD, FADA
Coordinator, Clinical Research
GI/Nutrition Service
Memorial Sloan-Kettering Cancer Center
New York, New York

Peter Burke, MD
Assistant Professor in Surgery
Harvard Medical School
Department of Surgery
Beth Israel Deaconess Medical Center
Boston, Massachusetts

Kathleen A. Burk-Shull, MEd, RD
PA Student
Saint Francis College
Loretto, Pennsylvania

Karen Buzby, RD
Nutrition Consultant
Bala Cynwyd, Pennsylvania

Pamela Charney, MS, RD, CNSD
Bassett Healthcare
Cooperstown, New York

Ronni Chernoff, PhD, RD, FADA
Associate Director
Geriatric Research Education and Clinical
    Center
Professor, Nutrition and Dietetics
John L. McClellan Memorial Veterans Hospital
College of Health Related Professions
University of Arkansas for Medical Sciences
Little Rock, Arkansas

Judith A. Fish, MMSc, RD, CNSD
Nutrition Support Dietitian
Nutrition/Gastroenterology
Geisinger Medical Center
Danville, Pennsylvania

Sharlene Gaffka
Eastern Michigan University
Ypsilanti, Michigan

Sharon L. Gallagher, MEd, RD, CDE
Nutritionist
Harvard Pilgrim Health Care
Quincy, Massachusetts

**Michele Morath Gottschlich, PhD, RD,
    CNSD**
Director, Nutrition Services
Shriners Burns Institute
Cincinnati, Ohio

Coral R. Grigas, RD, CNSD, LD*
Clinical Dietitian
Martin Memorial Hospital South
Stuart, Florida

Jeanette Hasse, PhD, RD, FADA, CNSD
Transplant Nutrition Specialist
Baylor Institute of Transplantation Sciences
Baylor University Medical Center
Dallas, Texas

Carol S. Ireton-Jones, PhD, RD, LD, CNSD
Nutrition Therapy Specialist
Carrollton, Texas

Lucinda K. Lysen, RD, RN, BSN
Registered Dietitian Consultant
Stuart, Florida

Edward A. Mascioli, MD
Assistant Professor of Medicine
Harvard Medical School
Cambridge, Massachusetts

Laura E. Matarese, MS, RD, LD, FADA, CNSD
Manager, Nutrition Support Dietetics
Cleveland Clinic Foundation
Cleveland, Ohio

Jo Ann McCrae, MS, RD, CNSD
Nutrition Support Consultant
Philadelphia, Pennsylvania

Kathy Pesce-Hammond, MD, RD, LD, CNSD, RN, C
Clinical Nutrition Specialist/Consultant
Atlanta, Georgia

Janice Raymond, MS, RD, CNSD
Manager of Enteral/Part B Services
Northwest Pharmaceutical Services
Port Orchard, Washington

Susan R. Roberts, MS, RD, LD, CNSD
Clinical Dietitian
Baylor University Medical Center
Dallas, Texas

Michelle M. Romano, RD, LD, CNSD
Clinical Dietitian/Nutritionist
Nutrition Services
Martin Memorial Medical Center
Stuart, Florida

Patricia Queen Samour, MMSc, RD
Director
Department of Dietetics
Beth Israel Deaconess Medical Center,
    West Campus
Boston, Massachusetts

Denise B. Schwartz, MS, RD, FADA, CNSD
Nutrition Support Specialist
Food and Nutrition Services
Providence Saint Joseph Medical Center
Burbank, California

Deborah Silverman, MS, RD, LD, FADA
Assistant Professor/Program Director
Human Nutrition Programs
Eastern Michigan University
Ypsilanti, Michigan

Kathy Stone, MBA, RD, FADA, CDE
Owner, Strictly Nutrition
Boca Raton, Florida

Wendy S. Swails, RD, CNSD
Research Dietitian
Beth Israel Deaconess Medical Center
Boston, Massachusetts

Joan R. Ullrich, RD
Nutrition Coordinator
Home Enteral Program
UCLA Home Care Pharmacy
University of California Los Angeles Medical
    Center
Los Angeles, California

Christina J. Valentine, MS, RD, LD
Instructor in Pediatrics
Neonatal Nutritionist
Department of Pediatrics
Baylor College of Medicine
Houston, Texas

Christine Wanke, MD
Assistant Professor of Medicine
Harvard Medical School
Infectious Disease, Department of Medicine
Beth Israel Deaconess Medical Center
Boston, Massachusetts

Marion F. Winkler, MS, RD, LDN, CNSD
Surgical Nutrition Specialist
Department of Surgery and Nutritional
Support Service
Rhode Island Hospital and Brown
    University
Providence, Rhode Island

*Thanks to Ms. Grigas for her contributions in
 reviewing sections of this book.*

Introduction

In today's environment of health care reform and managed care, practitioners who are committed to providing high quality care must pay close attention to the value of nutrition. In the acute care setting, nutrition intervention does reduce length of stay, mortality and morbidity, and other complications, particularly associated with malnutrition and weight loss. Nutrition intervention also affects the quality of a patient's life. Patients are discharged much sooner than ever before with a concurrent increased use and need for more high technological therapies such as parenteral and enteral nutrition in home care. Sicker patients are being discharged to subacute, rehabilitation, transition care, or long-term care facilities more than ever before. Caregivers in these settings require new skills and knowledge bases for providing high quality care including nutrition. The practitioner today, and in the future, needs to know more than the nutrition management issues specific to each patient's medical condition(s). Other skills are essential for managing more complex patients who require parenteral and/or enteral nutrition. Nutritional needs must be determined and suitable products, equipment, and supplies must be evaluated and selected for each patient. The health care provider must also keep updated on the latest literature, legislative issues that affect the health care arena, and other subjects such as reimbursement, critical pathways, and case management.

This book is divided into several sections in a logical progressive order from the management of patients with various diseases/conditions to nutrition support, discharge planning, and management of the patient outside the hospital setting. Basic guidelines for normal nutrition, neonatal nutrition, and feeding the pediatric patient are included in the text. Numerous diets, charts, tables, algorithms, and other general resources are provided at the end of the book.

The disease/disorder specific sections in Chapter 3 have been written to focus attention on the latest approaches to nutrition management of numerous conditions such as acquired immune deficiency syndrome (AIDS), obesity, and transplantation. The section on nutrition support addresses specific and practical issues relating to using parenteral and enteral nutrition, as well as transitional feedings. Some of the newer health care topics of case management and clinical pathways are addressed later in the book. Since discharge planning starts with a patient's admission and is often under the direction of a case manager, all health care providers must work together to meet the goals for each patient. As such, the dietitian is actively involved in clinical pathways, determining needed services after discharge, and handling reimbursement issues with the patient, case manager, and other involved parties. Once the patient is discharged from the hospital, the continuum of care does not stop. To ensure quality health care and positive outcome, nutrition management must continue into the home or other setting.

This book is an easy to use and concise reference on clinical dietetics in the hospital and home setting. The reader, whether a health care practitioner, student, or teacher will find this book comprehensive and up-to-date.

George L. Blackburn
Patricia Queen Samour
Beth Israel Deaconess Medical Center

CHAPTER 1

Screening and Assessment

- Nutrition Screening
- Nutrition Assessment

Nutrition Screening

Lucinda K. Lysen

DESCRIPTION

Nutrition screening should be required for any patient in the hospital, receiving home care, or at an extended-care facility. Screening identifies the patient at nutritional risk and the steps required for nutrition consultation and nutrition assessment. An ongoing nutrition screening will alert the health care practitioner to changes in patient condition that will ultimately affect nutrition status. The objective of nutrition screening is to identify risk factors that can lead to nutrition compromise.

INITIAL SCREENING

Initial screening with the patient and/or significant other should cover the following areas:

- physical ability to ingest food
- food tolerance and/or intolerance
- previous diet history and/or dietary modifications
- change in weight/weight history
- alcohol use/abuse
- polypharmacy
- possible food/drug interactions

REVIEW OF MEDICAL HISTORY

A review of medical history should cover the following areas:

- Past and current diagnoses and/or problem list that may alter nutrition status of the patient
  1. changes in requirements for certain nutrients due to respiratory, cardiac, gastrointestinal, and other diseases
  2. any interference with the ability to ingest or digest food, absorb nutrients, or excrete waste
- Objective evidence of nutrition status
  1. weight history
     - weight at admission
     - height
     - usual body weight
     - percentage of weight change
  2. laboratory data
     - serum albumin level
     - hemoglobin and hematocrit
     - disease-specific blood work
  3. physical assessment (see Physical Assessment section in Chapter 3)
     - edema/skin turgor
     - cachexia/muscle wasting

1

–obesity
–presence of lesions/wounds/pressure sores
–skin color
• Medical treatments that may affect nutritional status
  1. drug/nutrient interactions
  2. chemotherapy
  3. radiation therapy
  4. dialysis
  5. surgery
• Type of diet patient is ingesting
  1. number of days NPO
  2. oral supplementation
  3. enteral tube feeding
  4. parenteral nutrition

RISK IDENTIFICATION

Nutritional risk is based upon results of nutrition screening. Patients identified as being at nutritional risk need nutrition assessment. Patients not at nutritional risk are periodically reevaluated on the basis of criteria established by the individual institution.

Specialized nutrition support may be required in the following instances:

• poor nutrient intake—inability to meet nutrient and food requirements for greater than 5 days
• weight loss
  a. unintentional weight loss of 10% of usual weight in 6 months, or
  b. involuntary weight loss of greater than 5 lb in 1 month
• serum albumin level of less than 3.5 g/dL

REFERENCE

Winkler MF, Lysen LK. *Suggested Guidelines for Nutrition and Metabolic Management of Adult Patients Receiving Nutrition Support.* Chicago, Ill: American Dietetic Association; 1993:2–5.

Nutrition Assessment

Lucinda K. Lysen

DESCRIPTION

The purpose of nutrition assessment is to investigate the nutrition status of the patient when nutrition screening indicates the need for comprehensive nutrition consultation. Nutrition assessment enables one to determine the safest, most convenient, and most economical means by which nutrient intake can be provided to the patient. It also enables one to manage the nutritionally compromised patient for the best nutritional outcome.

Areas of nutrition assessment are listed below.

COMPREHENSIVE INTERVIEW WITH THE PATIENT AND/OR SIGNIFICANT OTHER

• Extent and duration of physical factors affecting food ingestion
• Exploration of food tolerances and intolerances
  1. appetite changes
  2. anorexia
  3. difficulty swallowing
  4. gastrointestinal compromise, such as vomiting, nausea, diarrhea, or malabsorption
  5. food allergies or aversions

- Previous diet history, including the use of nutrition supplements and prior use of enteral and parenteral support
- Estimation of nutrient intake based on diet history
- Weight history
  1. usual body weight
  2. history of weight loss or gain and time frame

REVIEW OF MEDICAL MANAGEMENT OF THE PATIENT

- Medical diagnoses and/or problem list
  1. indications for medical nutrition therapy
  2. disease-specific problems requiring adjustments in nutrient intake
  3. indications for enteral nutrition support, such as cancer of the head or neck, chewing disorders, difficulty swallowing, tooth or jaw injuries, or benign obstructions of the upper gastrointestinal tract
- Metabolic gastrointestinal tract dysfunction, such as pancreatitis, radiation enteritis, or chemotherapy that would impair the ability to digest some nutrients
- Increased metabolism, causing an increase in nutrient needs beyond the level that can be achieved by regular oral means
- Respiratory failure
- Anorexia
- Psychiatric disorders
- Neurologic disorders
- Cardiac and/or pulmonary disorders/cachexia

REVIEW OF CONTRAINDICATIONS TO ORAL OR ENTERAL NUTRITION

- Intractable vomiting
- Upper gastrointestinal hemorrhage
- Severe intractable diarrhea
- Intestinal obstruction
- Upper gastrointestinal high-output fistula
- Pertinent laboratory data
  1. blood glucose level

  2. blood urea nitrogen (BUN) level/creatinine level
  3. electrolyte abnormalities
  4. serum albumin level
  5. hemoglobin and hematocrit levels

CRITERIA TO EVALUATE

- Review of systems
  1. cardiac
  2. pulmonary
  3. renal
  4. hepatic
  5. gastrointestinal
  6. endocrine
- Enteral nutrition risk profile
  1. aspiration
  2. dehydration
  3. diarrhea
- Anthropometric evaluation
  1. weight on admission, usual body weight, desirable body weight, ideal body weight
  2. height
  3. body mass index (see Body Mass Index in Appendix H)
- Physical assessment
  1. cachexia/muscle wasting
  2. obesity
  3. edema/skin turgor
  4. ascites
  5. dehydration
  6. skin lesions and/or pressure sores
  7. signs of vitamin and/or mineral deficiencies

Refer to the section on Physical Assessment in Chapter 3 for more specific details.

REFERENCE

Winkler MF, Lysen LK. *Suggested Guidelines for Nutrition and Metabolic Management of Adult Patients Receiving Nutrition Support.* Chicago, Ill: American Dietetic Association; 1993:6–9.

Physical Assessment

Kathy Pesce-Hammond

DESCRIPTION

Physical examination is part of a comprehensive approach to the assessment of nutritional status. Key information is gathered through interviewing, observation, and hands-on examination techniques and measurements.

EXAMINATION TECHNIQUES

Inspection

- Critical observation to assess color, shape, texture, and size
- Most frequently used technique
- Uses the senses of smell, sight, and hearing

Palpation

- Touching to assess texture, temperature, size, and mobility of a body part
- Two types:
  1. Light—uses the fingertips for maximum sensitivity
  2. Deep—uses the hand for heavier pressure

Percussion

- Palpation by tapping fingers and hands quickly and sharply against body surfaces
- Produces sounds to locate the border, shape, and position of organs
- Determines if an organ is solid or filled with fluid or gas
- Two types:
  1. Direct—tapping the fingertips or hand directly against the body structure
  2. Indirect—using the nondominant hand as the stationary hand while hyperextending the middle finger and placing the distal portion against the skin; the middle finger of the dominant hand is used to strike against the hyperextended middle finger

Auscultation

- Last technique to be used in assessment (except when assessing the abdomen, in which it is performed after inspection)
- The stethoscope is used to listen to different sounds produced by lungs, heart, liver, and intestines

INSTRUMENTS

- Thermometer
- Stethoscope
- Sphygmomanometer
- Penlight
- Wooden tongue depressor
- Tape measure/ruler
- Scales
- Skin calipers
- Reflex hammer
- Nasoscope
- Otoscope
- Cotton balls
- Magnifying glass

PREPARATION

- Gather all needed equipment.
- Provide privacy for the client.
- Expose only the area being examined.
- Explain purpose and each process as the examination progresses.

ASSESSMENT

General Survey

- Reflects overall nutritional status
- Notes general state of health including orientation, speech, body type, and mobility
- Notes signs of nutritional depletion, such as skeletal muscle wasting, especially in the quadriceps and deltoids; subcutaneous fat

wasting in the face, triceps, thighs, and waist; and overall weight loss

Anthropometric Measurements (also see Appendix D)

- Height
- Weight, including usual, ideal, and current. Usual body weight is more useful than ideal weight in ill populations. Percent deviation from usual weight assists in determining degree of malnutrition.
- Knee-height calipers can be used to estimate height and weight measurements for non-ambulatory patients, especially in the home, where weights may be difficult to impossible to obtain.
- Body mass index (BMI): determined by weight in kilograms divided by height in meters squared (see BMI chart in Appendix H)
- Waist-hip ratio: a measure that correlates with risk for diabetes mellitus, stroke, coronary artery disease, and early mortality if over 0.8 for women or over 1.0 for men
- Subcutaneous fat measurements (triceps, biceps, subscapular, and suprailiac skinfolds): a measure of somatic fat stores
- Midarm muscle circumference: a measure of skeletal protein mass

Vital Signs

- Temperature
- Pulse
- Respiration
- Blood pressure

Skin

- Inspect/palpate for the following: color changes, pigmentation, lesions, and bruises. Also assess texture, moisture, temperature, and turgor. Assess wounds and ulcers for size, color, drainage, smell, and warmth.
- Skin should be warm, dry, and smooth to the touch, pinkish in color, and without color changes, lesions, bruises, or rashes. Skin is the first line of defense.

Nails

- Inspect/palpate the nails for the following: color, shape, contour, angle, lesions, and circulation.
- The nail plate is pink in the white population and bluish in dark-skinned populations.
- The nail surface should be smooth with a translucent plate. The surface may be flat or slightly curved. When squeezed, the nail should appear white and then return to its pinkish color when released.

Hair

- Inspect/palpate for the following: color, shine, quantity, and texture.
- Hair should be consistent in color, quantity, and texture. Natural shine should be present.

Face

- Inspect/palpate for the following: color, lesions, texture, and moisture.
- Face should be consistent in color, warm and dry, pinkish in color, smooth, and without lesions.
- Assessment of cranial nerve V (trigeminal) is performed by having the patient clench teeth and noting muscle contraction. Cranial nerve VII (facial) is tested by having the patient show upper and lower teeth. These nerves are important in the eating process.

Eyes

- Inspect/palpate for the following: moisture; color of surrounding skin; condition of conjunctiva, cornea, and sclera.
- The skin surrounding the eye should be warm, dry, and consistent in color. The conjunctiva should be red and without drainage. The sclera is normally white, and the cornea is clear without opacities.

Nose: Internal and External

- Inspect/palpate for the following: shape, discharge, patency, septum deviation, and condition of mucous membranes.
- Note any discharge from the nose, including color and consistency.
- Do internal inspection by tilting the head slightly back and assessing nasal passages for patency; lack of patency may influence the passage of enteral feeding devices.
- Mucous membranes should be pink.

Jaws

- Inspect/palpate for the following: opening and closing of the jaw, movement from side to side, and condition of the parotid gland.
- The upper and lower front teeth should align, and the jaw should be able to move from side to side without making a "popping" sound. This is important in assessing chewing ability. Also assess the parotid gland, located anterior to the ear lobes, for enlargement.

Lips

- Inspect/palpate for the following: color, symmetry, and lesions.
- The lips should be pink, symmetrical, and without lesions.

Tongue

- Inspect/palpate for the following: symmetry, color, moisture, and texture.
- Inspection is performed by having the patient stick the tongue out. Symmetry can then be noted if the tongue protrudes in midline without deviations or tremors. The tongue should be pink and should appear moist. The tongue is slightly rough in texture from taste buds present.

Buccal Mucosa

- Inspect/palpate for the following: color, moisture, and lesions.

- The oral mucosa should have a pink or red undertone in white populations and may have a bluish undertone in black populations. The mucosa should appear moist and smooth without lesions.
- Assess the gag reflex by touching the back of the pharynx with a tongue blade to elicit a response.

Teeth

- Inspect/palpate for the following: color, state of repair, absence, and inflammation.
- The teeth should be some shade of white in a state of good repair without mottling or patches noted. No inflammation should be present.

Gums

- Inspect/palpate for the following: color, moisture, and lesions.
- The gums should be pink and moist, without lesions or sponginess noted.

Neck

- Inspect/palpate for the following: neck vein distention, condition of the thyroid gland, parotid gland, and presence of feeding devices.
- The neck veins should be flat and nondistended. Assess the thyroid gland by standing behind the patient, placing the right fingers between the trachea and sternomastoid muscle, and, while slightly retracting the muscle, asking patient to swallow. Repeat for the left side. The thyroid should move slightly up. No hardened nodules or growths should be present.
- Feeding devices should be noted.

Thorax

- Inspect/palpate for the following: muscle development and respiratory rate, depth, and rhythm.
- Auscultate for breath sounds. Breath sounds should be clear with high quality.

- Assess the thorax for adequate muscle and fat stores. Respiratory rate should be within a normal range (adults = ~ 16–20 breaths/minute). Depth should be even and rhythm regular.
- When auscultated, the breath sounds should be clear with a high quality.

Heart

- Inspect for the following: muscle and fat wasting and the presence and condition of vascular access and surrounding skin.
- Adequate muscle and fat stores should be noted in the general assessment, including the supraclavicular and temporal areas of the body.
- Auscultate heart sounds for presence of normal and abnormal sounds and evaluation of rate and rhythm.

Abdomen

- Inspect for the following: color, warmth, moisture, symmetry, contour, shape, and muscle development; placement and inversion of umbilicus; movements and presence of any feeding devices and/or ostomies. The abdomen should be pink, warm, and dry. The abdomen should be symmetrical bilaterally; contour may range from flat to rounded, depending upon nutritional status, gas, and the presence of fluid. The umbilicus should be midline and inverted. Feeding devices and/or ostomies should be noted, including condition of device, drainage, inflammation, or swelling.
- Auscultate for bowel sounds, using a stethoscope. Dividing the abdomen in four quadrants, begin to listen for bowel sounds in the right lower quadrant where the iliocecal valve is located. Proceed in a clockwise position around the abdomen. Normal bowel sounds occur 5–34 times per minute and are high pitched, with gurgling sounds occurring at irregular intervals. Bowel function such as diarrhea or constipation should also be assessed.

- Percuss the four quadrants to assess the density of abdominal contents. Tympany is present over the intestines, indicating the presence of air and over the stomach, since a gastric air bubble is present. Solid organs and masses produce a dull sound.
- Palpate all four quadrants lastly to determine the size and location of specific organs and the presence of tenderness or pain. Perform light palpation in all four quadrants, using circular motions. The liver may be palpated if necessary. No masses or tenderness should be present.

Renal

- Inspect urine for color and turbidity.
- Urine is normally yellow to amber-yellow in color and clear in appearance.

Musculoskeletal

- Inspect/palpate for fat stores, muscle mass, range of motion, and joint changes, swelling, pain, and tenderness. Also assess motor skills.
- Adequate fat and muscle stores should be present. Triceps skinfold measurements and midarm muscle circumference measurements can assist in this determination. In addition, examination of the gastrocnemius muscle for muscle mass is appropriate along with examination of the deltoid muscle. Degree of mobility of the fingers, wrist, hand, elbow, and shoulder can indicate the need for adaptive equipment to assist with eating.
- No pain, swelling, or tenderness should be present.

Neurological

- Inspect for the following: mental alertness, orientation, motor status, coordination, weakness, and reflexes.
- Observation during general conversation will reveal alertness and orientation. Assess motor status by observing gait and performance with utensils. Hand-to-mouth coordination can eas-

ily be observed during mealtime. Any weakness should be noted.

- Assess reflexes to note central nervous system functioning. A reflex hammer may be used. Reflexes to assess include the biceps, brachioradialis, and patella. Reflexes are graded from 0 to 4, where 2+ is normal response, 0 is absence of response, and 4+ is hyperactivity.

PROBLEMS

General Survey

- Loss of weight, muscle mass, and fat stores
- Excess fat stores in obesity
- Anemia and fatigue

Skin

- Poor wound healing, decubitus ulcers
- Red, swollen, and/or with lesions
- Rash, pellagrous dermatitis
- Bleeding, poor skin turgor
- Xerosis (dry, shedding skin) and follicular hyperkeratosis (spinelike plaques that feel like sandpaper on the buttocks, thighs, elbows, and knees)
- Lesions with irregular borders, asymmetry, or unusual size, color, and/or diameter (usually non-nutritional related)

Nails

- Koilonychia (spoon-shaped, concave nails); be sure to rule out any cardiopulmonary disease
- Dull and lackluster appearance, with transverse ridging across the nail plate
- Bruising and bleeding
- Pallor, poor blanching, irregular shape

Hair

- Lack of shine, luster; thin and sparse distribution with wide gaps between hairs; alopecia
- Dyspigmentation (R/O bleaching)

- Easily plucked hair
- Alternating bands of light and dark hair (Flag sign)
- Corkscrew hair

Face

- Diffuse pigmentation
- Swelling
- Moon face
- Paresthesia
- Temporal wasting
- Maxillary wasting

Eyes

- Visual changes
- Bitot's spots
- Conjunctival xerosis (inner lids and whites are dull and dry in appearance)
- Keratomalacia (softening of the cornea)
- Pale conjunctiva
- Angular palpebritis (cracked corners of the eye)
- Corneal arcus (grayish-white ring or arc surrounding cornea due to lipid deposition)
- Xanthelsasma (soft, raised yellow plaques on the eyelids)

Nose

- Seborrhea
- Obstruction; deviated septum
- Inflamed mucous membranes

Jaws

- Malocclusion
- Enlarged parotid gland (bilateral)

Lips

- Cheilosis (vertical cracks, red, swollen)
- Angular stomatitis (cracks and redness at corner of mouth)

Tongue

- Asymmetry
- Atrophic filiform papillae
- Glossitis (beefy red, atrophied tongue)
- Magenta or scarlet color
- Fissures

Mucous Membranes

- Pallor
- Lesions
- Texture

Teeth

- Mottling
- Decay
- Missing teeth; poor teeth repair
- Inflammation

Gums

- Sponginess
- Receding gumline
- Bleeding
- Lesions

Neck

- Distended veins
- Enlarged thyroid

Thorax

- Depressed muscle mass
- Decreased muscle strength
- Shortness of breath
- Fatigue
- Decline in pulmonary function

Cardiac

- Heart failure, irritability, other disease
- Volume overload
- Hyperlipidemia

Gastrointestinal

- Anorexia, nausea
- Vomiting
- Diarrhea
- Constipation
- Absent bowel sounds
- Sluggish bowel sounds
- Hyperactive bowel sounds
- Poor wound healing
- Scaphoid abdomen (loss of subcutaneous fat)
- Protuberant abdomen (obesity, gaseous distention)
- Ascites
- Pain

Urinary

- Dark, concentrated urine
- Light, dilute urine
- Presence of blood in urine

Musculoskeletal

- Rickets
- Craniotabes (softening of back and sides of skull in infants less than 1 year of age)
- Enlargement of epiphyses
- Osteomalacia
- Osteoporosis
- Muscle wasting
- Fat store depletion
- Painful, swollen joints
- Limited range of motion

Neurological

- Listlessness, apathy
- Confusion
- Dementia
- Paresthesia in hands and feet
- Lack of coordination
- Tetany
- Hyperactive reflexes
- Hypoactive reflexes

Mucous Membranes

- Iron and B$_6$ for microcytic anemia
- Folate for macrocytic anemia
- B$_{12}$ for megaloblastic anemia

Teeth

- Adequate fluoride
- Avoiding excess simple sugars

Gums

- Vitamin C to maintain healthy tissues

Neck

- Adequate iodine to prevent thyroid enlargement
- Maintenance of appropriate fluid status

Thorax

- Adequate protein to maintain muscle mass and strength
- Adequate calories and phosphorus to provide necessary energy

Cardiac

- Adequate protein, calories, thiamine, phosphorus, selenium, potassium, calcium, and magnesium for cardiac muscle
- Maintenance of fluid balance
- Avoidance of excess fat intake

Gastrointestinal/Hepatic

- Adequate magnesium and B$_{12}$ for anorexia
- Adequate fluid and fiber for bowel function
- Appropriate access for feeding: small-bowel option for feeding in many cases of gastric paresis, vomiting, early postoperative feeding
- Protein, calories, zinc, and vitamin C to promote wound healing
- Maintenance of appropriate fluid status and sodium and chloride balance with ascites

Urinary

- Giving adequate fluid for age and disease state to prevent dark, concentrated urine
- Avoiding excess fluid intake to prevent light, dilute urine

Musculoskeletal

- Adequate vitamin D and calcium to ensure proper bone development and prevention of rickets, osteomalacia, and osteoporosis
- Adequate vitamin C for joints
- Adequate protein for growth

Nervous System

- Protein to maintain alertness and prevent listlessness, apathy, and confusion
- Pantothenic acid, biotin, and folate for lethargy
- Thiamine to assist with mental confusion, weakness, and peripheral neuropathy (beriberi)
- B$_6$ to treat polyneuritis
- Niacin and B$_{12}$ to assist in prevention of dementia
- Calcium and magnesium to prevent tetany, tremors, and some behavioral disturbances

---

REFERENCES

Bates B, Bickley LS, Hoekelman RA, eds. *A Guide to Physical Examination and History Taking.* 6th ed. Philadelphia, Pa: JB Lippincott Co; 1995.

Cecere C, McCash K. Health history and physical examination. In: *Medical-Surgical Nursing.* St Louis, Mo: CV Mosby; 1992:29–49.

Curtas S, Chapman G, Meguid NM. Evaluation of nutritional status. *Nurs Clin North Am.* 1989;24:301–313.

Czajka-Narin DM. The assessment of nutritional status. In: Mahan LK, Arlin M, eds. *Krause's Food, Nutrition, and Diet Therapy.* Philadelphia, Pa: WB Saunders Co; 1992: 293–313.

Flory C. Skin assessment. *RN.* June 1992:22–26.2

Fuller J, Schaller-Ayers J, eds. *Health Assessment: A Nursing Approach.* 2nd ed. Philadelphia, Pa: JB Lippincott Co; 1994:115–184.

Grant A. *Nutrition Assessment Guidelines.* Seattle, Wash: Northgate Station; 1979.

Herbert J. Health history and physical assessment. In: Bauxbaum BS, Mauro E, Norris CG, eds. *Illustrated Manual of Nursing Practice.* 2nd ed. Springhouse, Pa: Springhouse; 1994:48–75.

Hopkins B. Assessment of nutritional status. In: Gottschlich MM, Matarese L E, Shronts EP, eds. *Nutrition Support Dietetics Core Curriculum.* 2nd ed. Silver Spring, Md: American Society for Parenteral and Enteral Nutrition; 1993:15–70.

Jarvis C. *Physical Examination and Health Assessment.* Philadelphia, Pa: WB Saunders Co; 1992.

Konstantinides N. Nutritional care. In: Bauxbaum BS, Mauro E, Norris CG, eds. *Illustrated Manual of Nursing Practice.* 2nd ed. Springhouse, Pa: Springhouse; 1994: 789–835.

Owen G. Physical examination as an assessment tool. In: Simko MD, Cowell C, Gilgride JA, eds. *Nutrition Assessment: A Comprehensive Guide for Planning Intervention,* 2nd ed. Gaithersburg, Md: Aspen Publishers, Inc; 1995: 85–90.

Poncar PJ. Who has time for a head to toe assessment? *Nurs.* 1995;25:59.

Sherman JL, Fields SK. *Guide to Patient Evaluation.* Garden City, NY: Medical Examination; 1982.

Weinsier RI, Morgan SL, eds. *Fundamentals of Clinical Nutrition.* St Louis, Mo: CV Mosby; 1993.

CHAPTER 2

Indirect Calorimetry

Carol S. Ireton-Jones

DESCRIPTION

Indirect calorimetry is the determination of heat production (energy expenditure) through measurements of the oxygen consumption and carbon dioxide production during respiratory gas exchange. Unlike energy expenditure formulas, it measures actual energy expenditure of a specific individual in a specific state of health/disease. Thus it is a valuable clinical tool. It enables the clinician to assess more accurately a patient's energy requirements and thus to make better decisions regarding the patient's dietary program. Because all energy is derived from the oxidation of protein, carbohydrate, and fat and because the amounts of oxygen consumed and carbon dioxide produced are characteristic and constant for each fuel, indirect calorimetry measurements can help to determine not only recommended caloric intake but also proportions of specific nutrients in the diet. The clinician can prevent underfeeding and harmful overfeeding that may lead to hepatic steatosis. The extra carbon dioxide and fluid loads produced as a result of excess nutrient intake exert deleterious effects on patients with impaired ventilator function.

COMPONENTS OF TOTAL DAILY ENERGY EXPENDITURE

- *Basal energy expenditure* or *basal metabolic rate (BMR)* is the approximate energy cost of maintaining basic physiologic activities such as heartbeat, respiration, kidney function, osmotic balance, brain activity, and body temperature. It is determined 12–14 hours after the ingestion of food and with the individual at complete rest.
- *Resting energy expenditure (REE)* includes the BMR and any increases that occur following awakening and with minimal activity.
- *Diet-induced thermogenesis* (the "thermic effect" of food) accounts for a 5%–10% increase above REE in daily energy expenditure. It includes an obligatory process due to the inevitable energy costs of digestion, absorption, and processing or storage of substrates and a component that involves stimulation of the sympathetic nervous system.
- *Shivering* and *nonshivering cold-induced thermogenesis* play a minor role in everyday life. Nonshivering thermogenesis is difficult to demonstrate in adult individuals and therefore is considered to be of little or no consequence in overall daily energy expenditure.
- *Physical activity* adds energy costs that are proportionate to the rate of sustained muscle contraction.
- *Stress from injury or illness* is caused by specific diseases such as acquired immune deficiency syndrome (AIDS) or cancer, by fever, or by the therapeutic interventions of pharmacotherapy and chemotherapy. It also adds energy costs.

PHYSIOLOGY OF ENERGY EXPENDITURE

- The maintenance of body functions is dependent on a constant amount of voluntary and involuntary energy expenditure and varies among individuals.

- Energy expenditure is proportionate to the body surface area and to the percentage of lean body mass.
- Males typically have higher metabolic rates than do females.
- Energy expenditure is generally depressed during starvation and in chronic dieters and anorexics.
- Energy expenditure is higher in people residing in cold climates as compared to those in warmer climates, in the obese, in smokers, and under conditions of stress and disease.

INDIRECT CALORIMETRY PROCEDURE

There are two methods of performing indirect calorimetry:

- *Open-circuit method:* The subject is permitted to breathe air from the environment, while his or her expired air is collected for volumetric measurement by a metabolic cart. The gas volume is then corrected for standard conditions and is analyzed for its oxygen and carbon dioxide content, with a subsequent calculation being done to determine oxygen consumption and carbon dioxide production. This is the method of indirect calorimetry most commonly used today.
- *Closed-circuit method:* The subject is isolated from outside air and breathes from a reservoir containing pure oxygen. The decrease in the gas volume in the closed system is related to the rate of the oxygen consumption.

In either method, the Weir equation is then used to calculate energy expenditure in kcal from the 1-minute volume of oxygen consumed and carbon dioxide produced.

Energy expenditure can be accurately determined under the following standard conditions:

- The patient should be measured when he or she is awake and 2 hours after a meal unless on continuous nutritional support. Water or a noncaloric beverage is acceptable intake before a test. If a patient is on continuous feeding, feeding is not discontinued for the test.
- Measurements should be taken at least 1 hour following strenuous activity such as a dressing change, chest physiotherapy, or physical therapy: ie, a patient must be at rest for 1 hour prior to the test.

The following is a protocol for taking indirect calorimetry measurements:

- The patient is connected to the metabolic cart:
  1. A spontaneously breathing patient is connected to the cart using a canopy.
  2. A ventilator-dependent patient is connected to the cart using a single-piloted exhalation valve to collect expired gas. Inspired gas is sampled on the "dry side" of the ventilator humidifier.
- When measuring pediatric patients or neonates with a metabolic measurement cart, one must use appropriate technique and equipment to account for lower ventilatory volumes.
- Measurements of oxygen consumption and carbon dioxide production are made in 1-minute intervals until a steady state is achieved. This is indicated by 3–5 consecutive 1-minute measurements in which the measured energy expenditures (MEEs; calculated from the Weir equation) are within 10% of each other and the corresponding respiratory quotients (RQs; calculated from the ratio of carbon dioxide produced [VCO_2] to oxygen consumed [VO_2]) are within 5% of each other or by maintenance of the resting state for 10–15 minutes. The 1-minute measurements of MEE and RQ are then averaged.
- Long-term measurements of greater than 2 hours and up to 24 hours can be done with most metabolic carts, depending on the patient's medical status and cooperation.

INTERPRETATION OF RESULTS

- Since MEE represents resting energy expenditure, it may need to be modified to account for daily energy requirements. In general, nutritional support is inadequate when MEE × an activity factor exceeds caloric intake. Adjustments to specific conditions are:

1. Light activity, inactive disease state: MEE × 1.1–1.2
2. Light activity, active disease state: MEE × 1.2–1.5
3. High activity, inactive disease state: MEE × 1.5
4. AIDS: MEE × 1.5–2.0
5. Cancer: MEE × 1.35–1.5

- RQ has been used to determine the efficacy of specific nutritional support regimens for hospitalized patients. Oxidation of each major nutrient class occurs at a known RQ, ranging from 0.7 for fat oxidation to 1.0 for glucose oxidation. Net fat synthesis, and thus overfeeding, can be identified by the occurrence of an RQ greater than 1.0. Nutritional support is inadequate when RQ is less than 0.83 (see box).

RQ (Respiratory Quotient) (specific fuel utilization)	
Substrate	*RQ*
Fat	0.70
Protein	0.80
Carbohydrate	0.95–1.00
Mixed diet	0.85

USES

Hospital

- All patients receiving intensive nutritional support should have their energy expenditure measured using indirect calorimetry as a part of the initial nutritional assessment.
- Patient prioritization for indirect calorimetry:
  1. all intensive care unit (ICU) patients receiving nutrition support
  2. patients receiving parenteral nutrition other than those in the ICU
  3. all other patients
- MEE should be done weekly for ICU patients; all other patients should have their energy expenditures reassessed biweekly unless other-

wise indicated. Any patient's energy expenditure should be reassessed when a significant change affecting the condition occurs, such as a change in the route of nutritional support from parenteral to enteral or in the method of ventilation from mechanical ventilator support to spontaneous breathing.

- Reassessment of MEE should be done following each major surgical procedure, following each change in medical status, or by a standard protocol.

Home

- Because the types and complexity of cases of patients seen at home are increasing, the use of indirect calorimetry in the home can be an important part of initial and follow-up assessments for people who are receiving nutrition support or are at nutritional risk.
- Patients on home total parenteral nutrition may be inadequately nourished if the Harris-Benedict equations are used to estimate their energy requirements. The Harris-Benedict equations were developed from MEEs of adult normal subjects, not acutely ill or chronically ill people.
- Most metabolic carts are too cumbersome and are not portable enough to take into the patient's home. One metabolic cart has been successfully used in home care applications because it is small and because, although heavy, it can be carried into a patient's home.

Other

- Indirect calorimetry can be used not only for patients receiving intensive nutritional support but also for patients whose energy requirements are difficult to assess (obese patients, children).
- Inpatient and outpatient centers dealing with eating disorders will find the assessment of energy expenditure a useful adjunct to therapy.
- Study protocols may be devised to examine segments of the patient population in conjunction with specific diseases or injury.

• Indirect calorimetry may be used in other programs such as wellness programs.

LIMITATIONS OF USE

• A patient who is ventilator dependent receiving pressure support, high-frequency ventilation, or levels of F_{IO2} greater than 60% often cannot be accurately measured.
• In some cases, isolation techniques will prevent the use of the measurement equipment.
• Patient cooperation is necessary for the connection of most spontaneously breathing patients to the metabolic carts.
• Presence of an incompetent tracheal cuff will invalidate the measurement data because of the potential for dilution by room air or other sources of air.
• A patient receiving dialysis should not be measured during treatment.
• A patient with leaking chest tubes should not be measured.
• When indirect calorimetry is not available, appropriate energy equations should be used to predict the energy expenditures of hospitalized and home care patients. Sections in Chapter 3 discuss means to estimate energy requirements for specific conditions, such as disease states, injuries, pregnancy, old age, and prematurity.
• When a steady state is not achieved or there is wide variability in 1-minute measurements of MEE and RQ, this is indicative of an inaccurate indirect calorimetric measurement, and the resulting MEE and RQ data should not be used.

EQUIPMENT

• Metabolic measurement carts
  1. Examples are Horizon System, Delta Trac, the 2900 Energy Measurement System (SensorMedics, Anaheim, California), and the CCM (Medical Graphics Corporation, St. Paul, Minnesota)
  2. Advantages: easy to use, accurate among various operators, reproducible results, instantaneous results, can be used with a variety of patients in many settings
  3. Disadvantages: expensive
  4. Characteristics to consider in selection
     –the population the metabolic cart will be applied to: ventilator-dependent and spontaneously breathing adult and/or pediatric patients
     –the type of measuring technique the metabolic cart uses (mixing chamber or breath by breath)
     –the type and ease of connections to ventilator-dependent patients
     –the type and ease of connections to spontaneously breathing patients (mask, canopy)
     –special considerations such as ease of movement, warranty, training, and support services, both technical and scientific
• Douglas bags/pulmonary physiology lab
  1. Advantages: considered by some to be the "gold standard" for performing indirect calorimetry
  2. Disadvantages: cumbersome; accuracy relies on the operator's skills in obtaining and analyzing the data; results are not usually available quickly; not often used in the hospital or home care settings
• Ventilators that are able to perform indirect calorimetry
  1. Advantages: Patient can be measured 24 hours per day without additional equipment.
  2. Disadvantages: Only the patient using the ventilator can be measured because the indirect calorimetry is part of the ventilator; expensive.

REFERENCES

American Society for Parenteral and Enteral Nutrition. Dietitian specialty session: Indirect calorimetry. In: *18th Clinical Congress Program Manual*. Silver Spring, Md: American Society for Parenteral and Enteral Nutrition; 1994:456–480.

Feurer I, Mullen JL. Bedside measurement of resting energy expenditure and respiratory quotient via indirect calorimetry. *Nutr Clin Pract*. 1986;1:43–49.

Ireton-Jones CS. Indirect calorimetry. In: Skipper A, ed. *The Dietitian's Handbook of Enteral and Parenteral Nutrition.* Rockville, Md: Aspen Publishers, Inc; 1989:205–218.

Ireton-Jones CS, Borman KR, Turner WW. Nutrition considerations in the management of ventilator-dependent patients. *Nutr Clin Pract.* 1993;8:60–64.

Ireton-Jones CS, Long A, Garritson B. The use of indirect calorimetry in the assessment of energy expenditure in patients receiving home nutrition support. *J Am Diet Assoc.* 1994;94(no 9, suppl):A30. Abstract.

Ireton-Jones CS, Turner WW. The use of respiratory quotient to determine the efficacy of nutritional support regimens. *J Am Diet Assoc.* 1987;87:180–183.

Ireton-Jones CS, Turner WW, Liepa GU, et al. Equations for the estimation of energy expenditures in patients with burns with special reference to ventilatory status. *J Burn Care Rehabil.* 1992;13:330–333.

Jequier E. Measurement of energy expenditure in clinical nutritional assessment. *JPEN.* 1987;11:86S–89S.

Kinney JM. Indirect calorimetry in malnutrition: nutritional assessment or therapeutic reference? *JPEN.* 1987;11:90S–94S.

Makk LJ, McClave SA, Creech PW, et al. Clinical application of the metabolic cart to the delivery of total parenteral nutrition. *Crit Care Med.* 1990;18:1320–1327.

McClave SA, Snider HL. Use of indirect calorimetry in clinical nutrition. *Nutr Clin Pract.* 1992;7:202–221.

McClave SA, Snider HL, Greene L, et al. Effective utilization of indirect calorimetry during critical care. *Intern Care World.* 1992;9:194–200.

Porter C, Cohen NH. Indirect calorimetry in critically ill patients: role of the clinical dietitian in interpreting results. *J Am Diet Assoc.* 1996;96:49–57.

Sedlet KL, Ireton-Jones CS. Energy expenditure and the abnormal eating pattern of a bulimic: a case report. *J Am Diet Assoc.* 1989;89:74–77.

Weissman CW, Sadar A, Kemper MA. In vitro evaluation of a compact metabolic measurement instrument. *JPEN.* 1990;12:216–221.

CHAPTER 3

Nutrition Management for Specific Medical Conditions

- Burns
- Cardiovascular Disorders
- Diabetes Mellitus
- Gastrointestinal Disorders
- Geriatric Conditions
- HIV/AIDS
- Neonatal Conditions
- Obesity
- Oncology
- Otolaryngology

- Pediatric Conditions
- Physical Assessment
- Pregnancy and Lactation
- Pulmonary Conditions
- Renal Conditions
- Solid Organ Transplantation
- Transplantation of Bone Marrow and Peripheral Blood Stem Cells
- Trauma/Sepsis

Burns

Michele Morath Gottschlich

DESCRIPTION

Burns, as commonly defined, represent tissue destruction resulting in circulatory and metabolic alterations that characterize the compensatory response to injury (see Table 3–1). These events have important effects on nutritional status.

CAUSE

The causes of burn wounds include excessive exposure to thermal (heat or cold), chemical (acids or alkalis), electrical, and radioactive agents.

ASSESSMENT

Classification

Burns are usually classified according to depth of skin involvement:

- First-degree burns: limited involvement of outer epidermal layers only
- Second-degree burns: damage extending through the epidermis into varying depths of the dermis
- Third-degree burns: full-thickness injury with destruction of all epithelial elements

Initial Assessment of Nutritional Status

Obtain diet/medical history to determine if the patient presents with significant risk factors that may further compromise nutritional status (eg, inadequate intake prior to burn, > 20% burns, concomitant injury, sepsis, or recent weight loss > 10%).

Estimation of Nutritional Requirements

Energy
- Alterations in metabolism

19

Table 3–1 Metabolic Alterations Following Burns

		Flow Response	
	Ebb Response	Acute Phase	Adaptive Phase
Dominant factors	Loss of plasma volume Poor tissue perfusion Shock Low plasma insulin levels	Heightened total body blood flow Elevated catecholamines Elevated glucagon Elevated glucocorticoids Normal or elevated serum insulin High glucagon-insulin ratio	Stress hormone response subsiding Convalescence
Metabolic and clinical characteristics	Decreased oxygen consumption Depressed resting energy expenditure Decreased blood pressure Cardiac output below normal Decreased body temperature	Catabolism Hyperglycemia Increased respiratory rate Increased oxygen consumption and hypermetabolism Increased carbon dioxide production Increased body temperature Redistribution of polyvalent cations such as zinc and iron Increased urinary excretion of nitrogen, sulphur, magnesium, phosphorus, potassium, and creatinine Accelerated gluconeogenesis Fat mobilization Increased use of amino acids as oxidative fuels	Anabolism Normoglycemia Energy expenditure diminished Nutrient requirements approaching preinjury needs

Source: Reprinted with permission from MM Gottschlich, JW Alexander, RH Bower. Enteral nutrition in patients with burns or trauma. In: *Clinical Nutrition Enteral and Tube Feeding,* JL Rombeau and MD Caldwell, eds. p 307, © 1990, WB Saunders Co.

1. The increased energy expenditure of burns exceeds that of any other injury.
2. Oxygen consumption is near normal during resuscitation, then rises and peaks around postburn day 10, with a maximum level 2–2.5 times greater than the normal metabolic rate.
3. Chronic elevation of catecholamines seems to be the dominant stimulus for increased oxygen consumption and enhanced energy needs.
4. The greater the percentage of body surface area burned, the more pronounced the hypermetabolic response; other factors also affect the response (ie, fever, sepsis, surgery, nutrient intake, environmental temperature, body composition, physical activity, drugs).
5. Metabolic rate returns to normal after wound coverage is achieved.

• Guidelines for meeting caloric needs
1. Many mathematical equations exist for estimating energy expenditure.
   – *Curreri formula* for children > 3 years old and adults: $(25 \times$ kg of body weight$) + (40 \times \%$ burn$)$
   – *Polk formula* for children < 3 years old: $(60 \times$ kg of body weight$) + (35 \times \%$ burn$)$

−*Harris-Benedict equation* to derive basal energy expenditure (BEE); BEE × (activity factor) × (injury factor) will estimate total caloric needs.

Activity factor
Confined to bed = 1.2
Out of bed = 1.3
Injury factor
Burns = 2.1

2. Indirect calorimetry permits a more accurate, individualized measure of energy expenditure.
   −Multiply resting energy expenditure by activity factor 1.2–1.3 to estimate daily needs.
   −Reassess at least twice weekly.
   −If respiratory quotient (RQ) is > 1.0, reduce total caloric intake, and/or reduce carbohydrate-to-lipid ratio; if RQ < 0.80, increase total caloric intake.

Protein

- Alterations in metabolism
  1. Protein may be the most important nutrient compromised by a burn injury.
  2. Protein provides the amino acid building blocks for healing.
  3. Gluconeogenesis from alanine and other gluconeogenic amino acids is increased during the acute phase.
  4. The plasma concentration of arginine decreases, whereas levels of plasma phenylalanine and leucine are frequently elevated.
  5. Extensive nitrogen losses occur in exudate and urine.
  6. Protein catabolism, like energy expenditure, is related to the size of the injury; aberrations normalize after the wound is covered.
- Guidelines for intake
  1. Considerable evidence supports the use of high-protein regimens (20%–25% of caloric needs), which inherently contain a low calorie-nitrogen ratio.
  2. The protein source should be of high biologic value.

3. Intact protein is superior to predigested/elemental amino acids in enteral nutrition.
4. Arginine enrichment improves cell-mediated immunity and wound healing and decreases morbidity and mortality in burns; glutamine is a key fuel for the intestinal mucosa and therefore should be included in nonvolitional feeding regimens for burns; branched-chain amino acid supplementation has not shown beneficial effects.

Carbohydrate

- Alterations in metabolism
  1. Increased glucose production from gluconeogenesis occurs in response to the altered hormonal environment.
  2. There is little evidence to suggest impaired glucose oxidation occurs.
  3. The burn wound metabolizes large quantities of glucose, largely to lactic acid, a pathway apparently favored by healing wounds.
  4. During the acute phase following major thermal injury and during periods of infection, the tendency for hyperglycemia has resulted in terms such as *stress diabetes* and *diabetes of injury*.
- Guidelines for intake
  1. Carbohydrate has beneficial effects as a nutritional substrate.
     −It stimulates insulin release, a key anabolic hormone.
     −Protein is best utilized when abundant carbohydrate is present.
  2. Potential side effects of excessive carbohydrate intake are
     −hyperglycemia
     −osmotic diuresis, resulting in dehydration and hypovolemia
     −excess carbon dioxide production with potential respiratory insufficiency

Fat

- Alterations in metabolism
  1. Reduced lipolysis during the acute phase, with preferential oxidation of lean body mass for fuel

2. Elevated levels of serum free fatty acids
3. Increased serum triglycerides
4. Decreased levels of serum cholesterol
- Guidelines for intake
  1. Conservative ingestion of fat is beneficial; diets containing 15%–20% of nonprotein calories as fat seem to be optimal.
  2. Supplementation with fatty acids of the omega-3 family (eg, fish oil) has been correlated with improved immunocompetence and tube-feeding tolerance; this may be due to their inhibitory effect on the omega-6 fatty acid conversion to the 2-series of prostaglandins or an unrecognized omega-3 dietary requirement.
  3. Complications related to excessive fat intake are
     - hepatomegaly
     - fat overload syndrome
     - impaired clotting
     - impaired host defense
     - decreased resistance to infection
     - increased incidence of diarrhea

Micronutrients

- Protein and energy cannot be efficiently utilized if micronutrient intake is inadequate.
- Current knowledge supports daily multivitamin supplementation.
- Further enrichment with vitamins A and C along with zinc is also important.
  1. Vitamin A
     - Vitamin A is important for maintenance of immunologic response and epithelialization.
     - Dietary guidelines should approximate 5000 IU of Vitamin A per 1000 kcal of enteral nutrition.
  2. Ascorbic acid
     - Ascorbic acid is an important coenzyme involved in collagen synthesis and immune function.
     - Ingestion of 1 g of ascorbic acid per day (500 mg twice daily) should be routine protocol.

3. Zinc
   - Zinc is a cofactor in energy metabolism and protein synthesis.
   - Supplementation with 220 mg of zinc sulfate daily is recommended.

PROBLEMS

- Underfeeding has a direct negative impact on wound healing, immunocompetence, and mortality.
- Overfeeding can cause complications such as hyperglycemia, fatty liver, and elevated carbon dioxide production (respiratory insufficiency).

TREATMENT/MANAGEMENT

Enteral Nutrition

- Adequate oral intake is probable with burns ≤ 20% of the surface area.
- Feeding tubes should usually be inserted for patients with a burn area exceeding 20% or patients presenting with significant nutritional risk factors.
- Begin enteral nutrition as soon as possible postburn.
  1. Delayed enteral feeding is associated with loss of gastrointestinal mucosal mass, decreased tube-feeding tolerance, elevated catabolic hormones, increased metabolic rate, and increased risk of postburn malnutrition.
  2. Tube feeding bypassing the stomach into the small intestine makes enteral nutrition possible during times of gastric ileus.
  3. Selection of enteral feeding products must consider the unique energy, protein, fat, and micronutrient needs of burn patients; many commercial tube-feeding products are unacceptable for burns.
  4. A moderately low-fat, high-protein diet therapy program is recommended.
  5. Since digestive and absorptive capabilities are intact in burns (assuming that enteric feeding is implemented early), hydrolyzed products are not warranted.

Table 3–2 Nutrition Parameters To Monitor in Burn Patients

Parameter	Frequency	Comments
Diet history	On admission	Look for evidence of preinjury malnutrition, food allergies, and intolerances that could put a critically ill patient at heightened risk.
Indirect calorimetry	Biweekly	Valuable indicator of severity of hypermetabolism. Nutrition support is inadequate when resting energy expenditure (REE) $\times$ 1.3 exceeds caloric intake or when respiratory quotient (RQ) is less than 0.83.
Weight	Three times weekly	Weight loss in excess of 10% of preinjury weight represents a nutritional emergency. A weight change greater than 1 lb/day indicates fluid imbalances and will skew interpretation of visceral proteins. Corrections must be made for amputations, supportive apparatus, occlusive dressings, and major escharotomies.
Triceps skinfold, midarm muscle circumference	Weekly	Detect long-term changes in lean body mass and fat stores. In the absence of physical therapy, the immobile patient will lose somatic protein even with aggressive nutritional support.
Nitrogen balance	Daily	Amount of urine urea nitrogen excreted in 24 hours is a valuable index of severity of hypercatabolism. Nitrogen balance indicates whether nitrogen intake is exceeding body mass breakdown. Nutrition support is considered inadequate if nitrogen balance is negative.
Serum albumin, transferrin, prealbumin, retinol binding protein levels	Weekly	Indicative of extent of depletion of visceral proteins. Delivery of a large quantity of blood products or the long half-life of certain secretory proteins can complicate interpretation.
Delayed hypersensitivity skin testing, total lymphocyte count, C3, IgG	Optional	Suboptimal nutritional status can cause deficits in immune function, and infection can cause derangements in nutrition parameters.
Serum glucose	Daily until stable, then twice weekly	Some patients with previously normal glucose tolerance prior to injury may require sliding-scale insulin therapy during aggressive nutritional support.
Fluid status, blood urea nitrogen, and serum creatinine	Daily until stable, then twice weekly	Need to be monitored for all patients receiving high-protein regimens because of high renal solute load. If azotemia develops, increase the delivery of free water, decrease the protein content of nutrient substrate, or both.
Nutrient intake from all sources (oral, tube feeding, parenteral)	Daily	Immediate modification in nutrition support should be made if deviation of actual intake from goal is detected. The use of a computer can greatly improve speed and sophistication of nutrient analysis (eg, vitamin intake).
Follow reports of skin graft adherence, healing process, or percent open wound	Weekly	Poor wound healing may suggest inadequate consumption of protein and/or micronutrients. Reassess needs/intake and supplement as indicated.

Source: Adapted with permission from MM Gottschlich, JW Alexander, RH Bower. Enteral nutrition in patients with burns or trauma. In: *Clinical Nutrition Enteral and Tube Feeding*, JL Rombeau and MD Caldwell, eds. p 318, © 1990, WB Saunders Co.

- Enteral nutrition is favored over parenteral because of specific advantages derived from alimentation by the enteral route:
  1. Decreased incidence of complications such as pneumothorax, bleeding, and infection
  2. Lower cost
  3. Maintenance of optimal intestinal anatomy and function

Parenteral Nutrition (PN)

- If calorie requirements cannot be entirely met by enteral feedings, PN can save burn patients from the morbidity and mortality of malnutrition. However, PN implemented during the first 10 days postburn has no positive effect on immune function or survival.
- Conservative administration of intravenous fat is recommended in view of its hyperlipidemic and immunosuppressive tendencies.
  1. Intravenous lipids are unnecessary if enteral support containing fat is delivered simultaneously.
  2. When PN is the sole source of nutrition, 500 mL of 10% fat emulsion three times weekly is adequate.

Monitoring

Monitoring to determine tolerance and effectiveness of the diet therapy program is important. Table 3–2 lists clinical and laboratory parameters that should be monitored.

REFERENCES

Alexander JW, MacMillan BG, Stinnett JD, et al. Beneficial effects of aggressive protein feeding in severely burned children. *Ann Surg.* 1980;192:505–517.

Alexander JW, Saito H, Trocki O, Ogle CK. The importance of lipid type in the diet after burn injury. *Ann Surg.* 1986; 204:1–8.

Bell SJ, Molnar JA, Krasker WS, Burke JF. Prediction of total urinary nitrogen from urea nitrogen for burned patients. *J Am Diet Assoc.* 1985;85:1100–1104.

Gottschlich MM. Assessment and nutrition management of the patient with burns. In: Winkler MF, Lysen LK, eds. *Suggested Guidelines for Nutrition and Metabolic Management of Adult Patients Receiving Nutrition Support.* Chicago, Ill: American Dietetic Association; 1993:64–70.

Gottschlich, MM. Nutrition in the burned pediatric patient. In: Queen P, Lang C, eds. *Handbook of Pediatric Nutrition.* Gaithersburg, Md: Aspen Publishers, Inc; 1993:536–559.

Gottschlich MM, Jenkins M, Warden GD, et al. Differential effects of three enteral regimens on selected outcome variables in burn patients. *JPEN.* 1990;14:225–236.

Gottschlich MM, Mayes T, Khoury J, Warden GD. Significance of obesity on nutritional, immunological, hormonal and clinical outcome parameters in burns. *J Am Diet Assoc.* 1993;93:1261–1268.

Gottschlich MM, Warden GD, Michel MA, et al. Diarrhea in tube-fed burn patients: incidence, etiology, nutritional impact, and prevention. *JPEN.* 1988;12:338–345.

Herndon DN, Stein MD, Rutan TC, Abston S, Linares H. Failure of TPN supplementation to improve liver function, immunity, and mortality in thermally injured patients. *J Trauma.* 1987;27:195–204.

Hildreth M, Gottschlich MM. Nutritional support of the burned patient. In: Herndon DN, ed. *Total Burn Care.* Philadelphia, Pa: WB Saunders Co., 1996:237–245.

Ireton CS, Hunt JL, Liepa GU, Turner WW. Evaluation of energy requirements in thermally injured patients. *JPEN.* 1982;6:577.

Ireton-Jones C, Gottschlich MM. The evolution of nutrition support in burns. *J Burn Care Rehabil.* 1993;14:272–280.

Jenkins M, Gottschlich M, Baumer T, Khoury J, Warden GD. Enteral feeding during operative procedures. *J Burn Care Rehabil.* 1994;15:199–205.

Kravitz M, Woodruff J, Petersen S, Warden G. The use of the Dobhoff tube to provide additional nutritional support in thermally injured patients. *J Burn Care Rehabil.* 1982; 3:226–228.

Mayes T, Gottschlich MM. Burns. In: Matarese L, Gottschlich M, eds. *Contemporary Nutrition Support Practice.* Philadelphia, Pa: WB Saunders Co. In press.

Mayes T, Gottschlich MM, Khoury J, Warden GD. An evaluation of predicted and measured energy. *J Am Diet Assoc.* In press.

Mochizuki H, Trocki O, Dominioni L, Alexander JW. Reduction of postburn hypermetabolism by early enteral feeding. *Curr Probl Surg.* 1985;42:121–125.

Morath MA, Miller SF, Finley RK, Jones LM. Interpretation of nutritional parameters in burn patients. *J Burn Care Rehabil.* 1983;4:361–366.

Saffle JR, Medina E, Raymond J, Westenskow D, Kravitz M, Warden GD. Use of indirect calorimetry in the nutritional management of burned patients. *J Trauma.* 1985; 25:32–39.

Waxman K, Rebello T, Pinderski L, et al. Protein loss across burn wounds. *J Trauma.* 1987;27:136–140.

Wilmore DW, Long JM, Mason AD, Skreen RW, Pruitt BA. Catecholamines: mediator of the hypermetabolic response to thermal injury. *Ann Surg.* 1974;180:653–669.

Cardiovascular Disorders

Deborah Silverman and Sharlene Gaffka

DESCRIPTION

This category includes any disorder associated with abnormal functioning of the heart and blood vessels—arteries, capillaries, and veins. A properly functioning cardiovascular system adequately delivers oxygen, hormones, and immunologic substances in nutrient-rich blood throughout the body. The cardiovascular system is also responsible for the removal of metabolic waste products from tissues. In the United States cardiovascular disease is the leading cause of death. These diseases can be caused from genetic and environmental factors or a combination of these. To improve the health status of the population of the United States, a nutrition-related health status objective for the year 2000 is to reduce coronary heart deaths from an age-adjusted baseline of 135 per 100,000 in 1987, to no more than 100 per 100,000 people.

- The heart weighs only 250–350 grams and is about the size of a fist.
- With each beat the heart pumps an average of 148 ml, or a total of more than 6,813 liters per day.

Each heartbeat pumps blood through the systemic and pulmonary circulations. Cardiac function is based on the adequacy of the cardiac output (CO), which is the amount of blood pumped from the left ventricle per minute.

- CO is calculated by multiplying the amount of blood ejected from one ventricle with one heartbeat (stroke volume, or SV) by the heart rate (HR, the number of times the heart beats per minute, or bpm)
- CO (ml / min) = SV (ml / beat) × HR (beats / min)
- Cardiac output of an adult male is between 4.5 and 8 liters per minute.

GENERALIZED ASSESSMENT

The assessment of any individual with a cardiovascular disorder provides an important baseline of information that can be used to prioritize problems, develop a care plan for the delivery of medical nutrition therapy, monitor progress, and evaluate effectiveness of treatment/outcome. Elements of the nutritional assessment of individuals with cardiovascular disorders include

- *Family History:* for determination of genetic risk factors/cause of death in first-degree relatives and data on second-degree relatives; age and time of onset or diagnosis of each major risk factor of the disorder.
- *Psychosocial Assessment:* for accurate identification of the individual's problems and needs, and the ability to establish an effective counseling relationship and ensure successful outcomes; areas for inquiry should include
  - home life and meal patterns
  - cultural and economic background
  - appetite relative to food-, diet-, and health-related aspects
  - allergies, intolerances, or food avoidances
  - dental and oral health problems
- *Anthropometric Assessment:* Markers should be obtained as to their appropriateness, the ability of the individual to cooperate, weight history, and the ability to reassess and monitor these markers on a regular basis; markers that should be considered include
  - height, which may include knee height in older Americans
  - weight: desirable for given gender and frame size, and expressed as relative to desirable or ideal body weight and/or body mass index
- *Nutrition History:* Reported in as comprehensive manner as possible or appropriate, and including information on the following components of the diet:

−Calories/Energy
−Fat, expressed as percent of total calories, and differentiated by mono-, poly-, and saturated components, including cholesterol
−Fiber
−Sodium
−Caffeine and Alcohol
• *Clinical Assessment—General:* Evaluate for signs of malnutrition, correlate general health status with chronological age, blood pressure (see box)
• *Skin and Extremities:* Evaluate for color, turgor, temperature, and moisture; evaluate for signs and symptoms of chronic arterial insufficiency such as uneven hair distribution or hair loss, ischemia of the lower extremities, presence of edema.
• *Nails:* Assess for color, shape, thickness, symmetry, and nail adherence.
• *Cardiovascular:* Examine arterial pulses and jugular veins for information on overall function of the ventricles, the quality of the arterial blood vessels, and the condition of the aortic valve; jugular veins provide information regarding the volume and pressure of the right side of the heart.
  −Arterial pulses include the carotid, radial, brachial, femoral, popliteal, dorsalis pedis, and posterial tibial

Biochemical Assessment: A general lipid profile should be obtained on individuals, particularly those with identified risk factors (see box).

In assessment of the biochemical markers of individuals, the nutrition practitioner should

• Understand what is being measured
• Make sure the measure of low density lipoprotein (LDL)-cholesterol was obtained in the fasting state
• Make sure the samples were prepared and stored properly
• Appreciate the need for serial measurements

SELECTED CARDIAC DISORDERS WITH NUTRITIONAL SIGNIFICANCE

Coronary Artery Disease

• Atherosclerosis
• Arteriosclerosis

Hypertension

• Cardiac Failure
• Myocardial Infarction

CORONARY ARTERY DISEASE

Coronary artery disease (CAD) is any disorder of the coronary arteries that leads to an interference in blood supply to the myocardium. Permanent disruption of blood flow causes myocardial dysfunction and can include sudden death. CAD is characterized by the attachment of plaques, (composed primarily of lipids and cholesterol) to the inner arterial wall, thus altering the lumen size and functional capacity of the coronary artery. The cavity of the artery de-

---

Classification of Blood Pressure for Adults Age 18 Years and Older

Category	Systolic (mm Hg)	Diastolic (mm Hg)
Normal	< 130	< 85
High Normal	130–139	85–89
Hypertension		
Stage 1 (Mild)	140–159	90–99
Stage 2 (Moderate)	160–179	100–109
Stage 3 (Severe)	180–209	110–119
Stage 4 (Very Severe)	≥ 210	≥ 120

NCEP Adult Treatment Panel II Categories for Total and LDL-Cholesterol Concentrations for Individuals with and without Coronary Heart Disease

Individuals without Coronary Heart Disease

Total Cholesterol Category	Total Cholesterol in mg/dL (mmol/L)	LDL-Cholesterol Category	LDL Cholesterol in mg/dL (mmol/L)
Desirable	< 200 (5.17)	Desirable	< 130 (3.36)
Borderline High	200–239 (5.17–6.18)	Borderline High Risk	130–159 (3.64–4.11)
High	≥ 240 (6.21)	High Risk	≥ 160 (4.13)

Individuals with Coronary Heart Disease

LDL Cholesterol Category	LDL Cholesterol in mg/dL (mmol/L)
Optimal	≤ 100 (2.6)
Higher than Optimal	> 100 (2.6)

creases in diameter therefore diminishing the flow of oxygen and nutrient-rich blood to the myocardium. The attachment of the yellowish plaques inside the vessels also causes them to lose their elasticity.

Lesions are categorized into three forms:

- The *fatty streak* is presumed to be a type of reversible lesion that will not occlude the affected vessel, commonly discovered in young people. The earliest atherosclerotic lesion is a flat, yellow, lipid-filled smooth muscle cell.
- *Fibrous plaque* is the representative lesion of progressing atherosclerosis. It is composed of smooth muscle cells that are loaded with lipids, encompassed by elastic fibers, collagen, and a mucophage matrix. The raised lesion is white and projects into the cavity of the artery, thus narrowing the intravascular space.
- *Complicated or advanced lesions* result when fibrous plaques are transformed by blood clots (which occlude the intimal layer), hemorrhage, calcification, and cellular necrosis. The lesion enlarges and hardens, creating an inflexible, intricate structure often producing vascular occlusion.

Clinical sequelae includes myocardial infarction, the leading cause of morbidity and mortality in the United States. The leading cause of CAD is atherosclerosis. Risk factors for the development of atherosclerosis include

- Heredity or family history
- Age
- Gender, particularly male and menopausal females without hormone replacement
- Hypertension
- Lipid levels, specifically hypercholesterolemia and low high density lipoproteins (HDL)
- Obesity
- Smoking
- Sedentary lifestyle
- Diabetes mellitus
- Psychosocial factors that include aggressiveness, competitiveness, and an urgent sense of time

Effects of diet on risk of CAD have been documented in observational studies and clinical trials. Most recently, observational studies have recognized a relationship between dietary antioxidants (particularly vitamin E, beta-carotene, selenium, and ascorbic acid) and CAD. It is not recommended that general recommendation or use of supplements of these nutrients be utilized until clinical trial data are available.

Possible side effects from the use of supplements include

- Vitamin C: cramping, diarrhea, kidney stones
- Vitamin E: can interfere with action of Coumadin

A more generalized recommendation can be made to the general public to consume at least five or more servings of fruits and vegetables daily.

Treatment with Medical Nutrition Therapy

High risk individuals should begin a medical nutrition therapy program in consultation with a nutrition practitioner and their physician. Minimal medical nutrition therapy goals are to lower LDL-cholesterol to below 160 mg/dL if other risk factors are absent; or below 130 mg/dL if two or more risk factors are present, one of which is male gender (see box).

Three nutritional factors contribute to elevated cholesterol

- Saturated fat (reduces LDL receptor activity)
- Dietary cholesterol (suppresses LDL receptor synthesis)

- Obesity (decreases HDL cholesterol and causes an overproduction of lipoprotein)

The Step I Diet emphasizes the choice of fruits, vegetables, grains, cereals, and legumes, as well as poultry, fish, lean meats, and low-fat dairy products instead of foods high in saturated fat and cholesterol. Most individuals can adhere to these dietary recommendations with only moderate changes in dietary habits.

The Step II Diet further reduces saturated fat and cholesterol. Sufficient reduction in saturated fat and cholesterol should lower LDL cholesterol, reduce hypercholesterolemia, and reduce body weight to a desirable level.

Any dietary modifications that are utilized as a component of medical nutrition therapy must be nutritionally adequate and meet the Recommended Dietary Allowances. Successful medical nutrition therapy outcomes for individuals with CAD must include

- interventions that require a concerted effort by the entire health care team

---

Medical Nutrition Therapy for Hypercholesterolemia

Nutrient	Step I Diet	Recommended Intake	Step II Diet
Total Fat		30% or less of Total Calories	
Saturated Fatty Acids	8–10% of Total Calories		> 7% of Total Calories
Polyunsaturated FA		Up to 10% of Total Calories	
Monounsaturated FA		Up to 15% of Total Calories	
Carbohydrates		55% or more of Total Calories	
Protein		Approximately 15% of Total Calories	
Cholesterol	Less than 300 mg/day		Less than 200 mg/day
Total Calories		To achieve and maintain desirable weight	

TREATMENT/MANAGEMENT (see Appendixes F and G for Assessment of Mineral and Trace Element Nutriture and Assessment of Vitamin Nutriture Tables)

General Survey

- Adequate protein and calories to ensure adequate protein and fat stores
- Avoidance of overfeeding
- Adequate iron intake to prevent microcytic hypochromic anemia and fatigue

Skin

- Adequate protein, vitamin C, and zinc to assist with wound healing and prevention of decubitus ulcers
- Adequate B vitamins, especially niacin, to prevent swollen, red skin
- Adequate biotin and zinc to prevent rashes
- Adequate niacin to assist with prevention of pellagrous dermatitis
- Adequate vitamin A and essential fatty acids to assist with maintaining skin
- Vitamin K and C to prevent excessive bleeding, petechiae, and purpura
- Adequate fluid intake to prevent dehydration

Nails

- Adequate iron to prevent koilonychia
- Adequate protein and calories for nails to have a healthy shine and smoothness
- Vitamins A and C to prevent mottling, irregularities, and poor blanching

Hair

- Adequate protein to prevent dull, dry hair and thinning
- Adequate calories and protein to assist with preventing alopecia that is not related to disease or treatment
- Protein and copper to prevent dyspigmentation and to prevent hair from being easily plucked
- Copper to maintain texture

Face

- Adequate calories and protein to prevent temporal and maxillary wasting
- Protein to maintain color and to prevent dyspigmentation and swelling
- Calcium to prevent paresthesia

Eyes

- Vitamin A for various disorders, including visual changes, Bitot's spots, xerosis, and keratomalacia
- Iron, folate, and B_{12} to prevent potential for anemias
- Niacin, riboflavin, and pyridoxine for angular palpebritis
- Prevention and/or control of hyperlipidemia

Nose

- Adequate vitamin B (riboflavin, niacin, pyridoxine) for seborrhea
- Obstructions or deviated septum will influence decision of feeding tube placement

Jaws

- Malocclusion will influence feeding (textures and types of food)
- Enlarged parotid gland may signal eating disorders, such as bulimia from vomiting

Lips

- Adequate niacin and riboflavin to prevent cheilosis
- Adequate riboflavin, pyridoxine, niacin, and iron to prevent angular stomatitis

Tongue

- Zinc for taste atrophy
- B vitamins such as riboflavin, folic acid, B_6, iron, and B_{12} for glossitis
- Niacin for scarlet tongue

- a positive attitude, knowledge, and skills in motivating the individual and in organizing a team approach by both the physician and nutrition practitioner
- individuals who have had difficulty in adhering or responding to the Step I Diet should receive counseling by a registered dietitian.
- practical approaches that may be used by the physician and registered dietitian to promote adherence include
  - assessment of nutritional status and eating habits
  - initial instructions for dietary modifications
  - strategies for behavior modification
  - weight reduction
  - physical activity

Success with medical nutrition therapy requires the use of long-term monitoring and investigation as to reasons behind an inadequate response to the dietary management by the individual.

Components of the dietary modifications for hypercholesterolemia include

- *Saturated Fatty Acids:* tend to raise serum cholesterol but differ in their cholesterol-raising potential. Major sources of saturated fatty acids are the following: animal fats (dairy products such as butter, whole milk, ice cream, cheese), beef, pork, poultry, and plant oils (coconut oil, palm kernel oil, palm oil, cocoa butter)
- *Monounsaturated Fatty Acids:* lower serum cholesterol when used as part of a low-saturated fat diet. They do not appear to lower HDL cholesterol. The trans versions of monounsaturated fatty acids do not lower LDL cholesterol. Major sources of monounsaturated fatty acids are the following: olive oil, canola oil, peanut oil, rice oil, hazelnut oil, avocado. Sunflower, safflower and soybean oils with high oleic acid content are also commercially available.
- *Polyunsaturated Fatty Acids:* lower serum cholesterol and tend to lower HDL cholesterol. Major sources of polyunsaturated fatty acids include omega 6 polyunsaturates (linoleic acid) of corn oil, safflower oil, sun-

flower oil, and soybean oil, and omega 3 polyunsaturated fish oils. An increased intake of omega 3 fatty acids is associated with a disruption of platelet aggregation, which may reduce the risk of coronary thrombosis. Omega 3 fatty acids appear to be more effective at lowering triglyceride levels than lowering serum cholesterol. In some individuals, omega 3 supplements have been an effective treatment for hypertriglyceridemia.

- *Soluble Fiber:* is considered an adjunct to a cholesterol-lowering diet.
- *Alcohol:* increases triglycerides and HDL cholesterol in many individuals but does not affect LDL cholesterol. Excessive alcohol intakes may have significant adverse effects on health.

Children with acceptable total cholesterol and LDL cholesterol levels should follow dietary recommendations for the general, healthy population. Children with borderline or high lipid levels need to follow the Step 1 Diet, then the Step 2 Diet if their lipids do not change to satisfactory levels. Children at risk may also need to follow other risk factor intervention strategies.

Factors affecting both adults' and children's ability to comply with dietary modifications include

- Food likes and dislikes
- Time of eating
- Location of meals
- Food preparation and shopping habits, who shops and prepares the meals (see box for terms used on food labels)
- Previous experiences with dietary change

Individuals can lower the fat content of food selections in fast food restaurants by selecting food items such as

- Low fat frozen yogurt
- Low fat or skim milk
- Salads, using dressing sparingly or in a low fat variety
- Lean roast beef sandwiches
- Plain cheese or vegetable pizza
- Grilled chicken entrees

Terms Used on Food Labels for Calories, Fat, Cholesterol, and Sodium

Calorie Free	< 5 calories per serving
Light (Lite)	1/3 less calories or ≤50% of the fat of the regular or reference product; or sodium content has been reduced by at least 50%
Fat Free	<0.5 grams of fat per serving
Low Fat	≤ 3 grams of fat per serving
Reduced or Less Fat	At least 25% less fat per serving than the regular or reference product (cannot be used if product meets definition for low fat)
Lean	<10 grams of fat, < 4 grams of saturated fat, and < 95 mg of cholesterol per serving
Extra Lean	< 5 grams of fat, < 2 grams of saturated fat, and < 95 mg of cholesterol per serving
Low in Saturated Fat	≤ 1 gram saturated fat per serving and ≤ 15% of calories from saturated fatty acids
Cholesterol Free	< 2 mg of cholesterol and ≤ 2 grams of saturated fat per serving
Low Cholesterol	≤ 20 mg of cholesterol and ≤ 2 grams of saturated fat per serving
Reduced Cholesterol	At least 25% less cholesterol than the regular or reference product and ≤ 2 grams of saturated fat per serving (cannot be used if product meets definition for low cholesterol)
Sodium Free (No Sodium)	< 5 mg of sodium per serving and no sodium chloride in ingredients
Very Low Sodium	≤ 35 mg of sodium per serving
Low Sodium	≤ 140 mg of sodium per serving
Reduced or Less Sodium	At least 25% less sodium per serving than the regular or reference product (cannot be used if product meets definition of low sodium)

- Plain grilled hamburgers with no mayonnaise, cheese, or special sauces

MYOCARDIAL INFARCTION (MI)

Infarction is more commonly referred to as a heart attack. MI occurs when the complete occlusion of the coronary arteries causes tissue death to an area of the myocardium following prolonged oxygen deprivation. Myocardial cells begin to die after about 20 minutes of oxygen deprivation. After this period, the ability of the cells to produce adenosine triphosphate (ATP) aerobically is exhausted, and the cells fail to meet their energy demands. Without ATP, the sodium-potassium pump quits, and the cells fill with sodium ions and water, eventually causing them to lyse. With lysis, cells release intracellular potassium stores and intracellular enzymes, which injure neighboring cells. Intracellular proteins gain access to the general circulation and the interstitial space, contributing to interstitial edema and swelling around the myocardial cells. With cell death, inflammatory reactions are initiated. At the site of inflammation, platelets accumulate and release clotting factors. Mast cell degranulation occurs, resulting in the release of histamine and various prostaglandins. Some are vasoconstrictive and some stimulate clotting.

Signs and symptoms include

- an abrupt onset of pain often described as severe and crushing in nature and that may radiate anywhere in the upper body, but most often radiates to the left arm, neck, or jaw
- nausea and vomiting
- feeling of weakness as a result of decreased blood flow to skeletal muscles
- cool, clammy pale skin due to sympathetic vasoconstriction
- decreased urine output related to decreased renal blood flow and increased aldosterone and antidiuretic hormone (ADH)
- tachycardia due to increased cardiac sympathetic stimulation
- mental state of great anxiety and feelings of doom

Diagnosis

- Decreased blood pressure, depending on extent of myocardial damage, increased heart rate
- Electrocardiogram may show acute changes in the ST and T waves
- Cardiac enzymes (creatinine phosphokinase, serum glutamic oxaloacetic transaminase, and lactic dehydrogenase) are increased as a result of myocardial cell death.

Complications may include thromboembolism, congestive heart failure, dysrhythmias, cardiogenic shock, myocardial rupture, pericarditis, and scar tissue of myocardial cells.

Medical Nutrition Therapy

Intervention should be started early in the hospitalization. The most potent prognostic variables are relating the extent of myocardial damage after the infarction: heart size, release of cardiac enzymes, pulmonary congestion, and left ventricular ejection fraction. Identification

and modification of the primary risk factors for atherosclerosis to reduce the progression and to inhibit the new development of atherosclerosis over the long-term should be accomplished.

Cholesterol levels above 250 mg/dL are associated with an increased cardiovascular risk. LDL cholesterol levels above 160 mg/dL are approximately equivalent to a total cholesterol level of above 250 mg/dL. Aggressive dietary efforts to lower the total cholesterol level to below 200 mg/dL, especially in patients with cholesterol levels above 250 mg/dL should be the first step. This dietary approach includes a caloric restriction in obese individuals, a reduction in cholesterol intake to less than 250 mg per day, a decrease in intake of saturated fat to 10% of total calories, an increase in the proportion of dietary protein derived from vegetable sources, and an increased intake of foods rich in fiber.

Caffeine restriction and avoidance of alcohol have also been suggested as appropriate dietary interventions. Individuals should be encouraged to adhere to their prescribed regimen of medical nutrition therapy.

CARDIAC FAILURE

Cardiac failure is also referred to as heart failure, cardiac decompensation, and congestive heart failure. This is a state in which there is inadequate cardiac output to meet the body's metabolic demands, resulting in poor perfusion to all organ systems. It is responsible for close to one million admissions to acute care facilities on an annual basis. Between 50% and 68% of individuals hospitalized with cardiac failure have significant impairment in their nutritional status based upon

- anthropometric measurements
- total body weight
- plasma protein status

Cardiac contractility is reduced and the ventricle is unable to pump as much blood out during systole as what comes in during diastole. It results in progressive increase in ventricular and diastolic volume. Left ventricular failure occurs when left ventricle cannot pump blood efficiently from the lungs into systemic circulation. Right failure occurs when the right ventricle cannot pump blood efficiently from the venous return into the pulmonary system.

Cardiac failure is often associated with undernutrition and other specific nutritional deficiencies. Nutritional factors may cause, precipitate, or aggravate cardiac failure. It is important to maintain adequate nutritional status in individuals who are at risk to avoid cardiac cachexia. Cardiac cachexia is a loss of total lean body mass and fat stores accompanied by hypoalbuminemia, proteinuria, and edema. This weight loss is different from simple starvation.

Depletion of lean body tissue causes a decline in strength, performance, and immune competence. Factors that contribute to the development of cardiac cachexia include

• anorexia leading to insufficient intake
• impaired absorption of ingested nutrients
• increased nutrient losses through metabolic wastes
• cytokine-mediated host response to the underlying disease

Repeated episodes of acute cardiac failure may compromise an individual's ability to achieve nutritional needs and thereby lead to compromised nutritional status.

Any condition or disease that changes fluid and/or electrolyte balance can contribute to cardiac failure. Primary imbalances include fluid volume excess related to compromised regulatory mechanisms, activity intolerance related to decreased cardiac reserve, hyponatremia, hypo- and hyperkalemia, hypomagnesemia, metabolic alkalosis (if potassium losing diuretics are used), metabolic acidosis, and respiratory acidosis resulting from impaired gas exchange caused by decreased cardiac output, increased preload, and transudation of fluid into the alveoli.

Assessment includes

• General complaints of dyspnea, fatigue, restlessness, insomnia, anorexia, nausea, vomiting
• Past history that determines dates and time of onset, and associated conditions such as pain, fatigue, edema, syncope, dyspnea, orthopnea, palpitations, cyanosis, intermittent claudication, and clubbing of fingernails
• Medication history of use of over-the-counter medications and products that may have significant sodium content
• Social history that should include information on the individual's exercise and recreational activities, use of tobacco, alcohol, recreational drugs, caffeine, and other potential stressors
• Family history for presence of diabetes mellitus, hypertension, cardiovascular disease, renal disease, hypertension, obesity, peripheral vascular disease

Physical examination should include

• General examination for signs of breathing or circulation difficulties, level of consciousness, vital signs, respiratory rate, and blood pressure.
• *Skin:* evaluate for signs of peripheral cyanosis in the nailbeds, earlobes, tip of nose, lips, hands, and feet; determine if edema is present.
• *Cardiovascular:* evaluate hemodynamic status for systolic murmurs, cardiomegaly, orthopenia, decreased cardiac output, increased pressures.
• *Pulmonary:* evaluate gas exchange, observe for signs of dyspnea.
• *Gastrointestinal:* observe for ascites, decreased motility, diarrhea, constipation, nausea, vomiting, anorexia, evaluate weight gain and signs of protein and fat malabsorption.
• *Endocrine/Metabolic:* evaluate for increased energy, macronutrient, and micronutrient requirements; evaluate metabolic state of balance including electrolyte and acid-base balances.
• *Renal:* evaluate urine output, signs of proteinuria, specific gravity, urinary sodium, nocturia, fluid balance.
• *Neuro/Muscular:* observe for level of consciousness, fatigue, muscle strength.

Diagnostic tests used in the Nutritional Status Assessment include

• Electrolytes
• Blood urea nitrogen and creatinine

- Liver function tests
- Prothrombin time
- Serum glucose
- Arterial blood gases
- Serum thiamin, folate, and iron
- Malabsorption tests may also serve as useful markers to determine any degree of protein losing enteropathy associated with cardiac failure
- Urine volume and specific gravity
- Noninvasive tests include a chest X-ray, electrocardiogram, echocardiogram, and hemodynamic monitoring

GOALS OF MEDICAL NUTRITION THERAPY

Management should be individualized as to the severity, acuity of presentation, etiology, presence of coexisting illness, and precipitating factors and work to

- achieve and maintain optimal gas exchange
- achieve and maintain adequate cardiac output and function
- reduce and prevent excess fluid volume
- achieve and maintain a tolerance to activity that does not induce hypoxemia, weakness, or diminish cardiac reserve
- prevent recurrent episodes of cardiac failure through maintaining an optimal state of health.

Implementation of the Medical Nutrition Therapy Care Plan

Individual and family should be involved in a counseling program that contains a curriculum on both the preventive and treatment aspects of cardiac failure. This program should include information as to the signs and symptoms associated with unusual fatigue, shortness of breath, inability to sleep lying flat, swelling of the extremities, weight gain associated with rapid fluid retention (more than 2–3 pounds in 1 day), the importance of weight monitoring by weighing themselves at the same time each day and with

the same amount of clothing and with an empty bladder, and considerations for management of nocturia and persistent coughing.

Weight management and/or weight loss in obese individuals is necessary with cardiac failure to reduce systemic vascular resistance as well as myocardial oxygen demand.

Care should be taken to minimize any drug-induced anorexia. Individuals who are unable to consume their nutrient needs with an oral diet should receive supplementation. Studies have determined that a continuous rather than bolus feeding administration method is preferable as it minimizes myocardial oxygen consumption.

Additional elements of the prescription for medical nutrition therapy include

- Sodium restriction at levels of 2.0–2.5 gm / day with adjustments made that range from 0.5–4.0 gm, depending on level of acuity.
- Provision of adequate potassium to balance losses from drug therapies

Individuals should receive counseling on how to avoid high-sodium containing foods such as processed, packed, and cured meats, prepared and canned foods, salty snack foods, and the use of a water softener attached to the drinking/cooking water source. The individual should be counseled on methods used to enhance the flavors and tastes of foods without utilizing sodium-containing condiments and seasonings as diets containing < 4 grams of sodium per day are generally unappealing to Americans since unrestricted intakes can be as much as 10 grams per day.

Overall composition of the diet should be at 35% fat, 50% carbohydrate, and 15% protein. Individuals with moderate to severe cardiac failure or who have been diagnosed with cardiac cachexia are generally unable to consume energy at levels > 40 kCal/kg body weight and 1.5–2.0 grams of protein/kg body weight without adjunctive nutrition support. Caution should be taken when feeding individuals who present at ≤ 85% of their dry body weight as they may experience difficulty in managing the metabolic load delivered to the heart with the nutrition prescription established to replete body stores.

Energy levels may be initiated at resting energy expenditure levels for these individuals and gradually increased, based upon their improved clinical condition. Care should be taken to adjust meal times around periods of exercise, or tests conducted in a health care setting to avoid tiring the individual and producing early satiety. Fluid restriction should be initiated for the management of hyponatremia and volume overload. Fluid intake should be restricted to 20–25 ml/kg/day. Additional considerations should be made as to the appropriateness of restriction of caffeine and alcohol in individuals with cardiac failure, particularly during acute episodes of the condition.

Individuals receiving diuretics that inhibit sodium and chloride reabsorption in the thick ascending limb of the loop of Henle are at-risk for onset of thiamin deficiency (see box). Careful assessment of these individuals is necessary to differentiate the diagnosis of thiamin deficiency rather than other adverse cardiovascular effects. Individuals with thiamin deficiency can exacerbate signs and symptoms such as peripheral vasodilatation leading to high-output cardiac failure, biventricular low output failure, and retention of sodium and water, resulting in edema.

HYPERTENSION

As many as 50 million Americans have elevated blood pressure (systolic blood pressure 140 mm Hg or greater and/or diastolic blood pressure 90 mm Hg or greater), or are taking antihypertensive medication. The prevalence of hypertension increases with age, is greater for African Americans than Caucasians, and in both races is greater in less educated than more educated individuals. Nonfatal and fatal cardiovascular diseases, including coronary heart disease and stroke, as well as renal disease, and all-cause mortality, increase progressively with higher levels or both systolic blood pressure and diastolic blood pressure (see box).

Hypertension should not be diagnosed on the basis of a single measurement. Initial elevated readings should be confirmed on at least two subsequent visits during one to several weeks. Risks of coronary heart disease at any level of high blood pressure are increased several-fold for persons with target-organ disease (see box).

Assessment should include

- Family history for hypertension, premature coronary heart disease, stroke, diabetes, and dyslipidemia

Diuretics Used To Treat Heart Failure		
Drug	Dose Range (mg)	Frequency
Thiazide diuretics		
Hydrochlorothiazide	25–50	weekly to daily
Chlorthalidone	25–100	weekly to daily
Loop diuretics		
Furosemide	20–200	daily or twice daily
Bumetanide	0.5–4	daily or twice daily
Ethacrynic acid	25–100	daily or twice daily
Torsemide	5–100	daily
Thiazide-related diuretic		
Metolazone	2.5–10	daily or twice daily
Potassium-sparing diuretics		
Triamterene	50–100	daily or twice daily
Amiloride	5–10	daily
Spironolactone	25–100	daily or twice daily

ACE Inhibitors Used To Treat Heart Failure

Drug	Dose Range (mg)	Frequency	Target Dose for Survival Benefit
Captopril	6.25–150	three times daily	50 mg three times daily
Enalapril	2.5–20	twice daily	10 mg twice daily
Lisinopril	2.5–40	daily	-----
Ramipril	2.5–10	once or twice daily	5 mg twice daily
Quinapril	5–20	twice daily	-----
Zofenopril	-----	-----	30 mg twice daily
Trandolapril	-----	-----	4 mg daily

- Medical history or symptoms of cardiovascular, cerebrovascular, or renal disease; diabetes mellitus; dyslipidemia; or gout
- Known duration and levels of elevated blood pressure
- History of weight gain, physical activity, smoking or use of tobacco
- Nutrition history with assessment of intake as to levels of sodium, alcohol, and intake of cholesterol and saturated fats
- History of results and side effects of previous antihypertensive therapies
- Symptoms suggesting secondary hypertension
- Psychosocial and environmental factors such as family situations, employment status, work conditions, and educational level that may influence control of blood pressure

Biochemical assessment should include

- Urinalysis
- Complete blood count
- Serum glucose, fasting if possible
- Electrolytes (potassium, calcium)
- Uric acid
- Cholesterol (total and HDL)
- Triglyceride level

MEDICAL NUTRITION THERAPY

Elements of the prescription for medical nutrition therapy include

- *weight reduction:* excessive body weight is correlated closely with increased blood pressure.
  - Deposition of excess fat in the upper body (increased waist-to-hip ratio above 0.85 in women and 0.95 in men) has been correlated with hypertension.
  - Weight reduction reduces blood pressure in a large proportion of hypertensive individuals with as little as 10 pounds of loss.

Classification of Blood Pressure for Adults Age 18 Years and Older

Category	Systolic (mm Hg)	Diastolic (mm Hg)
Normal	< 130	< 85
High normal	130–139	85–89
Hypertension		
Stage 1 (mild)	140–159	90–99
Stage 2 (moderate)	160–179	100–109
Stage 3 (severe)	180–209	110–119
Stage 4 (very severe)	≥ 210	≥ 120

Manifestations of Target-Organ Disease

Organ System	Manifestations
Cardiac	Clinical, electrocardiographic, or radiologic evidence of coronary heart disease
	Left ventricular hypertrophy or "strain" by electrocardiography or left ventricular hypertrophy by echocardiography
	Left ventricular dysfunction or cardiac failure
Cerebrovascular	Transient ischemic attach or stroke
Peripheral vascular	Absence of one or more major pulses in the extremities (except for dorsalis pedis) with or without intermittent claudication; aneurysm
Renal	Serum creatinine $\geq$ 130 µmol / L (1.5 mg/dL)
	Proteinuria (1+ or greater)
	Microalbuminuria
Retinopathy	Hemorrhages or exudates, with or without papilledema

---

−Use of dietary regimens should be individualized and monitored.

−It is recommended that dietary therapy be utilized for at least 3–6 months prior to initiating pharmacologic therapy.

• *moderation of alcohol intake:* excessive alcohol intake can raise blood pressure and cause resistance to antihypertensive therapy.

−individuals should be counseled to limit their daily intake to 1 ounce of ethanol (2 ounces of 100 proof whiskey, 8 ounces of wine, or 24 ounces of beer)

• *moderation of dietary sodium:* multiple therapeutic trials document a reduction of blood pressure in response to reduced sodium intake.

−The impact on dietary sodium on blood pressure depends on the provision of sodium as the chloride salt.

−African Americans, older individuals, and individuals with hypertension are more sensitive to changes in dietary sodium chloride.

−The average American consumes in excess of 150 mmol per day of sodium.

−Moderate dietary sodium chloride reduction to a level of < 6 grams NaCl or < 2.3 grams sodium per day is recommended.

• *increase in potassium content:* dietary potassium intake may protect against developing hypertension, and potassium deficiency may increase blood pressure and induce ventricular ectopy. Several potential mechanisms have been proposed including a natriuretic effect; inhibition of renin release; antagonism of angiotension II, direct vasodilation, decreased thromboxane production; and increased kallikrein production.

−Levels should be administered that maintain serum levels.

• *Increase in calcium content:* calcium deficiency is associated with an increased prevalence of hypertension, and a low calcium intake may amplify the effects of a high sodium intake on blood pressure. An increased calcium intake may lower blood pressure in some patients with hypertension.

−Recommended calcium intakes in excess of the recommended daily allowance of 20–30 mmol (800–1200 mg) in an attempt to lower blood pressure.

• *Increase in magnesium content:* evidence suggests an association between lower dietary magnesium intake and higher blood pressure.

- An increased magnesium intake should be encouraged in an effort to lower blood pressure.

Other dietary factors with bearing on control of hypertension include

- dietary fats
- caffeine
- dietary carbohydrates and protein
- garlic and onion

The medical nutrition therapy program should be integrated within a total program for modifications in lifestyles that control hypertension and/or overall reduce cardiovascular risk.

- Lose weight if overweight
- Limit alcohol intake to no more than 1 ounce of ethanol per day
- Exercise (aerobically) on a regular basis
- Reduce sodium intake to less than 100 mmol per day (< 2.3 grams of sodium or < 6 grams of sodium chloride)
- Maintain adequate dietary potassium, calcium, and magnesium intake
- Stop smoking and reduce dietary saturated fat and cholesterol intake for overall cardiovascular health. Reducing fat intake also assists in the reduction of energy intake, which is important for control of weight and Type II diabetes mellitus.

DRUG THERAPY IN HYPERTENSION

Diuretics and beta-blockers have been shown to reduce cardiovascular morbidity and mortality in controlled clinical trials. These two classes of drugs are preferred for initial drug therapy. Due to the nature of antihypertensive drug therapies, the individual should be assessed for possible drug-nutrient interactions.

Prevention, Monitoring, and Address of Problems of Adherence

Treatment plans should include elements that address

- education about conditions and treatment
- individualization of regimen
- provision of reinforcement
- promotion of social support
- collaboration with other professionals

REFERENCES

Anderson KN, Anderson LE, Glanze WD. *Mosby's Medical, Nursing, and Allied Health Dictionary.* 4th ed. St. Louis, Mo:. Mosby-Year Book, Inc; 1994.

Avioli LV, Bassi JA, Bistrian BR, Halpern SL. *Quick Reference to Clinical Nutrition.* Philadelphia, Toronto. J.B. Lippincott Co; 1979:123–136.

Blackburn GL, Gibbons GW, Bothe A, et al. Nutritional support in cardiac cachexia. *J Thor Cardiovasc Surg.* 1977;73:489–496.

Brady JA, Rock CL, Horneffer MR. Thiamin status, diuretic medications, and the management of congestive heart failure. *J Am Diet Assoc.* 1995;95:541–4.

Canobbio MM. Brottmiller WG, Adkisson S. *Cardiovascular Disorders.* St. Louis, Mo: The C.V. Mosby Co; 1990: viii, 76–91.

Freeman LM, Roubenoff R. The nutrition implications of cardiac cachexia. *Nutr Rev.* 1994;52:340–347.

Huether SE, McCance KL. Schrefer S, Brower G, Hazelwood B. *Understanding Pathophysiology.* St. Louis, Mo: Mosby-Year Book, Inc; 1996.

Rothenberg MA, Chapman CF. *Dictionary of Medical Terms for the Nonmedical Person.* 3rd ed. Hauppauge, NY: Barron's Educational Series, Inc; 1994.

Schwengel RH, Gottlieb SS, Fisher ML. Protein-energy malnutrition in patients with ischemic and nonischemic dilated cardiomyopathy and congestive heart failure. *Am J Cardiol.* 1994;73:908–910.

Diabetes Mellitus

Pamela Charney

DESCRIPTION

Diabetes mellitus is the most common serious metabolic disease, affecting more than 11 million individuals in the United States alone. It is characterized by abnormal glucose metabolism due to relative or absolute insulin deficiency; protein and fat metabolism is also affected. It is also characterized by pre- and postprandial hyperglycemia.

Serious long-term complications include retinopathy, neuropathy, and nephropathy. Life expectancy of individuals with diabetes is only 2/3 that of the general population.

Hormones involved with carbohydrate metabolism include the following:

- *Insulin* is secreted in response to elevated serum glucose and acts to lower blood glucose levels by facilitating glucose entry into cells, suppressing gluconeogenesis, and stimulating glycogen synthesis; an oral glucose load may lead to greater insulin release than an IV dose, possibly due to effects of gastrointestinal (GI) hormone release.
- *Glucagon* is secreted in response to a low serum glucose level—e.g., during a short fast. It acts to increase blood sugar levels by stimulating glycogenolysis and gluconeogenesis, thus ensuring available energy sources during the postabsorptive period.
- The *catecholamines* (epinephrine and norepinephrine) are released in response to stress and act to increase blood glucose levels.
- *Cortisol* leads to relative insulin resistance and may increase glucose production.

Glucagon, cortisol, and the catecholamines are known as the *counterregulatory hormones*.

Diabetes takes the following forms:

- Insulin-dependent diabetes mellitus (IDDM)
  1. Patients require insulin for immediate survival.
  2. Typical onset is at an early age (usually less than 40 years of age).
  3. Patients are prone to development of diabetic ketoacidosis.
  4. Symptoms include polyuria, polydipsia, and polyphagia, often of acute onset.
  5. Condition may be diagnosed after development of diabetic ketoacidosis.
- Non–insulin-dependent diabetes mellitus (NIDDM)
  1. Insulin is not required for immediate survival.
  2. Patient may require oral hypoglycemic agents and/or insulin for adequate blood glucose control.
  3. Patient is often older and overweight at diagnosis.
  4. Patient is not prone to ketoacidosis.
  5. Condition is more common; > 80% of patients with diabetes are non–insulin dependent
- Secondary diabetes
  1. Stress-induced hyperglycemia
  2. Gestational diabetes; impaired glucose tolerance with onset during pregnancy
  3. Diabetes due to medications or pancreatic disorders

Normal carbohydrate metabolism

- Blood glucose levels normally maintained within a narrow range (80–120 mg/dL)
- Insulin levels increase after meals and promote entry of glucose into cells as well as glycogen synthesis
- During a short fast, glucagon levels stimulate gluconeogenesis and glycogenolysis
- During stress or injury, counterregulatory hormones lead to increased gluconeogenesis and glycogenolysis as well as peripheral insulin resistance

CAUSE

Insulin-Dependent Diabetes Mellitus

- IDDM may be genetic in some cases.
- There is an autoimmune connection; IDDM may be related to development of antibodies to beta cells.
- Some trigger, such as viral illness, may be required for expression of diabetes.

Non–Insulin-Dependent Diabetes Mellitus

- There is insulin resistance at both hepatic and peripheral levels.
- Pancreatic dysfunction leads to abnormal insulin secretion.
- Consistent elevated blood glucose may lead to "exhaustion" of beta cells of pancreas that may be reversed with insulin therapy in some individuals.
- Some overweight individuals may develop peripheral resistance to the actions of insulin; weight loss improves insulin resistance.

NUTRITION ASSESSMENT

- Nutrition assessment of diabetic patients is similar to that of nondiabetic patients.
- Monitor current weight status and recent changes in weight.
- Review medical and surgical history and current problems; assess for complications of long-standing diabetes (retinopathy, neuropathy, and nephropathy).
- Medication history should include timing and doses of medications.
- Monitor laboratory data to include albumin and glucose; Hgb A1c for long-term glucose control; and other laboratory data as appropriate for the clinical condition.
- Assess level of stress; adequate blood glucose control may be difficult in critically ill patients.
- Nutrient requirements
    1. Use the Harris-Benedict equation with appropriate stress factors. Avoid overfeeding.

Indirect calorimetry allows for accurate measurement of energy requirements.
2. A quick rule of thumb is to provide no more than 25–30 kcal/kg body weight for most hospitalized patients.
3. Provide 0.8 g of protein/kg for nonstressed patients.
4. Protein requirements may be as high as 1.5–1.75 g/kg body weight in metabolic stress.
5. There is controversy over the need for protein restriction in renal failure. Many now suggest 0.6–0.8 g of protein/kg body weight for stable patients not on dialysis; patients on dialysis require increased protein intake.

PROBLEMS

Effect of Stress and Illness on Glycemic Control

- Stress and illness increase levels of counterregulatory hormones.
- Hepatic glucose production increases, while peripheral glucose uptake decreases.
- Peripheral insulin resistance often complicates management, leading to hyperglycemia that is difficult to control.
- Decreased oral intake during illness contributes to suboptimal glycemic control.

Diabetic Ketoacidosis

- Diabetic ketoacidosis is a potentially life-threatening complication that is seen in IDDM. It probably is related to insulin deficiency in the face of elevated counterregulatory hormones.
- Oxidation of fatty acids leads to increased levels of the ketone bodies (betahydroxybutyric acid and acetoacetic acid).
- Osmotic diuresis leads to dehydration, electrolyte abnormalities, and metabolic acidosis; if untreated, it has adverse effects on cardiovascular and renal function.
- The condition is treated with insulin as well as fluid and electrolyte replacement.

Hyperosmolar, Hyperglycemic, Nonketotic Coma

- This is a complication seen in NIDDM, most often in those with a concurrent serious illness.
- Residual insulin secretion is thought to prevent the development of acidosis.
- The condition is characterized by extreme hyperglycemia (> 600 mg/dL) and serum osmolality > 330 m Osm/kg, mild acidosis, and serum bicarbonate > 20 mEq/L; patients may be obtunded.
- Treatment is with insulin in addition to fluid and electrolyte replacement.
- Prompt recognition and treatment are vital, as mortality may be as high as 50%.

Hypoglycemia

- May occur as a result of overzealous insulin administration.
- Other causes include missed meals after insulin administration.
- Repeated severe hypoglycemia may have adverse neurological effects.

Neuropathy

- Delayed gastric emptying, or *gastroparesis*, occurs in 45%–75% of individuals with diabetes.
- Gastroparesis may be asymptomatic in some individuals. In others, it may be characterized by acute exacerbations with symptom-free intervals.
- Pharmacologic therapy includes erythromycin, domperidone, metaclopramide, and cisapride.
- Bowel rest and parenteral nutrition are rarely necessary; enteral feedings are often possible with tube placement in the duodenum.

Nephropathy

- Proteinuria is the first sign of diabetic nephropathy.

- Protein-restricted diets (0.6–0.8 g of protein/kg body weight) are often recommended prior to the initiation of dialysis; patients should be monitored closely to prevent development of malnutrition.
- Patients receiving maintenance dialysis treatment require adequate protein intake (up to 1.5 g of protein/kg body weight).

Dislipidemia

- The most common abnormality is elevated triglycerides along with low levels of high-density lipoprotein (HDL) cholesterol.
- Hypertriglyceridemia may improve with glycemic control.
- Patients with triglyceride levels > 2000 mg/dL may be at risk for pancreatitis.
- Treatment includes weight loss (in obese individuals), exercise, and a low-fat, limited–simple sugar diet.

TREATMENT/MANAGEMENT

- Treatment includes diet, exercise, oral hypoglycemics, and insulin if needed.
- Exercise enhances weight loss and may improve metabolic control in some individuals.
- Use of alcohol is discouraged.
- Results of the Diabetes Control and Complications Trial (DCCT) show that good control may prevent or delay onset of complications.

Diet

- Improved insulin sensitivity with weight loss in obese individuals may lead to improvement in glycemic control as well as decreased reliance on pharmacologic therapy.
- Increased fiber intake is often recommended, but glycemic response to fiber varies. Up to 50 g of dietary fiber per day has been recommended.
- Approximately 10%–20% of calories should come from protein.
- Diet should also include less than 30% of total calories from fat; saturated fat should be re-

duced. Recently, there has been increased interest in diets high in monounsaturated fat; more research is needed on long-term effects.

- The remainder of calories should be supplied by carbohydrate; moderate sucrose consumption is allowed as part of a well-balanced diet in patients with good blood glucose control.
- Consistency in timing of meals is important for patients on insulin therapy; however, intensive therapy and home blood glucose monitoring allow for more flexibility. Meal planning must be determined according to the patient's lifestyle and habits.
- A diabetic exchange system is often used in meal planning for patients with diabetes; other meal planning systems are also available.
- Results of the DCCT indicate the need for a multidisciplinary approach to nutrition management to optimize compliance.

Oral Hypoglycemic Agents

- Oral hypoglycemic agents are used in patients with NIDDM.
- Sulfonylureas act to stimulate insulin secretion and potentially reduce insulin resistance.
- Metformin, a biguanide, has recently been approved for use in the United States.
- Long-acting agents have been associated with the development of hypoglycemia and should not be used in the elderly or those at risk for hypoglycemia.

Insulin

- In normal individuals, insulin is secreted as a bolus dose in response to a meal as well as a constant basal level; most adults secrete approximately 30–35 units/day.
- Patients with IDDM require exogenous insulin for survival; patients with NIDDM may require insulin to achieve blood glucose control.
- Currently, beef, pork, and human insulins are available; beef and pork differ from human insulin by 1 and 3 amino acids.
- Short-acting (regular), intermediate (NPH), and long-acting insulins are available; they differ in timing of peak action as well as duration of action.

- Currently, there is no "ideal" recommended insulin regimen. Insulin therapy in IDDM may be initiated with 0.6–0.8 units/kg per body weight and adjusted according to blood sugar levels. Traditionally, patients are managed with both A.M. and P.M. injections of a combination of short- and intermediate-acting insulin per day.
- Many physicians now recommend "intensive" management with multiple insulin injections each day; insulin pumps may be used in some patients to avoid the need for multiple needlesticks each day.
- Patient lifestyle, blood glucose levels, and desires must be considered when designing an insulin regimen.
- Accurate home blood glucose monitoring is needed for optimal glycemic control.

NUTRITION SUPPORT IN PATIENTS WITH DIABETES MELLITUS

- Indications for nutrition support are the same as those for patients without diabetes.
- Enteral feedings are preferred over parenteral feedings for several reasons: enteral feeding provides for a more physiologic route of feeding, maintenance of the gut mucosal barrier, and fewer potentially serious complications.
- Glycemic control should be optimized prior to initiating enteral or parenteral feedings.
- Insulin is the preferred pharmacologic agent for glycemic control; oral hypoglycemic agents are not recommended except for those patients who are stable on long-term enteral feedings.

Enteral Nutrition Support

- Feedings should be given into the small intestine, particularly in those patients with gastroparesis.
- Balanced polymeric formulas are appropriate for most patients, including those with mild to moderate gastrointestinal impairment.

- Disease-specific formulas are expensive and not well tested.
- Feedings should not be diluted unless additional free water is needed.
- For guidelines on insulin use in enteral nutrition, see Exhibit 3–1.

Parenteral Nutrition Support

- Initiate total parenteral nutrition with 100–150 g of dextrose; advance dextrose by 50–75 g/d only after blood sugar is stable at the desired level.
- Less than 30% of nonprotein calories as lipid is a safe level and may decrease the need for insulin in some patients.
- For guidelines on insulin use in parenteral nutrition, see Exhibit 3–2.

Exhibit 3–1 Insulin Use in Enteral Nutrition

If the patient has not previously been on insulin:

- Check blood glucose levels every 6 hours.
- Initiate sliding scale insulin as needed.
- Add 1/4 to 1/2 of the previous day's sliding scale as NPH.
- Continue sliding-scale coverage.
- Split doses of NPH with sliding-scale insulin as needed.

If the patient has previously been on insulin:

- Check blood glucose levels every 6 hours.
- Patient may require increased insulin with enteral feedings, particularly if critically ill.
- Give 1/4 of usual NPH dose every 12 hours while initiating continuous feedings.
- Give sliding-scale regular insulin to maintain blood glucose levels < 200 mg/dL.
- Add 1/4 to 1/2 of the previous day's sliding scale as NPH.
- Monitor insulin dose as well as enteral formula intake daily to prevent sudden fluctuations of insulin or formula intake.

Exhibit 3–2 Insulin Use in Parenteral Nutrition

If the patient has not previously been on insulin:

- Do not give insulin in initial total parenteral nutrition (TPN).
- Check blood glucose levels every 6 hours.
- Give sliding-scale insulin to maintain blood glucose levels < 200 mg/dL.
- Add 1/4–1/2 of previous day's sliding scale as regular insulin to the next day's TPN.
- Continue to adjust regular insulin in TPN according to sliding-scale insulin needs and blood glucose monitoring.

If the patient has previously been on insulin:

- Initiate TPN with 100–150 g of dextrose.
- Add approximately 1/4 usual NPH dose as regular insulin in TPN.
- Check blood sugar every 6 hours.
- Give sliding-scale insulin to maintain blood glucose levels < 200 mg/dL.
- Add 1/4–1/2 of previous day's sliding scale as regular insulin to the next day's TPN.

REFERENCES

Anderson JW, Gustafson NJ, Bryant CA, Tietyen-Clark J. Dietary fiber and diabetes: a comprehensive review and practical application. *J Am Diet Assoc.* 1987;87:1189–1197.

Charney PJ. Diabetes mellitus. In: Gottschlich MM, Matarese LE, Shronts EP, eds. *Nutrition Support Dietetics Core Curriculum.* 2nd ed. Silver Spring, Md: American Society for Parenteral and Enteral Nutrition; 1993:377–388.

Diabetes Control and Complications Trial Research Group. The effects of intensive treatment of diabetes on the development and progression of long term complications in insulin-dependent diabetes mellitus. *N Engl J Med.* 1993;329:977–986.

Franz MJ, Horton ES, Bantle JP, et al. Nutrition principles for the management of diabetes and related complications. *Diabetes Care.* 1994;17:490–518.

Garg A. High-monounsaturated fat diet for diabetic patients. *Diabetes Care.* 1994;17:242–246.

Henry RR. Protein content of the diabetic diet. *Diabetes Care.* 1994;17:1502-1513.

Ilarde A, Tuck M. Treatment of non-insulin-dependent diabetes mellitus and its complications: a state of the art review. *Drugs Aging.* 1994;4:470–491.

Lebovitz HE. Oral antidiabetic agents. In: Kahn CR, Weir GC, eds. *Joslin's Diabetes Mellitus.* 13th ed. Philadelphia, Pa: Lea & Febiger; 1994:508–525.

Nutritional care in diabetes mellitus and reactive hypoglycemia. In: Mahan LK, Arlin M, eds. *Food, Nutrition, and Diet Therapy.* 8th ed. Philadelphia, Pa: WB Saunders Co; 1992:527–555.

Page SR, Tattersall RB. How to achieve optimal diabetic control in patients with insulin-dependent diabetes. *Postgrad Med J.* 1994;70:675–681.

Riccardi G, Rivellese AA. Effects of dietary fiber and carbohydrate on glucose and lipoprotein metabolism in diabetic patients. *Diabetes Care.* 1991;14:1115–1125.

Rosenzweig JL. Principles of insulin therapy. In: Kahn CR, Weir GC, eds. *Joslin's Diabetes Mellitus.* 13th ed. Philadelphia, Pa: Lea & Febiger; 1994:460–487.

Tal A. Oral hypoglycemic agents in the treatment of type II diabetes. *Am Fam Physician.* 1993;48:1089–1095.

Gastrointestinal Disorders

Deborah Silverman

DESCRIPTION

The major function of the gastrointestinal tract is to convert foodstuffs into a form that can be readily assimilated and used by the body.

Gastrointestinal disorders often result in maldigestion and malabsorption of nutrients, which often presents as diarrhea. Diarrhea can have severe nutritional consequences through loss of essential nutrients such as water, minerals, vitamins, electrolytes, and micronutrients. Severe diarrhea can disrupt nutrient absorption to such an extent that malnutrition can occur.

Gastrointestinal disorders can be both the cause and the end result of life-threatening conditions. Disruption of the normal processes of nutrient digestion and absorption causes malnutrition, which may lead to serious clinical complications.

The gastrointestinal tract includes organs that comprise the alimentary canal and certain accessory organs, primarily the pancreas, liver, and gallbladder.

- The upper gastrointestinal tract is composed of
  1. the mouth and pharynx (or oral cavity)
  2. the esophagus
  3. the secretory glands
  4. the stomach
- The lower gastrointestinal tract is composed of
  1. the duodenum
  2. the jejunum
  3. the ileum
  4. the colon
- The accessory organs are composed of
  1. the liver
  2. the gallbladder
  3. the pancreas
  4. the cecum
  5. the appendix

The functions of different parts of the gastrointestinal tract are as follows:

- The *alimentary canal* begins the digestive process with chewing, salivating, and swallowing.
- The *stomach* stores food, mixes food with gastric juices, and regulates transport into the small intestine for continued digestion and absorption.
- The *small intestine* (duodenum, jejunum, and ileum) completes the digestive process by absorbing the end products of digestion.

- The *large intestine* (colon, cecum, and appendix) absorbs water and forms feces.
- *Secretory glands*, which are distributed throughout the gastrointestinal tract, with the exception of the colon, release secretions into a duct (*exocrine*) or release secretions into the blood (*endocrine*).
- *Sphincters*—circular muscles located in the gastrointestinal tract—assist in regulating passage of contents from one segment of the tract to another.

Digestion

Table 3–3 shows the digestive process.

Absorption

Table 3–4 shows sites of absorption for different nutrients.

Secretion

- Fluids fluctuate in volume from the mouth to that which is lost in stool.
- Of the approximate 2 L of fluid ingested daily, approximately 7 L are added from endogenous secretions, for a total of 9 L.
  1. 3–5 L of this fluid is absorbed in the jejunum.
  2. 3–4 L of this fluid is absorbed in the ileum.
  3. 1–2 L of this fluid is absorbed in the colon.
  4. 0.2 L of this fluid is lost in stool.
- Refer to Table 3–5 for a breakdown of the composition of different gastrointestinal fluids.

Motility

- Many factors may alter the motility of the gastrointestinal tract and influence gastric emptying.
- Return of normal activity may precede return of bowel sounds in postoperative patients.
- The digestive organs resume normal activity postoperatively at different times:
  1. The stomach's propulsive functions should return in 48–72 hours.
  2. The small intestine's propulsive function can be seen within 12 hours, making the small intestine the best site for early postoperative enteral feeding.
  3. The colon may require about 72 hours for propulsive function to be seen and for contractions to be sustained that move gas and bowel contents.
- Factors that may prolong postoperative ileus include
  1. Sympathetic hyperactivity, usually due to pain
  2. Abdominal distention
  3. Intraperitoneal irritation
  4. The administration of autonomic, cardiac, or psychotropic drugs
  5. Electrolyte imbalances
  6. Concomitant disease in the gastrointestinal tract
- The passage of flatus commonly indicates the end of a postoperative ileus.

Adaptation

Maintenance of the trophic effects found in the mucosa of the gastrointestinal tract is best accomplished through provision of enteral nutrient sources. Provision of specific gastrointestinal tract–preferred fuel sources, such as glutamine to the enterocyte and short-chain fatty acids to the colonocyte during periods of growth following resection or injury, is advantageous in achieving adaptation.

Immunologic Barrier

The mucosa of the gastrointestinal tract provides a protective barrier against bacterial translocation and potential toxins. Failure to maintain a normal mucosal barrier can lead to breakdown of barrier function and increase gastrointestinal tract permeability.

NUTRITIONAL IMPLICATIONS IN ASSESSMENT OF THE GASTROINTESTINAL TRACT

Assessment of an individual with a gastrointestinal disorder should cover the following areas:

Table 3–3 Digestive Process

Source of Secretion	Enzyme(s)	Substrate(s)	End Products
Salivary glands	Salivary amylase	Starch Glycogen	Maltose plus 1:6 glucosides plus maltotriose
Lingual glands	Lingual lipase	Short-chain primary ester link at omega-3	Fatty acids plus 1, 2-diacylglycerols
Stomach glands	Pepsin A (fundus) Pepsin B (pylorus) Rennin	Protein Casein of milk	Peptides Coagulates of milk
Pancreas	Trypsin	Protein Peptides	Polypeptides Dipeptides
	Chymotrypsin	Protein Peptides	Same as trypsin
	Carboxypeptidase	Polypeptides at the free carboxyl end of the chain	Lower peptides; free amino acids
	Pancreatic amylase	Starch Glycogen	Maltose plus 1:6 glucosides plus maltotriose
	Lipase	Primary ester linkages of triacylglycerol	Fatty acids, monoacylglycerols, diacylglycerols, glycerol
	Ribonuclease	Ribonucleic acid	Nucleotides
	Deoxyribonuclease	Deoxyribonucleic acids	Nucleotides
	Cholesteryl ester hydrolase	Cholesteryl esters	Free cholesterol plus fatty acids
	Phospholipiase A_2	Phospholipids	Fatty acids, lysophospholipids
Liver and gallbladder	Bile salts and alkali	Fats, neutralize acid chyme	Fatty acid-bile salt conjugates and finely emulsified neutral fat-bile salt micelles and liposomes
Small intestine	Aminopeptidase	Polypeptides at the free amino end of the chain	Lower peptides; free amino acids
	Dipeptidases	Dipeptides	Amino acids
	Sucrase	Sucrose	Fructose, glucose
	Maltase	Maltose	Glucose
	Lactase	Lactose	Glucose, galactose
	Phosphatase	Organic phosphates	Free phosphate
	Isomaltase or 1:6 glucosidase	1:6 glucosides	Glucose
	Polynucleotidase	Nucleic acid	Nucleotides
	Nucleosidases	Purine or pyrimidine nucleosides	Purine or pyrimidine bases, pentose phosphate

Source: Adapted from RK Murray, DK Granner, PA Mayes, VW Rodwell. In: *Harper's Biochemistry,* 21st ed., pp. 584–585, © 1988, Appleton & Lange.

Table 3–4 Absorption Process

Site	Nutrient(s) Absorbed
Esophagus	None
Stomach	Water, ethyl alcohol, copper, iodide, fluoride, molybdenum
Duodenum	Calcium, phosphorus, magnesium, iron, copper, selenium, thiamin, riboflavin, niacin, biotin, folate, vitamins A, D, E, K
Jejunum	Lipids, monosaccharides, amino acids, small peptides, thiamin, riboflavin, niacin, pantothenate, biotin, folate, vitamin B_6, vitamin C, vitamins A, D, E, and K, calcium, phosphorus, magnesium, iron, zinc, chromium, manganese, molybdenum
Ileum	Vitamin C, folate, vitamin B_{12}, vitamin D, vitamin K, magnesium, bile salts and acids
Colon	Water, vitamin K, biotin, sodium, chloride, potassium, short-chain fatty acids

- *Chief complaint:* If the patient presents with gastric pain, heartburn, vomiting, or altered bowel habits, ask questions about
  1. Onset, duration, and severity of the complaint
  2. What precipitates the symptoms
  3. What makes symptoms worse
  4. What makes symptoms better
- *Medical history:* Ask about
  1. History of disorders of the mouth, throat, abdomen, and rectum
  2. Long-term gastrointestinal conditions such as ulcerative colitis
  3. Major disorders, including neurologic disorders that can impair movement of the tongue, mouth, and throat and gastric motility and disease conditions such as diabetes, hypothyroidism, and constipation
  4. Allergies to foods
  5. Surgical history for procedures of the gastrointestinal tract, particularly resections

  6. Ingestion of vitamins, mineral supplements, laxatives, and mineral oil
- *Family history:* Check for a history of Crohn's disease, ulcerative colitis, colon cancer, gallbladder disease, alcoholism, or gastric ulcers.
- *Psychosocial history:* Investigate situations that might have emotional implications, including implications for self-image.
- *Functional status/activities of daily living:* Ask about
  1. Nutrition history (detailed)
  2. Appetite changes
  3. Ability to purchase and prepare food
  4. Special dietary restrictions
  5. Ability to exercise regularly
  6. Smoking and drinking history
  7. Dental history
- *Physical examination* for nutritional status
  1. Obtain height, weight, and weight history (particularly related to recent changes associated with vomiting and diarrhea).

Table 3–5 Composition of Gastrointestinal Fluids in mEq/L

Source	Volume per Day	Sodium	Potassium	Chloride	Bicarbonate
Gastric	2000 at pH < 4	60	10	90	0
	2500 at pH > 4	100	10	100	0
Pancreatic	1000	140	5	75	90
Bile	1500	140	5	100	35
Small bowel	3500	100	15	100	25
Diarrhea	1000–4000	60	30	45	45

2. Mouth: Inspect the individual's mouth for dental caries and problems of the gums, tongue, and lips.
3. Abdomen: Use techniques of inspection, auscultation, percussion, and palpation to detect such markers as bowel sounds and location(s) of pain.

- *Review of assessments/history/physical examinations by other health care professionals:* Look for abnormal findings such as dysphagia, nausea and vomiting, distention and protrusion, abdominal pulsations related to intestinal obstruction, abnormal abdominal sounds (hyper- or hypoactive bowel), ascites, abdominal pain, constipation, and diarrhea.
- *Pertinent diagnostic tests*
  1. Liver function tests, including prothrombin time and ammonia levels
  2. Prealbumin
  3. Hydration status indicators (patient may have a propensity to become dehydrated)
  4. Stool analysis
  5. Radiography: abdominal films, barium swallows, upper gastrointestinal series, small-bowel series and enema, barium enema
  6. Endoscopy
  7. Ultrasonography, computed tomography (CT) scan, magnetic resonance imaging (MRI)

Optimally, to assess/determine problems of the gastrointestinal tract, one should have a solid knowledge of the normal processes of digestion, absorption, and metabolism.

If the individual is experiencing symptoms that do not appear to be normal, then the nutrition care plan should be based on achievement of an outcome as close to normal as possible.

SIGNIFICANT FACTORS THAT MAY AFFECT THE ABILITY TO DELIVER APPROPRIATE NUTRITION SUPPORT

- *Jejunal resection, intact ileum, intact colon.* Individuals rarely need aggressive nutrition support and can usually be fed immediately.
- *Less than 100 cm of ileum resected; colon largely intact.* Individuals have bile acid diarrhea but can usually be managed by controlled oral intake and medication therapy.
- *100–200 cm of ileal resection with colon largely intact.* Individuals have both bile acid diarrhea and steatorrhea but can usually be treated by a managed oral diet.
- *More than 200 cm of small bowel resected or lesser resection with colostomy.* Individuals require a well-managed oral diet following a graduated regimen for adaptation.
- *Less than 60 cm of small bowel remaining or only duodenum.* Individuals require parenteral nutrition support and may also receive adjunctive oral or tube feedings.
- *Surgical removal of portions of the upper gastrointestinal system secondary to tumor, trauma, achalasia, or esophageal stricture.* Management will vary depending upon the extent of the surgical removal, the portion(s) of the upper gastrointestinal system removed, and the nature of possible postoperative therapy.
- *Partial obstruction, eg, secondary to tumor, stricture (scleroderma), or inflammation.* Individuals rarely need aggressive nutrition support and can be managed by controlled oral intake.
- *Oral cavity abnormality, such as lesions or poor dentition.* Individuals rarely need aggressive nutrition support and can be managed by controlled oral intake.
- *Gastroparesis as a result of diabetes mellitus, pancreatic cancer, a medication side effect, aging, neuromuscular disorders such as ALS, chemotherapies such as vinblastine and vincristine, or uremia.* Individual management will vary depending on the etiology of the gastroparesis.
- *Diseases that have a high risk for swallowing disorders, such as Parkinsonism, dementia, Alzheimer's, coma, cerebrovascular disease, multiple sclerosis, head trauma, or muscular dystrophies.* Individual management will vary depending on the etiology and extent of the swallowing disorder.

SPECIFIC DISORDERS OF THE GASTROINTESTINAL TRACT: THE ORAL CAVITY AND ESOPHAGUS

On entering the mouth, food is chewed by the action of the jaw muscles and is made ready for swallowing by mixing with the secretions released from the salivary glands. The passage of food from the mouth through the pharynx into the esophagus constitutes *swallowing*. Swallowing is divided into four stages:

- anticipatory
- oral (or voluntary)
- pharyngeal
- esophageal

Swallowing is a reflex response initiated by a voluntary action and regulated by the swallowing center in the medulla of the brain. As the food passes through the pharynx, the swallowing center acts to inhibit the respiratory center, thereby preventing food from being aspirated into the larynx and lungs.

When food moves into the esophagus, both the striated muscles of the upper portion of the esophagus and the smooth muscles of the distal portion are stimulated by cholinergic (parasympathetic) nerves. The result is *peristalsis*, or a progressive wavelike motion that moves the food through the esophagus into the stomach.

At the lower end of the esophagus, just above the upper end of the stomach, lies the lower esophageal sphincter (LES). Normal LES pressure is higher than intragastric pressure. On swallowing, the LES pressure drops, relaxing the sphincter so that food may pass from the esophagus into the stomach. The musculature of the LES possesses increased tonic pressure that functions between meals to prevent gastroesophageal reflux.

Swallowing Difficulties/Dysphagia

Disruption of any phase of the swallowing process can result in dysphagia, either with or without aspiration. It is necessary to evaluate the disturbance via fluoroscopic swallow study and to prescribe a nutrition therapy modality that is individualized to the consistency of a diet that enables safe mastication and swallowing. Modifications in consistencies of foods include the following:

- Use of thin liquids that do not require mastication and require only minimal pharyngeal or esophageal peristalsis
- Use of thick liquids that do not require mastication but require tongue control to form and propel the bolus through the oral cavity, and require some pharyngeal and esophageal peristalsis to keep the mass from lodging in the esophagus
- Use of mashed solid foods that do not require mastication but contain more bulk than liquids, that are easily controlled by the tongue, and that require more pharyngeal and esophageal action.
- Use of semisolid foods that require some degree of mastication but can be formed into a soft mass so that they can be held and controlled by the tongue. Foods of this consistency also require adequate pharyngeal movement to complete the swallow.
- Use of soft chunk foods that require mastication but do not result in the individual's becoming fatigued during the feeding process. These foods tend to stick together to form a cohesive bolus and may then trigger the pharyngeal swallow response. They should not stick to the palate or tongue and should be easy for the tongue to control.

Reflux Esophagitis or Gastroesophageal Reflux Disease

Gastroesophageal reflux, manifested as heartburn, results from LES incompetence (a decrease in pressure at the LES), which occurs when LES pressure is decreased or the LES is relaxed. Recurring reflux of hydrochloric acid into the esophagus can damage the esophageal mucosa. Multiple mechanisms, including neural and hormonal, regulate LES pressure. Certain foods and/or food-related substances appear to increase, probably indirectly, the relaxation of the LES. Fat-containing foods increase relaxation by decreasing LES pressure and delaying gastric emptying. Other foods with this effect include chocolate, alcohol, mint, carbonated beverages, citrus, tomato juices, and possibly coffee.

Nutritional management should be aimed at

- avoiding substances that can further lower LES pressure, which is already low due to the condition
- avoiding substances that may promote the secretion of acid, which would then be present in higher concentrations than normal if refluxed
- avoiding high-fat foods or meals, chocolate, coffee, alcohol, peppermint, spearmint, and other plants with volatile oils
- avoiding high-protein diets; the digestion of protein stimulates the release of gastrin, which increases LES pressure but is also a potent stimulator of hydrochloric acid secretion
- consuming small meals and consuming fluids between meals to decrease gastric volume

Achalasia

Achalasia is a motility disorder of the esophagus associated with dysphagia or difficulty in swallowing. The sphincter may fail to relax and open properly when swallowing occurs, thereby impairing passage of the food bolus from the pharynx into the stomach and possibly precluding aspiration.

Nutritional management should have the opposite aim from that for gastroesophageal reflux disease: ie, to reduce gastrin secretion, thereby lowering LES pressure and facilitating relaxation of the sphincter:

- reducing carbohydrate and protein in the diet and increasing fat
- incorporating low-fiber foods that are easier to swallow
- avoiding use of citrus juices and highly spiced foods to prevent irritation of the mucosa
- avoiding use of caffeine and theophylline, which increase LES pressure

Other Esophageal Disorders

Esophageal Perforation

Esophageal perforation may be caused by blunt injury to the chest, abdominal trauma, convulsions, endoscopic study, or a surgical procedure. Nutritional consequences include weight loss due to inability to ingest adequate oral nutrition and excessive protein loss because of catabolism and/or loss of protein-rich fluid.

In nutritional management:

- Enteral nutrition is the preferred modality, but the use of a nasogastric/enteric feeding route should be avoided so as not to increase esophageal irritation and reflux.
- Percutaneous endoscopically placed feeding sites should also be avoided because the esophagus must be invaded for placement.
- Gastrostomy or jejunostomy feedings are appropriate.

Esophageal Obstruction

The esophagus may be obstructed by cancer, congenital abnormalities, or strictures. Nutritional consequences include weight loss, dysphagia, and sepsis (aspiration pneumonia).

In nutritional management:

- Enteral nutrition is the preferred modality. Parenteral nutrition is not indicated because the gastrointestinal tract is functional.
- Use of percutaneous endoscopically placed feeding tubes, gastrostomy, and jejunostomy feeding sites is appropriate.
- Polymeric formulas are generally well tolerated.

Esophageal Varices

This is a condition of portal hypertension with multiple etiologies. Its nutritional consequence is malnutrition.

Nutritional management includes

- use of a soft diet excluding high-roughage foods that can cause irritation
- use of enteral nutrition support (but nasoenteric feeding tube placements are contraindicated due to risk of esophageal bleeding)

• use of percutaneous or gastrostomy-placed feedings only in absence of ascites

Esophageal Resection/Replacement

Esophageal resection or replacement may be required because of tumor, congenital abnormalities, or trauma. Nutritional consequences include swallowing difficulties due to differences in musculature and innervation between the colon/jejunum and the normal esophagus.

In nutritional management

• Give small, frequent feedings of nutrient-dense foods to optimize intake.
• An antidumping regimen may be indicated.
• Have feeding jejunostomies placed at the time of the operative procedure.
• Oral daily intake may be augmented with nocturnal feedings.

SPECIFIC DISEASES OF THE GASTROINTESTINAL TRACT: THE STOMACH

The bolus of swallowed food enters the stomach through the LES. The stomach connects the esophagus with the small intestine and is divided functionally and histologically into the following parts:

• cardis
• fundus
• body
• antrum
• pylorus

The fundus and body contain most of the acid- and pepsin-secreting cells, the antrum contains cells that secrete gastrin, and the neck cells throughout the stomach produce intrinsic factor.

Blood supply arrives from the celiac trunk and the major branches of the celiac, left gastric, common hepatic, and splenic arteries, splitting off into numerous branches that provide a very rich supply to the organ. Autonomic innervation is primarily parasympathetic through the vagus nerve and sympathetic through fibers that arise from T-6 to T-10.

The stomach has two curvatures, the lesser and the greater, with the lesser being shorter than the greater. The shape of the stomach allows it to serve as an excellent food reservoir.

One of the most important functions of the stomach is the production of hydrochloric acid. The gastric mucosal barrier prevents hydrochloric ions from flowing back through the gastric mucosa and also lubricates the passage of solids and undigested food. It protects the epithelium from mechanical damage, delays the passage of chyme into the intestine so that the intestine is not overwhelmed, and enables food to be properly mixed for initial digestion. Hyper- and hypo-osmotic solutions as well as fats appear to delay emptying of the stomach as a result of a reflux mechanism from receptors situated in the duodenum. Between meals, gastric motor function works to empty any residual of recently ingested food.

Peptic Ulcer Disease

Peptic ulcer disease is an ulceration of the gastrointestinal tract in areas that come in contact with gastric acid. Treatment is directed at the reduction of gastric secretions and the buffering of gastric acid. Chronic antacid therapy, however, may affect nutritional status in the following ways:

• Excessive and prolonged use of calcium antacid products may induce hypercalcemia and development of renal calculi.
• Phosphorus depletion may occur with use of magnesium hydroxide and aluminum hydroxide.
• Cimetidine may decrease vitamin B_{12} absorption.
• Pain, bleeding, hypermotility, and/or gastric outlet obstruction may occur.
• Iron-deficiency anemia may develop secondary to poor intake, blood loss, impaired breakdown of iron-rich foods, and altered gastric pH.
• Progression to oral intake and the variety of food items included is based on individual tolerance.

Gastritis

Gastritis is the acute or chronic inflammation of the mucosal lining of the stomach. Etiologies vary but include alcohol abuse, ingestion of corrosives, bacterial or viral infection (food poisoning), anemia, shock, and chronic drug use.

The clinician should take into consideration the following implications for nutritional status:

- Pain on eating may prevent adequate oral intake.
- Stimulation of gastric secretions should be reduced; modifications to the diet include avoidance of caffeine and excess liquids.
- Reduced secretion of intrinsic factor may result from chronic gastritis, increasing the risk of inadequate vitamin B_{12} absorption.

Vomiting

Aside from obvious impairment of intake, prolonged vomiting can lead to a metabolic alkalosis.

- Intractable vomiting may require parenteral support until oral intake or enteral support can be reestablished

Hiatal Hernia

Hiatal hernia is herniation of a portion of the stomach through the hiatus of the diaphragm into the esophagus.

- Anatomical ramifications of this condition may complicate or contraindicate nasogastric or orogastric tube feedings.
- Progression of oral feeds requires frequent small feedings, upright positioning during ingestion, avoiding food intake prior to retirement, and often elevation of the head of the bed to avoid regurgitation and aspiration.

Gastric Outlet Obstruction

Gastric outlet obstruction is a disturbance in the normal emptying of the stomach. It may be

- *Anatomical*, as in pyloric stenosis, stricture, or swelling near a pyloric or duodenal ulcer,
- *Functional*, occurring, eg, postvagotomy.

The patient may require parenteral support while diagnostic evaluation is in progress. If the disturbance is prolonged, the patient may require enteral feeding via jejunostomy.

GI Bleed

GI bleed may be accompanied by nausea and hematemesis.

- With resolution of hemorrhage, resume enteral infusions or oral intake as tolerated.
- Chronic low-grade gastric bleeding or recurring gastrointestinal bleeds can induce iron-deficiency anemia.
- Scleroderma is thickening of the gastric lining that may interfere with secretion of gastric juice.
- Vasomotor involvement may affect gastric motility.
- Gastric carcinoma is often asymptomatic initially, then characterized by anorexia and weakness progressing to early satiety, pain, and vomiting.
- Surgical resection may be indicated.

General Surgery

Gastric surgeries may be indicated in cases of tumor, ulcer disease, perforation, hemorrhage, Zollinger-Ellison syndrome, gastric polyposis, and Menetrier's disease.

Vagotomy

Truncal vagotomy has the following effects:

- The resting tone of the stomach (*gastric stasis*) is altered, and the pyloric sphincter is widely patent.
- Poor gastric emptying is the result of a disturbance in normal antral peristalsis.
- Emptying of solids is slowed and emptying of liquids is accelerated.
- Hypertonic fluids leave the stomach undiluted.
- The grinding of solid foods and the sieving action of the pylorus are not normal, resulting in the emptying of larger masses of solid food into the small intestine.

- The stomach is less able to perform the functions of storage, mixing, liquefying, digesting, and delivering the resulting chyme to the duodenum in a controlled fashion.
- There is early satiety because of reduced storage capacity.

Selective and parietal cell vagotomies have the following effects:

- There is minimal acceleration of liquid emptying.
- Emptying of solids is not altered.
- There is early satiety because of reduced gastric capacity.
- Vagotomy of the fundus will impair receptive relaxation.
- Release of catecholamines or any means of sympathetic stimulation causes relaxation of fundic tone and occasionally gives rise to acute gastric dilatation (*adynamic ileus*).
- Once the process has resolved, all liquids are handled by the stomach in the same fashion, so the common practice of progression from a clear liquid to a full liquid to a soft diet in the postoperative period has no physiologic rationale.

Pyloroplasty

- This surgery is commonly used to widen the opening of the pylorus.
- Hypertonic fluids flow into the duodenum.

Total Gastrectomy

In cases of total gastrectomy (removal of the entire stomach), a reservoir may be created by using a section of the jejunum to form a pouch.

- The limitations of a reduced gastric pouch, however, dictate a need for small, frequent, nutrient-dense feedings.
- The loss of the pyloric sphincter can result in dumping syndrome (described later in this section).

Subtotal or Partial Gastrectomy

This procedure is removal of a portion of the stomach (amount removed varied) accompanied by a reconstruction procedure. There are several varieties of partial gastrectomy:

- Gastroduodenostomy (Billroth I)—anastomosis of the proximal end of the intestine (duodenum) to the distal end of the stomach, causing bypassing of pyloric sphincter
  1. Dumping syndrome may occur.
  2. Some compromise of digestion may result as chyme rapidly mixes with duodenal, pancreatic, and biliary secretions.
- Gastrojejunostomy (Billroth II)—anastomosis of the stomach to the side of the jejunum, creating a blind loop and resulting in bypassing of the pyloric sphincter
  1. Dumping syndrome may occur.
  2. Some compromise of digestion, particularly fat, may occur as chyme mixes with duodenal, pancreatic, and biliary secretions in abnormal synchronization.
- Gastric Bypass—gastroenterostomy created surgically so that food bypasses most of the stomach
  1. Dumping syndrome may occur.
  2. Other complications include steatorrhea, gallstones, and the potential for iron and B_{12} deficiency.
- Gastric Stapling—surgical division of the stomach, leaving a small partition open to food passage. Cautious feedings limited in volume (with increased frequency) are progressed to a maximum of approximately 600 kcal/day plus vitamin and mineral supplements to achieve weight loss.

Dumping Syndrome

This condition results from alteration, ablation, or bypass of the pyloric sphincter.

- Approximately ½ of gastric surgery patients develop dumping.

The syndrome has two phases:

- *Early dumping* occurs 10 to 15 minutes after ingesting a meal (especially if the meal is high in carbohydrates).
- Symptoms include diaphoresis, nausea, vomiting, dizziness, palpitations, flushing, weak-

ness, abdominal bloating, cramping, and diarrhea (within 1 hour after a meal).
* *Late dumping* occurs 1 to 2 hours after a meal.
* Symptoms include perspiration, tachycardia, mental confusion, and syncope. This phase is thought to be the result of insulin-induced hypoglycemia.

The exact etiology of dumping syndrome is unknown but is thought to be related to

* Extravascular fluid depletion resulting from rapid reflux of hypertonic gastric contents into the jejunum
* Release of intestinal hormones (serotonin, bradykinin, enteroglucagon, GIP, neurotensin)

Management of oral progression involves a low-carbohydrate, high-protein, modified-fat diet, limiting fluids to between meals.

* Meals served dry; liquids consumed 1 to 2 hours postprandially
* Avoidance of simple sugars to reduce osmolality of food contents directly entering the small bowel
* Increase in the concentration of complex carbohydrates
* Avoidance of lactose-containing foods

Generally these dietary modifications are needed only for a short term, as most individuals can resume a general diet. However, some individuals may need to adhere to this diet indefinitely.

Dumping syndrome may be seen with initial enteral infusions following gastrectomy, gastroduodenostomy, or gastrojejunostomy. Enteral feeding requires attention to osmolality, related to small or predigested molecules of carbohydrate (sucrose), protein (amino acids), and fat medium chain triglycerides (MCT). Introduction of enteral products at isotonic concentration or of hypertonic solutions at low volume is recommended.

Bezoar Formation

This condition is the formation of masses of retained food and vegetable matter in the stomach and intestine. It occurs because of reduced gastric motility, decreased mixing and churning of the stomach, delayed gastric emptying, and reduction of gastric secretions. It is treated with digestive materials such as papain, cellulase, and pancreatic enzymes, using an endoscope.

SPECIFIC DISORDERS OF THE GASTROINTESTINAL TRACT: THE INTESTINES

The adult has approximately 350 to 650 cm (11.5–21.5 ft) of small intestine, depending on the method and circumstances of the measurement.

The enterocyte is highly susceptible to injury, so provision of nutrients is essential for gastrointestinal function. The presence of food in the small intestine plays an integral part in the maintenance of normal villous structure and function.

During periods of stress, particularly critical illness, the mucosa of the gastrointestinal tract is susceptible to ulceration and bleeding.

The ileocecal valve protects the small intestine from a more rapid transit time of food and from the anaerobic bacterial flora of the colon. Loss of the valve permits bacterial reflux, which results in increased small intestinal colonization of a highly anaerobic bacteria that can

* Deconjugate bile salts, leading to diarrhea
* Convert fatty acids to hydroxy fatty acids that impair water absorption by the colon

Carbohydrate malabsorption may add to the diarrhea due to the increased osmotic concentration caused by breakdown of unabsorbed carbohydrate.

The severity of nutritional problems resulting from disorders of the intestines is multifactorial:

* length and location of the remaining bowel
* presence or absence of the ileocecal valve
* concomitant colonic disease
* mucosal integrity and function of the remaining gut
* time since onset of the syndrome/disorder

Nutritional management of maldigestive/malabsorptive disorders is summarized in Table 3–6.

Disorders of Absorption

Disorders of absorption generally involve a defect in the mucosal absorptive mechanisms.

- A selective defect in specific transport systems for protein, lipid, or carbohydrate
- Disorders such as celiac sprue or conditions that invade the mucosa, such as intestinal lymphoma
- A marked decrease in absorptive surface area and a derangement in cellular maturation, genetic expression, and differentiation that results in an impairment in global absorptive function
- Bacterial overgrowth related to the stasis associated with motility disorders, multiple jejunal diverticula, or blind loops

Small Intestinal Obstruction

Small intestinal obstruction is a mechanical obstruction of the lumen resulting from adhesions, tumor, or hernia.

- Net absorption decreases in its early phase ($\leq$ 12 hours), while net secretion remains constant.
- The late phase begins after 12 hours, with net absorption decreasing further and net secretion increasing, thereby further exacerbating intestinal distention.
- The resulting third-spacing of isosmolar fluid leads to an isosmolar volume contraction.
- Intestinal distention, stasis, and accumulation of desquamated cells and debris allow intraluminal bacteria to flourish.
- Partial or incomplete intestinal obstruction results from conditions that intermittently allow proximal intestinal content and gas to pass the point of obstruction.

Table 3–6 Nutritional Management of Maldigestive/Malabsorptive Disorders

Disorder	Nutritional Management
Acute malabsorption	Parenteral nutrition or hydrolyzed enteral nutrition
Disaccharidase deficiency	Lactase replacement with lactose; sucrose restriction
Bile salt diarrhea	Moderate to normal fat, medium chain triglycerides, cholestyramine
Primary pancreatic insufficiency	Low fat, medium chain triglycerides, pancreatic enzymes
Pancreatic insufficiency, secondary to rapid transit	Low fat, medium chain triglycerides, pancreatic enzymes, low osmolality, low lactose
Bacterial overgrowth	Antibiotics
Ileal impairment	Low fat, medium chain triglycerides, low osmolality
Mucosal alterations	Low fat, medium chain triglycerides, low lactose
Resection of < 100 cm of the ileum	Moderate to low fat, medium chain triglycerides, low oxalate, low osmolality
Resection of > 100 cm of the ileum	Low fat, medium chain triglycerides, low oxalate, low osmolality
Massive resection	Hydrolyzed enteral nutrition or parenteral nutrition

Source: ME Shils. Nutritional repletion after major gut excision. In JJ DeCosse and P Sherlock (eds): *Clinical Management of Gastrointestinal Cancer,* © 1984, Martinus Nijhoff.

- The individual presents with crampy abdominal pain and intermittent diarrhea.
- Nutritional management should proceed with caution. The individual should remain without enteral nutrition support until the nature and extent of the obstruction can be determined and medical/surgical management is implemented. Advancement of nutrition support may use a transitional modality, with incorporation of parenteral nutrition support and enteral nutrition support individualized to the appropriate levels.

Lactase Deficiency

Lactase deficiency is the most common mucosal brush border enzyme deficiency. Nutritional consequences include abdominal pain, bloating, flatulence, and diarrhea after lactose ingestion. The amount of lactose tolerated by each individual can vary considerably in a range of < 3 g to as great as 15 g. Diagnosis should be confirmed by a lactose tolerance test, a hydrogen breath test, or an intestinal biopsy.

Nutritional management must include a reduction of dietary lactose as the major aspect of treatment, with the amount of reduction adjusted to the individual's ability to tolerate lactose.

- The individual should be counseled on foods that contain lactose, how to read nutrition labels, how to watch for "hidden sources," and how to adjust ingestion of lactose to avoid symptoms.
- Reduction of exposure by the mucosa to a quantity of lactose can be accomplished by dividing the total dose into smaller portions throughout the day.
- Since a number of foods that contain lactose are also good sources of calcium, individuals should be counseled on how to incorporate other calcium-rich food sources into their dietary intake or advised to take a calcium supplement.
- Tolerance to milk may be enhanced by adding a lactase-enzyme preparation to foods with lactose per the manufacturer's recommendations.

- Yogurt that contains live bacteria cultures may be well tolerated by these individuals since the bacteria synthesize beta-galactosidase, which ferments lactose in the intestinal lumen.

Inflammatory Bowel Disease

Inflammatory bowel disease is inflammatory disease that can cause ulceration of the colonic mucosa (*ulcerative colitis*) or affects both the large and small intestines (*Crohn's disease*).

Nutritional consequences include malnutrition, diarrhea, abdominal pain, bloody stools, steatorrhea, malabsorption, limited oral intake, anorexia, avoidance behavior, possibility of micronutrient deficiencies, and possible lactase deficiency.

- *Crohn's disease:* steatorrhea; loss of calcium, magnesium, and possibly zinc in the stool; excessive absorption of uncomplexed oxalate, hyperoxaluria, and increased risk of calcium oxalate stones; small intestinal malabsorption; weight loss; and possible hypoalbuminemia
- *Ulcerative colitis:* constipation, bloody diarrhea, abdominal pain, fever, dehydration, weight loss, anemia

Nutritional management varies depending upon individual severity of symptoms and the extent of mucosal involvement.

- The patient may have increased energy requirements. Adjust for degree of hypermetabolism and need for weight maintenance/repletion.
- The patient may have increased protein needs secondary to enteric losses and/or use of corticosteroids in medical treatment modality. Required levels of intake may be 1.3 to 2.0 g/kg per body weight.
- Bowel rest may alleviate some of the acute symptoms, with parenteral nutrition support used during these time periods to provide adequate nutritional intake.
- When the disease is in remission, use of a standard oral diet, offered in small, frequent feeding intervals, should be encouraged.

- When enteral nutrition support is indicated, mild to moderate inflammation may benefit from use of polymeric diets, and moderate to severe inflammation may benefit from monomeric (defined or elemental) diets.
- Avoidance of specific foods should be entirely dependent on the individual's needs and the food's influence on the severity of disease.
- Other dietary modifications that may be efficacious include
  1. restriction of fiber in the diet to less than 30 g
  2. restriction of fat in the presence of steatorrhea, with the use of medium-chain triglycerides to augment caloric intake and monitoring of individuals receiving MCT for nausea, vomiting, abdominal discomfort, and osmotic diarrhea
  3. lactose restriction if the individual is lactase deficient
  4. supplementation of vitamins and minerals (see Table 3–7)
  5. use of oral rehydration therapy solutions when individuals with malabsorption cannot maintain fluid and electrolyte homeostasis

Short Bowel Syndrome

Short bowel syndrome is an array of metabolic and physiologic consequences that occur as a result of massive surgical resection, bypass, or intrinsic disease of the bowel. It is generally defined as having less than 150 cm of small intestine remaining.

Nutritional Consequences

Nutritional consequences are entirely dependent upon the degree and location of resection, and the subsequent rehabilitation of the individual is dependent upon overall health status. Metabolic consequences include anemia, bile salt depletion, osteomalacia, cholelithiasis, dehydration, diarrhea, steatorrhea (particularly if the ileocecal valve is resected), cholerheic (bile salt) diarrhea, hypocalcemia, hypomagnesemia, oxalate stones, trace mineral deficiencies, vitamin (A, D, E, K, B_{12}) deficiencies, and protein-energy malnutrition.

Nutritional Management

Nutritional management varies depending on site and extent of intestinal resection. Prior to initiation of nutritional therapy, assess the functional capacity of the remaining sections of the bowel, and note the stool pattern and volume. Resections of 70%–80% are associated with the most severe nutritional problems and necessitate aggressive nutritional support.

Management of any individual, independent of degree of resection, includes

- Replacement of fluids and electrolytes
- Use of total parenteral nutrition in the initial postoperative phase
- Once diarrhea has stabilized, transition to an enteral route of nutrition support with gradual transition to enteral/oral feedings and parenteral nutrition tapered

Table 3–7 Recommended Vitamin and Mineral Supplementation for Patients with Inflammatory Bowel Disease

Nutrient	Recommended Dose
Multivitamin and mineral supplement	1 tablet per day
Vitamin A	10,000–50,000 U/d
Vitamin D	1,600 U/d
Vitamin E	30 U/d
Vitamin K	5 mg/d
Vitamin B_{12}	200 μg/mo
Calcium	0.5 g of elemental calcium 3–4 times a day
Magnesium	150 mg of elemental magnesium, 4 times a day
Zinc	25 mg of elemental zinc, 4 times a day
Iron	60 mg of elemental iron, 3 times a day

1. Use of continuous infusion of enteral nutrition may be better tolerated than bolus feedings.
2. Monomeric diets may be efficacious in the early adaptive period, with consideration given to the osmotic concentration and the rate of feeding.
3. Polymeric diets have been demonstrated as efficacious, with attention paid to the content of fat (MCT may be useful).

- An oral diet consumption that is low in fat and high in carbohydrates, except for individuals with osmotic diarrhea
- Estimation of energy requirements at 1.5–2.0 times the basal energy expenditure
- Estimation of protein requirements at levels that maintain nitrogen balance
- Individualized restriction of soluble fiber content and lactose in the oral diet
- For individuals with hyperoxaluria, possible restriction of high-oxalate foods such as chocolate, cola drinks, tea, carrots, celery, spinach, pepper, nuts, plums, figs, and strawberries

Long-term management for nutritional consequences should include monitoring of

- Electrolytes, fluid status, vitamin/mineral status (especially calcium, magnesium, sodium, potassium, zinc, phosphate, and iron), with replacement as necessary
- Weight status
- Tolerance to enteral feeding regimen, with adjustment as necessary
- Protein nutriture status, using appropriate biochemical markers such as prealbumin or albumin

REFERENCES

Allard JP, Jeejeebhoy KN. Nutritional support and therapy in the short bowel syndrome. *Gastroenterol Clin North Am.* 1989;18:589–601.

Bristol JB, Williamson RCN, Chir M. Nutrition, operations, and intestinal adaptation. *JPEN.* 1988;12:299–309.

Desai MB, Jeejeebhoy KN. Nutrition and diet in management of diseases of the gastrointestinal tract. In: Shils ME, Young VR, eds. *Modern Nutrition in Health and Disease.* Philadelphia, Pa: Lea & Febiger; 1988:1092–1128.

Frankenfield DC, Beyer PL. Dietary fiber and bowel function in tube-fed patients. *J Am Diet Assoc.* 1991;91:590–596.

Klein S, Jeejeebhoy KN. Long term nutritional management of patients with maldigestion and malabsorption. In: Sleisenger MH, Fordtran JS, eds. *Gastrointestinal Disease: Pathophysiology/Diagnosis/Management.* 5th ed. Philadelphia, Pa: WB Saunders Co; 1993:2048–2061.

Lacey JM, Wilmore DW. Is glutamine a conditionally essential amino acid? *Nutr Rev.* 1990;8:48:297–309.

Messing B, Pigot F, Rongier M, et al. Intestinal absorption of free oral hyperalimentation in the very short bowel syndrome. *Surg Clin North Am.* 1987;67:551–571.

Podolsky DK. Inflammatory bowel disease. *N Engl J Med.* 1991;325:928–937.

Podolsky DK. Inflammatory bowel disease. *N Engl J Med.* 1991;325:1008–1016.

Purdum PP, Kirby DF. Short-bowel syndrome: a review of the role of nutrition support. *JPEN.* 1991;15:93–101.

Geriatric Conditions

Ronni Chernoff

POPULATION DESCRIPTION

The geriatric population is defined as those people aged 65 and older. Although this is an arbitrary designation, it has been used in common law to define retirement age, age of eligibility for federal and state entitlement programs, and demographic strata. In the over-65 population, there are stratifications for the "young-old" (65–74), "old" (75–84), and "very old" (85 and older). It is noteworthy that the most significant growth among the over-65 group has been among the very old.

The geriatric population as a percentage of the American population is expanding more rapidly than any other group. It is expected to increase further when the oldest people of the "baby boom" generation, born between 1946 and 1964, reach the age of 65 in approximately 15 years.

Longitudinal studies have described changes that are part of the normal human aging process that influence the standard approaches to assessing nutritional status, defining nutrient requirements, selecting nutrition interventions, and providing nutrition support to older people. This chapter will briefly describe these issues.

PHYSIOLOGY OF HUMAN AGING

Humans are very heterogenous in genetic profile, predisposition to disease, health behaviors, cultural behaviors, and social and environmental factors, all of which contribute to the rate and manner in which individuals age. However, there are common physiologic alterations that occur with age, although they may happen at a different rate among individuals. The following are the major changes associated with advancing age:

- decrease in body protein compartments
- decrease in total body water content
- loss of bone density
- increase in proportion of body fat

Decrease in Body Protein Compartments

The decrease in body protein compartments may contribute to the following effects:

- decrease in muscle mass, with an associated reduction in muscle strength, coordination, and functional independence
- reduction in organ function, including cardiac, pulmonary, renal, hepatic, gastrointestinal (including peristalsis), bladder, and urinary tract function
- decrease in basal metabolic rate and oxygen consumption, contributing to a decrease in the need for dietary energy
- impairment of immune responses
- reduction in production of hormones, enzymes, metabolic substrates, and blood cell types
- decline in the rate of physiologic response to both internal and external events; possibly slower recovery from illness, trauma, or surgery

Decrease in Total Body Water

In young adulthood, water is approximately 80% of body composition, but it may decrease to 60%–70% in older people. Water is an important compartment of the human body because it is involved in the

- maintenance of cellular integrity
- regulation of body temperature
- transportation of nutrients
- dilution and transport of medications
- maintenance of normal body waste removal

Decrease in Bone Density

Loss of bone density occurs in males and females, although the primary focus has been on the pathologic loss of bone that may occur in women who are postmenopausal.

Decreased bone density contributes to the likelihood of fractures resulting from, or contributing to, falls. In advanced osteoporosis, collapse of the vertebrae contributes to a compression of the abdominal cavity, with subsequent displacement and constriction of vital organs.

Reduction in bone density can be minimized by a lifelong health plan that includes adequate dietary calcium, vitamin D, and weight-bearing exercise. In postmenopausal women, current therapy for avoiding excess bone loss includes hormone replacement therapy, which should be undertaken under the direction of a physician.

Increase in Proportion of Body Fat

Although the actual amount of body fat may not increase significantly, reductions in all the other major compartments contribute to this change. There is also a shift in fat tissue deposition, with more fat deposited in the abdominal area and an increase in the density of organ fat pads.

NUTRITIONAL REQUIREMENTS OF OLDER ADULTS

The physiologic changes that occur with advancing age and changes in body composition, chronic disease, level of physical activity, medication use, and social and economic conditions all contribute to whether individuals meet their daily nutritional requirements. The need for specific nutrients is affected uniquely by age, and generalizations cannot be made for most nutrients.

Energy

- Calorie needs are determined by the amount of energy needed to sustain basal metabolic function, to sustain lean body mass, and to support physical activity.
- Energy needs tend to decrease with advancing age due to the reduction in total body protein and decreased physical activity.

- Energy needs increase when there is a demand for tissue synthesis to heal a wound, repair a bone fracture, or fight infection.

Protein

- Protein needs actually increase with advancing age.
- The recommended dietary allowance (RDA) for adults (0.8 g/kg of body weight) will not achieve nitrogen equilibrium in healthy, ambulatory elderly people.
- One g/kg of body weight is a better base level for dietary protein intake.
- There may be greater demands for protein for tissue synthesis, bone repair, or infection resistance.

Carbohydrate

- There are no significant changes in carbohydrate requirements with age.
- Recommendations are the same for older adults as they are for younger adults—55%–60% of calories from complex carbohydrates.
- Due to a decrease in bowel motility, emphasis should be placed on dietary intake of carbohydrates that are rich in fiber.

Fat

- Dietary fat should be eaten in amounts adequate to provide needed energy, fat-soluble vitamins, and essential fatty acids.
- There is some controversy about restricting dietary fats, such as cholesterol, in elderly people.
- Risk factors for coronary heart disease change in the early 60s, with systolic hypertension becoming a greater predictor than serum lipid profiles.

Water

- Thirst sensitivity decreases with advancing age, and there is a risk of dehydration in older people.
- Requirements for free fluid are approximately 30 ml/kg of body weight.
- Minimum fluid intake should be approximately 1500 ml/day.

Vitamin B$_1$ (Thiamine)

- RDA for adults is 1.2 mg/day for men and 1.0 mg/day for women.
- There is no known decrease in absorption or alteration in metabolism of vitamin B$_1$ associated with age.
- Epidemiologic studies reveal that approximately 50% of people over age 65 are ingesting less than 2/3 of the RDA for thiamine.
- The greatest risk factor for vitamin B$_1$ deficiency is alcoholism, which interferes with intake, absorption, and utilization.

Vitamin B$_2$ (Riboflavin)

- RDA for adults is 1.4 mg/day for men and 1.2 mg/day for women.
- There is no known decrease in absorption or alteration in metabolism of vitamin B$_2$ associated with age.
- Inadequate dietary intake is the greatest risk factor for the elderly, due to decreased consumption of milk products, the primary source of riboflavin, associated with lactose intolerance.

Niacin

- RDA for niacin is 15 mg of niacin equivalents (NE) per day for men and 13 mg NE per day for women, which appears to be adequate for older adults.

Vitamin B$_6$

- RDA for vitamin B$_6$ is 2.0 mg/day for men and 1.6 mg/day for women.
- Many studies have demonstrated an inadequate intake of vitamin B$_6$ among elderly people.
- There have been suggestions that vitamin B$_6$ requirements may be too low for elderly people because atrophic gastritis, more common among the elderly, may interfere with absorption, but this has yet to be supported by research.
- Alcoholism and liver disease are risk factors for vitamin B$_6$ deficiency among older adults.

Folate

- RDA for folate is 200 µg/day for men and 180 µg/day for women.
- There is no age-related impact on folate requirements.
- Alcoholism is a risk factor for folate deficiency in the elderly.

Vitamin B$_{12}$

- RDA for vitamin B$_{12}$ is 2 µg/day for both men and women.
- Atrophic gastritis and bacterial overgrowth may contribute to deficiency in older adults due to impaired absorption.
- There is some controversy over whether the RDA should be increased to the pre-1989 level of 3 µg/day for the elderly, but individuals at risk due to gastrointestinal problems should be monitored regularly.

Vitamin C

- RDA for vitamin C is 60 mg/day for both men and women.
- Elderly subjects have lower blood, plasma, and serum levels than do younger adults.
- Low blood levels of vitamin C can be corrected with supplementation, but when supplements are stopped, low levels return rapidly.
- There do not appear to be any age-related alterations in the absorption or utilization of vitamin C.
- Stress, smoking, and some medications may increase vitamin C requirements, so it is important to review dietary intake of vitamin C with individuals who may be at risk of inadequate intake.

Vitamin A

- RDA is 1000 mg of retinol equivalents (RE) for men and 800 mg of RE for women.
- It is rare to identify a vitamin A deficiency in older adults.

- Chronic hypervitaminosis may be a problem in elderly people who take large doses of supplementary vitamin A.
- High levels of vitamin supplementation has been associated with increased levels of circulating retinyl esters, which may indicate vitamin toxicity or liver damage.
- Conversion of beta carotene to vitamin A is a well-regulated reaction that prevents hypervitaminosis with high levels of beta carotene intake.
- Beta carotene supplementation has been promoted to quench free radicals; although this suggestion has not been fully investigated, large doses of beta carotene do not appear to be toxic.

Vitamin D

- RDA for vitamin D is 5 μg/day (200 IU) for both men and women over age 51.
- Vitamin D can be obtained from dietary sources or from sunlight exposure on the skin.
- Elderly people are at risk for vitamin D deficiency because of inadequate diets, lack of sun exposure, decreased 7-dehydrocholesterol levels in skin, and impaired conversion of vitamin D precursors in liver and kidney.
- Vitamin D is needed to facilitate calcium absorption.
- Vitamin D has an important role in immune function, and deficiency may contribute to increased susceptibility to communicable disease.
- Vitamin D supplementation at the RDA level should be considered for housebound or institutionalized elderly people.

Vitamin E

- RDA for vitamin E is 10 mg of α-tocopherol equivalents for men and 8 mg α-tocopherol for women.
- There does not appear to be any age-related alteration in the absorption or metabolism of vitamin E.
- Vitamin E is a nutrient that is frequently taken as a supplement because of its antioxidant properties.

- Other claims made for the benefits of vitamin E in ischemic heart disease have yet to be scientifically confirmed.

Vitamin K

- RDA of 1 μg/kg of body weight is considered sufficient.
- Vitamin K is derived from diet and synthesized by bacteria in the jejunum and ileum.
- Elderly persons at risk of developing a deficiency are those receiving sulfa drugs and anticoagulant therapy.
- People taking large supplements of vitamins A and E may develop an induced hemorrhagic condition associated with a vitamin K deficiency.

Calcium

- RDA for calcium is 800 mg/day for both men and women. This is controversial, and suggestions have been made that the RDA for calcium be increased to 1000, 1200, or 1500 mg/day.
- The condition most closely associated with calcium metabolism in older adults is osteoporosis; this occurs in both males and females.
- Postmenopausal osteoporosis is currently treated with hormone replacement therapy, calcium, and vitamin D.
- Plasma calcium levels are not reflective of calcium status due to the close regulation of plasma calcium by several homeostatic mechanisms.
- Hypercalcemia in elderly people is usually indicative of malignant disease, hyperparathyroidism, overuse of thiazide therapy, or immobilization.

Sodium

- There is no RDA for sodium.
- Hyponatremia is a common finding among hospitalized and institutionalized elderly.
- Hypernatremia is often indicative of an acute disease process, but elderly individuals are prone to dehydration due to decreased thirst sensitivity.

- Sodium-restricted diets should be used with caution in older patients.

Potassium

- There is no RDA for potassium.
- Hypokalemia may occur in older adults who are on diuretic therapy.
- Hyperkalemia is most likely to occur in individuals with impaired renal function.
- There is some evidence that a diet rich in potassium may have a protective effect against cerebrovascular accidents.

Iron

- RDA for iron is 10 mg/day for men and women.
- Iron stores tend to increase with advancing age.
- Iron-deficiency anemia is most likely related to gastrointestinal blood loss from malignancies, peptic ulcer disease, or nonsteroidal anti-inflammatory drugs (aspirin, indomethacin).

Zinc

- RDA is 15 mg/day for both men and women.
- Evidence of zinc deficiency in elderly people is variable.
- Many elderly people have a decrease in taste sensitivity (*hypogeusia*) that has been associated with zinc deficiency, but the hypogeusia seen in elderly subjects is attributed to many factors other than zinc nutriture.
- Zinc requirements increase with a demand for tissue synthesis, but large doses for extended periods will interfere with absorption of other trace minerals (eg, copper).

NUTRITIONAL ASSESSMENT OF THE ELDERLY

Assessing the nutritional status of older adults is often a challenge due to the physiologic, physical, and disease-related changes that are associated with advanced age. An assessment that gathers as much information as possible, without making comparisons to standards that do not include equivalent populations, is an appropriate goal.

Physical Assessment

- Review condition of hair and skin, skin turgor, and signs of edema.
- An oral exam is important; the condition of the oral mucosa, tongue, gums, and teeth and the presence of dentures or of lesions all may be a clue to nutritional status.
- Evaluation of physical disabilities should be part of a physical assessment.
- Obtain a history of past illnesses that might affect nutritional status.

Anthropometric Measures

- Weight for height is best evaluated by using a measure of body mass index: weight (kg)/ height (m^2).
- Fluctuations in weight should be monitored closely; weight gain or loss may be an indication that physical conditions are changing.
- Height should be measured with the individual standing erect; if that is not possible, recumbent length, knee-to-heel, or segmental measurements should be used.
- Measures that have standards derived from young adult populations are not reliable or valid in assessing nutritional status of older adults; these measurements can be used to gauge baseline data and track changes over time.
- Skinfold measures and midarm muscle circumference may not be reliable measures in older people because of the age-associated loss of lean body mass and loss of cutaneous elasticity.

Biochemical Assessment

- Serum albumin is the most reliable measure of visceral protein status in older adults.
- Transferrin is not reliable because older adults have increased iron stores and transferrin is

more sensitive to iron nutriture than to protein status.

- When available, thyroxine-binding prealbumin and retinol-binding protein are the most sensitive indicators of protein status or response to nutrition intervention.

Hematologic Measures

- Hematocrit, hemoglobin, and total lymphocyte count should be monitored regularly; these measures are not affected by advancing age.
- Anemia is common among elderly people, although its etiology is unknown.

Immunologic Measures

- The immune system does not function as efficiently in older adults.
- The ability to respond to recall antigens diminishes with age as it does with chronic protein energy malnutrition; the only way to distinguish between age-related and malnutrition-related energy is to renourish the individual and retest with recall antigens.

Functional Assessment

Many instruments are available to assess functional status. The basic skills that they address include

- *Bathing:* ability to manage personal hygiene
- *Dressing:* ability to dress oneself
- *Toileting:* ability to get to toilet without help
- *Transferring:* ability to transfer from bed to a chair and from a chair to an upright position
- *Continence:* ability to control bladder and bowel function
- *Feeding:* ability to feed oneself

These dimensions are measured on 3- or 4-point scales that allow the clinician to evaluate patients' skills at self-care. There is a strong correlation between the score on these activities of daily living and both serum albumin levels and measures of utilization of health resources, such as many hospitalizations or institutionalization.

There is a supplemental scale that assesses "instrumental" activities of daily living which include:

- using the telephone
- shopping
- preparing food
- housekeeping
- laundry
- transportation (ie, driving)
- managing medications
- managing finances

These dimensions are also measured on a scale that assesses the ability of patients to live independently.

Medication Profile

Polypharmacy is a common problem in elderly people and must be considered as part of a comprehensive geriatric assessment. A medication profile should be kept on each patient.

- Medications, both prescription and over the counter, can have direct effects on the absorption, metabolism, and excretion of nutrients.
- Drugs can affect food intake by altering appetite, taste, or smell.
- Food can interfere with the absorption or utilization of medications.
- Drug-drug interactions may also impair nutritional intake.

Social History

- Assess socioeconomic status along with place and type of residence.
- Assess living situation, including with whom the patient is residing (spouse, adult children, relatives, friends, acquaintances, alone).
- Obtain a history of smoking and alcohol use.
- Ascertain whether the individual can afford to purchase adequate food or whether there is need for social intervention that provides access to senior meal programs, food stamps, food assistance programs, or home-delivered meals.

MODIFIED DIETS

It is well known that older people often have at least one, and frequently more than one, chronic condition that requires dietary modification. It is common for physicians to prescribe dietary modifications for many of these conditions (eg, diabetes, coronary heart disease, hypertension, obesity). Additionally, some older adults assume responsibility for altering their own diets as a health promotion measure.

- The patient's comprehension of the modifications required by the diet should be apparent to the counselor.
- Careful assessment of the value of dietary modification should be conducted, particularly if medications are also prescribed to manage the same condition.
- Some dietary modifications may affect the nutritional value of the individual's usual intake; if this occurs, appropriate supplements should be offered so that nutritional deficiencies do not create new health problems or compound existing health problems.
- For many older people, dietary modifications may contribute to chronic undernutrition.
- Serious consideration of restricting food selection must be given, particularly when older people are institutionalized, undernourished, or terminally ill.
- There should be a compelling medical indication to modify by restriction the diet of a frail elderly person.

CONSIDERATIONS IN FEEDING THE ELDERLY

Whenever possible, encouraging eating patterns close to usual for the individual is the best option when feeding elderly people. However, many factors must be reviewed in selecting the best route through which to feed someone.

Oral Feeding Considerations

- Is the person able to self-feed? Are modified utensils, plate slip guards, double-handled cups, nonspill glasses or other devices needed to aid in independent feeding?
- Is impaired vision or neurologic function a factor that requires the individual to be helped with feeding or to be fed?
- Can the individual chew and swallow food? Is there a need for dental intervention? Is there a need for altering the consistency of food to accommodate any chewing or swallowing impairment?
- Are there religious or cultural dietary considerations? Are there medically related problems in digestion or absorption of food? Is there a requirement to modify the diet to address unique, disease-related needs?
- Is the individual eating a diet that meets nutrient requirements, or is a nutrient supplement needed? For diets that are nutritionally inadequate, a multivitamin/mineral supplement should be considered.
- If the individual cannot eat enough, a meal supplement may be a reasonable addition to the diet.
- Oral liquid feedings can supplement a diet by contributing protein, calories, vitamins, and minerals; they may be a viable option for between-meal feedings for individuals who have a limited capacity and experience early satiety at meals.
- For individuals who are unable to eat due to their medical conditions, another feeding route must be considered, such as enteral or parenteral feeding.

Enteral Feeding Considerations

- Determination of length of feeding should be part of feeding route selection. Short-term feeding can use nasal access; long-term feeding should consider placement of an indwelling tube (ie, percutaneous endoscopic gastrostomy).
- Mental status should be evaluated because confused and agitated people resist tube placement and may pull out tubes and harm themselves.
- Gastrointestinal tract function must be evaluated to ensure best tube placement to maxi-

mize nutrient digestion and absorption.

- Formula selection depends on tolerance for volume, ability to digest and absorb nutrients, medical condition, nutritional requirements, and patient prognosis.
- Cost may be a factor in selecting enteral feeding. Reimbursement for enteral feeding exists through a durable medical equipment (DME) component of Medicare. Enteral feeding is less expensive than parenteral nutrition interventions.
- Complications of enteral feeding must be minimized by regular careful monitoring. Such complications may include
  1. gastric retention
  2. gastric reflux
  3. mucosal ulceration
  4. pulmonary infusion
  5. pulmonary aspiration
  6. hyperglycemia/dehydration
  7. hyperatremia
  8. hyperchloremia
  9. azotemia
- Patency of feeding tube should be a high priority. Only enteral formula should be infused through the tube, and the tube should be flushed regularly with water.

Parenteral Feeding Considerations

- Anticipated patient prognosis must be evaluated in the decision to provide parenteral nutrition support to an elderly patient.
- Venous access may present a problem in older adults.
- Parenteral solutions consist of hypertonic glucose solutions, aqueous protein solutions, lipid emulsions, vitamins, minerals, and trace elements.
- Elderly individuals are more likely to have a glucose intolerance. Although it is an accepted practice to infuse insulin with hypertonic glucose solution, this technique would require very close monitoring in older patients.
- Lipid clearance rates should be assessed before infusion of large volumes of lipid emulsions.

- Tolerance to large-volume fluid infusion must be judged because elderly adults are more sensitive to shifts in fluid compartments and volume expansion than are younger adults.
- Careful, close monitoring is necessary when supporting older patients on parenteral nutrition.

Home Nutritional Support

- Social circumstances must be carefully evaluated before sending an elderly patient home with either enteral or parenteral support.
- Finances, space for storage, caregiver support, and access to medical care all must be evaluated.
- When possible, options for home nutrition support should include visiting nurses, support from hospital personnel, support from family or close friends, or a home nutrition support company.
- Maintaining elderly patients who require nutrition support in their own homes is an acceptable and desirable option if all the requirements for safety, cleanliness, adequate storage (including refrigeration), and close medical supervision and monitoring are met.

REFERENCES

Chernoff R. Thirst and fluid requirements. *Nutr Rev.* Washington, DC; 1995.

Food and Nutrition Board, National Research Council. *Recommended Dietary Allowances.* 10th ed. Washington, DC: National Academy Press; 1989.

Fosmire GJ. Trace metal requirements. In: Chernoff R, ed. *Geriatric Nutrition: The Health Professional's Handbook.* Gaithersburg, Md: Aspen Publishers, Inc; 1991;77–106.

Fosmire GJ, Manuel PA, Smiciklas-Wright H. Dietary intakes and zinc status of an elderly rural population. *J Nutr Elderly.* 1984;4:19–30.

Gersovitz M, Motil K, Munro HN, et al. Human protein requirements: assessment of the adequacy of the current recommended allowance for dietary protein for men and women. *Am J Clin Nutr.* 1982;35:6–14.

Gilford DM, ed. *The Aging Population in the Twenty-First Century: Statistics for Health Policy.* Washington, DC: National Academy Press; 1988.

Katz S. Assessing self maintenance: activities of daily living, mobility, and instrumental activities of daily living. *J Am Geriatr Soc.* 1983;31:721–727.

Katz S, Akpom CA. A measure of primary sociologic functions. *Int J Health Serv.* 1976;6:493–508.

Krasinski SD, Russell RM, Ostradovec CL, et al. Relationship of vitamin A and vitamin E to fasting plasma retinol, retinol-binding protein, retinyl esters, carotene, α-tocopherol, and cholesterol among elderly people and young adults: increased plasma retinyl esters among the vitamin A supplement users. *Am J Clin Nutr.* 1989;49:112–120.

Lindeman RD, Beck AA. Mineral requirements. In: Chernoff R, ed. *Geriatric Nutrition: The Health Professional's Handbook.* Gaithersburg, Md: Aspen Publishers, Inc; 1991;53–76.

Lipschitz DA. Impact of nutrition on the age-related declines in hematopoiesis. In: Chernoff R, ed. *Geriatric Nutrition: The Health Professional's Handbook.* Gaithersburg, Md: Aspen Publishers, Inc; 1991.

Manolagas SC. Immunoregulatory properties of 1,25 $(OH)_2D_3$: cellular requirements and mechanisms. In: Norman AW, Schaefer K, Grigoleit HG, et al, eds. *Vitamin D: Molecular, Cellular and Clinical Endocrinology.* New York: Walter de Gruyter & Co; 1988.

Mitchell CO, Chernoff R. Nutritional assessment of the elderly. In: Chernoff R, ed. *Geriatric Nutrition: The Health Professional's Handbook.* Gaithersburg, Md: Aspen Publishers, Inc; 1991;363–396.

Nutrition screening initiative. Green, Margolis, Mitchell & Greenwald, Washington, DC.

Shock NW, Greulich RC, Andres R, et al. *Normal Human Aging: Baltimore Longitudinal Study on Aging.* Washington, DC: Government Printing Office; 1984. NIH Publication No 84-2450.

Sullivan DH, Patch GA, Walls RC, et al. Impact of nutrition status on morbidity and mortality in a select population of geriatric rehabilitation patients. *Am J Clin Nutr.* 1990;51: 749–758.

Suter PM. Vitamin requirements. In: Chernoff R, ed. *Geriatric Nutrition: The Health Professional's Handbook.* Gaithersburg, Md: Aspen Publishers, Inc; 1991;25–52.

HIV/AIDS

Stacey J. Bell, Wendy S. Swails, Bruce R. Bistrian, Christine Wanke, Peter Burke, and R. Armour Forse

DESCRIPTION

Human immunodeficiency virus (HIV) infection directly affects the immune system, ultimately rendering it ineffective by drastically reducing the number of T helper cells, which are an essential component of host resistance to infections and malignancies. The direct consequences of the immunosuppression are numerous because the body becomes prone to a wide variety of opportunistic bacterial and parasitic infections, other pathogenic viruses, and certain types of tumors. These conditions and the HIV virus itself may affect the function of many organ systems in the body, particularly the gastrointestinal tract, bone marrow, lungs, eyes, brain, and skin.

The Centers for Disease Control and prevention (CDC) in Atlanta has defined various states of HIV infection as follows. An individual infected with the virus is considered to have the acquired immune deficiency syndrome (AIDS) when he or she develops one of the AIDS-associated illnesses or when his or her CD4 count falls below 200 cells/mm³.

There are three CD4+ T-lymphocyte categories:

- *Category 1:* ≥ 500 cells/mm³
- *Category 2:* 200–499 cells/mm³
- *Category 3:* < 200 cells/mm³

There are three clinical categories of HIV infection:

- *Category A:* One or more of the following conditions:
  1. Asymptomatic HIV infection
  2. Persistent generalized lymphadenopathy
  3. Acute (primary) HIV infection with accompanying illness or history of acute HIV infection
- *Category B:* Symptomatic conditions that meet at least one of the following criteria:
  1. The conditions are attributed to HIV infection or are indicative of a defect in cell-mediated immunity.
  2. The conditions are considered by physicians to have a clinical course or to require management that is complicated by HIV infection.
- *Category C:* Clinical conditions listed in the AIDS surveillance case definition (eg, candidiasis, cryptococcosis, Kaposi's sarcoma, cryptosporidiosis, cytomegalovirus, histoplasmosis, lymphoma, mycobacterium, *pneumocystis carinii* pneumonia, toxoplasmosis of brain, progressive multifocal leukoencephalopathy, wasting syndrome due to HIV)

CAUSE

HIV infection is usually contracted through sexual contact with an infected partner, intravenously through blood products or contaminated needles, or through maternal transmission in utero or from breast milk.

ASSESSMENT

Because HIV infection is a chronic disease, each marker of nutritional status should be made serially: ideally, every 6 months beginning at the time of diagnosis and, with evaluation of selected parameters, more frequently as the disease progresses.

Anthropometric Measures

- Actual weight
- Percent weight lost over time

- Body composition as
  1. extracellular water/body cell mass
  2. body fat obtained from bioelectrical impedance

Biochemical Parameters

- Serum albumin concentrations
- Serum cholesterol concentrations
- Serum triglyceride concentrations
- Serum electrolyte concentrations
- Complete blood count with differential

Immune/HIV Related Parameters

- CD4 and CD8 cell counts

Gastrointestinal Symptoms

- To be checked routinely:
  1. stool number and consistency
  2. incidence of abdominal pain, cramping, or bloating
- To be performed when signs (weight loss, chronic diarrhea) or symptoms (anorexia, pain, dysphagia, etc) prompt:
  1. stool culture and/or stool examination for routine or opportunistic pathogens within the gastrointestinal tract
  2. stool nitrogen measurement
  3. fecal fat measurement: qualitative or 72-hour fecal fat measurement following a 100-g–fat diet
  4. D-xylose test
  5. upper/lower endoscopy and biopsy

Appetite

- Presence of anorexia, nausea, vomiting, or diarrhea
- Difficulty swallowing or chewing
- Mouth sores
- Poor dentition
- Gum inflammation

Diet History

- Food frequency
- 24-hour recall
- Oral supplement use

Medications

- Prescription, including route of administration: oral, subcutaneous, transdermal patch, or intravenous
- Nonprescription, including vitamins/minerals and herbs

Employment/Exercise

- Workplace and schedule
- Exercise routine

Financial Status/Meal Preparation

- Access to food
- Preparation and storage of food
- Support system

Alternative Therapies

- Mind/body classes
- Yoga
- Acupuncture

Other Medical Diagnoses

- Pulmonary
  1. *Pneumocystis carinii* pneumonia (PCP)
  2. Tuberculosis (TB)
  3. Cytomegalovirus (CMV)
- Neurologic
  1. Central nervous system (CNS) involvement
  2. Peripheral neuropathy
  3. Visual problems
- Hematologic
  1. Anemia
  2. Neutropenia
  3. Thrombocytopenia
- Tumors
  1. Kaposi's sarcoma
  2. Lymphoma
- Cardiac
  1. Cardiomyopathy
- Renal
  1. Nephropathy
- Other non–AIDS-related diagnoses

PROBLEMS

Weight Loss

- Disproportionate depletion of body cell mass compared to fat mass
- Timing of death has been related to loss of body cell mass (BCM), with death occurring when BCM is 54% of normal
- Fat mass depletion (end-stage disease only)
- Associated with elevated levels of cytokines (specifically tumor necrosis factor and interferon gamma) in some instances
- Possible causes:
  1. Impaired oral intake
  2. Impaired deglutition
  3. Malabsorption
  4. Metabolic alterations

Diarrhea

- Chronic diarrhea defined as a change in bowel habits that persists for > 28 days
- Causes
  1. gastrointestinal pathogens (bacterial, viral, parasitic)
  2. gastrointestinal Kaposi's sarcoma
  3. medication side effects
  4. dysfunction of intestinal tract due to primary HIV virus infection
- 50%–80% of HIV infected patients have diarrhea; the majority of diarrhea is chronic.
- 30%–40% of HIV patients with chronic diarrhea have no recognizable etiology despite undergoing an intensive intestinal workup, including biopsies.

Malabsorption

- Exacerbated by high-fat diet (particularly long chain triglycerides (LCT))
- May inhibit absorption of fat-soluble vitamins
- Often results in impaired absorption of minerals and other vitamins (eg, zinc and vitamins B_1, B_6, and B_{12})

Anorexia

- Causes
  1. fatigue
  2. medications
  3. depression
  4. elevated levels of cytokines (particularly tumor necrosis factor) in serum and/or tissues
- Results in progressive weight loss

Esophageal/Oral Lesions

- Causes
  1. oral hairy leukoplakia
  2. oral candidiasis
  3. oral Kaposi's sarcoma or lymphoma
  4. herpetic or aphthous ulcers
  5. HIV-associated gingivitis or periodontitis
  6. HSV, CMV, or Candidal esophagitis

Taste Changes

- Causes: medications (Acyclovir, Amphotericin B, chemotherapy)

Dysphagia

- Causes: oral and esophageal infections
- Leads to decreased oral intake

Nausea/Vomiting

- Causes
  1. medications
  2. gastritis/esophagitis

3. upper–small-bowel disease or infection (giardia, microsporidia)
- May result in electrolyte imbalances and/or dehydration

Metabolic Derangements

- Causes
  1. diarrhea
  2. vomiting
- Cytokine activity leading to
  1. hypertriglyceridemia
  2. decreased protein synthesis
  3. increased muscle breakdown
  4. increased energy expenditure in relation to BCM

Micronutrient/Trace Element Deficiencies

- Causes
  1. diarrhea
  2. intestinal infections with impaired absorption
- May result in poor immune function and impaired protein synthesis

Anemia

- Types and causes:
  1. *Macrocytosis:* vitamin B_{12} or folate deficiency due to enteropathy
  2. *Normocytic:* anemia or chronic disease secondary to HIV infection, bone marrow suppression by opportunistic infections, or medications
  3. *Microcytosis:* chronic blood loss from gastrointestinal tract secondary to neoplasms or infectious enteropathies

Pancreatitis

- Causes
  1. medications (Pentamidine, Dideoxyinosine/ddI)
  2. hypertriglyceridemia

Serum Lipid Abnormalities

- Types: hypertriglyceridemia and hypocholesterolemia
- Causes:
  1. Elevated circulating levels of tumor necrosis factor (TNF) and interferon gamma increase adipose tissue lipolysis and hepatic lipogenesis.
  2. Increased synthesis of very low density lipoproteins (VLDLs) in the liver and decreased lipoprotein lipase activity impair triglyceride clearance.
- Hypertriglyceridemia is associated with a poor prognosis.

TREATMENT/MANAGEMENT

Weight Loss

- High-calorie, high-protein diet
  1. Caloric requirements: 30–40 kcal/kg body weight
  2. Protein requirements: 1.2–1.5 g/kg body weight
- Oral supplements
  1. Standard, polymeric formulas may be used if no diarrhea, malabsorption, or metabolic abnormalities are present.
  2. Elemental or partially hydrolyzed formulas with low amounts of LCT but abundant amounts of medium-chain triglycerides (MCT) are acceptable in the presence of diarrhea/malabsorption.
  3. Specialized diet for HIV infection; for pre-AIDS patients, a diet with hydrolyzed proteins and fish oil preliminarily has been shown to improve weight maintenance and decrease the number of hospitalizations.
- Tube feeding
  1. Only appropriate for anorectic patients without malabsorption of multiple nutrients.
  2. Nasogastric or nasoenteric tube for short-term feeding or if patient is motivated to insert tube daily for long-term use.
  3. Endoscopically or surgically placed gastrostomy or jejunostomy tube for long-term feeding.
  4. Same guidelines for formula selection as with oral supplements.
  5. Provision of diet during night by pump is convenient for most patients but with gastric feedings, small boluses every 4–6 hours may be possible.
- Parenteral nutrition
  1. Indicated when patient has failed enteral support or when fluid and electrolyte losses are excessive and cannot be met via enteral intake.
  2. To be initiated only if patient has reasonable prognosis, desires therapy, and is malnourished; most effective in patients who have isolated gastrointestinal (GI) infection or GI disease that precludes oral intake or absorption (eg, microsporidia).
  3. Infusions made centrally via Hickman or Groshong catheter, venous access disc, or PICC line.
  4. Provision of diet overnight, usually for 10–16 hours.
  5. Under investigation
     - growth hormone
     - insulinlike growth factor
     - progestational agents

Diarrhea

- Low-fat diet (20% of total calories), or add limited amounts of MCT oil (up to 30 cc TID or QID) to foods.
- Low-lactose diet if lactose intolerance is present.
- Low-fat or MCT-rich oral liquid supplements.
- Increase fiber (eg, psyllium, pectin, or guar) intake.
- Increase intake of electrolyte-repleting fluids such as broths, diluted fruit juices, and oral rehydration drinks.
- Small, frequent meals with vitamin supplementation.
- Avoid caffeinated beverages.

- Dilute sorbitol-containing medications before ingestion.
- Antidiarrheal medications.
- If diarrhea persists and has no treatable etiology, parenteral support may be indicated.
- Patients may malabsorb medications; therefore, liquid preparations or crushed tablets should be used when feasible.
- Under investigation
  1. Glutamine supplemented diets
  2. Asacol

Malabsorption

- Low-fat diet.
- Use MCT oil and/or MCT-containing oral supplements.
- Exogenous pancreatic enzymes.

Anorexia

- The following are suggestions for appetite enhancement:
  1. small, frequent meals
  2. high-calorie, high-protein foods and supplements
  3. relaxing while eating
  4. eating favorite foods
  5. ordering takeout food, having someone else cook, or eating at a restaurant
  6. taking appetite stimulants (eg, Megace, Marinol)
- If significant weight loss occurs, enteral or parenteral support may be indicated.

Esophageal/Oral Lesions

- Soft foods, fluids with meals, and oral liquid supplements can allow nutrient intake without exacerbation of lesions.
- Extremely hot foods and spicy or highly acidic foods should be avoided.
- Cold foods (eg, popsicles) may be soothing.
- Good oral and dental hygiene should be practiced.
- Rinses with a topical anesthetic may be helpful.

Taste Changes

- Taste-altering medications should be taken between meals if possible.
- Spices and flavorings can be added to food.
- Oral supplements in metal cans should be avoided if taste is metallic.

Dysphagia

- Foods can be moistened with sauces.
- Soft foods should be provided.
- Sticky (eg, peanut butter) or dry (eg, toast) foods that are difficult to swallow should be avoided.
- Liquids should be taken with solids.
- Artificial saliva may be used.

Nausea/Vomiting

- Treat dehydration and electrolyte imbalances before taking calorie-rich foods and beverages.
- Meals should be small and frequent.
- The patient should remain seated upright for at least 30 minutes after eating.
- Foods should be served at room temperature to diminish odor of food.
- Foods with strong odors (eg, fish, coffee) should be avoided.
- Clear, cool liquids and gelatin may be tried between meals.
- The patient should eat slowly.
- Low-fat foods should be chosen over greasy, fried foods.
- The patient can try eating salted, dry, high-carbohydrate foods between meals (eg, crackers).
- The patient should eat meals before taking medications that cause nausea.
- The patient should take antiemetic medications prior to meals.

Metabolic Derangements

- The patient may require significant acetate supplementation if diarrhea is severe.

- Under investigation is the use of omega 3–containing oils to decrease cytokine activity.

Micronutrient/Trace Element Deficiencies

- All patients should take a daily multivitamin/mineral supplement that supplies 100% of the RDAs for each nutrient.
- If the patient receives total parenteral nutrition (TPN), selenium supplementation may be increased by an additional 40 mEq/d (in addition to the standard trace element dose of 60 mEq/day).
- Oral zinc and/or calcium supplementation may be needed in the presence of severe diarrhea.
- Under investigation are megadoses of selected vitamins, especially antioxidants (beta carotene, vitamins C and E) and B-complex (vitamins B_6 and B_{12}).

Anemia

- Consolidate blood draws.
- Provide colony-stimulating factors, such as granulocyte-macrophage colony-stimulating factor (GM-CSF).
- Provide erythropoietin.
- Provide blood transfusions.
- Evaluate medications and other contributing factors.

Pancreatitis

- Evaluate medications.
- Prescribe a low-fat diet if the patient complains of symptoms with a regular diet.
- Withhold intravenous lipids if the patient's serum triglyceride level rises above 1000 mg/dL.

Hypertriglyceridemia

- No treatment

REFERENCES

Bell SJ, Chavali S, Forse RA. Cytokine influence on the human immunodeficiency virus (HIV): action, prevalence, and treatment. In: Forse RA, Bell SJ, Blackburn GL, Kabbash LG, eds. *Diet, Nutrition, and Immunity.* Boca Raton, La: CRC Press; 1994:115–126.

Bell SJ, Mascioli EA, Forse RA, et al. Nutrition support and the human immunodeficiency virus (HIV). *Parasitol.* 1993;107:553–567.

Chlebowski RT, Beall G, Grosvenor M, et al. Long-term effects of early nutritional support with new enterotropic peptide-based formula vs standard enteral formula in HIV-infected patients: randomized prospective trial. *Nutr.* 1993;9:507–512.

Chlebowski RT, Grosvenor MB, Bernhard NH, et al. Nutritional status, gastrointestinal dysfunction, and survival in patients with AIDS. *Am J Gastrol.* 1989;84:1288–1293.

Dworkin BM, Rosenthall WS, Wormser GP, et al. Selenium deficiency in the acquired immunodeficiency syndrome. *JPEN.* 1986;10:405–407.

Dwyer JT, Bye RL, Holt PL, et al. Unproven nutrition therapies for AIDS: what is the evidence? *Nutr Today.* March/April 1988:25–33.

Ellis W, Basinger G, Paul J, et al. The use of home total parenteral nutrition in a patient with AIDS. *AIDS Patient Care.* 1994;8:6–10.

Feingold KR, Serio MK, Adi S, et al. Tumor necrosis factor stimulated hepatic lipid synthesis and secretion. *Endocrinol.* 1989;124:2336–2342.

Galvin TA. Micronutrients: implications in human immunodeficiency virus disease. *Top Clin Nutr.* 1992;7:63–73.

Grunfeld C, Feingold KR. Metabolic disturbances and wasting in the acquired immunodeficiency syndrome. *N Engl J Med.* 1992;327:329–337.

Kotler DP, Tierney AR, Wang J, et al. Magnitude of body-cell-mass depletion and the timing of death from wasting in AIDS. *Am J Clin Nutr.* 1989;50:444–447.

Kotler DP, Wang J, Pierson RN. Body composition studies in patients with acquired immunodeficiency syndrome. *Am J Clin Nutr.* 1985;42:1255–1265.

Trujillo EB, Borlase BC, Bell SJ, et al. Assessment of nutritional status, nutrient intake, and nutrition support in AIDS patients. *J Am Diet Assoc.* 1992;92:477–478.

Tuttle-Newhall JE, Verrabagu MP, Mascioli E, et al. Nutrition and metabolic management of AIDS during acute illness. *Nutr.* 1993;9:240–244.

Neonatal Conditions

Christina J. Valentine

DESCRIPTION

Neonates are classified by their age in gestation and birth weight. Full-term infants are described as infants > 37 weeks' gestation; premature infants are infants < 37 weeks' gestation. Physical examination using Dubowitz or Ballard developmental criteria objectively describes the infant's age in weeks' gestation. Weight status is then categorized by use of intrauterine growth charts to determine if the infant is appropriate (AGA), small (SGA), or large (LGA) for his or her gestational age. A frequently used curve for this purpose is the Battaglia growth chart. The gestational age of the infant can then be used to predict the level of function of the infant's gastrointestinal system.

Unlike the healthy full-term infant, the premature infant is born without many hormonal, enzymatic, motor, and digestive processes, making feeding difficult. In addition, the premature infant misses that last trimester in utero, which is vital for accretion of nutrients. Consequently, the premature infant in the extrauterine environment is likely to exhibit inadequate nutrient delivery or intake, shorter stature, poor bone mineralization, cholestasis of the liver, and changes in visual acuity. Therefore, quality as well as quantity of nutrients becomes a particularly important consideration when choosing a feeding plan for the premature infant.

In addition, a timely intervention with parenteral nutrition enhances nitrogen balance for the infant, and a timely initiation of enteral nutrition support can result in earlier nipple feeding and significant cost savings. Early initiation of enteral feeding can also promote feeding tolerance, produce gastrointestinal hormone surges, and enhance intestinal motor activity. Specialized nutritional support is therefore warranted if it is both systematic and timely. The following chapter will describe neonatal nutrition support recommendations and will designate differences for gestational age or weights when necessary.

NUTRITION ASSESSMENT

To begin a systematic and timely approach, a thorough nutrition assessment strategy should be formulated. Assessment of the nutritional status and plan for the infant should be done on a routine schedule by a registered dietitian competent in the area of neonatal nutrition.

Requisite Dietitian Competencies

Competencies should be evaluated by a senior neonatologist and should include

- ability to assess the nutritional status of the neonate
- knowledge of all American Academy of Pediatrics nutrition and breastfeeding recommendations and expert statements
- ability to integrate scientific recommendations into intravenous and enteral support recommendations
- knowledge of parenteral nutrition solutions used in the neonatal unit: composition, uses, contraindications, and advantages and disadvantages
- knowledge of initiation of and transition from parenteral feeding to enteral feeding
- knowledge of human milk and breastfeeding
- knowledge of formula types; quantity and quality of nutrient composition
- ability to formulate clinical research projects independently
- ability to teach and present lectures on the subject of high-risk and general neonatal nutrition

Components of Nutrition Assessment

The initial approach to nutrition assessment of the neonate requires the following:

- maternal profile
- infant profile
- evaluation parameters
- consistent routine for monitoring
- variances of nutritional risk to screen and prioritize infants
- assessment tools

From these components, a basis for individualized feeding strategies can be determined.

Maternal Profile

Data to be gathered on the mother include

- mother's age, parity, gravida
- prenatal care
- substance abuse, smoking, or alcohol use
- medications, tocolytics, or steroids
- complications during pregnancy or at delivery
- plans to breast- or bottle-feed

Infant Profile

Data to be gathered on the infant include

- gestational age and intrauterine developmental stage—what enzymes, motor ability, and digestive maturity the infant has
- weight and weight for age—AGA, SGA, or LGA status
- Apgar scores at 1, 5, and 10 minutes (estimated level of asphyxia)
- C-section or vaginal delivery
- complications during pregnancy or at delivery
- in-born (at the same hospital as the nursery) or transported into the hospital
- diagnosis, medical treatment and plan
- respiratory status—mechanical ventilation, nasal continuous positive airway pressure, surfactant use, and/or oxygen
- bed type—warmer, isolette, or crib

Evaluation Parameters

- Fluid and electrolyte needs, based on the infant's age, respiratory status, bed type, phototherapy use, and renal function
- Growth needs, based on reference data for calories, protein, fat, vitamins, minerals, and trace elements

- Gastrointestinal status and ability to tolerate enteral feeding, based on developmental markers and clinical status
- Parenteral nutrition support—site, infusion rates, adequacy, and time frame to start and progress
- Enteral feeding plan—mode, volume, milk type, and progression
- Transition plan from parenteral to full enteral feeding
- Medication delivery and interaction possibilities
- Potential nutrient supplement needs over baseline as a result of limited volumes or excess losses
- Tolerance to parenteral infusions—line patency, precipitation concerns, growth, and laboratory monitors
- Tolerance to enteral feeding—gastric residuals, emesis, stool number, stool consistency, stool color, and respiratory changes (incidence of apnea and bradycardia associated with feeding)
- Growth
  - Weight gain—evaluate infants > 2 kg (g/day) and infants < 2 kg (g/kg/day)
  - Length gain (cm/wk)
  - Head circumference velocity (cm/wk)
  - Knemometer measurement of knee-heel velocity (mm/day average)

Routine for Monitoring

The following parameters should be assessed daily:

- weight (g)
- intake volume (cc/kg/day), calories (kcal/kg/day), protein (g/kg/day), fat (g/kg/day); for other nutrients, calculate per kg/day
- output in urine (cc/kg/hr); stool output in number, volume (cc/kg) if applicable, consistency, and color
- gastric residuals—number and volume
- other losses, ie, chest tube drainage, ventricular tap losses, ostomy, or Penrose drain losses—record and use to assess need for fluid and/or nutrient replacement

The following parameters should be checked weekly:

- weight gain average—infants > 2 kg (g/day) and infants < 2 kg (g/kg/day)
- length gain (cm/wk)
- head circumference velocity (cm/wk)
- knemometry velocity (mm/day)

Accurate and timely serum biochemistries can help determine the status of nutritional therapy. Currently, the text *Pediatric Clinical Chemistry*, by the American Association of Clinical Chemists, provides a valuable reference for infant laboratory standards. True "norms" for the preterm population are, however, scarce, making interpretation difficult. Become familiar with the populations used for each reference value.

Infants have a small blood volume available, so blood draws should be limited.

The following schedule offers a practical approach for serum evaluations:

- *Electrolytes*—Initially check every day (sodium, potassium, bicarbonate, and chloride) until the infant is stable; then change to every week.
- *Triglycerides*—Initially check 4 hours after each lipid infusion change; then discontinue when the infant is stable, or just check periodically if the infant is continuing on long-term (> 3 weeks) parenteral nutrition.
- *Mineral*—Initially check ionized calcium each morning until the infant is on full parenteral nutrition; then switch to serum calcium, phosphorus, alkaline phosphatase (ALK-Phos), and magnesium every week. After transition to full enteral feeding, switch to evaluations every other week.
- *Protein*—Initially check blood urea nitrogen (BUN) along with creatine every other day; then just check BUN every week. Once the infant is stable and growing on enteral feeds, switch to every other week and then to once a month.
- *Protein/Calorie*—Check serum albumin (half-life 14–21 days) starting on day 14 of

life, and then switch to every other week. Serum prealbumin has a shorter half-life (1.9 days), is more sensitive, and can be used to monitor acute changes in protein or calorie nutrition.

- *Liver*—Evaluate direct bilirubin, gamma glutamyl transferase (GGT), and alanine amino transferase (ALT) if the infant is on long-term (> 3 weeks) parenteral nutrition.
- *Vitamin A Status*—Serial serum retinol levels and retinol-binding protein may be important if the infant is on long-term (> 3 weeks) parenteral nutrition without adequate enteral sources.
- *Zinc Status*—To establish zinc nutriture, it is recommended to evaluate zinc losses in relation to the infant's intake. Prealbumin and alkaline phosphatase changes can also be used to monitor status. Serum zinc is not predictive of zinc status. Ostomy, or stool output of zinc, should be evaluated if the infant has had gastrointestinal surgery. If the infant has chest tube drainage and/or ventricular taps, consider assessment for zinc loss as well.

Variances of Nutritional Risk

To use the dietitian's time efficiently, screening for high-risk infants can be done initially by a technician. Infants with any one of the parameters reflecting nutritional risk should be evaluated:

- NPO and no parenteral nutrition (PN) > 3 days
- enteral volume < 130 cc/kg/day and no supplemental PN
- weight gain
  1. < 15 grams per day (if weight > 2 kg)
  2. < 13 grams/kg/day (if weight < 2 kg)
  3. > 20% weight loss after first week of life
- albumin < 2.7 g/dl
- prealbumin < 18 mg/dl
- phosphorus < 4.8 mg/dl
- alkaline phosphatase > 600 IU/dl

Variations should also be noted when the infant's chart does not contain a growth chart with daily weights and weekly head circumferences documented. After reviewing the screening of all the infants, the dietitian can plan appropriate nutrition intervention strategies, with high-risk infants prioritized. An algorithm to describe and organize the flow of nutrition services in the neonatal intensive care unit is summarized in Figure 3–1.

Assessment Tools

Tools frequently helpful for assessment of the infant include the following:

- Weight scale, length board, steel tape measure, and knemometer
- Growth grids: plain graph paper, intrauterine growth charts, or extrauterine charts. Both intrauterine and extrauterine charts *should not be considered optimal and should be used with caution* since they were created using populations specific to the time period and individual nursery protocols.
- Pediatric laboratory standards from *Pediatric Clinical Chemistry* text
- Care plan and milestone documentation sheet
- Neonova computer program to help with nutrient calculations and data collection

NUTRITIONAL PROBLEMS OF THE PREMATURE INFANT

The premature infant has numerous difficulties that the full-term infant does not share. Glucose instability, immature renal threshold, poor respiratory status, and limited fat or glycogen stores all compromise the infant's condition and make management strategies difficult.

These clinical and immaturity issues lead to several unique problems for nutritional consideration:

- increased body water (80% vs full-term 60%)
- decreased body stores of protein (8% vs full-term 12%)
- decreased fat stores (1% vs full-term 16%)
- increased risk for catabolism and essential fatty acid deficiency
- increased risk for sepsis
- clinical instability

TREATMENT AND MANAGEMENT

Nutrition Goals

Three major goals should be emphasized for the neonate (keep in mind any unique problems of the premature infant).

- Provide fluid, calories, protein, and fats to avoid catabolism and deficiencies.
- Avoid toxic overload by using appropriate quality and quantity of nutrients.
- Achieve appropriate weight gain and skeletal growth.

To achieve these goals, fluids, calories, protein, and other nutrients must be administered both parenterally and enterally in a timely manner.

Intravenous Fluid Therapy

To begin, immaturity and elevated cutaneous insensible losses are major determinants of the infant's fluid needs. The goal for fluids is typically 150 cc/kg/day. (Extreme immaturity (< 26 weeks' gestation) may require volumes of 150–200 cc/kg.) This volume should be achieved in a stepwise fashion, beginning with 60–80 cc/day (for infants > 1500 g at birth) or 80–100 cc/kg/day (for infants < 1500 g) and increasing by 20–30 cc/kg/day until the goal of 150cc/kg/day is achieved.

It should be stressed that fluid needs can be altered by the infant's immaturity and environment. For example, phototherapy and radiant warmers can dramatically increase the infant's insensible water losses. Conversely, humidified environments or plastic wrap can decrease losses. Individualized plans should adjust for these factors.

Suggested Nutrient Intake

Full-term nutrient needs are based on recommended dietary allowances, whereas limited body stores, increased energy expenditure, and clinical status result in specific nutrient recommendations for the premature infant. With the

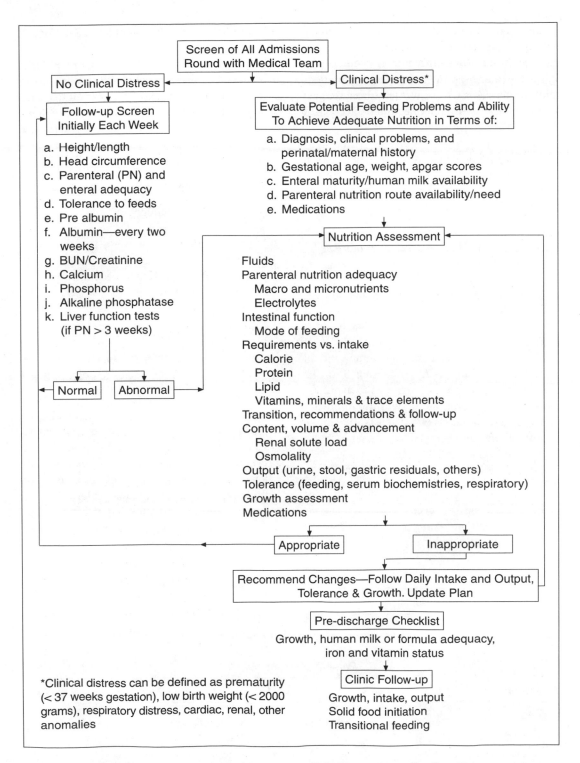

Figure 3–1 A Flow Chart of Events for Nutrition Services in the Neonatal Intensive Care Unit

exception of some of the light-sensitive, poorly delivery nutrients, parenteral needs are calculated to be less than the enteral needs of the infant for calories, protein, fat, electrolytes, vitamins, minerals, and trace elements because gastrointestinal losses do not need to be accounted for.

Tables 3–8 through 3–12 give nutrient recommendations for neonates. Additional nutrients to consider if infant has been on long-term parenteral support > 3 weeks without significant enteral source are iron and carnitine.

Parenteral Nutrition and Intravenous Fat Support

The initial mode of nutrition support for the high-risk infant is often PN and intravenous fat emulsions (IFE). This is indicated if the infant is unable to achieve full enteral feeding by day of life 3 and has urine output. The therapy should be initiated within 24–72 hours after birth. Its advantage is provision of nutrients to avoid catabolism and to promote growth. Its disadvantages are increased risks for sepsis, metabolic abnormalities, biochemical rickets, and cholestatic jaundice, as well as expense.

Guidelines for therapy are as follows:

• Use peripheral venous access if duration of therapy will be < 2 weeks. Use percutaneous access if duration of therapy will be > 2 weeks and peripheral sites have become a problem.

• Goal intake is 80–90 nonprotein cal/kg/day 3 g/kg/day protein.
• Use trophamine to boost essential and branched-chain amino acid delivery as well as to help with solubility of the PN solution and 3–4 g/kg/day fat.
• To calculate parenteral nutrition orders, use the following equation:

$$\left(\frac{\text{X amount/kg of nutrient desired}}{\text{Volume of solution/kg}} \right)$$

$$\times\ 100 = \text{amount to write}$$

For example:

$$\left(\frac{\begin{array}{c}\text{3 g/kg of protein desired for}\\\text{a 1.5-kg infant}\end{array}}{\text{130 cc/kg}} \right)$$

$$\times\ 100 = .023$$

$$\times\ 100 = 2.3\%\ \text{amino}$$
$$\text{acids to order}$$
$$\text{on PN sheet}$$

• Start with maintenance fluid therapy, and increase volume, calories, protein, and fat to goal intake for all infants by 3–7 days.
• Begin with 6 mg/kg/minute of dextrose (3.4 kcal per g), and increase daily to goal of 12 mg/kg/min and < 55% of total calories.
  1. Immature infants may require continuous insulin delivery to receive optimal dextrose and calories.

Table 3–8 Macronutrient Requirements for Neonates under and over 2 kg (unit/kg/day)

Macronutrient	Parenteral		Enteral	
	< 2 kg	> 2 kg	< 2 kg	> 2 kg
Calories (kcal)	80–90	80	120	98–108
Protein (g)*	3.0–4.0	2.0–3.0	3.0–4.0	2.0–2.5
Fat (g)	3.0–4.0	3.0	5.0–7.0	9.0

*Protein intake may be elevated with excess gastric, intestinal, ventricular, or chest tube losses.

Table 3–9 Vitamin Requirements for Neonates under and over 2 kg (unit/kg/day)

	Parenteral		Enteral	
Vitamin	*< 2 kg*	*> 2 kg*	*< 2 kg*	*> 2 kg*
Vitamin A (IU)*	700–1500	2300	1500	1500
Vitamin D (IU)	160	400	400	300–400
Vitamin E (IU)	3.5–7.0	7.0	6–25	3.0–4.0
Vitamin K (μg)**	100	200	7.0–9.0	5.0–10.0
Vitamin B$_1$ (μg)	200–350	1200	180–240	300–400
Vitamin B$_2$ (μg)	150–200	1400	250–360	400–500
Vitamin B$_{12}$ (μg)	0.3	1.0	0.3	0.3–0.5
Niacin (mg)	4.0–6.8	17.0	3.6–4.8	5.0–6.0
Folic acid (μg)	56	140	25–50	25

*Vitamin A delivery with current water-miscible bags in PN is poor; therefore, extra supplementation may be warranted.
**In addition, infants should receive vitamin K at birth: 1 mg of phylloquinone intramuscularly for infants > 1 kg and 0.3 mg of phylloquinone intramuscularly for infants < 1.0 kg.

2. Delivery of insulin is recommended when serum glucose > 180 mg/dL. Consider providing supplemental insulin at 0.06–0.10 U/h.
3. Prime the tubing with insulin, and use short tubing with a microinfusion pump to enhance insulin delivery.

- Begin with 1–2 g/kg/day of protein and increase daily to achieve goal of 3 g/kg. Infants with gastrointestinal, chest, or ventricular drainage may require up to 4.0 g/kg/day.
- Start IFE within the first 0–5 days of life, using 1 g/kg of the 20% concentration run over 24 hours (20% = 20 g of fat = 1.8 kcal/cc + glycerol in emulsion 0.2 kcal/cc = 2.0 kcal/cc total; 0.5 g/kg/day is required for essential fatty acid. Progress IFE to a goal intake of 3.0–4.0 g/kg/day.
- Add 30–40 mg of cysteine for every gram of protein in the PN; this practice will enhance solubility of PN.
- Provide electrolytes initially at 2–4 mEq/kg sodium and 1–2 mEq/kg/day potassium to maintain acid-based homeostasis. Also consider additional sodium acetate at 1 mmol/kg/day if using cysteine in PN.
- Begin calcium at 50–60 mg/dL and phosphorus at 40–45 mg/dL in the PN. Increase to maximum concentrations of 67 mg of calcium per deciliter and 62 mg of phosphorus per deciliter, which has been shown to enhance bone density in premature infants on PN. The calcium-to-phosphorus ratio should be provided in a 1.3:1.0 by weight or molar ratio of 1.0:1.0.

1. Maximum concentration is dependent on solubility or pH of the solution of PN.
2. Major factors in calcium and phosphorus solubility are
   - *Amino acids.* As the concentration increases, the pH will decrease and enhance solubility; conversely, as the concentration decreases, the pH will rise and the

Table 3–10 Electrolyte Requirements for Neonates (mEq/kg/day)

Electrolyte	Parenteral	Enteral
Sodium	2.0–3.0	2.0–3.0
Potassium	2.0–3.0	2.0–3.0
Chloride	2.0–3.0	2.0–3.0

Note: Excess losses due to gastric, intestinal, urine, diuretic use, or extreme immaturity may require increased supplementation.

Table 3–11 Mineral Requirements for Neonates under and over 2 kg (mg/kg/day)

Mineral	Parenteral		Enteral	
	< 2 kg	> 2 kg	< 2 kg	> 2 kg
Calcium	65–104	80–100	120–230	66.0
Phosphorus	60–81	46.0	60–140	50–56
Magnesium	4.3–7.2	4.3–7.2	7.9–15.0	6.7

Note: Calcium and phosphorus delivery with 1.8:1 by weight or 1:1 molar ratio is currently recommended.

solubility will fall. (General rule of thumb: At least 1.8% of amino acids per deciliter is needed to avoid precipitation of standard calcium and phosphorus delivery.) With maximal concentrations of calcium and phosphorus, it is best to use 2.5%–3.0% amino acids.

– *Cysteine.* Addition of 30–40 mg/g of protein will decrease pH and enhance solubility.

– *Temperature.* As the temperature of the surrounding environment increases, the pH will rise and result in less solubility. (General rule of thumb: Watch overhead warmer or vent placement.)

– *Acetate.* As acetate is provided, the pH will increase; therefore, the solubility will

decrease. (General rule of thumb: Use < 4.0 meq sodium acetate per deciliter of PN.)

• Add multivitamins using MVI-Pediatric at 40% of a vial per kilogram for infants < 2 kg and 100% of a vial for infants > 2 kg.

• Add trace elements to provide recommendations per kg.

Enteral Feeding Therapy

Direct and indirect benefits of enteral feeding include

• trophic effects on the intestinal tract
• luminal nutrients for hormonal stimulation
• hormonal stimulation of gastrin and trophic

Table 3–12 Trace Element Requirements for Neonates under and over 2 kg (unit/kg/day)

Trace Element	Parenteral		Enteral	
	< 2 kg	> 2 kg	< 2 kg	> 2 kg
Iron (mg)	0.1–0.2	0.1	2.0–6.0	1.0–2.0
Zinc (μg)*	400	100	1000	833
Copper (μg)**	20	10	120–150	67
Selenium (μg)***	1.5–2.0	1.5	1.3–3.0	1.6
Manganese**	10 μg	2.5 μg	7.5 μg	0.3–0.6 mg

*The infant may require increased intake if there are gastrointestinal, chest tube, or ventricular losses and may require decreased intake if there is renal failure.
**The infant may require decreased intake during severe cholestasis; monitor.
***The infant may require decreased intake if there is renal failure.

hormone with small (2 kcal/kg) feeds
- improved liver function versus PN
- enhanced motor activity—enhanced maturation of the small intestine
- fewer days NPO for infants fed "early" versus late (3 vs 15 days) and fewer days to achieve full enteral nutrition without an increased incidence in gastrointestinal disease

Potential concerns that may warrant delay with initiating feedings include

- *Questionable circulation*—Indomethacin use or patent ductus arteriosus
- *Unstable blood pressure*—mean < 30 or dopamine use at > 5.0 μg/kg
- *Severe acidosis*—blood pH < 7.2, lactate > 2.0, or arterial P_{O_2} < 40
- *Severely asphyxiated*—low 5-minute Apgar score < 5.0

Method of Feeding

- 33–35 weeks
  1. Breastfeeding—recommended by the American Academy of Pediatrics and the World Health Organization as the preferred feeding method. Also appears to be better tolerated than bottle for infants with respiratory compromise.
     - Assess latch, swallow, and weight gain.
     - Provide unlimited time to ensure that the infant gets to the latter, fat-rich hindmilk.
  2. Bottle feeding
     - Assess suck and swallow.
     - If infant has a grooved palate from long-term intubation or oral gastric tubes, then consider the Haberman feeder. The Haberman nipple has a longer shaft that may allow for a better nipple seal and intraoral pressure.
     - Consider one nipple feed at a time, and limit each in duration to 20 minutes.
- < 33 weeks' gestation
  1. Bolus/intermittent gavage
     - Direct delivery every 3–4 hours
     - "Physiologic" hormone stimulation

- Less time for milk to become infectious precipitate or, potentially, to interact with medications
  2. Continuous drip
     - Delivery every hour over 24 hours
     - May be better tolerated than bolus for infants < 1500 g
     - Provides less change in energy expenditure than the bolus method
     - May be better tolerated in infants with gastrointestinal disease or heart disease
     - Recommended delivery with automated syringe pump and short tubing, with syringes changed every 3–4 hours
     - Monitor for additive separation, medication interactions, or precipitation

Route of Feeding

- Oro/nasogastric
  1. "Physiologic" pattern of stimulation
  2. Lingual and gastric lipase stimulated; helpful in fat absorption
- Transpyloric:
  1. Useful in certain specific situations
     - For infants who have severe reflux that does not respond to medication therapy
     - For infants with a high risk of aspiration
     - As an alternative to long-term parenteral nutrition because of feeding failure on oral or nasogastric feeding
  2. Not recommended, however, for routine use
     - Bypassing the stomach can result in increased fat malabsorption and/or bacterial overgrowth.
     - Skill is required in tube placement, and X-ray exposure may be necessary to check tube placement.
     - Malposition and loss of tube placement are frequent problems.

Milk Type

Human milk has the following advantages:

- gives mother a role in infant's care
- has antiinfective properties—secretory IgA, IgG, lactoferrin, lysozymes

- has absorptive benefits—unique milk fat globule, bile-salt, stimulating lipase
- contains growth factors, long-chain polyunsaturated fatty acids, cholesterol
- transmits host-protective bacteriobacillus bifida flora in the mother's intestine

To collect the mother's milk for later use (milk banking):

- Instruct the mother on pumping her breasts.
- After colostrum, discard the first tablespoon of subsequent pumpings.
- Collect milk in glass bottles and label with name, date, time, and any medications used by the mother.
- Check all medications for safety in human milk.
- Have all milk delivered to the milk storage area on ice.
- Store the milk in the freezer until needed.

To fortify human milk:

- Thaw 24-hour volume and fortify if necessary (all infants < 2000 g should need fortification).
- Fortify human milk with powdered human milk fortifier.
- Initiate fortification with two packets per 100 cc of human milk, and after 24 hours increase fortification to four packets per 100 cc to provide full-fortified human milk.

Human milk fortifier contains corn syrup solids, whey protein, sodium caseinate, vitamins, minerals, electrolytes, and trace elements. Nutrients per packet are 3.5 calories, 0.175 g of protein, and < 0.025 g of fat.

The *hindmilk technique* can be used to boost caloric intake. Hindmilk is the latter part of the mother's milk expression. It contains the highest fat content and calories; therefore, to boost calories for infants on tube feedings or bottle feedings of human milk, instruct the mother as follows:

- Label a bottle "#1" and have the mother empty the first 2 minutes of pumping into this bottle. This is the foremilk. It will be saved in the freezer for later use.
- Label another bottle "#2" and have the mother completely finish expressing her milk into this bottle. This is the hind milk.
- Do this for each breast at each pumping.
- Next, pool all samples of bottles labeled "#2 and fortify as described earlier.

This simple technique can increase the fat and calories by 2–3 times. Weight gain has been shown to improve by 2–3 fold.

When human milk is not available, a formula must be used. Formulas should be assessed for

- nutrient quantity and quality
- bioavailability and absorptive considerations
- volume needed to meet infant's need
- supplements needed
- osmolality, renal solute load
- preservatives, emulsifiers, or contaminants
- cost

Premature infant formulas are recommended for use in the low–birth weight infant until a weight > 2 kg is reached. These formulations are designed to meet the fluid, calorie, protein, vitamin, mineral, and trace element needs of the premature infant. Both quality and quantity of nutrients have been formulated on the basis of intrauterine accretion rates. The standard infant formulas, soy formulas, and protein hydrolysates are not recommended for use for premature infants because of both quantitative and qualitative deficits. Full-term, standard formulas are not nutrient dense and require large volumes > 180 cc/kg/day of intake. Soy formulas have been associated with decreased phosphorus and bone density in premature infants, and most elemental formulas are casein based (with inappropriate amino acid profiles for the premature infant) and have concentrations of calcium, phosphorus, and zinc in particular that are below the recommendations for the premature infant. Therefore, to supply the premature infant with an appropriate nutrient source when breast milk is unavailable, premature infant formulas are the milk of choice.

For the full-term infant who is able to nipple-feed, a 20-kcal/oz, standard infant formula should be used. To ensure nutrient adequacy, infants on a standard 20-kcal/oz formula should receive minimum of 180 cc/kg/day. Density should be changed accordingly to 24-kcal/oz standard formula if the infant is receiving only 150 cc/kg/day. Similarly, the concentration should be changed to 27 kcal/oz if the infant is receiving only 130 cc/kg/day. Further concentration is not recommended due to hydration difficulties. Additions of oils, glucose polymers, or protein powders should only be used when absolutely necessary because they can cause bioavailability, delivery, and sedimentation problems.

Indications for use of formula types can be seen in the following summary:

- *Premature*—infants < 35 weeks' gestation and/or < 2000 g
- *Standard, cow's milk–based*—infants without special needs > 35 weeks' gestation and > 2 kg
- *Soy protein, non–cow's milk-based*—Full-term infants with documented galactosemia or true lactose intolerance; *not recommended for preterm infants* since they may decrease bone mineralization

- *Protein hydrolysates, special elemental formulas*—documented protein allergy or very severe malabsorption

Suggested Enteral Feeding Initiation and Advancement for Infants on Tube Feedings

For human milk:

- Use full-strength human milk.
- Start with 5–20 cc/kg/day (volume should never advance > 20 cc/kg/day.
- Titrate PN support accordingly; see Table 3–13 for example.
- Increase daily by 5–20 cc/kg/day.
- Goal volume is minimum 150 cc/kg/day.
- Fortify with two packets of human milk fortifier per 100 cc of human milk if the infant is < 2 kg or on a volume restriction of 150 cc/kg/day.
- After 24 hours of tolerance on 150 cc/kg/day of human milk with two packets per 100 cc of human milk, increase to four packets per 100 cc.
- Infants < 1 kg and infants > 2 kg may experience difficulty with full fortification. *Monitor serum calcium and phosphorus levels carefully.*

Table 3–13 Enteral Feeding Initiation and Parenteral Transition Guidelines

Time Period	Milk Volume (cc/kg/day)	Parenteral Volume (cc/kg/day)	Intravenous Fat Volume (cc/kg/day)
Milk start*	20	110	20
After 24 hours	40	90	20
48 hours later	60	90	0
72 hours	80	70	0
96 hours	100	50	0
120 hours	120	30**	0
144 hours	140	0	0
168 hours	150–160	0	0

*Initiation is based on a standard volume of 20 cc/kg/day started on day of life 5–15. If the infant is very immature (< 30 weeks' gestation) and unstable or is starting feedings in the first week of life, priming doses at < 20 cc/kg/d may be warranted.

**If needed, an intravenous dextrose solution can be hung instead of parenteral fluids at 30 cc/kg/day.

For formula

- Initiate feedings with 5–20 cc/kg/day half-strength formula—Sterile water does not initiate the same motility effects as starting with milk.
- Titrate PN support accordingly; see Table 3–13 for example.
- Increase to full-strength formula after 24 hours on half-strength.
- After another 24 hours of tolerance, begin advancement by 5–20 cc/kg/day. *Again, remember to avoid advancement > 20 cc/kg/day.*
- Goal intake is a minimum of 150 cc/kg/day for infants < 2 kg or for infants > 2 kg on a volume restriction.

Never advance concentration and volume on the same day. Monitor feeding tolerance, labs, and growth. Some infants on fortified human milk may require volumes from 160–180 cc/kg/day or hindmilk. Infants on premature formulas may require 160 cc/kg/day to grow. Infants > 2 kg, on standard 20-kcal/oz formula or breast milk require > 180 cc/kg/day.

Nutritional Status Monitors and Goals

Finally, feeding tolerance, laboratory values, and growth goals should be evaluated based on criteria described earlier. *Feeding tolerance markers* commonly include gastric residual volume, color, incidence of emesis, and stool pattern. Signs of intolerance are residuals that are green, bloody, and/or in a quantity > half of a 3-hour volume. Any occurrence of emesis is a concern, and the infant should be assessed. Stools that become frequent, loose, or irregular; contain glucose; and/or have a low pH (< 5.5) should also become a concern, and the infant should be evaluated for sepsis, drug interactions, or milk intolerance. Typical management strategies for any of these problems include a clinical exam of the infant and his or her situation. Check the feeding-tube position, or try changing the mode of feeding. Check the infant's position and medications, and/or consider changing the infant's milk strength or type.

Slow the rate of milk delivery, or consider decreasing the volume of feedings. Intravenous fluid replacement or PN support may need to be reinitiated if enteral volume drops to 130 cc/kg/day or less. Further workup for malabsorption problems may be warranted if the infant continues to have emesis, residuals, or stools with glucose, despite being septic free and on low volumes of a continuous milk drip.

Laboratory monitors should be evaluated as previously described, with the overall goal to include albumin > 2.9 g/dL, prealbumin > 19 mg/dL, and phosphorus > 5.0 mg/dL.

Growth monitors should include weight gain, length gain, and knee-heel length velocity. Overall goals should include average weight gain of > or equal to 15 g/kg/day if infants is < 2 kg, and 20–30 g/day if the infant is > 2 kg; length acceleration of > 0.5 cm/wk; and knee-heel length velocity of > 0.4 mm/day.

CONCLUSION

Nutritional influences on the neonate's respiration, development, and outcome necessitate timely and appropriate nutrition intervention strategies. Routine assessment and evaluation by a dietitian competent in the area of neonatal nutrition is therefore warranted and can produce favorable outcomes.

REFERENCES

American Academy of Pediatrics, Committee on Nutrition. Human milk banking. *Pediatr.* 1980;65:854–856.

American Academy of Pediatrics, Committee on Nutrition. Use of intravenous fat emulsions in pediatric patients. *Pediatr.* 1981;68:738–743.

American Academy of Pediatrics, Committee on Nutrition. The promotion of breastfeeding. *Pediatr.* 1982;69:654–661.

American Academy of Pediatrics, Committee on Nutrition. Commentary on parenteral nutrition. *Pediatr.* 1983;17:547–552.

American Academy of Pediatrics, Committee on Nutrition. Nutritional needs of low-birth-weight infants. *Pediatr.* 1985;75:976–984.

American Academy of Pediatrics, Committee on Nutrition. Transfer of drugs and other chemicals into human milk. *Pediatr.* 1989;84:924–936.

American Academy of Pediatrics and American College of Obstetrics and Gynecology. *Guidelines for Perinatal Care.* 3rd ed. 1992:10.

Anderson DM, Kliegman RM. The relationship of neonatal alimentation practices to the occurrence of endemic necrotizing enterocolitis. *Am J Perinatol.* 1991;8:62–67.

Antonson DL, Smith JL, Nelson RD, Anderson AK, Vanderhoof JA. Stability of vitamin and mineral concentrations of a low-birth-weight infant formula during continuous enteral feeding. *J Pediatr Gastroenterol Nutr.* 1983; 2:617–621.

Apgar V. A proposal for a new method of evaluation of the newborn infant. *Anesth Analg.* 1953;32:260.

Avens R, Reichman B. Grooved palate associated with prolonged use of orogastric feeding tubes in premature infants. *J Oral Maxillofac Surg.* 1992;50:64–65.

Aynsley-Green A, Adrian TE, Bloom SR. Feeding and the development of enteroisular hormone secretion on the preterm infant: effects of continuous gastric infusions of human milk compared with intermittent boluses. *Acta Pediatr Scand.* 1982;71:379–383.

Ballard JL, Novak KK, Driver M. A simplified score for assessment of fetal maturation of newly born infants. *J Pediatr.* 1979;95:769–774.

Battaglia FC, Lubchenko LO. A practical classification of newborn infants by weight and gestational age. *J Pediatr.* 1967;71:159–163.

Baumgart S, Fox WW, Polin RA. Physiologic implications of two different heat shields for infants under radiant warmers. *J Pediatr.* 1982;100:787–790.

Beale EF, Nelson RM, Bucciarelli RL, Donnelly WH, Eitzman DV. Intrahepatic cholestatis associated with parenteral nutrition in premature infants. *Pediatr.* 1979; 64:342–347.

Behrman RE, Shniono PH. Neonatal risk factors in neonatal-perinatal medicine. In: Fanaroff AA, Martin RJ, eds. *Diseases of the Fetus and Infant.* Vol 1. 5th ed. St Louis, Mo: Mosby Yearbook, Inc; 1992:4–5.

Berseth CL, Ittman PI. Antral and duodenal motor response to duodenal feeding in preterm and term infants. *J Pediatr Gastroenterol Nutr.* 1992;14:182–186.

Berseth CL, Nordyke CK, Valdes MG, Furlow BL, Liang V. Responses of gastrointestinal peptides and motor activity to milk and water feedings in preterm and term infants. *Pediatr Res.* 1992;31:587–590.

Bier J, Ferguson A, Anderson L, et al. Breastfeeding of very low birth weight infants. *J Pediatr.* 1993;123:773–778.

Bisset WM, Watt J, Rivers RPA, Milla PJ. Postprandial motor response of the small intestine to enteral feeds in preterm infants. *Arch Dis Child.* 1988;64:1356–1361.

Blondheim O, Abbasi S, Fox WW, Bhutani VK. Effect of enteral gavage feeding rate on pulmonary function of very low birth weight infants. *J Pediatr.* 1993;122:751–755.

Brans YW, Dutton EB, Andrew DS, Menchaca EM, West DL. Fat emulsion tolerance in very low birth weight neonates: effect on diffusion of oxygen in the lungs and on blood pH. *Pediatr.* 1986;78:79–84.

Brown MR, Thurberg BJ, Golub L, Manisleo WM, Cox C, Shapiro DL. Decreased cholestasis with enteral instead of intravenous protein in the very low birth weight infant. *J Pediatr Gastroenterol Nutr.* 1989;9:21–27.

Collins JW, Hoppe M, Brown K, Edidin D, Padbury J, Ogala ES. A controlled trial of insulin infusion and parenteral nutrition in extremely low birth weight infants with glucose intolerance. *J Pediatr.* 1991;118:921–927.

Consensus recommendations. In: Tsang RC, Lucas A, Uauy R, Zlotkin S, eds. *Nutritional Needs of the Preterm Infant: Scientific Basis and Practical Guidelines.* Pauling, NY: Caduceus Medical Publishers, Inc; 1993:288–295.

Cooper A, Jakobowski D, Spiker J, Floyd T, Ziegler MM, Koop CE. Nutritional assessment: an integral part of the preoperative pediatric surgical evaluation. *J Pediatr Surg.* 1981;16(suppl):554–561.

Dancis J, O'Connell JR, Holt LE. A grid for recording the weight of premature infants. *J Pediatr.* 1948;33:570–572.

Davidson M, Levine SZ, Bauer CH, Dann M. Feeding studies in low-birth-weight infants. I. Relationship of dietary protein, fat, and electrolyte to rates of weight gain, clinical courses, and serum chemical considerations. *J Pediatr.* 1967;70:695–713.

Eggert LD, Rusho WJ, MacKay MW, Chan GM. Calcium and phosphorus compatibility in parenteral nutrition solutions for neonates. *Am J Hosp Pharm.* 1982;39:49–53.

FitzGerald KA, MacKay MW. Calcium and phosphorus solubility in neonatal parenteral nutrient solutions containing trophamine. *Am J Hosp Pharm.* 1986;43:88–93.

Friel JK, Andrews WL, Hall MS, et al. Intravenous iron administration to very-low-birth-weight newborns receiving total and partial parenteral nutrition. *JPEN.* 1995;19:114–118.

Georgieff MK, Mills MM, Zempel CE, Chang PN. Catch-up growth, muscle and fat accretion, and body proportionality of infants one year after newborn intensive care. *J Pediatr.* 1989;114:2888–2892.

Gibson AT, Pearse RG, Wales JK. Knemometry and the assessment of growth in premature babies. *Arch Dis Child.* 1993;69:498–504.

Grant J, Denne S. Effect of intermittent versus continuous enteral feeding of energy expenditure in premature infants. *J Pediatr.* 1991;118:928–932.

Greene HL, Hambidge KM, Schanler R, Tsang RC. Guidelines for the use of vitamins, trace elements, calcium, magnesium, and phosphorus in infants and children receiving total parenteral nutrition: Report of the Subcommittee on Pediatric Parenteral Nutrient Requirements from the Committee of Clinical Practice Issues of the American Society for Clinical Nutrition. *Am J Clin Nutr.* 1988;48:1324–1342.

Greer FR, McCormick A, Loker J. Changes in the fat concentration of human milk during delivery by intermittent bolus and continuous mechanical pump infusion. *J Pediatr.* 1984;105:745–749.

Greer F, Steichen JJ, Tsang RC. Effects of increased calcium, phosphorus, and vitamin D intake on bare mineralization in very-low-birth weight infants fed formulas with polycose and medium chain triglycerides. *J Pediatr.* 1982; 100:951–955.

Hall RT, Callenbach JC, Sheehan MB, et al. Comparison of calcium and phosphorus supplemented soy isolate formula with whey-predominant premature formula in very low birth weight infants. *J Pediatr Gastroenterol Nutr.* 1984;3:571–576.

Hanosh M. Lipid metabolism in premature infants. *Biol Neonate.* 1987;52(suppl 1):50–64.

Haumont D, Deckelbaum RJ, Richelle M, et al. Plasma lipid and plasma lipo protein concentrations in low birthweight infants given parenteral nutrition with twenty or ten percent lipid emulsion. *J Pediatr.* 1989;115:787–793.

Heird WC, Hay W, Helms RA, Storm MC, Kashyap S, Dell RB. Pediatric parenteral amino acid mixture in low birth weight infants. *Pediatr.* 1988;81:41–50.

Heldt GP. The effect of gavage feeding on the mechanics of the lung, chest wall, and diaphragm of preterm infants. *Pediatr Res.* 1988;24:55–58.

Hey EN, Katz G. Evaporative water loss in the newborn baby. *J Physiol.* 1969;200:605–619.

Hughes CA, Talbot JC, Ducker DA, Harran MJ. Total parenteral nutrition in infancy: effect on the liver and suggested pathogenesis. *Gut.* 1983;24:241–248.

Hurst N. *Breast-Feeding Your Hospitalized Baby.* Houston, Tx: Texas Children's Hospital; 1988.

Kelsen SG, Ference M, Kapoor S. Effects of prolonged undernutrition on structure and function of the diaphragm. *J Appl Physiol.* 1985;58:1354–1359.

Klish WJ. Special infant formulas. *Pediatr Rev.* 1990;12:55–62.

Kovar I, Mayne P, Barltrop D. Plasma alkaline phosphatase activity: a screening test for rickets in preterm neonates. *Lancet.* Feb. 6, 1982:308–310.

Laine L, Shulman RJ, Pitre D, Liftschitz CH, Adams J. Cysteine usage increases the need for acetate in neonates who receive total parenteral nutrition. *Am J Clin Nutr.* 1991; 54:565–567.

Latimer JS, McClain CJ, Sharp HL. Clinical zinc deficiency during zinc-supplemented parenteral nutrition. *J Pediatr.* 1980;97:434–437.

Lemons PM, Miller K, Eitzen H, Strodbeck F, Lemons JA. Bacterial growth in human milk during continuous feeding. *Am J Perinatol.* 1983;1:76–80.

Lubchenko LO, Hansman C, Dressler M, Boyd E. Intrauterine growth as estimated from live born birth weight data at 24 to 42 weeks of gestation. *Pediatr.* 1963;32:793–800.

Lucas A. Does diet in preterm infants influence clinical outcome? Energy metabolism, nutrition, and growth in premature infants. *Biol Neonate.* 1987;52:141–146.

Lucas A, Bloom SR, Ansyley Green A. Gut hormones and minimal enteral feeding. *Acta Pediatr Scand.* 1986;75: 719–723.

Lucas A, Morely R, Cole TJ, Lister G, Leeson-Payne C. Breast milk and subsequent intelligence quotient in children born preterm. *Lancet.* 1992;339:261–264.

Lyon AJ, McIntosh N, Wheeler K, Williams JE. Radiological rickets in extremely low birthweight infants. *Pediatr Radiol.* 1987;17:56–58.

MacDonald PD, Skeoch CH, Dryburgh F, Alroomil G, Galea P, Gettinby G. Randomized trial of continuous nasogastric, bolus nasogastric, and transpyloric feeding in infants of birthweight under 1400 grams. *Arch Dis Child.* 1992;67:429–431.

Mayfield SR, Albrecht J, Roberts L, Lair C. The role of the nutritional support team in neonatal intensive care. *Semin Perinatol.* 1989;13:88–96.

Meetze WH, Valentine C, McGiugan JE, Canlon M, Sacks N, Neu J. Gastrointestinal priming prior to full enteral nutrition in very low birth weight infants. *J Pediatr Gastroenterol Nutr.* 1992;15:163–170.

Meier P, Anderson GC. Responses of small preterm infants to bottle and breastfeeding. *MCN.* 1987;12:97–105.

Michaelsen KF, Skov L, Badsberg JH, Jorgensen M. Short-term measurement of linear growth in preterm infants: validation of hand-held knemometer. *Pediatr Res.* 1991; 30:464–468.

Moskowitz SR, Pereira G, Spitzer A, Heaf L, Amsel J, Watkins JB. Prealbumin as a biochemical marker of nutritional adequacy in premature infants. *J Pediatr.* 1983;102: 749–753.

Mulvihill SJ, Stone MM, Fankalsrud EW, Debas HT. Trophic effect of amniotic fluid on fetal gastrointestinal development. *J Surg Res.* 1986;40:291–296.

Nanji AA. Absence of increase of serum alkaline phosphatase activity with parenteral nutrition-associated cholestasis: possible consequences of hypozincemia and hypomagnesenia. *Enzyme.* 1985;33:101–104.

National Research Council. *Recommended Dietary Allowances.* 10th ed. Washington, DC: National Academy Press; 1989.

Narayanan I, Mehta R, Choudhury DK, Jain BK. Sucking on the emptied breast: non-nutritive sucking with a difference. *Arch Dis Child.* 1990;65:241–244.

Neu J. Functional development of the fetal gastrointestinal tract. *Semin Perinatol.* 1989;13:224–235.

Neu J, Valentine C, Meetze W. Scientifically-based strategies for nutrition of the high risk, low-birth weight infant. *Eur J Pediatr.* 1990;150:2–13.

Neville MC, Keller RP, Seacat J, Casey CE, Allen JC, Archer P. Studies on human lactation, I: within-feed and between-breast variation in selected components of human milk. *Am J Clin Nutr.* 1984;40:635–646.

Ostertag SG, Jovanovic L, Lewis B, Auld PAM. Insulin pump therapy in the very low birth weight infant. *Pediatr.* 1986;78:625–630.

Parker P, Stroop S, Greene H. A controlled comparison of continuous versus intermittent feeding in the treatment of infants with intestinal disease. *J Pediatr.* 1981;99:360–364.

Pediatric Clinical Chemistry. 3rd ed. Washington, DC: American Association of Clinical Chemists; 1989.

Pereira GR, Lemons JA. Controlled study of transpyloric and intermittent gavage feeding in the small preterm infant. *Pediatr.* 1981;67:68–72.

Phelps SJ, Helms RA. Risk factors affecting infiltration of peripheral venous lines in infants. *J Pediatr.* 1987;3:384–389.

Prealbumin. In: Howanitz JH, Howanitz PJ, Cornbleat PJ, Schifman RB, Petz LD, eds. *Laboratory Medicine Test Selection and Interpretation.* New York, NY: Churchill Livingstone, Inc; 1991:165.

Prestridge LL, Schanler RJ, Shulman RJ, Burns P, Laine LL. Effect of parenteral calcium and phosphorus therapy on mineral retention and bone mineral content in very low birth weight infants. *J Pediatr.* 1993;122:761–768.

Raiha NCR. Biochemical basis for nutritional management of preterm infants. *Pediatr.* 1974;53:147–156.

Rivera A, Bell R, Bier D. Effect of intravenous amino acids on protein metabolism of preterm infants during the first three days of life. *Pediatr Res.* 1993;33:106–111.

Schanler RJ. Human milk for preterm infants: nutritional and immune factors. *Semin Perinatol.* 1989;13:69–77.

Schanler RJ, Abrams S, Garza C. Bioavailability of calcium and phosphorus in human milk fortifiers and formulas for very low birth weight infants. *J Pediatr.* 1988;113:95–100.

Schanler RJ, Hurst NM. Human milk for the hospitalized preterm infant. *Semin Perinatol.* 1994;18:476–484.

Schmidt GL, Baungatner TG, Fischlschweiger W. Cost containment using cysteine HCl acidification to increase calcium/phosphate solubility in hyperalimentation solutions. *JPEN.* 1986;10:203–207.

Schwarz SM, Gewitz MH, See CC, et al. Enteral nutrition in infants with congenital heart disease and growth failure. *Pediatr.* 1990;86:368–373.

Shaffer SG, Quimiro CL, Anderson JV, Hall RT. Postnatal weight changes in low birth weight infants. *Pediatr.* 1987;79:702–705.

Shenai JP, Chytil F, Jhaver A, Stahlman MT. Plasma vitamin A and retinol-binding protein in premature and term neonates. *J Pediatr.* 1981;99:302–305.

Shenai JP, Jhaveri BM, Reynolds JW, Huston RK, Babson G. Nutritional balance studies in very low-birth-weight infants: role of soy formula. *Pediatr.* 1981;67:631–637.

Shenai JP, Stahlman MT, Chytil F. Vitamin A delivery from parenteral alimentation solution. *J Pediatr.* 1981;99:661–663.

Shulman RJ, Laine LD, Petitt R, Rahman S, Reed T. Protein deficiency in premature infants receiving parenteral nutrition. *Am J Clin Nutr.* 1986;44:610–613.

Shulman RJ, Pokorny WJ, Martin CG, Petitt R, Baldaia L, Roney D. Comparison of percutaneous and surgical placement of central venous catheters in neonates. *J Pediatr Surg.* 1986;21:348–350.

Soliz A, Suguihara C, Huang J, Hehre D, Bancalari E. Effect of amino acid infusion on the ventilatory response to hypoxia in protein-deprived neonatal piglets. *Pediatr Res.* 1994;35:316–320.

Solomons NW. On the assessment of zinc and copper nurture in man. *Am J Clin Nutr.* 1979;32:856–871.

Sommerfeld ES, Penn D, Wolf H. Carnitine blood concentrations and fat utilization in parenterally alimented premature newborn infants. *J Pediatr.* 1982;100:260–264.

Sosenko IRS, Frank L. Nutritional influences on lung development and protection against chronic lung disease. *Semin Perinatol.* 1991;15:462–468.

Steichen JJ, Gratton TL, Tsang RC. Osteopenia of prematurity: the cause and possible treatment. *J Pediatr.* 1980;96:528–534.

Sulkers EJ, Goudever JB, Wattimera JLD, Sauer PJJ. Comparison of two premature formulas with and without addition of medical-chain triglycerides (MCT'S) I: effect on nitrogen and fat balance and body composition changes. *J Pediatr Gastroenterol Nutr.* 1992;15:34–41.

Thomas JL, Reichelderfer TE. Premature infants: analysis of serum during the first seven weeks. *Clin Chem.* 1968;14:272–280.

Thompson M, Price P, Stahle D. Nutrition services in neonatal intensive care: a national survey. *J Am Diet Assoc.* 1994;94:440–441.

Uauy RD, Birch DG, Birch EE, Tyson JE, Hoffman DR. Effect of dietary omega-3 fatty acids on retinal function of very-low-birth-weight neonates. *Pediatr Res.* 1990;28:485–492.

Valentine CJ. Neonatal nutrition in the 1990's: milking it for everything you can! *Building Blocks for Life.* 1994;18:1–6.

Valentine C, Hurst N, Schanler RJ. Hindmilk improves weight gain in low-birth-weight infants fed human milk. *J Pediatr Gastroenterol Nutr.* 1994;18:474–477.

Valentine C, Schanler RJ. Neonatal nutritionist intervention improves nutritional support and promotes cost containment in the management of low birth weight (LBW) infants. *ASPEN Clin Congress.* Baltimore, Md: 1993;46A:466.

Widdowson EM. Fetal and neonatal nutrition. *Nutr Today.* September/October (1987):16–21.

Wit JM, von Kalsbeek EJ, Van Wijk-hoek JM, Leppink GJ. Assessment of the usefulness of weekly knemometric measurements in growth studies. *Acta Pediatr Scand.* 1987;76:974–980.

Wu PYK, Hodgman JE. Insensible water loss in preterm infants: changes with postnatal development and non-ionizing radiant energy. *Pediatr.* 1974;54:704–712.

Ziegler EE, O'Donnell AM, Nelson SE, Fomon SJ. Body composition of the reference fetus. *Growth.* 1976;40:329–341.

Zlotkin SH, Bryan MH, Anderson GH. Intravenous nitrogen and energy intakes required to duplicate in utero nitrogen accretion in prematurely born human infants. *J Pediatr.* 1981;99:115–120.

Zlotkin SH, Buchanan BE. Meeting zinc and copper intake requirements in the parenterally fed preterm and full-term infant. *J Pediatr.* 1983;103:441–446.

Obesity

Sharon L. Gallagher, Edward A. Mascioli, and R. Armour Forse

DESCRIPTION

Obesity is a complex, serious medical disorder and a leading public health problem. It contributes to several chronic diseases and is associated with increased mortality rates. Despite decades of research and clinical attention, there is as yet no "cure" for this resistant disease. In fact, its prevalence continues to increase. Treatment is difficult, with inconsistent results. This section will address current thoughts on the clinical management of obesity and its associated complications.

Definition

Obesity is defined as an excess increase in body fat. It can be expressed (or estimated) in various forms:

- % Ideal (or Desirable) Body Weight (IBW, or DBW)
  1. *Mild obesity:* 120%–140% IBW
  2. *Moderate obesity:* 141%–200% IBW
  3. *Morbid or severe obesity:* > 200% IBW
  4. *Superobesity:* > 250% IBW

- Body Mass Index (BMI)—weight (in kg)/ height (in m^2) (see BMI Chart in Appendix H)
  1. *Mild obesity:* BMI > 25 but < 30 kg/m^2
  2. *Moderate obesity:* BMI of 30–40 kg/m^2
  3. *Morbid or severe obesity:* BMI > 40 kg/m^2
  4. *Superobesity:* BMI > 50 kg/m^2

Methods of Assessing Body Fat

- Anthropometry (skinfold measurements)
- Waist/Hip Ratio (WHR): classifies obesity based on fat distribution
- Bioelectrical Impedance (BIA)
- Total Body Electrical Conductivity (TOBEC)
- Densitometry (underwater weighing)
- Total Body Water (TBW)
- Total Body Potassium (TBK)
- Computer Tomography (CT)
- Infrared Interactance
- Magnetic Resonance Imaging (MRI)

Prevalence

- According to the third National Health and Examination Survey (NHANES III, 1988–1991), 33.4% of adults are overweight.

- Prevalence has increased from 25% since the NHANES II survey (1976–1980).
- Over 50 million adults (one third of the U.S. adult population) are classified as obese.
- Obesity tends to be more prevalent in minority populations (eg, African Americans, Hispanics, and Native Americans), women, and individuals with low socioeconomic status.

CAUSES

Although the causes of obesity are complex in each individual, obesity is always the result of an imbalance between energy intake and energy expenditure. Obesity probably involves a combination of genetics and environment. People may inherit the tendency to gain weight, but environment can be the "trigger" that allows the expression of the genetic background.

Genetics

- Childhood obesity is linked with higher parental body weights.
- One adoption study found a 70% correlation between adopted children and their biological parents; no correlation was seen with adoptive parents.
- Studies have shown that BMIs of identical twins were highly correlated even when the twins were reared in separate environments.
- The amount of visceral body fat may be more influenced by heredity than the amount of subcutaneous fat.
- Studies with certain populations suggest lower rates of energy expenditure in obese subjects.
- Recent discovery of a gene for obesity in mice may help researchers understand how the size of body fat stores can be regulated.

Environment

- Physical activity has decreased in our country with industrialization; decreasing physical activity may explain why we tend to get fatter as we age.
- The percentage of calories from fat has been increasing; dietary fat is converted to body fat with much greater efficiency than carbohydrate.
- Epidemiological evidence shows increasing prevalence of obesity with immigration to the United States.
- Our culture offers highly palatable foods accessible to all at a low cost.
- Obesity is associated with lower socioeconomic status, income, and education. One study concluded that obesity was the cause of lower income rather than the result.
- Some researchers have suggested that feeding behaviors are a result of learned responses during childhood or related to cultural influences, or that they are a learned method of coping with stress or anger.

Theories of Obesity

Several theories have delineated possible mechanisms accounting for excessive weight gain and failure to lose weight:

- *Set Point Theory.* Fat storage appears to be regulated to achieve stable body weight.
- *Fat Cell Theory.* Set point may be determined by the number of fat cells an individual has at critical development stages.
- *Weight Cycling Theory.* Repeated cycles of weight loss and weight gain may result in greater difficulty in maintaining weight loss.
- *Push-Pull Theory.* Obesity may be the result of consuming excess calories (push theory) or the result of a genetic predisposition that leads to excess fat deposition (pull theory).
- *Externality Theory.* Some people may respond more to external cues to eat (eg, established meal times) than to internal cues, such as hunger.
- *Deprivation or Restraint Theory.* Chronic dieting may lead to periods of binging.

Hypothesized Etiologic Factors

The following factors have been explored in terms of their etiologic role in obesity:

- *Metabolic Factors.* Altered thermogenesis and/or lipoprotein lipase (LPL) levels may promote obesity.
- *Calorie Consumption.* Most clinical studies have *not* found that obese individuals consume more calories than lean controls. However, other studies have discovered that individuals tend to underreport energy intake and overestimate physical activity. This is estimated to be present to a larger degree in the obese population than in lean persons.
- *Diet Composition:* High levels of dietary fat have been correlated with obesity in women.
- *Psychopathology:* Obese individuals have *not* been found to display significant differences from lean individuals in psychological functioning. In addition, any psychological disturbances noted (such as poor body image or poor self-esteem) may well be the result of obesity rather than the cause.
- *Physical Activity:* Obese individuals are clearly less active than nonobese peers; however, is this cause or effect?

ASSESSMENT

Consider the following upon initial encounter with the patient:

- weight history (highest weight, lowest adult weight, number of attempts to lose weight, number of pounds lost each time, age at onset of obesity)
- body fat distribution (WHR)
- dieting history (number of attempts, types of programs)
- medical history (any weight-related comorbid conditions? Any conditions in which obesity is a secondary problem?)
- eating habits (amount of dietary fat, total calories, size of meals/snacks, frequency of eating events, use of alcohol, frequency of eating foods purchased outside the home)
- current level of physical activity and opportunities/ability to exercise
- social factors (support systems, finances, daily activities, living environment)

- degree of overweight (overweight vs obese vs severely obese)
- patient's reasons for wanting to lose weight at this time (internal vs external motivation)
- patient's current knowledge level (knowledge of diet principles, behavioral techniques)
- patient's expectations regarding rate of weight loss, weight goals (realistic?)
- any psychological associations with eating problems
- presence of eating disorders, binge eating and/or purging behaviors—is it even appropriate for the patient to lose weight? (Binge eating disorders are estimated to exist in 20%–30% of people entering weight loss programs. They are very resistant to treatment.)

PROBLEMS

- Mortality risk increases with a BMI of ~ 22 or greater.
- An IBW > 120% is associated with increased risk for hypertension, coronary artery disease, cerebrovascular disease, lipid disorders, non–insulin-dependent diabetes mellitus, hyperinsulinemia, insulin resistance, some kinds of cancer, venous stasis ulcers, degenerative arthritis, gout, gallbladder disease, pulmonary disease (sleep apnea, obesity hypoventilation), infertility, and menstrual irregularities.
- The estimated economic cost of obesity in the United States is ~ $39 billion (1992).
- Android, or upper-body, obesity (WHR > 1.0 in men or > 0.8 in women) is associated with greater intra-abdominal fat and its adverse health effects: higher risks of heart disease, hypertension, insulin disorders, and diabetes.
- There is a current controversy regarding weight cycling. Epidemiological studies show an association of elevated health risk with repeated variations in weight. However, this interpretation has been challenged by those who state that the relationship is not one of cause and effect. Further research is needed.
- Discrimination against the obese is prevalent in the United States and has been demon-

strated to have negative social and economic consequences.

- "Blaming-the-victim" syndrome is prevalent in our culture, particularly among health professionals.

TREATMENT

Adults

The following general considerations should be kept in mind:

- The goal of treatment is not necessarily to achieve "ideal" weight but to reduce weight to control medical comorbid conditions.
- It must be understood that obesity is a chronic disorder requiring long-term care. Patients must be willing to alter their lifestyle permanently.
- Treatment options may be classified according to weight. The stepped-care approach can be a cost-effective tool in the decision-making process (see Figure 3–2). The challenge is to

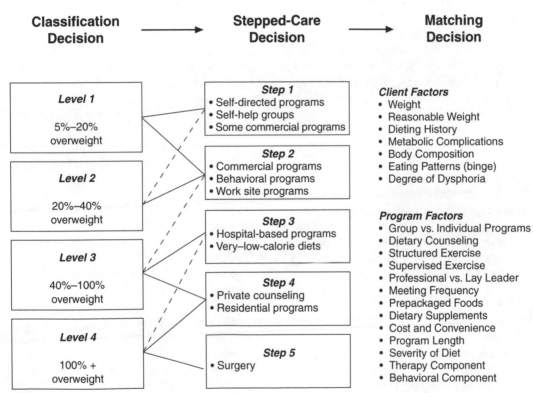

Figure 3–2 A conceptual scheme showing the three-stage process in selecting a treatment for an individual. The first step, the classification decision, divides individuals according to percentage overweight into four levels. These levels dictate which of the five steps would be reasonable in the second stage, the stepped-care decision. This indicates that the least intensive, costly, and risky approach will be used from among alternative treatments. The third stage, the matching decision, is used to make the final selection of a program and is based on a combination of client and program variables. The dashed lines with arrows between the classification and stepped-care stages show the lowest level of treatment that may be beneficial, but more intensive treatment is usually necessary for people at the specified weight level. *Source:* Reprinted with permission from KD Brownell and TA Wadden. The Heterogeneity of Obesity: Fitting Treatments to Individuals. *Behavior Therapy* 22. p. 163, © 1991, Association for the Advancement of Behavior Therapy; 1991:162.

match the diagnosis with optimal treatment, using the patient's input.

Dietary Therapy and Exercise

- The traditional dietary approach has been calorie restriction; however, this appears to be effective only under controlled conditions, with weight eventually regained slowly.
- Low-fat diets (< 30% calories from fat) or very–low-fat diets (< 20% calories from fat) may produce greater results since they promote a lifelong adaptation of eating habits rather than a temporary restriction of calories. This may translate into improved weight loss maintenance on a long-term basis.
- Current data on conservative dietary treatment show < 5% of participants maintain their weight loss 5 years later. However, these are data from formal programs and perhaps should not be generalized to individuals who diet on their own.
- Regular exercise is clearly a strong predictor of sustained weight loss, though it has not been demonstrated to result in dramatic weight losses.
- Exercise provides such benefits as promoting favorable body composition and changes in fat oxidation, not to mention general cardiovascular benefits, psychological advantages, and improvements in comorbid conditions, independent of weight loss.

Community-Based Diet Programs

- These programs may be used as a first-step, self-help approach.
- They provide peer support at a low cost.
- High attrition rates and lack of professional staff are disadvantages.

Pharmacological Therapy

- Current drug trials have shown a medically significant weight loss of 15% when drugs are used as part of a comprehensive program involving diet, exercise, and behavior modification.
- Past abuse of amphetamines has resulted in negative attitudes by many health profession-

als; these may be unfounded for newer protocols and drugs.
- An optimal drug does not yet exist.
- Combinations of drugs may be useful, as in the long-term treatment model for management of hypertension.
- Long-term effects of taking drugs are not known.
- Benefits of the drugs end when the drug is stopped, as in other chronic conditions such as hypertension, hypercholesterolemia, and Type II diabetes.

Psychotherapy/Behavioral Modification

- Useful strategies include cognitive restructuring, self-monitoring, stimulus control, skills training/problem solving, relapse prevention, positive reinforcement, contracts, assistance in developing support systems, and stress management.
- These strategies improve weight loss maintenance.
- Therapy may be most useful in conjunction with other treatment methods, such as diet and exercise, pharmacotherapy, or surgery.
- Patients with eating disorders or severe psychopathology may not be appropriate candidates for weight loss.

Very–Low-Calorie Diets

- Very–low-calorie diets are designed to produce rapid weight loss while preserving lean body tissue.
- They usually provide ~ 600–800 cal of liquid formula or lean protein foods per day (protein-sparing modified fast, or PSMF).
- They should be limited to patients > 130% IBW and have clear health risks related to their obesity.
- Such diets are contraindicated in pregnant women, children, elderly adults, or persons with recent myocardial infarction, severe congestive heart failure, unstable angina, renal/hepatic disease, severe psychiatric disturbances, eating disorders (eg, anorexia, bulimia), active alcoholism, or drug abuse.
- Generally programs will last ~ 12–16 weeks.

- The dieter will need medical supervision.
- Weight loss should not exceed 1%–2% of body weight (~ 3–4 lb/wk); weight loss should be at least ~ 75% fat and no more than ~ 25% lean body mass. Excessive loss of lean body mass is undesirable and unsafe.
- Exercise minimizes lean tissue loss during weight reduction.
- Provide adequate protein to spare lean body mass (1.2–1.5 g/kg IBW). Carbohydrate levels vary: generally < 100 g/day. Fat should be < 30% of calories from fat (20% may be ideal).
- Provide supplements: multivitamin, Ca^{++}, K^+, Mg^{++}. Patient should consume at least 64 oz of noncaloric fluids per day. Sodium, which may be indicated, can be added through bouillon.
- Monitor the period of reintroduction of food for "refeeding edema."
- Disadvantages include electrolyte imbalance, potential cardiac arrhythmias, weakness, fatigue, dizziness, dry skin, constipation or diarrhea, cold intolerance, nausea, and gallstone formation.
- Very–low-calorie diets are associated with high attrition rates, though generally lower than rates for commercial diet programs. Patient selection is critical.
- Though initial weight losses are often significantly large, most studies show that 90% of participants regain most of their weight 5 years later.
- The diet is most effective when combined with behavior modification and exercise.
- Regular contact with health care providers can improve maintenance.

Gastric Restrictive Surgery

- The most current procedures endorsed by the National Institutes of Health Consensus Conference on Gastrointestinal Surgery for Severe Obesity in 1991 are gastric bypass and vertical-banded gastroplasty.
- Technological advances have reduced many earlier problems with surgeries.
- Current success rates reported to be ~ 60% excess weight loss 5 years after surgery.

- Surgery should be reserved for severely obese patients (BMI > 40 kg/m^2) who have a history of intractable obesity and failed attempts at conservative dieting methods.
- Potential patients should be referred to interdisciplinary programs with experienced surgeons.
- Contraindications are the same as for very–low-calorie diet programs (see above section).
- Potential perioperative complications include wound infections, splenic injuries, anastomotic leaks, intra-abdominal sepsis, cardiac events, ulcerations, and pulmonary embolism.
- Potential long-term complications include staple line disruption, stomal stenosis, lactose intolerance, dehydration, dumping syndrome, vitamin/mineral deficiencies (especially B_{12}, iron, and folate), and persistent nausea/vomiting.
- Studies show significant weight losses leading to such health improvements as decreased lipid levels, improved heart function, and improvement or cure for sleep apnea, hypertension, and Type II diabetes. Other studies have showed resolved problems with arthritis, infertility, and venous stasis disease.
- Exhibit 3–3 contains typical diet stages for the first 2 months after gastric restrictive surgery

---

Exhibit 3–3 Dietary Stages after Gastric Restrictive Surgery

Stage 1: 1 oz of water every hour (this stage usually lasts 1 day)

Stage 2: 3 oz of water every hour, 3 oz of broth at meals (lasts 1 day)

Stage 3: 8 oz of sugar-free, nonfat milk products at meals; clear liquids between meals (lasts for 2–3 weeks)

Stage 4: 3 oz of lean protein foods at each meal, either pureed or very soft (lasts for 4–6 weeks)

Stage 5: Solid foods as tolerated, with an emphasis on low-fat, sugar-free foods (beginning at ~ 8 weeks post surgery)

(reflecting dietary protocol at the Beth Israel Deaconess Medical Center in Boston).

Children

- The overweight child is identified by a triceps skinfold measurement (TSF) > 85th percentile, a BMI > 85th percentile, or weight for height > 95th percentile.
- Childhood obesity is associated with parental obesity, higher socioeconomic status, increased parental education, small family size, television viewing, and family activity patterns.
- The clinician must rule out medical (endocrine) causes of obesity.
- "First of all do no harm": the goal is to maintain weight if the child is still growing or at least to slow the rate of weight gain. Weight loss has a risk of delaying growth.
- Be careful not to label children as overweight.
- Long-term emphasis should be on behavior modification and exercise.
- Present the condition as a family problem: the family needs to be involved in improving eating and exercise habits.
- Discourage highly restrictive or rigid diets except for severely obese adolescents.
- Allow for occasional treats.
- Be sensitive to the child's not wanting to be different from peers.

MANAGEMENT

Program Goals

- Develop screening criteria and ways to match patients to treatments.
- The ideal rate of weight loss in conservative therapy is 1–2 lbs. per week.
- A weight loss of just 10% of total weight may reduce many medical risks; it may not be necessary to reach ideal body weight (however, more clinical data are needed to support this theory). Start with a 10% weight loss and make sure patient can maintain it before progressing.

- Help the patient achieve a "reasonable" (and maintainable) weight, which may be different from aesthetic or "ideal" weights as mandated by cultural standards.
- Increase the length of treatment.
- Provide positive reinforcement for any and all successes.
- Schedule frequent follow-up visits for support.
- Adjust treatment goals as needed.
- Weight loss should *not* be the primary way to measure progress. In addition, use body measurements and behaviors to reinforce success. Have the patient focus on the positive effects of weight loss rather than the scale.

Education

- Correct misconceptions and myths about dieting and weight management.
- Emphasize the goal of developing healthier eating habits, not "dieting."
- Discuss the lipogenic potential of dietary fat; emphasize decreased fat over caloric restriction.
- Discuss the benefits of exercise; dispel myths of needing to meet an exercise threshold before benefits will occur.
- Incorporate behavioral management and cognitive restructuring techniques.
- Emphasize long-term treatment and commitment to weight control.
- Help the client set realistic goals.
- Challenge the client's beliefs (eg, that the body can be shaped at will to match cultural ideals).

Factors Predicting Success with Weight Maintenance

- Regular exercise
- Low-fat eating
- Self-monitoring activities (eg, food and activity records)
- Social support system
- Positive coping style
- Continued contact with health professionals

Maintenance

- Resting metabolic rate (RMR) temporarily declines with caloric restriction.
- Weight reduction suppresses the energy cost of physical activity. The formerly obese individual should be taught that with lost lean tissue mass, caloric intake must be less than when he or she was obese to maintain lost weight. The individual may be more liberal with calories if physical activity is much higher.
- Some studies claim that lowering of RMR can be minimized by promotion of weight training, though research is controversial in this area.
- Better results have been seen with longer treatment periods and closed groups as opposed to open groups.
- Relapse prevention planning uses a system of patient support similar to that used in treatment of chemical dependencies.
- Remind patients to return to the medical support system when necessary; reassure them they will not be chastised for what they consider "failure."

REFERENCES

Blackburn GL, Kanders BS, eds. *Obesity: Pathophysiology, Psychology and Treatment.* New York, NY: Chapman & Hall, Inc; 1994.

Bouchard C, Perusse L, LeBlanc C, Tremblay A, Theriault G. Inheritance of the amount and distribution of human body fat. *Int J Obesity.* 1988;12:205–215.

Bray GA. Use and abuse of appetite-suppressant drugs in the treatment of obesity. *Ann Intern Med.* 1993;119:707–713.

Brownell KD, Wadden TA. Etiology and treatment of obesity: understanding a serious, prevalent, and refractory disorder. *J Consult Clin Psychol.* 1992;60:505–517.

Colditz GA. Economic costs of obesity. *Am J Clin Nut.* 1992;55:503S–507S.

Croft JB, Strogatz DS, James SA, et al. Socioeconomic and behavioral correlates of body mass index in black adults: the Pitt County study. *Am J Public Health.* 1988;82:821–826.

Dietz WH, Robinson TN. Assessment and treatment of childhood obesity. *Pediatr Rev.* 1993;14:337–344.

Foreyt JP, Goodrick GK. Factors common to successful therapy for the obese patient. *Med Sci Sports Exercise.* 1991;23:292–297.

Frankle RT, Yang M, eds. *Obesity and Weight Control.* Gaithersburg, Md: Aspen Publishers, Inc; 1988.

Goldstein DJ, Potvin JH. Long-term weight loss: the effect of pharmacologic agents. *Am J Clin Nutr.* 1994;60:647–657.

Jeffery RW. Population perspectives on the prevention and treatment of obesity in minority populations. *Am J Clin Nutr.* 1991;53:1621S–1624S.

Kral JG. Surgical treatment of obesity. In: Wadden TA, Van Itallie TB, eds. *Treatment of the Seriously Obese Patient.* New York, NY: Guilford Press; 1992:497–506.

Kuczmarski RJ, Flegal KM, Campbell SM, Johnson CL. Increasing prevalence of overweight among U.S. adults: the National Health and Examination Surveys, 1960 to 1991. *JAMA.* 1994;272:205–211.

Lichtman SW, Pisarska K, Berman ER, et al. Discrepancy between self-reported and actual caloric intake and exercise in obese subjects. *N Engl J Med.* 1992;327:1893–1898.

National Institutes of Health Consensus Conference Panel. Gastrointestinal surgery for severe obesity. *Ann Intern Med.* 1991;115:956–961.

National Institutes of Health Technology Assessment Conference Panel. Methods for voluntary weight loss and control. *Ann Intern Med.* 1992;116:942–949.

National Task Force on the Prevention and Treatment of Obesity. Weight cycling. *JAMA.* 1994;272:1196–1202.

National Task Force on the Prevention and Treatment of Obesity. Towards prevention of obesity: research directions. *Obesity Res.* 1994;2:571–584.

Stunkard AJ, Foch TT, Hrubec Z. A twin study of human obesity. *JAMA.* 1986;256:51–54.

Stunkard AJ, Harris JR, Pedersen NL, McClearn G. The body mass index of twins who have been reared apart. *N Engl J Med.* 1990;322:1483–1487.

Stunkard AJ, Sorensen TIA, Hanis C, et al. An adoption study of human obesity. *N Engl J Med.* 1986;314:193–198.

Wadden TA, Foster GD, Letizia KA, Mullen JL. Weight reduction and metabolic rate: good news for obese patients? *Gastroenterol.* 1991;100:1146–1149.

Zhang Y, Proenca R, Maffel M, Barone M, Leopold L, Friedman JM. Positional cloning of the mouse obese gene and its human homologue. *Nature.* 1994;372:425–432.

Oncology

Abby S. Bloch

DESCRIPTION

As the second leading cause of death in the United States, soon to surpass heart disease, cancer is of concern to both health professionals and the public. Studies have shown that 40%–80% of all patients who are diagnosed with cancer will develop clinical malnutrition. The clinical effects of poor nutrition may compromise the individual's ability to heal surgical wounds, maintain skin turgor, prevent breakdown or decubiti, prevent anastomotic leaks or dehiscence, maintain metabolic balance, and maintain effective immune activity; they may also increase morbidity and mortality. Therefore, feeding the cancer patient should be an integral aspect of care and management.

CAUSE

Cancer is caused by uncontrolled growth and spread of abnormal cells. Both external (chemicals, radiation, viruses, procarcinogens and carcinogens ingested) and internal (hormones, immune conditions, inherited mutations) factors play a role in its development. Malnutrition in the cancer patient may be caused by any of the following:

* changes in dietary patterns, food intake, or appetite
* metabolic abnormalities caused by the disease process
* antineoplastic therapy (surgical resection of the gastrointestinal (GI) tract, chemotherapy, radiation therapy, hormones, or immunotherapy)
* functional status or logistical problems with food purchasing, preparing, and handling

ASSESSMENT

To determine the extent and depth of the nutritional problem, if any, a patient must be appropriately screened and assessed. The following are guidelines for performing a thorough, accurate assessment.

* Use the appropriate screening/assessment tool or measure to do the following:
  1. Establish risk category (Table 3–14 provides a screening tool).
  2. Flag nutritional deficits and problems.
  3. Develop a nutrition care plan and nutrient goals.
* Determine food intolerance, food aversions, and changes in taste perception or preferences.
* Assess the degree of decreased appetite, early satiety, head/neck or gastrointestinal discomfort, or symptoms affecting food intake or tolerance.
* Assess weight changes.
  1. Significant weight loss may be experienced by 45% or more of all adult hospitalized cancer patients.
  2. Assess preillness adult weight status, prior 6-month weight patterns, admission weight, and current weight.
  3. Consider influences such as edema, ascites, and hydration status.
* Assess medical status.
  1. Check for other clinical conditions such as diabetes, heart disease, hypertension, and renal disease.
  2. Obtain a list of all medications being taken.
  3. Obtain a history of previous therapy, treatments, or medical management.
* Evaluate nondietary factors affecting nutritional status:
  1. Age—if the individual is elderly, screening and assessment parameters should be appropriate for his or her age. Body composition, weight, and metabolic rate should be evaluated accordingly, using appropriate tables and algorithms.
  2. Functional status—mobility, dexterity, visual acuity, range of motion, mental status, pain status

Table 3–14 MSKCC Nutrition Care Process

Process	Low Risk	Moderate/High Nutritional Risk	
MSKCC Patient Assessment Summary Nursing Review of Patient History and Data Base	Patient without weight loss or nutritional complications	Nurse Referral to Dietitian: 1. Weight status: Patient has a weight loss of 10 or more lbs in the last 3 months and/or 2. A 2- or more week history of food intake decreased from normal, nausea/vomiting, diarrhea, mouth sores, or difficulty chewing or swallowing.	
		Adult Oncology Screening Tool	
Dietitian's Evaluation of Nutrition Risk/ Intervention Plan	*Low Risk Criteria* (patient does not meet nutritional risk criteria above; without weight loss/ nutritional complications): Rescreen on 6th day.	*Moderate Nutritional Risk Criteria* Nutritional Assessment completed within 24 hrs of referral Reassessment within 5 days.	*High Nutritional Risk Criteria* Nutritional Assessment completed within 24 hrs of referral. Reassessment within 3 days.
Diagnosis/ Complications	Nadir fever Comfort care Cancer of the: Prostate Bladder Ovarian Renal cell Lung Liver	AIDS/HIV Ascites Emesis > 3 days Diarrhea > 3 days Diabetes Decubiti Stage II Edema Esophageal stricture GBM (Glioblastoma) Odynophagia Renal insufficiency Mucositis	Acute weight loss during hospitalization Chylous ascites/chylous leak Dysphagia GI (fistula, ileus, upper GI bleed, malabsorption, obstruction, short gut/ dumping syndromes) Graft vs. host disease Liver failure/Hepatic encephalopathy New Onset Diabetes Pancreatitis Poor wound healing documented/Decubiti Stages III and IV Renal failure/dialysis

continues

Table 3–14 continued

Adult Oncology Screening Tool

Dietitian's Evaluation of Nutrition Risk/ Intervention Plan	Low Risk Criteria	Moderate Nutritional Risk Criteria	High Nutritional Risk Criteria
Treatment/Surgery	Biopsy Bronchoscopy One day chemotherapy Head and Neck Surgery (without complications) including: Partial Thyroidectomy, Neck Dissection, Parotidectomy, Craniofacial, Small Check, Oral Lesions, Nasal Polyps, Sinus Surgery, Biopsy, Tonsillectomy	Autologous Bone Marrow Transplant (BMT) Head & Neck Surgery: Craniotomy Total Thyroidectomy Free Flap, Skin Grafts, Bone Grafts, Palate Surgeries Base of Tongue, Floor of Mouth, Partial Glossectomy	Allogenic BMT Surgery for Esophageal Cancer Pancreatic Cancer Head & Neck Surgery: Commando Procedures, Mandibulectomy, Laryngectomy, Laryngopharyngoesophogastrectomy/ Gastric Pull-Up After Loading Catheters Head and Neck Brachytherapy
Weight status	(% UBW) > 90% UBW	(Loss) (1) 1%–2% UBW (over 1 wk) (2) < 5% UBW (over 1 mo) (3) < 10% UBW (over 6 mo)	(Loss) (1) > 2% UBW (over 1 wk) (2) > 5% UBW (over 1 mo) (3) > 10% UBW (over 6 mo)
Diet orders	Patient does not require diet instruction.	Patient requires diet instruction for diet modification or drug-nutrient interaction.	Enteral Nutrition TPN/PPN Dysphagia Diet Renal Diet NPO/Clear liquids ≥ 5 days (without nutrition support) (Exceptions: nephrectomy, cystectomies, hemicolectomies)

Note: UBW = usual body weight.
Source: Courtesy of Memorial Sloan-Kettering Cancer Center, Food Service Department, New York, New York.

3. Adequate means accessible to the patient to obtain, prepare, and ingest food
4. Financial, psychological, and social conditions that may influence eating
- Obtain laboratory parameters from the medical record that will provide insight on the clinical status of the patient.
- Assess the effect of the disease process on nutritional status.
  1. Tumors within the GI tract may obstruct the passage of food.
  2. Tumors outside the GI tract may press on or obstruct organs or parts of the GI tract.
  3. Systemic effects of the tumor may cause anorexia, early satiety, or aversions to certain foods.

PROBLEMS

Metabolic Alterations Affecting Nutritional Status

- *Energy expenditure* may increase (sarcomas, leukemia, lymphomas, lung, head/neck, small-cell lung carcinoma, and gastric), decrease (pancreatic), or remain normal (colon). Resting energy expenditure cannot explain fully the cachexia seen in many cancer patients.
- *Carbohydrate metabolism* appears to be altered in the cancer patient, preventing him or her from adapting to a starved state in which glycogen stores and ketone bodies can supply needed fuel to the brain, sparing glucose and muscle protein. Insulin resistance or impaired insulin sensitivity may be seen in wasting cancer patients.
- *Lipid metabolism* is altered in the malnourished cancer patient, as seen in the depletion of fat stores. Increased lipolysis and fatty acid oxidation may be related to the insulin resistance of the patient. Cancer patients do not suppress lipolysis after a glucose load is given, leading to body fat depletion of the cachectic cancer patient.
- *Protein metabolism* is also altered in the cancer patient. Malnourished cancer patients have protein metabolism similar to traumatized or infected noncancer patients. Most of these patients are in negative nitrogen balance that becomes more pronounced with the severity of the malignancy. Patients may have increased liver synthesis, decreased synthesis in the muscles causing muscle wasting, decreased serum protein levels, and increased whole-body protein turnover favoring the tumor over the host.

Treatments Affecting Nutritional Status

- *Chemotherapy* may cause nausea, vomiting, anorexia, diarrhea, mucositis, stomatitis, constipation, abdominal pain, pain on swallowing, generalized pain, altered taste, food aversions, cardionephrohepatotoxicity, and electrolyte and fluid abnormalities (see Table 3–15 for emetogenic potential of specific chemotherapy agents).
- *Radiation* may cause nausea, vomiting, anorexia, stenosis, radiation enteritis/malabsorption, decreased taste, decreased smell, problems with chewing/swallowing/mouth blindness, mucositis, dental caries, oral infections, inability to swallow, dry mouth, and mouth sores.
- *Surgery* may induce metabolic or nutritional compromise of the patient by altering or removing parts of the GI tract that play a role in digestion, absorption, or utilization of foodstuffs or nutrients. Surgical resection may compromise the physical capability of the patient, as in head/neck surgery, or create tolerance problems such as cramping, rapid transit, diarrhea, or fat malabsorption.

TREATMENT/MANAGEMENT

Nutritional Requirements

Calories

Caloric requirements should be established to ensure adequate energy and nutrients needed by the patient. To determine caloric levels, the following estimates are a quick guide that will meet

Table 3–15 Emetogenic Potential of Individual Chemotherapy Agents

Incidence	Agent	Dose (mg/m²)	Onset (h)	Duration (h)
V—High > 90%	HD-Carboplatin (CDPCA)	≥ 1 gm/m²		
	Carmustine (BCNU)	> 200	2–4	4–24
	Cisplatin (CDDP)	≥ 70	1–6	24–120
	Cyclophosphamide (CTX)	≥ 1000	4–12	12–24
	Cytarabine (ARA-C)	> 1000	Related to rate	2–4
	Dacarbazine (DTIC)	≥ 500	1–3	1–12
	Dactinomycin (ACT-D)			
	Ifosfamide	≥ 3 gm/m²		
	Lomustine (CCNU)	> 60	2–6	4–6
	Melphalan (L-PAM)	> 140	3–6	6–12
	Nitrogen mustard (Mechlorethamine)	6	0.5–2.0	8–24
	Streptozocin	> 500	1–4	12–24
	HD-Thiotepa	Cont. infusion		
	Tirapazamine			
IV—Moderate-High 60%–90%	5-Azacytidine*	200	1–3	3–4
	Carboplatin (CDBCA)	500–< 1000		
	Carmustine (BCNU)	≤ 200	2–4	4–24
	Cisplatin (CDDP)	< 70	1–6	24–120
	Cyclophophamide (CTX)	≥ 750–< 1000	4–12	12–24
	Cytarabine	250–1000	6–12	3–5
	Dacarbazine (DTIC)	< 500	1–3	1–12
	Daunorubicin	≥ 75		
	Doxorubicin (ADRIA)	≥ 45	4–6	6+
	HD-Edatrexate*			
	Idarubicin			
	Ifosfamide	≥ 1200–< 3000		
	Loboplatin*			
	Lomustine (CCNU)	< 60	2–6	4–6
	Mesna			
	Methotrexate	≥ 1000	4–12	3–12
	Mitomycin	10	1-4	48–72
	Mitotane			
	Procarbazine	100	24–27	Variable
III—Moderate 30%–60%	Aldesleukin			
	Asparaginase	> 5000 U	1–3	—
	Bleomycin			
	Busulfan	148 (4 mg/kg)	—	—
	Carboplatin (CDBCA)	< 300	6–12	24
	Carmustine (BCNU)			
	Cyclophosphamide (CTX)	< 750	4–12	12–24
	(PO)	100		
	Cytarabine	20–< 250		

continues

Table 3–15 continued

Incidence	Agent	Dose (mg/m²)	Onset (h)	Duration (h)
	Doxorubicin (ADRIA)	> 20–< 45	4–6	6+
	Etoposide (VP-16)	> 100 or infusion	3–8	—
	5-Fluorouracil (5-FU)	> 1000	3–6	—
	Hexamethylmelamine*			
	Ifosfamide	< 1200	1–2	—
	Methotrexate	250–< 1000	4–12	3–12
	Mitoxantrone			
	Pentostatin	2–4		
	Teniposide (VM-26)*	60–170	3–8	—
II—Mild	9-AC*	Cont. infusion		
10%–30%	Bleomycin	10 U	3–6	—
	Camptothecan (CPT-11)*			
	Cytarabine	< 20	6–12	3–5
	Docetaxel*			
	Doxorubicin (ADRIA)	< 20	4–6	6+
	5-Fluorouracil (5-FU)	< 1000	3–6	—
	Hydroxyurea	1000–6000	6–12	—
	Irinotecan*			
	6-Mercaptopurine	100	4–8	—
	Methotrexate	< 250	4–12	3–12
	Mitomycin			
	Mitomycin-C	Intrahepatic		
	Mitoxantrone	10–14	—	—
	Paclitaxel			
I—Minimal	Altetamine			
< 10%	Asparaginase			
	Busulfan	2–6	—	—
	Chlorambucil	1–3	48–72	—
	Cladribine (2-CDA)	Cont. infusion		
	Edatrexate			
	Estramustine			
	Etoposide (VP-16)			
	Floxuridine (FUDR)	IP		
	Fludarabine			
	Fluorouracil (5-FU)	Cont. infusion		
	Goserelin			
	Idarubicin			
	Interferon (α, β, γ)	Variable	—	—
	Leuprolide acetate			
	Megestrol acetate			
	Mitotane			
	Navelbine (Vinorelbine)			
	Pegaspergase			

continues

Table 3–15 continued

Incidence	Agent	Dose (mg/m²)	Onset (h)	Duration (h)
	PBA			
	Plicamycin			
	Suioi*	Cont. infusion		
	Suramin*			
	Tamoxifen			
	Taxotere			
	Teniposide (YM-26)*			
	Thioguanine			
	Topotecan*			
	Vinblastine (Velban)	6	4–8	—
	Vincristine			
	Vinorelbine			

Note: Where dosage, onset, or duration information is not provided, the health professional working with a specific agent should fill in the blanks for that agent on the basis of clinical practice at his or her facility and personal experience of patients receiving the agent. — means value is insignificant.

Source: Adapted from CM Lindley, S Bernard, and SM Fields. *J Clin Oncology*, 1989. Modified and Updated by Abby S. Bloch, MS, RD and Jane Nolte, PharmD. Memorial Sloan-Kettering Cancer Center Antiemetic Subcommittee, Pharmacy and Therapeutics Committee, New York, New York, 1995.

the needs of the majority of patients being managed:

- 25–30 kcal/kg body weight for nonambulatory or sedentary adults
- 30–35 kcal/kg body weight for slightly hypermetabolic patients, for weight gain, or for an anabolic patient
- 35 kcal/kg body weight for hypermetabolic or severely stressed patients or patients who have malabsorption

Protein

Adequate protein should be provided to meet protein synthesis and minimize protein degradation. Most malnourished cancer patients will be in negative nitrogen balance despite adequate nitrogen given.

- 0.6–0.75 g/kg body weight: Recommended Dietary Allowance (RDA) reference protein value
- 0.8–1.0 g/kg body weight: normal maintenance level
- 1.0–1.2 g/kg body weight: safe intake for a nonstressed cancer patient

- 1.5–2.5 g/kg body weight: intake if increased protein demands exist, eg, protein-losing enteropathy, hypermetabolism, or extreme wasting

Fluids

Fluid status should be considered in the overall dietary or nutrition plan. Hydration status may affect the clinical response of the patient and induce untoward clinical effects. The patient who is not at liberty to consume fluid ad libitum needs to have hydration status monitored closely to prevent hydration problems. Individuals with drainages or high output from fistulas, diarrhea, or other conditions that could dehydrate them should also be closely monitored.

Nutrition Support Modalities

Oral Intake

If the patient is struggling to meet nutritional and caloric needs, he or she may require modification in caloric density; modification in amounts, types, and volumes of food at each feeding; and supplements to augment total intake. Separation of fluids and solids may prevent early satiety or dumping symptoms if present. Pain and nausea should be managed by adequate medication at least 30 minutes prior to meals. (Exhibit 3–4 shows the antiemetic regimens recommended by the Memorial Sloan-Kettering Cancer Center.) This approach should be tried before alternative methods are used. However, the time period in which the patient attempts to meet nutritional needs with these techniques should not permit significant nutritional and weight deterioration before oral intake is abandoned for an alternative nutrition plan.

Enteral Management

This method of feeding is very safe, easy to administer, and cost-effective. Several types of enteral support may be chosen on the basis of the clinical and logistical needs of the patient.

- *Nasoenteric tube feeding*—for short-term management (ie, if the patient will be able to eat adequately within 2–4 weeks). Placement is easily done at the bedside without equipment or special procedures involved. Placement should be verified before feedings begin.
- *Gastrostomy feeding tube*—for longer-term management of patients with a functional

---

Exhibit 3–4 1995–1996 Memorial Sloan-Kettering Cancer Center Adult Acute Antiemetic Regimens*

Recommended Antiemetic Regimens Based on the Emetic Potential of Specific Chemotherapy Programs

Grade	Emetogenic Classification	Antiemetic Regimen
V	High	Granisetron 2 mg PO + Dexamethasone 20 mg PO/IV
V-CI	High-Continuous Infusion	Ondansetron 8 mg IVPB loading dose 30 minutes before chemotherapy × 1 dose only followed by 1 mg/hour × 24 hours for _____ days. Dexamethasone 20 mg IVPB.
IV	Moderately High	Granisetron 2 mg PO + Dexamethasone 20 mg PO/IV
III	Moderate	Granisetron 1 mg PO + Dexamethasone 20 mg PO/IV or Ondansetron 16 mg PO + Dexamethasone 20 mg PO/IV
II	Mild	Dexamethasone 20 mg PO/IV
I	Minimally	PRN antiemetics only

Breakthrough Antiemetic Regimen:
If a patient requests additional antiemetics or vomits > 3 times, give: Metoclopramide 2 mg/kg IVPB × 1 dose, and every 3–4 hours as needed + Diphenhydramine 50 mg IV every 30 minutes, PRN only, for dystonic reactions.

Delayed Antiemetic Regimen:
To begin at 6 am the day following chemotherapy: Dexamethasone 8 mg PO BID × 2 days; taper to 4 mg PO BID × 1 day + Metoclopramide 0.5 mg/kg PO × 2 days, OR Prochlorperazine spansule 15 mg BID × 3 days

NOTE: Patients should receive dexamethasone PO or IV concurrently with a serotonin antagonist where specified. For leukemia, lymphoma, multiple myeloma, and bone marrow transplant patients, refer to individual protocols for dexamethasone use. Patients may not tolerate metoclopramide and/or prochlorperazine in delayed emesis regimens; however, dexamethasone should be used if possible.

*Antiemetic regimens are likely to change as new and more effective agents become available.

stomach. Several types of gastrostomy tubes are available:

1. A percutaneous endoscopic gastrostomy (PEG) tube can be placed as an outpatient procedure.
2. A surgically placed enterostomy tube can be placed at the time of a surgical procedure.
3. A skin-level, low-profile feeding device (button) may replace a PEG tube after initial success with gastrostomy feeding is determined and when the patient will require such a tube for nutrition support in the future.

• *Jejunostomy feeding tube*—for longer-term management of patients who have compromised gastric function. Two types of jejunostomy tubes, similar to gastrostomy tubes, are available: percutaneous endoscopic jejunostomy (PEJ) tubes and surgically placed tubes. A button may replace the initial tubes once the procedure is established.

Parenteral Nutrition

If the GI tract has been used unsuccessfully to maintain nutritional needs of the patient or the clinical indications of the patient preclude the use of the GI tract for feeding, then total parenteral nutrition may be considered. In conjunction with an active plan of therapy, some appropriate indications for parenteral support are as follows:

• severe malnutrition unable to be corrected by enteral support
• chronic malabsorption, severe diarrhea
• short-bowel obstruction
• high-output fistula
• short-bowel secondary to bypass surgery
• radiation enteritis
• patient undergoing anticancer therapy that will be compromised if malnutrition interferes with treatment schedule
• patient NPO for 10 days or longer post surgery and at risk for potential complications following surgery, such as wound dehiscence, anas-

tomotic leak, infection, and compromised skin turgor

Nutrition Support Management

Feeding Options

• Oral intake
  1. Provide small, frequent feedings.
  2. Provide high–caloric density foods.
  3. Separate liquids and solids if appropriate.
  4. Make food consumption as easy, painless, and stress-free as possible.
• Enteral support
  1. Formula selection
    –General, intact formulas should be well tolerated. If the patient is lactose intolerant or if volume limitations or gastric discomfort exists, appropriate modifications should be implemented.
    –Predigested or specialty formula is indicated if a metabolic abnormality exists or if the patient has a clinical condition such as short-bowel syndrome.
    –Most cancer patients have difficulty with adequate intake, so providing a feeding with adequate volume (enough calories) to meet nutritional needs is important.
    –If the cancer patient requires a higher protein content or a caloric density greater than 1 kcal/cc on the basis of determination of clinical status, then the appropriate formula should be selected.
    –A huge array of commercial formulas is available for specific medical needs and clinical requirements.
• Parenteral support
  1. Formula should contain adequate intravenous hypertonic glucose, protein, fat emulsion, vitamins, minerals, and electrolytes to meet the nutritional needs of the patient.
  2. Parenteral nutrition may be administered in the hospital or in an outpatient setting, including the home.
  3. If not contraindicated, oral intake should be encouraged for gut stimulation and the prevention of stasis, sludge, and gallstones.

4. Delivery methods
   - *The bolus method* is the easiest, fastest, and physiologically closest to normal eating. If the patient has a normal-functioning stomach but has a mechanical limitation, anorexia, early satiety, or some other nonmetabolic reason for poor intake, then bolus feeding is recommended. The feedings may be scheduled 3–6 times daily, depending on the total daily volume needed to be consumed, the lifestyle of the patient, availability of others for assistance, time constraints, and other logistical issues. Each feeding should be administered over a 10- to 20-minute period.
   - *The gravity dump method* is an option for the patient who cannot manipulate the syringe or tube during bolus administration or requires a little slower administration of each feeding. The patient may not be as mobile or active as the patient on bolus feeding; therefore, a gravity feeding may be more convenient. A feeding generally runs over an hour or so.
   - *Pump-assisted, continuous feeding* over extended periods of time may be beneficial to patients who are fragile or very ill or who need the feeding in slow, controlled volumes, as in the case of patients with short-bowel syndrome or radiation enteritis. Patients who want to be free of the feeding during the day may prefer to receive their feeding at night while they sleep. Therefore, pump-assisted feedings may provide a controlled, regulated volume continuously throughout the night.

5. There are two delivery methods:
   - The formula may be *infused over a 24-hour period* using a volumetric pump.
   - The formula may be *infused cyclically* depending on lifestyle and clinical status of the patient.

Nutrition Support in the Home Setting

- A nutritional care plan should be developed and reviewed with the patient and/or caregiver prior to home management.
- Patients and/or caregivers should be thoroughly trained and knowledgeable in the management, care, potential complications, and outcome goals of enteral support.
- Ongoing monitoring of nutritional, clinical, and functional status of the patient should occur. When changes in the status of the patient are noted, adjustments should be implemented to meet the recent needs of the patient to prevent deterioration or complications from developing.

REFERENCES

American College of Physicians. Parenteral nutrition in patients receiving cancer chemotherapy. *Ann Intern Med.* 1989;110:734–736.

American Society for Parenteral and Enteral Nutrition. Standards for home nutrition support. *Nutr Clin Pract.* 1992; 7:65–69.

American Society for Parenteral and Enteral Nutrition, Board of Directors. Guidelines for the use of parenteral and enteral nutrition in adult and pediatric patients. *JPEN.* 1993;17(suppl):15A–525A.

Bloch AS. Cancer. In: Gottschlich MM, Matarese LE, Shronts EP, eds. *Nutrition Support Dietetics Core Curriculum.* 2nd ed. Silver Spring, Md: American Society for Parenteral and Enteral Nutrition; 1993:213–227.

Bloch AS. Feeding the cancer patient: Where have we come from, where are we going? *Nutr Clin Prac.* 1994;9:87–89.

Brennan MF, Burt ME. Nitrogen metabolism in cancer patients. *Cancer Treat Rep.* 1981;65 (suppl):67–78.

Cancer Facts and Figures. Atlanta, Ga: American Cancer Society; 1996.

Daly JM, Redmond HP, Gallagher H. Perioperative nutrition in cancer patients. *JPEN.* 1992;16:100S–105S.

Daly JM, Shinkwin M. Nutrition and the cancer patient. In: Murphy GP, Lawrence W, Lenhard RE, eds. *American Cancer Society Textbook of Clinical Oncology.* 2nd ed. Atlanta, Ga: American Cancer Society; 1995:580–596.

Hansell DT, Davies JW, Burns HJ. The relationship between resting energy expenditure and weight loss in benign and malignant disease. *Ann Surg.* 1986;203:240–245.

Harvey KB, Moldawer LL, Bistrian BR, Blackburn GL. Biological measures for the formation of a hospital prognostic index. *Am J Clin Nutr.* 1981;34:2013–2022.

Heber D, Byerley LO, Tchekmedyian NS. Hormonal and metabolic abnormalities in the malnourished cancer patient: effects on host-tumor interactions. *JPEN.* 1992;16: 60S–64S.

Heber D, Chlebowski RT, Ishibashi DE, Herrold JN, Block JB. Abnormalities in glucose and protein metabolism in noncachectic lung cancer patients. *Cancer Res.* 1982;42: 4815–4819.

Holroyde CP, Reichard A. Carbohydrate metabolism in cancer cachexia. *Cancer Treat Rep.* 1981;65(suppl):55–59.

Jeevanandam M, Horowitz GD, Lowry SF, Brennan MF. Cancer cachexia and rate of whole body lipolysis in man. *Metab.* 1986;35:304–310.

Kern KA, Norton JA. Cancer cachexia. *JPEN.* 1988;2:286–298.

Klein S, Koretz RL. Nutritional support in patients with cancer: what do the data really show? *Nutr Clin Prac.* 1994; 9:91–100.

Kokal WA, McCulloch A, Wright PD, Johnston ID. Glucose turnover and recycling in colorectal carcinoma. *Ann Surg.* 1983;198:601–604.

Norton JA, Stein TP, Brennan MF. Whole body protein synthesis and turnover in normal and malnourished patients with and without known cancer. *Ann Surg.* 1981;194:123–128.

Ollenschlager G, Viell B, Thomas W, Konkol K, Burger B. Tumor anorexia: causes, assessment, treatment. *Recent Results Cancer Res.* 1991;121:249–259.

Pisters PW, Pearlstone DB. Protein and amino acid metabolism in cancer cachexia: investigative techniques and therapeutic interventions. *Crit Rev Clin Lab Sci.* 1993;30: 223–272.

Schein PS, Kisner D, Haller D, Blecher M, Hamosh M. Cachexia of malignancy: potential role of insulin in nutritional management. *Cancer.* 1979;43:2070–2076.

Shaw JM, Humberstone DM, Wolfe RR. Energy and protein metabolism in sarcoma patients. *Ann Surg.* 1988;207: 283–289.

Shaw JH, Wolfe RR. Whole body protein kinetics in patients with early and advanced gastrointestinal cancer: the response to glucose infusion and total parenteral nutrition. *Surg.* 1988;103:148–155.

Shike M, Russell DM, Detsky AS, et al. Changes in body composition in patients with small cell lung cancer: the effect of total parenteral nutrition as an adjunct for chemotherapy. *Ann Intern Med.* 1984;101:303–309.

Shils ME. Principles of nutritional therapy. *Cancer.* 1979; 43: 2093–2102.

Shils ME. Nutrition and diet in cancer management. In: Shils ME, Olson J, Shike M, eds. *Modern Nutrition in Health and Disease.* 8th ed. Philadelphia, Pa: Lea & Febiger; 1994:1317–1348.

Warnold I, Lundholm K, Schersten T. Energy balance and body composition in cancer patients. *Cancer Res.* 1978; 38:1801–1807.

Waterhouse C, Kemperman JH. Carbohydrate metabolism in subjects with cancer. *Cancer Res.* 1971;31:1273–1278.

Wilson AW, Kirk CJC, Goode AW. The effect of weight loss, operation and parenteral nutrition on fat clearance in patients with colorectal cancer. *Clin Sci.* 1987;73:497–500.

Young VR. Energy metabolism and requirements in the cancer patient. *Cancer Res.* 1977;37:2336–2347.

Otolaryngology

Judith A. Fish and Kathleen A. Burk-Shull

DESCRIPTION

- Cancers of the head and neck region include tumors of the oral cavity, oropharynx, and larynx.
- Oral cancer can occur in or near the mouth, including the lips, tongue, labial mucosa, buccal mucosa, hard palate, gingival retromolar trigone, mandible, or mouth floor (Figure 3–3).
- Oropharyngeal cancer may involve the soft palate, palatine tonsils, base of the tongue, or posterior pharyngeal wall (Figure 3–4).
- Laryngeal cancer may occur on the epiglottis, vallecula (crevice between base of tongue and epiglottis), piriform fossa, or glottis.
- Nearly 95% of cancer in the upper aerodigestive tract is squamous cell cancer that involves the epidermis. Basal cell cancer is most common in lip cancer.

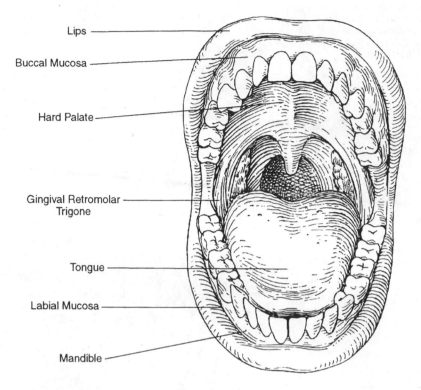

Figure 3–3 Anterior View of Oral Cavity. *Source:* Courtesy of the Medical Photography Department at Geisinger Medical Center, Danville, Pennsylvania.

- Sometimes complicating oral, pharyngeal, and laryngeal cancer are regional metastases in the neck lymph nodes and distal metastases in the lungs, bone, brain, liver, and other organs.
- Head and neck cancers most commonly occur in men 50 to 70 years of age.

CAUSE

The uncontrolled cell division that results in oral, pharyngeal, or laryngeal cancer is linked to

- tobacco and alcohol use
- chronic irritation of the oral cavity by sharp teeth, ill-fitting dentures, or a pipe
- poor dental hygiene
- excessive sun exposure (contributing to lip cancer)

NUTRITION ASSESSMENT

History

- A complete diet history should include evaluation of appetite, swallowing ability, and quantity and quality of diet. Many patients with cancer of the head and neck region have a history of heavy alcohol intake; therefore, amount and kind of alcohol intake is an essential part of the diet history.
- Dysphagia may include a wide range of problems, from decreased saliva production to aspiration. A swallowing evaluation can help define the swallowing disorder and direct therapy. A speech or swallowing therapist can help patients improve their swallowing with effective rehabilitation therapy.

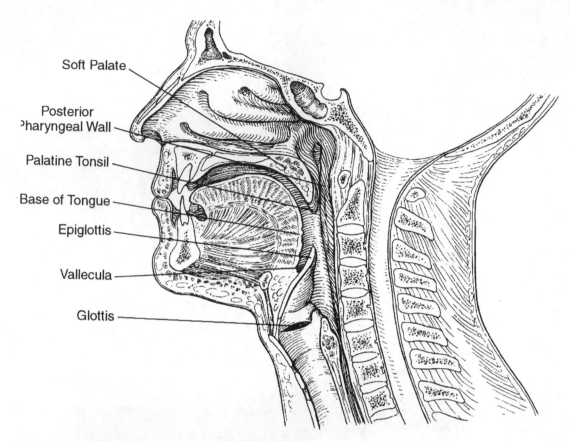

Soft Palate

Posterior
Pharyngeal Wall

Palatine Tonsil

Base of Tongue

Epiglottis

Vallecula

Glottis

Figure 3–4 Sagittal View of Oropharynx. *Source:* Courtesy of the Medical Photography Department at Geisinger Medical Center, Danville, Pennsylvania.

Warning signs and manifestations of dysphagia are as follows:

- Dysarthria (slurred speech)
- Labial and facial weakness and asymmetry
- Difficulty managing secretions/drooling
- Breathy and hoarse vocal quality
- Wet vocal quality
- Difficulty managing food orally
- Coughing during meals
- Slow and labored eating
- Increased temperature several hours following a meal
- History of aspiration pneumonia

Lower gastrointestinal (GI) function is usually good in this population group unless there is an additional unrelated diagnosis (eg, Crohn's disease). Signs and symptoms to be noted in a GI evaluation include

1. diarrhea
2. nausea
3. vomiting
4. constipation
5. esophageal reflux

- When establishing a history, it is helpful to evaluate both recent and past history for changes with diseases and therapy. One of the best indicators of malnutrition is weight loss. A weight loss of greater than 10% of usual body weight over 6 months is an indicator of risk for malnutrition. Patients weighing 85%–90% of their usual body weight are considered mildly malnourished, those weighing 75%–84% of their usual body weight are moderately malnourished, and those weighing less than 74% of their usual body weight are severely malnourished.

Physical Exam

- The physical exam often reveals clues to nutrition deficiencies that may be masked in a diet history. Table 3–16 lists signs and symptoms of vitamin and mineral deficiencies. Of special concern in this population are nutrient deficiencies associated with high alcohol intake (thiamin, folate, vitamin B_{12}, and zinc).

- Anthropometrics (height, weight, and skinfold measures) should be evaluated over a 6-month period. These measurements can be compared to standard values but are most useful as serial measures. A patient's maximum weight can

Table 3–16 Signs and Symptoms of Vitamin and Mineral Deficiencies

Vitamin	Deficiency Symptom	Vitamin	Deficiency Symptom
Thiamin	Beriberi:	Iron	Microcytic anemia
	mental confusion		Fatigue
	weakness		Angular stomatitis
	peripheral neuropathy	Zinc	Impaired wound healing
	heart disease		Alopecia
	edema		Skin rash
	muscle wasting		Impaired taste
	Wernicke's encephalopathy	Vitamin B_{12}	Megaloblastic anemia
Riboflavin	Angular stomatitis		Neuropathy
	Cheilosis		Stomatitis
	Glossitis		Glossitis
Niacin	Pellagra:		Anorexia
	diarrhea		Diarrhea
	dementia	Vitamin C	Hemorrhaging
	dermatitis		Weakness
	death		Irritability
	Scarlet tongue		Bleeding gums
	Tongue fissuring	Vitamin A	Poor night vision
Biotin	Skin rash		Bitot's spots
	Alopecia		Xerosis
	Lethargy	Vitamin D	Osteomalacia
	Anorexia		Rickets
	Paresthesia	Vitamin K	Purpura
Folic acid	Macrocytic anemia		Bleeding
	Stomatitis	Vitamin E	Hemolysis
	Glossitis		Anemia
	Lethargy		Myopathy
	Diarrhea	Calcium	Osteomalacia
Phosphorus	Cardiac failure		Rickets
	CNS dysfunction		Osteoporosis
	Respiratory failure		Tetany
Magnesium	Anorexia		
	Hypokalemia		
	Hypocalcemia		
	Vomiting		

be useful in evaluating weight goals in underweight patients. Edema or dehydration may alter weight assessment. Signs of edema include ankle swelling or swollen hands. Dehydration is usually characterized by tenting, complaints of thirst, decreased urination, or orthostatic blood pressure.

- Poor dentition may be a cause for decreased food intake. Patients may require teeth extraction prior to radiation therapy or surgery. Also, patients may have ill-fitting dentures secondary to weight loss. Evaluating dentition will help in advising patients on food consistency.
- Functional status is often forgotten but is an essential part of a physical exam. All patients should be monitored for their strength and ability to obtain and prepare food. A decline in functional status often leads to decreased food intake and may necessitate a consult to social services to obtain assistance.

Laboratory Measurements

- Laboratory measurements are necessary for metabolic monitoring in the unstable patient but can also contribute to baseline assessment.
- Visceral proteins (albumin, prealbumin, transferrin) have been described as nutrition markers but are also influenced by stress/injury and organ failure. Postsurgery patients will have a drop in the visceral proteins. Visceral proteins generally improve with adequate nutrition and recovery from stress/injury.
- Cholesterol has recently been recognized as a nutrition marker. Serum cholesterol below 160 mg/dl is associated with other indicators of malnutrition and morbidity.
- Baseline serum electrolytes, glucose, phosphorus, magnesium, and complete blood count may give clues to vitamin or mineral deficiencies. Measurement of thiamin, folate, and zinc may be imprecise or delayed secondary to laboratory limitations. If a patient has a history of chronic alcohol intake, it is reasonable to supplement these nutrients prophylactically:

1. Thiamine: 100 mg/day, IV or IM, for 3 days
2. Folate: 1 mg/day
3. Zinc: zinc sulfate, 220 mg/day

Assessment of Nutritional Requirements

- Calorie requirements can be easily estimated by 25–35 kcal/kg/day of ideal body weight (IBW). Estimates within this range are based on stress level, activity, and degree of malnutrition. Although these calculations are useful, they are only estimates and require adjustments according to weight changes. Indirect calorimetry is useful for patients for whom it is difficult to estimate calorie requirements, such as those who are severely under or over IBW.
- Protein requirements range from 1.0–2.5 g/kg IBW. Postoperative patients require approximately 1.5 g of protein per kilogram per day. Adjustments can be initiated based on nitrogen balance studies. Stable patients who are several weeks post surgery will require 1.0–1.5 g of protein per kilogram of body weight.
- Vitamins and minerals should be evaluated at initial evaluations if deficiencies are expected. Deficiencies in vitamin C, vitamin A, and zinc can delay wound healing post surgery. If deficient, these nutrients should be replaced (vitamin C, 500 mg twice daily; vitamin A, 10,000 IU daily; zinc sulfate, 50–100 mg daily). Diets and tube feeding should provide 100% of the U.S. recommended dietary allowance (RDA). If not, a multivitamin and mineral supplement should be recommended.
- Fluid requirements are 30–35 ml/kg for most patients. Fluid restrictions (1–1.2 L/day) may be necessary for patients with congestive heart failure, liver failure, refeeding risk, or renal dysfunction. Increased fluid may be necessary for elderly patients or patients with fluid losses from drains, wounds, or diarrhea.
- Refeeding syndrome is a life-threatening event that occurs when a malnourished patient is aggressively fed. Patients with cancer of the head and neck region often delay treatment

and present with significant weight loss. For this reason, these patients can be at risk for refeeding syndrome. Refeeding is characterized by fluid retention leading to cardiac decompensation and rapid drop in serum levels of phosphorus, magnesium, and potassium. To prevent refeeding syndrome:

1. Initial calorie assessments should be based on maintaining current body weight and not repletion (25–35 kcal/kg usual body weight).
2. Fluid should be restricted to 1.2–1.5 L daily.
3. Serum phosphorus, magnesium, and potassium should be measured prior to feeding and supplemented as necessary. Daily monitoring of these nutrients is essential in the first 3 days of feeding.
4. Patients should also be monitored for excessive weight gain and edema.
5. After several days of good tolerance of feeding and stable laboratory values, prescribed calories can be increased for repletion (30–35 kcal/kg IBW).

PROBLEMS

Approximately 40% of patients newly diagnosed with oral, pharyngeal, or laryngeal cancer are malnourished. These patients may be malnourished because of alcoholism and the resulting liver disease and/or because of diminished intake due to dysphagia or long-standing poor dental hygiene. Unfortunately, treatment for head and neck cancer further compromises nutritional intake and status.

* *Oral Cancers.* Early lesions may be asymptomatic, but more advanced tumors can severely inhibit oral intake. Tumors of the mandible or retromolar trigone can result in loose teeth, trismus (muscle spasm), and pain when chewing. Advanced tongue lesions can inhibit tongue mobility, thus affecting swallowing and speech. Often oral lesions are irritated by dentures and foods, especially sour, salty, spicy, and hot foods. Such discomfort and difficulties can cause the patient to restrict intake of some or all foods.
* *Oropharyngeal Cancers.* Advanced lesions of the soft palate can result in oronasal fistulas. Tonsillar lesions can cause dysphagia, odynophagia, and sore throat. Tumors in the base of the tongue may cause dysphagia by restricting tongue mobility. Large base-of-tongue tumors can result in greatly diminished intake, weight loss, and malnutrition. By comparison, oropharyngeal wall lesions are often asymptomatic.
* *Laryngeal Cancer.* Laryngeal cancer typically presents as hoarseness progressing to sore throat and odynophagia. More advanced lesions cause dysphagia, hemoptysis, and weight loss.

MEDICAL/SURGICAL TREATMENT

* Tumors in the head and neck are treated primarily by radiation therapy and/or resection of the tumor. Chemotherapy, used alone, has not been proven effective in eradicating head and neck tumors. Clinical trials continue to determine the adjunctive therapeutic benefit of chemotherapy in head and neck cancer.
* The decision between radiation and resection is made by the head and neck surgeon in consultation with the patient. Factors influencing this decision include the patient's age, surgical risk, and anticipated level of function after treatment.
* Radiation can be used alone to eradicate or palliate tumor, before surgery to shrink a large tumor, or after surgery to eliminate a known or suspected residual tumor. Radiation can be administered to the cancerous area via external beam or interstitial implants. Radiation to the head and neck region may cause a number of problems, which are described later in this chapter.
* Surgery involves removal of the diseased structure and a margin of tissue around the tumor and, if metastasis to the neck lymph nodes is suspected, dissection of the neck and removal of diseased lymph nodes. Surgery of

the upper aerodigestive tract can severely affect an individual's appearance and ability to swallow, smell, speak, and breathe. Fortunately, newer reconstruction techniques and extensive rehabilitation allow patients to resume reasonable appearance, speech, swallowing, and quality of life.

NUTRITIONAL MANAGEMENT

Oral Diet

Eating can be a major challenge for the person with head and neck cancer before, during, and after treatment. The nutritional implications of surgical resection and radiation and the corresponding nutrition therapy are described in Table 3–17. Many patients with oral, pharyngeal, or laryngeal cancer benefit from nutrition counseling and speech therapy, which helps them cope with the side effects of tumors and tumor treatment. Some patients are able to fill their nutrition requirements and gain weight through diet alone. Those who are unable to take adequate nutrients orally will require tube feeding. Such nutrition repletion is critical preoperatively, postoperatively, and during radiation therapy.

Tube Feeding

- Indications for tube feeding include inability to swallow or consume adequate calories. Patients immediately post surgery may be unable to swallow because of swelling. Patients receiving radiation therapy may be unable to take in adequate calories because of poor appetite and mucositis.
- Regardless of the patient's ability to swallow, tube feeding is only possible if the patient has a functional lower GI tract. Signs of adequate GI function include bowel sounds, soft abdomen, bowel movements (1–3 daily), no abdominal pain, and no nausea or vomiting.
- There are several routes for administering tube feeding (see Table 3–18):

1. nasogastric tube
2. nasoenteric tube
3. gastrostomy or percutaneous endoscopic gastrostomy (PEG) tube
4. jejunostomy

- Factors used to determine the appropriate tube-feeding route include
1. risk of aspiration and gastroesophageal reflux
2. need for gastric decompression
3. expected length of tube feeding
- A more permanent tube, such as a gastrostomy, PEG, or jejunostomy tube, is reserved for patients requiring more than 3 months of therapy. Previous abdominal surgeries may preclude placement of these tubes. Several authors have described positive outcome (economical and psychological) with use of PEG tubes for feeding in this population.
- Those patients who require less than 3 months of tube feeding can be fed via a nasal tube. For this population, the end of a feeding tube can usually be placed in the stomach. Small-bowel feeding is indicated in patients with increased risk of aspiration or poor gastric motility. A small-bowel feeding tube can be placed by waiting for peristalsis to move the tube into the small bowel and confirming placement with an X-ray. The most efficient method to place nasoenteric tubes is by fluoroscopy or with an endoscope.
- Method of administration of tube feeding is determined by the route of feeding, GI function, and appetite. Small-bowel feeding requires a continuous administration of tube-feeding formula. Bolus feeding into the small bowel is poorly tolerated. An example of small-bowel feeding is 75 ml of a polymeric formula per hour, administered over 24 hours. If a patient is transitioning to an oral diet and complains of fullness during the day, the feeding can be changed to a nighttime cycle (125 ml per hour for 12 hours). Maximum rate of tube feeding is individual for each patient. Generally, most patients in this population can tolerate a rate that provides their caloric requirement over 12 hours.

Table 3–17 Effects of Therapy for Head/Neck Cancer and Corresponding Nutrition Therapy

Therapy	Potential Complications	Nutrition Therapy
Radiation to mouth*	Xerostomia**	Drink adequate fluids (preferably nutrient-dense fluids). Use artificial saliva. Try sourballs or tart juices to stimulate saliva production.
	Diminished taste Metallic taste, bitter taste, or increased threshold for sweetness	Eat favorite foods.
	Dental caries Mucositis/stomatitis Osteonecrosis Oral infections Mouth sores/ulcers	Practice good oral hygiene, using a soft toothbrush and fluoride. Use rinses daily. Remove dentures. Try soothing mouth rinses ($\leq$ half-strength H_2O_2 or baking soda) or plain water rinses.
	Diminished nutrient intake Nausea Vomiting Trismus (lockjaw)	Try bland, room temperature foods. Drink nutrient-dense beverages. Try soft foods; avoid spicy, crunchy, hard, and hot foods. Try small, more frequent meals. Have others prepare meals/snacks. Have foods ready to consume. Condition may require tube feeding.
Radiation to neck	Dysphagia Odynophagia Diminished nutrient intake	Drink nutrient-dense beverages. Try soft foods or food consistency recommended by speech pathologist. Try small, more frequent meals.
Anterior tongue and anterior floor of mouth resection	Temporary, minimal difficulty manipulating food	Place food on nonoperative side. Check mouth for food after meals. Try soft food and thick liquids until swelling subsides.
Hard and soft palate resection	Nasal regurgitation of food and liquids	Try soft food until swelling subsides. Use intraoral prosthetic device.
Lip resection	Drooling and inadequate lip seal	Elevate chin when chewing and swallowing.

continues

Table 3–17 continued

Therapy	Potential Complications	Nutrition Therapy
Anterior mandible resection	Drooling and inability to bite	Mandible may need to be reconstructed. Avoid biting into foods; cut food into bite-size pieces.
Mandible (posterior) resection	Difficulty chewing	Mandible may need to be reconstructed. Try pureed or soft foods and liquids.
Hemiglossectomy	Temporary swelling, making manipulating food difficult	Place food on nonoperated side. Try soft foods and thick liquids until swelling subsides.
Total glossectomy	Inability to manipulate or propel food Aspiration (unless total laryngectomy performed)	Transfer small amounts of pureed food and liquids to pharynx by tilting head back or using large syringe and catheter. Clear larynx using Valsalva maneuver and coughing after the swallow. Some patients chronically aspirate and require permanent tube feedings.
Resection of base of tongue, tonsil, or pharyngeal wall	Dysphagia (due to removal of normal structures or stricture)	Do tube feeding until incision heals (5–7 days) and/or until normal swallowing is achieved. Provide swallowing therapy (turning head to operative side or tilting head toward normal side while swallowing). Strictures may require mechanical dilation.
Partial laryngectomy (supraglottic or hemi)	Dysphagia and aspiration likely, especially when postoperative edema and pain are present	Do tube feeding until incision heals (5–7 days). Provide swallowing therapy (supraglottic swallow: cough, inhale, bear down, place food in mouth, swallow hard, cough, swallow, breathe). Try semisolids or pureed foods until new swallowing techniques are mastered, then solids and liquids as tolerated.
Total laryngectomy	No aspiration risk Esophageal stricture possible	Do tube feeding until incision heals (5–7 days). Advance diet as tolerated after surgery. Provide esophageal dilation as needed.
All neck surgeries	Postoperative swelling Tracheostomy may impair swallowing	Do tube feeding until swelling subsides and tracheostomy is removed/replaced with a lighter model.

*Side effects may be temporary or permanent.

**Xerostomia is most severe when radiation is directed to the posterior oral cavity (retromolar trigone, tonsil, and superior pharynx).

Table 3–18 Routes for Administering Tube Feeding

Route	Advantages	Disadvantages
Nasogastric tube	Can tolerate gravity feeding Easy placement	May increase risk of aspiration Discomfort
Nasoenteric tube	May decrease risk of aspiration and gastric esophageal reflux Can administer feeding with gastric decompression	Can be difficult to place Requires a feeding pump Must be administered continuously
Gastrostomy or PEG tube	Can tolerate gravity feeding Comfort Appearance	Requires an additional procedure for placement May increase risk of aspiration and gastroesophageal reflux, site infection, or leakage
Jejunostomy	May decrease gastroesophageal reflux Can administer with gastric decompression Comfort Appearance	Requires surgery for placement Requires a feeding pump Must be administered continuously Site infection or leakage

- Intermittent tube feedings are administered via gravity over 30 minutes to 1 hour. Most patients require 3–5 feedings daily. Because intermittent feeding is a large volume of formula over a short period of time, it can only be administered into the stomach. Intermittent feeding into the small intestine will produce a dumpinglike syndrome. Many home patients prefer this mode of tube feeding because it is simple and can allow more time away from feeding.
- Formula selection should be based on individual patient requirements. Factors to consider include
  1. fluid restriction
  2. history of constipation
  3. digestion or absorption difficulties
  4. protein requirements
  5. availability (for home)
- Most patients in this population will tolerate a polymeric, 1.0-kcal/ml formula. Calorically dense formulas are indicated only for patients with fluid restrictions (eg, congestive heart failure, renal failure, or syndrome of inappro-priate secretion of antidiuretic hormone [SIADH]). Fiber-containing formulas can be helpful to maintain regular bowel movements in patients with a history of constipation. If a fiber-containing formula is selected, it is ideal to use a feeding tube no smaller than 10 French. Formulas are available to meet many different protein requirements. Postoperative patients may require a higher protein formula for wound healing. Specialized formulas are rarely necessary for this population but may be indicated if there is a concurrent illness. Often availability for home is an important factor when selecting a formula. Many of the formula companies now offer a mailing service by which formula can be purchased via the telephone.

Parenteral Nutrition

- Parenteral nutrition is indicated only in patients who require bowel rest (eg, Crohn's disease or chylous leak), have a nonfunctional GI tract (eg, pancreatitis), or have no access to the

GI tract (eg, obstructing esophageal tumor). Most patients in this population tolerate enteral feeding and rarely require parenteral nutrition. Occasionally, patients may require preoperative parenteral nutrition because of severe malnutrition and inability to place a feeding tube because of an obstructing tumor.

- Parenteral nutrition can be provided peripherally or centrally. Peripheral parenteral nutrition (PPN) can be provided only in solutions of 800–1000 mOsm or less. This limits the caloric and protein concentration of these solutions. PPN is most useful for transitional support for 5–7 days.
- Central access for parenteral nutrition requires placement of a central venous catheter in the subclavian or internal jugular vein. Central access is necessary for administering high osmolar solutions such as total parenteral nutrition (TPN). Patients who have had extensive surgery in the head and neck region may have limited locations for central access. Peripherally inserted central (PIC) catheters can also be used for TPN solutions. Because PIC catheters are placed peripherally, these catheters may be more appropriate for the patients who have had recent head and neck surgery.
- When TPN is indicated, TPN solutions can be designed to meet individual patient requirements. In general, this population tolerates solutions containing dextrose, amino acids, and lipids. Amounts of these substrates should be based on assessment of nutrient needs.

Home Nutrition Support

- Many patients in this population will require close monitoring of nutritional status and support. Some patients may benefit from instruction of a high-caloric diet on home tube feeding prior to surgery. Many patients will require home tube feeding after surgery until oral intake is adequate.
- Patients requiring home tube feeding and caregivers will require detailed instruction on home–tube-feeding administration. Many instruction booklets are available for purchase from pharmaceutical companies and hospitals. Instruction on managing potential complications is also important.
- Social services are often helpful in coordinating home–tube-feeding supplies and visiting nurses. Third-party reimbursement is variable and should be investigated on an individual basis.
- Documenting the medical necessity of tube feeding is essential for obtaining financial assistance.

REFERENCES

American Society for Parenteral and Enteral Nutrition, Board of Directors. Guidelines for use of enteral nutrition in the hospitalized adult patient. *JPEN.* 1987;11:430–439.

American Society for Parenteral and Enteral Nutrition, Board of Directors. Guidelines for use of total parenteral nutrition in the hospitalized adult patient. *JPEN.* 1993; 10:441–445.

Apovian CM, McMahon MM, Bristrian BR. Guidelines for refeeding the marasmic patient. *Crit Care Med.* 1990;18: 1030–1033.

Barades S, Blitzer A. Nutritional considerations in the management of head and neck cancer patients. *Otolaryngol Clin North Am.* 1984;17:725–733.

Bassett MR, Dobie RA. Patterns of nutritional deficiency in head and neck cancer. *Otolaryngol Head Neck Surg.* 1983;91:119–125.

Brookes GB, Clifford P. Nutritional status and general immune competence in patients with head and neck cancer. *J Roy Soc Med.* 1981;74:132–139.

Chencharick JD, Mossman KL. Nutritional consequences of the radiotherapy of head and neck cancer. *Cancer.* 1983; 51:811–815.

Close LG, Lee NK. Cancer of oral cavity and oropharynx. In: Meyerhoff WL, Rice DH, eds. *Otolaryngology: Head and Neck Surgery.* Philadelphia, Pa: WB Saunders Co; 1992:611–629.

Davis RK. Prognostic variables in head and neck cancer. *Otolaryngol Clin North Am.* 1985;18:411–419.

Droughton ML, Krech RL. Head and neck cancer resection and reconstruction: from past to present. *Today's OR Nurse.* 1992;14:25–34.

Fietkav R, Iro H, Saver R. Percutaneous endoscopically guided gastrostomy in patients with head and neck cancer. *Recent Results Cancer Res.* 1991;121:269–282.

Goichot B, Schlienger JL, Gruenberger F, et al. Low cholesterol concentrations in free-living elderly subjects: relations with dietary intake and nutritional status. *Am J Clin Nutr.* 1995;62:547–553.

Goodwin WJ, Byers PM. Nutritional management of the head and neck cancer patient. *Med Clin North Am.* 1993; 77:597–610.

Grant M, Rhiner M, Padilla GV. Nutritional management of the head and neck cancer patient. *Semin Oncol Nurs.* 1989;5:195–204.

Hopkins B. Assessment of nutritional status. In: Gottschlich MM, Matarese LE, Shronts EP, eds. *Nutrition Support Dietetics Core Curriculum.* 2nd ed. Silver Spring, Md: American Society for Parenteral and Enteral Nutrition; 1993:15–70.

Indeno KT. Enteral nutrition. In: Gottschlich MM, Matarese LE, Shronts EP, eds. *Nutrition Support Dietetics Core Curriculum.* 2nd ed. Silver Spring, Md: American Society for Parenteral and Enteral Nutrition; 1993:71–103.

Johns ME. The nutrition problem in head and neck cancer. *Otolaryngol Head Neck Surg.* 1980;88:691–694.

Kaiser TN, Gershon JS. Tumors of the larynx and laryngopharynx. In: Ballenger JJ, ed. *Diseases of the Nose, Throat, Ear, Head and Neck.* 14th ed. Philadelphia, Pa: Lea & Febiger; 1991:682–746.

Koehler J, Buhl K. Percutaneous endoscopic gastrostomy for postoperative rehabilitation after maxillofacial tumor surgery. *Int J Oral Maxillofac Surg.* 1991;20:38–39.

Kyle V. Nutritional considerations in the head and neck cancer patient. *Dietitians Nutr Support.* 1988;10:1–7.

Lebovics RD. Malignant tumors of the head and neck. In: Isselbacher KJ, Braunwald E, Wilson JD, Martin JB, Fauci AS, Kasper DL, eds. *Harrison's Principles of Internal Medicine.* 13th ed. New York, NY: McGraw-Hill; 1994:1850–1853.

Lindenbaum J. Folate and vitamin B_{12} deficiencies in alcoholics. *Semin Hematol.* 1980;17:119–128.

Logemann JA. *Evaluation and Treatment of Swallowing Disorders.* San Diego, CA: College-Hill Press; 1983.

Logemann JA. Physiology: mechanisms of normal and abnormal swallowing. In: Cummings CW, ed. *Otolaryngology: Head and Neck Surgery.* 2nd ed. Philadelphia, Pa: Mosby Year Book; 1993:1704–1712.

National Cancer Institute. *Oral Cancers: Research Report.* Bethesda, Md; 1991.

Ryder M. Peripherally inserted central venous catheters. *Nurs Clin North Am.* 1993;4:937–971.

Sigler BA. Nursing care for head and neck tumor patients. In: Thawley SE, Panje WR, eds. *Comprehensive Management of Head and Neck Tumors.* Philadelphia, Pa: WB Saunders Co; 1987:79–99.

Stokes MA, Hill GL. Peripheral parenteral nutrition: a preliminary report on its efficacy and safety. *JPEN.* 1993;17: 145–147.

Summers GW. Physiologic problems following ablative surgery of the head and neck. *Otolaryngol Clin North Am.* 1974;7:217–250.

Tannock IF, Bowman G. Lack of evidence for a role of chemotherapy in the routine management of locally advanced head and neck cancer. *J Clin Oncol.* 1986;4:1121–1126.

Thawley SE, O'Leary M. Malignant neoplasms of the oropharynx. In: Cummings CW, ed. *Otolaryngology: Head and Neck Surgery.* 2nd ed. Philadelphia, Pa: Mosby Year Book; 1993:1351.

Tomaiolo PP, Krause VK. Nutritional status of hospitalized alcoholic patients. *JPEN.* 1980;4(no 2):1–3.

Weckworth J, Nelson JK, O'Shea R. Home nutrition support. In: Gottschlich MM, Matarese LE, Shronts EP, eds. *Nutrition Support Dietetics Core Curriculum.* 2nd ed. Silver Spring, Md: Aspen Publishers, Inc; 1993:467–474.

Wenig BL, Gibson SE, Watkins JL. Complications of percutaneous endoscopic gastrostomy in head and neck cancer patients. *Ann Otol Rhinol Laryngol.* 1992;101:46–50.

Wilson PR, Herman J, Chubon SJ. Eating strategies used by persons with head and neck cancer during and after radiotherapy. *Cancer Nurs.* 1991;14:98–104.

Winkler MF, Mandry KM. Nutrition and wound healing. *Support Line.* 1992;14(no 3):1–4.

Pediatric Conditions

Lucille Beseler

DESCRIPTION

Feeding the pediatric patient poses a unique challenge to the health professional. Feeding and nutrition support become more complex in the still-developing child. Growth is a critical determinant of how a child is progressing. Pediatric nutrition interventions, due to this growth factor, are often highly complex and require individual evaluation. The following information is presented as guidelines. Criteria for feeding the pediatric patient should be based on medical history and stage of development. The goals of medical nutrition therapy for all pediatric patients are

- attainment of nutritional needs for macro/micronutrients
- attainment of normal growth and development
- nutrition rehabilitation with catch-up growth
- improved clinical outcomes

The following nomenclature is generally accepted to categorize pediatric patients:

- *Infants:* birth to 1 year
- *Children:* 1–10 years
- *Adolescents:* 11–18 years

Unless otherwise noted, references to pediatric patients will encompass all age categories.

CAUSE

A wide range of pediatric disorders require nutrition intervention. Advances in medical technology have made it possible for infants and children with comprehensive congenital anomalies and chronic catastrophic disease to survive. The existence of any chronic disease can interfere with a pediatric patient's nutritional status.

Screening criteria should be established to identify the pediatric patient at nutritional risk. Patients identified at nutrition risk should undergo a comprehensive nutrition assessment.

ASSESSMENT

Review of Medical History

Include the following:

- gestational age
- gastrointestinal symptoms, stool patterns, emesis
- growth/weight history
- social history

- existence of developmental delay
- stage of development
- activity level
- medications; any drug/nutrient interactions (eg, of anticonvulsant drugs)
- vitamins, mineral supplements

Anthropometrics

Anthropometrics should be measured and plotted on a standard gender-specific National Center for Health Statistics (NCHS) growth chart. The procedure for weighing and measuring should be consistent, using appropriate instrumentation. The patient should be gowned, infants should be measured without clothes. A stadiometer should be used for children over 3 years and a recumbent stadiometer for children under 3 years of age.

The following measures should be taken:
- weight for age (correct for gestational age; 40 weeks is baseline age for full-term gestation).
- height/length for age (recumbent length for children up to 3 years old)
- weight for height/length
- head circumference (up to 36 months of age)
  Additional measures that may be used are
- midarm circumference
- midarm muscle circumference
- triceps skinfold

Nutritional Intake

Dietary intake analysis can be derived from the following methods, using standardized questionnaires:

- 24-hour recall
- 3-day intake
- 7-day intake
- food frequency

Include a feeding history, with attention to the following:

- whether type and quantity of food are appropriate for age
- method of feeding by caretaker

- history of oral-motor problems
- timing of snacks and meals
- feeding environment, where meals are consumed, and food preparation practices
- allergies/intolerances

For infants, feeding history questions should cover

- type of feeding—formula or breast milk
- volume and frequency of feeding
- formula preparation
- whether method of feeding is appropriate and whether there are inadequate feeding practices or formula dilution errors
- description of the location and equipment used during feeding

Labs

Lab measures may include

- hemoglobin/hematocrit
- albumin/prealbumin
- other nutritionally significant laboratory findings based on specific disease

PROBLEMS

- Failure to thrive: drop of 2 percentiles in 6 months for weight or height; may require a multidisciplinary evaluation that includes a pediatric gastroenterologist
- Inadequate weight gain/growth failure or weight for age and weight for height below the 5th percentile (NCHS)
- Intolerance of feeding protocol
- Nutritional risk secondary to chronic disease
- Family or patient's inability to achieve goals of medical nutrition therapy
- Financial inability to purchase special formulas or supplements

TREATMENT/MANAGEMENT

Establishing Dietary Requirements

- Evaluate nutrient requirements—calories, protein, fat, carbohydrate, fluid, vitamins, and minerals—using Recommended Dietary Allowances (RDAs) for age (Table 3–19).
- In establishing nutrient requirements, an evaluation of activity level, disease state, and the need for catch-up growth must be considered. The RDAs must be adjusted on the basis of this information. In the case of children with developmental disabilities, caloric requirements will be lower than RDAs. To estimate caloric requirements for catch-up growth, use the following equation:

$$\frac{\text{Ideal weight:height} \times \text{RDA kcal/kg for weight age}}{\text{Actual weight}}$$

Weight age refers to the age at which present weight would equal the 50th percentile on the NCHS growth chart.

- Assessment must also include evaluation of fluid needs. Review existence of conditions requiring fluid restriction or fluid replacement.
  1. For children 1–10 kg = 100 ml/kg/day
  2. For children 11–20 kg = 1000 ml plus 50 ml/kg for each kg above 10
  3. For children > 20 kg = 1500 ml plus 20 ml/kg for each kg above 20

Table 3–19 Recommended Dietary Allowances of Protein and Calories for Infants, Children, and Adolescents

	Age	Protein g/kg	Cal/kg
Infants	0–6 mo	2.2	108
	6–12 mo	1.6	98
Children	1–3 yr	1.2	102
	4–6 yr	1.1	90
	7–10 yr	1.0	70
Females	11–14 yr	1.0	47
	15–18 yr	0.8	40
Males	11–14 yr	1.0	55
	15–18 yr	0.9	45

Source: Reprinted from *Recommended Dietary Allowances. 10th ed.* Washington, DC: National Academy Press; 1989.

General Guidelines for Medical Nutrition Therapy

- Establish goals of medical nutrition therapy, including the need for nutrient modification.
- Carefully consider if nutrient modification will cause inadequate intake or compromise the integrity of the child's diet.
- Develop a nutrition care plan based on assessment data and the disease process, with recommendations for how the plan can be implemented (oral or tube feeding).
- Set realistic goals for the caregiver.
- Evaluate the adequacy of the child's weight gain, on the basis of average weight gain for age, while the child is in the hospital and as an outpatient at regular intervals (monthly) until growth pattern improves to catch-up levels. Refer to a community-based health agency if you are unable to provide ongoing follow-up care.
- Revise the nutrition care plan to parallel changes in stage of development (see Pipes and Trahms for development of feeding behaviors).
- Evaluate the parents' and the patient's understanding of nutrition care plan, including infant formula preparation.
- Provide anticipatory guidance on effective feeding techniques and diet for age based on recommendations from the Academy of Pediatrics. Discourage early feeding of solid foods to infants and toddlers. Food selection should be based on the infant's or toddler's chewing and swallowing ability. Early introduction of solid food has many disadvantages, including

---

Average Daily Weight Gain

0–3 mo	20–30 g/day
3–6 mo	15–21/day
6–12 mo	10–13 g/day
1–6 yr	5–8 g/day
7–10 yr	5–11 g/day

---

a potential for increased risk of allergies. A method for identification of food allergies should be outlined.
- In cases of growth failure unresponsive to oral nutrition therapy, consider the need for tube feedings for the pediatric patient with a functioning gastrointestinal tract.

Treatment/Management for Infants with Growth Failure (Failure To Thrive)

- Evaluate appropriateness of formula with regard to type and caloric density.
  1. Standard infant formulas are available in ready-to-feed, concentrated, or powdered preparations. Standard caloric density of infant formulas is 20 kcal/oz. The caloric density of infant formulas often needs to be altered to meet the unique requirements of the medically complex pediatric patient. This may include patients with increased caloric needs or fluid restriction. Addition of modular fat, carbohydrate, and/or protein may be necessary. Infant formulas may be concentrated to 24 kcal/oz or more in special circumstances.
  2. Guidelines for altering caloric density of infant formula:
     - Concentrate formula base to 24 kcal/oz (concentrate or powdered formula).
     - Add modular fat as medium chain triglyceride (MCT) oil/corn oil/emulsified safflower oil.
     - Add carbohydrate as glucose polymers/maltodextrin.
  3. Evaluate
     - Renal solute load
     - Macronutrient distribution (should remain within normal range: CHO 35%–65%, protein 7%–16%, and fat 30%–55%; > 3% as essential fatty acids)
     - Osmolality (not to exceed 400 mOsm/kg H_2O)
  4. Protein hydrolysate formulas for special nutritional needs:

-*Alimentum* (Ross Labs): indicated for protein intolerance/allergy and fat malabsorption

-*Nutramigen* (Mead Johnson): indicated for protein intolerance/allergy and sucrose intolerance

-*Pregestimil* (Mead Johnson): indicated for protein intolerance/allergy, sucrose intolerance, and fat malabsorption

• Evaluate the possibility of improving nutrient composition of oral intake. To alter the caloric density of infant food:

1. Encourage use of energy-dense infant foods, and discourage use of infant foods with low caloric density such as fruit, desserts, and juice.
2. Add fats such as butter, margarine, and corn oil to boost calories of infant food if tolerated.

• Evaluate the need for vitamin/mineral supplementation, including iron, calcium, and fluoride.

1. Oral intake, children and adolescents
   -Increase oral feedings and include calorically dense snacks.
   -Increase caloric density of food with calorie boosters.
   -Evaluate need for oral supplements, including homemade and commercial varieties.
2. Enteral formulas
   -*Pediasure*, 30 kcal/oz (Ross Laboratories): for children aged 1 to 6 years; tube feeding or oral supplement
   -*Kindercal*, 30 kcal/oz (Mead Johnson): for children aged 1–10 years; tube feeding or oral supplement
   -*Nutren Jr.*, 30 kcal /oz (Clintec) for children aged 1–10 years, tube feeding or oral supplement.
3. Elemental formulas (for children aged 1–10)
   -*Peptamen Junior*, 30 kcal/oz (Clintec)
   -*Vivonex Pediatric*, 24 kcal/oz (Sandoz)
   -*Neocate One+*, 30 kcal/oz (Scientific Hospital Products)

Nutritional Support

Tube Feedings

• Tube feedings are indicated for the pediatric patient when oral intake is contraindicated or nutritional rehabilitation cannot occur without nutritional support due to inadequate oral intake or hypermetabolic needs. Hospitalized, normally nourished children with suboptimal nutrient intake for 5–7 days should receive nutrition support. Consultation with a pediatric gastroenterologist is necessary.

• If nutrition support will be continued after hospitalization, home care must be coordinated before hospital discharge. Once discharged from the hospital, the patient must be referred to an appropriate health professional for monitoring.

• Nasogastric tube feedings

1. Indicated for patients requiring
   -short-term feeding
   -continuous infusion feedings
   -nocturnal feedings to supplement oral intake
2. Contraindicated for patients at risk for aspiration, including those with gastroesophogeal reflux, neurological disorders, recurrent vomiting, impaired gastric emptying, and esophageal injury
3. Guidelines
   -Use small-bore soft pediatric nasogastric tube (#5–#8 French).
   -Monitor gastric residuals.
   -Secure tube to prevent patient removal.
   -Position patient to minimize risk of aspiration.

• Gastrostomy tube feedings

1. Indicated in cases of
   -prolonged use in children unable to attain adequate oral intake, on the basis of increased nutrient needs
   -neurologic inability to suck or swallow
2. Can be used for bolus or continuous feeds. Determine which method should be used on the basis of nutrient needs, GI function, and existence of fundoplication.

- Jejeunostomy tube feedings
  1. Indicated when
     - There is impaired gastric function with normal distal bowel.
     - Pediatric elemental or semielemental formula is required.
  2. General guidelines
     - Determine nutrient requirements: calories, protein, and fluid.
     - Determine the type of feeding to be used.
     - If tube feeding will require home management, consider the parent and/or caregiver's and child's lifestyle/schedule. Evaluate the parent's and the child's ability to handle complexity of nutritional support. Recommend social service evaluation if psychosocial problems prevail.
     - Consider supplies, including formula, home care company, and cost-benefit factors. Is the home care company determined by insurance company? Communicate with the home care company.
     - Select the formula.
     - Evaluate the need for pediatric multivitamins, including calcium and phosphorus (information on infants' and children's vitamins can be found in the *Physician's Desk Reference Handbook on Nonprescriptive Drugs*).
     - To preserve oral function and development, a speech/feeding therapy consult is recommended.
     - Communicate with pediatric subspecialists and the primary care physician. Determine who will provide ongoing nutrition care for patient after discharge (outpatient services, community-based pediatric nutritionist).
- To initiate continuous tube feedings:
  1. Start at 1–2 cc/kg/h.
  2. Advance by 0.5–1.0 cc/kg every 8–12 hours as tolerated until final volume is achieved.
  3. Do not advance formula volume and concentration simultaneously.
- To initiate bolus feedings:
  1. Start at 25%–50% of fluid volume per day.

  2. Determine number of feedings (usually every 3–4 hours).
  3. Divide volume equally between feedings.
  4. Gradually advance.
  5. Check residuals before each feeding.

Pediatric Parenteral Nutrition

Total parenteral nutrition (TPN) represents a complex intervention for the pediatric patient and requires professionals skilled and experienced in this area. Refer to Queen and Lang's *Handbook of Pediatric Nutrition* for a comprehensive guide to this subject.

Peripheral parenteral nutrition (PPN) is indicated when

- The pediatric patient is unable to obtain adequate nutrition via oral or enteral means.
- Use will be short term (2 weeks).

TPN is indicated when

- The pediatric patient is unable to tolerate enteral feedings.
- There is limited peripheral access.
- Nutrient needs are greater than PPN can supply.
- Parenteral support will last longer than 2 weeks.
- There is a condition requiring fluid restriction.

REFERENCES

American Academy of Pediatrics, Committee on Nutrition. *Pediatric Nutrition Handbook*. 3rd ed. Elk Grove Village, Ill: American Academy of Pediatrics; 1993.

American Society for Parenteral and Enteral Nutrition, Board of Directors. Guidelines for the use of parenteral and enteral nutrition in adult and pediatric patients. *JPEN*. 1993; 17(no 4, suppl):15A–525A.

Evkall S. *Pediatric Nutrition in Chronic Diseases and Developmental Disorders: Prevention, Assessment, and Treatment*. New York, NY: Oxford University Press; 1993.

Food and Nutrition Board, National Research Council. *Recommended Dietary Allowances*. 10th ed. Washington, DC: National Academy of Sciences; 1989.

Friscancho A. *Anthropometric Standards for the Assessment of Growth and Nutritional Status.* Ann Arbor, Mich: University of Michigan Press; 1990.

Mahan L, Rees J. *Nutrition in Adolescence.* St Louis, Mo: Mosby-Year Book, Inc; 1984.

Pipes P, Trahms C. *Nutrition in Infancy and Childhood.* 5th ed. St Louis, Mo: Mosby-Year Book, Inc; 1993.

Queen P, Lang C. *Handbook of Pediatric Nutrition.* Gaithersburg, Md: Aspen Publishers, Inc; 1993.

Walker A, Hendrick K. *Manual of Pediatrics.* Philadelphia, Pa: WB Saunders Co; 1985.

Woolridge N, Spinozzi N. *Quality Assurance Criteria for Pediatric Nutrition Conditions: A Model.* Chicago, Ill: American Dietetic Association; 1993.

Pregnancy and Lactation

Kathy Pesce-Hammond

PREGNANCY

Description

Pregnancy is an anabolic state in the life cycle occurring in women of childbearing age. Adequate nutrition during pregnancy influences a favorable course and outcome. Women who enter pregnancy with a nutritional risk or develop one during pregnancy increase the risk of developing complications.

Cause of Complications

Nutritional risk factors at the onset of pregnancy include age under 17 years or over 35 years; frequent pregnancies (less than 1 year apart); previous history of poor obstetric or fetal performance; economic deprivation (income below the poverty level; reception of local, state, or federal assistance); restricted dietary intake for social, religious, medical, or cultural reasons; substance abuse (tobacco, alcohol, drugs); chronic disease state (such as diabetes mellitus, kidney disease, hypertension, or gastrointestinal disorders); eating disorders; prepregnant weight 90% or below for standard weight for height or a body mass index (BMI) below 19.8; pregnant weight 120% or above for standard weight for height or a BMI greater than 26; and certain medications, such as Dilantin or oral contraceptives.

Nutritional risk factors during pregnancy include anemia, inadequate or excessive weight gain, multiple gestations, gestational diabetes, hypertension, and hyperemesis gravidarum.

Assessment

Current Medical Status and History

- Age
- Obstetric history (frequency, miscarriages, hyperemesis gravidarum)
- Chronic disease states (inflammatory bowel disease, diabetes mellitus, pancreatitis)
- Substance abuse
- Eating disorders
- Medications

Weight

- Obtain a history of gain and loss patterns.
- Record present weight.
- Determine pregravid weight.
- Determine BMI based on pregravid weight.
- Determine recommended weight gain, based on pregravid weight and BMI (see Table 3–20): approximately 2–5 lbs in the first trimester and 0.67–1.07 lb/wk during the second and third trimester. Maternal weight gain has the strongest influence on fetus birth weight.

Dietary Intake

- Evaluate prepregnancy intake via diet history and recall methods.
- Evaluate present intake.
- Evaluate for special modifications such as vegetarianism.
- Evaluate intake of caffeine and alcohol.
- Evaluate for pica intake.
- Compare intake with the dietary recommendations for pregnancy made by the Food and Nutrition Board, National Academy of Sciences National Research Council.
- Consider socioeconomic status.
- High-risk factors.

Nutritional Requirements

- An additional 300 kcal/day are required during the second and third trimester in normal-nourished women or 35–38 kcal/kg of actual body weight as recommended by the National Research Council.
- Additional calories may be needed in cases of metabolic stress.
- Additional 10 g of protein required (total of 60 g/day).
- Additional protein for stress and/or extraordinary losses may be required. Total protein intake should not exceed 1.5 kg body weight.

Table 3–20 Recommended Weight Gain in Pregnancy

Pregravid Weight	Recommended Total Gain in Pregnancy
Underweight (BMI < 19.8)	28–40 lb (12.5–18 kg)
Normal weight (BMI 19.8–26)	25–35 lb (11.5–16 kg)
Overweight (BMI 26–29)	15–25 lb (7.0–11.5 kg)
Obese (BMI > 29)	at least 15 lb (6 kg)
Twins	35–45 lb (16–20.5 kg)

- Requirements for iron, folate, and vitamin D increase 100% over nonpregnant levels.
- Calcium, phosphorus, thiamine, and B_6 increase 33%–50% over nonpregnant levels.
- Protein, zinc, and riboflavin increase 20%–25% over nonpregnant levels.
- Energy, selenium, magnesium, iodine, niacin, B_{12}, and Vitamins C and A increase 18% or less over nonpregnant levels.
- Several studies have suggested folate periconception to reduce risk of neural tube defects.

Nutritional Requirements during Lactation

- With proper weight gain during pregnancy, fat storage should be adequate to furnish 200–300 kcal/d for milk production during the first 3 months. The diet should be increased by 500 kcal/d to allow for the use of the fat storage.
- Protein requirement during the first 6 months of lactation is 65 g/day and then decreases to 62 g/day during the second 6 months.
- For Recommended Dietary Allowances for Vitamins during Lactation, see Table 3–21.

Biochemical Parameters

- Obtain hemoglobin and hematocrit.
- Maternal anemia early in pregnancy is associated with an increased risk of preterm labor. Iron-deficiency anemia should be diagnosed early.
- A glucose challenge test should be given between the 24th and 28th weeks of gestation.
- With a 30% to 40% increase in maternal blood volume during the last trimester, there may be a 12–15% decrease in hemoglobin and hematocrit per deciliter of blood. The mean corpuscular volume (MCV) and mean corpuscular hemoglobin concentration (MCHC) remain relatively unchanged.
- Albumin is also decreased due to a dilutional factor.
- Nutrients that are water soluble follow the de-

Recommended Dietary Allowances for Vitamins during Pregnancy for Women 25–50 Years of Age

Vitamin D	10 micrograms	Vitamin E	10 mg alpha-TE
Vitamin C	70 milligrams	Thiamin	1.5 milligrams
Riboflavin	1.6 milligrams	Niacin	17 milligrams NE
Folate	400 micrograms	Vitamin B_{12}	2.2 micrograms
B_6	2.2 milligrams	Vitamin A	800 micrograms (RE)
Vitamin K	65 micrograms		

Recommended Dietary Allowances for Minerals during Pregnancy

Calcium	1200 milligrams	Phosphorus	1200 milligrams
Magnesium	320 milligrams	Iron	30 milligrams
Zinc	15 milligrams	Iodine	175 micrograms
Selenium	65 micrograms (RDA)		

cline of albumin, including serum levels of vitamin C, folic acid, and vitamins B_6 and B_{12}.

- Urinary excretion of end products of folate, niacin, and pyridoxine metabolism is increased.
- Alterations in lipid metabolism occur, resulting in the doubling of serum levels of cholesterol, triglycerides, and blood-clotting factors.

Table 3–21 Recommended Dietary Allowances for Vitamins during Lactation

	1st 6 months	2nd 6 months
Vitamin A (µg RE)	1300	1200
Vitamin D (µg)	10	10
Vitamin E (mg alpha-TE)	12	11
Vitamin K (µg)	65	65
Vitamin C (mg)	95	90
Thiamine (mg)	1.6	1.6
Riboflavin (mg)	1.8	1.7
Niacin (mg NE)	20	20
Vitamin B_6 (mg)	2.1	2.1
Folate (µg)	280	260
Vitamin B_{12} (µg)	2.6	2.6
Minerals:		
Calcium (mg)	1200	1200
Phosphorus (mg)	1200	1200
Magnesium (mg)	355	340
Iron (mg)	15	15
Zinc (mg)	19	16
Iodine (µg)	200	200
Selenium (µg)	75	75

Physical Assessment

- Evidence of clinical deficiencies, including appearance of arms, legs, face, and neck, should be noted—especially signs of muscle wasting.

Problems

Nausea/Vomiting

- Common in early pregnancy due to hormonal changes. Usually referred to as "morning sickness."
- If excessive, then potential for protein and calorie depletion, along with vitamin, mineral, and electrolyte depletion.
- Prolonged, persistent vomiting after the 14th week of pregnancy is referred to as *hyperemesis gravidarum* and may require hospitalization. Dehydration, electrolyte imbalance, ketonuria, and significant weight loss may occur.

Heartburn

- Usually occurs during the latter period of pregnancy.
- Results from the pressure of the enlarged uterus on the stomach and a relaxed esophageal sphincter that allows reflux of stomach contents into the esophagus.

Constipation

- Usually caused by decreased gut motility, pressure of the enlarged uterus on the bowel, and decreased physical activity.
- Hemorrhoids may develop from the weight of the fetus and downward pressure of veins in the rectal region.

Gestational Diabetes

- The stress of pregnancy may result in diabetes during pregnancy. Changes in plasma insulin result in alterations in glucose metabolism.
- Routine screening by a fasting blood glucose (FBG) should be done at 24 to 28 weeks of pregnancy. If the FBG is > 140 mg/dL, then a 3-hour oral glucose tolerance test is done. Gestational diabetes is diagnosed if the following criteria are met: FBG of ≥ 105 mg/dL; 1-hour glucose of ≥ 190 mg/dL; 2-hour glucose of ≥ 165 mg/dL and/or 3-hour glucose of ≥ 145 mg/dL.
- Usually resolves after delivery.
- Etiology not completely understood.

Pregnancy-Induced Hypertension (PIH)

- PIH is a syndrome characterized by hypertension, proteinuria, and edema. It is defined by a systolic blood pressure of 140 mm Hg or greater or a diastolic pressure of 90 mm Hg or greater, or both. In young women who have low prepregnancy blood pressure, it is more useful to look at blood pressure changes during pregnancy. A systolic increase of 20 to 30 mm Hg or a diastolic increase of 10 to 15 mm Hg or both on at least two separate occasions may indicate PIH.
- Proteinuria varies with the severity of PIH. The presence of 500 mg of protein in a 24-hour urine specimen or 2+ on random collection indicates preeclampsia; eclampsia is indicated by 5 g of protein in a 24-hour urine specimen or 3+–4+ on random collection.
- Edema is present in preeclampsia and is associated with dizziness, headache, facial edema, anorexia, nausea, and vomiting. Eclampsia is a more severe form of edema that may be characterized by convulsions.
- PIH usually develops in the third trimester.
- Hypoalbuminemia, hypovolemia, and hemoconcentration may also be present.
- Proposed nutritional causes include protein deficiency and calcium deficiency.

Treatment/Management

General Guidelines Using the Food Guide Pyramid

- 6–11 servings daily from bread, cereal, rice, and pasta group
- 3–5 servings daily from vegetable group
- 2–4 servings daily from fruit group (at least 1 serving of dark greens, 2 servings of vitamin C–rich fruits or vegetables, and 2 servings of other)
- 4 servings daily from the milk, yogurt, and cheese group (pregnant adolescents should have 5–6 servings daily)
- 3 servings daily from the meat, dry beans, eggs, and nuts group
- Use of sugar and salt sparingly

General Guidelines Using the Food Guide Pyramid

- Follow the Food Guide Pyramid guidelines for pregnancy, with an increase in milk/milk products to 4–5 servings daily.
- Take approximately 2 L of fluid per day in the form of water, foods, and beverages. Forcing fluids may decrease milk production.
- Cigarettes and caffeine may cause gastroesophageal reflux.

Nausea and Vomiting

- Small, frequent, dry meals of easily digested carbohydrates.

- Fluids between meals if dry feedings are tolerated. Fluids should not be taken 1 hour before or 1 hour after meals.
- Eat as soon as hunger is felt.
- Eat saltines or other dry carbohydrate foods prior to rising in the morning.
- Avoid high-fat foods. A low-fat diet should be adhered to until fats can be tolerated.
- Avoid highly seasoned foods.
- Be careful with cooking odors that may be bothersome.
- Fluids and fats can gradually be added to meals as nausea subsides.
- Fluid and electrolyte replacement or parenteral nutrition may be indicated in cases of prolonged vomiting or hyperemesis gravidarum.

Heartburn

- Small, frequent meals.
- Do not skip meals.
- Chew adequately and eat slowly.
- Avoid being in a reclined position while eating. Wait 30 minutes after eating to recline.
- Decrease fat in meals.
- Drink fluids between meals.
- Avoid chewing gum, since swallowing air may cause heartburn.
- Avoid caffeine, spices, and alcohol intake.

Constipation

- Increase consumption of high-fiber foods, such as whole grains and fruit.
- Increase fluid intake to at least 6–8 glasses/day.
- Maintain physical activity as directed by physician.

Gestational Diabetes

- Nutritional needs are the same as for the normal pregnant woman.
- Maintain euglucemia to decrease or prevent losses of water, sodium, amino acids, and minerals seen with glycosuria.
- Restrict intake of simple carbohydrates.

- Daily food composition should contain 45%–60% of kilocalories from carbohydrate, 20% of kilocalories from protein, and 20%–35% of kilocalories from fat.
- Three meals and snacks should be provided daily, according to the type of insulin management, food preferences, and activity.
- Monitor blood glucose levels; urine glucose is not recommended.
- Gestational diabetes is usually treated by diet alone. If diabetes cannot be controlled by diet, then insulin may be required. Oral agents are not used due to harmful effects on the fetus.

Pregnancy-Induced Hypertension

- Avoid severe sodium restriction.
- Provide adequate calcium intake to meet the Recommended Dietary Allowance for pregnancy.
- Provide adequate protein intake for pregnancy.

REFERENCES

Committee on Nutritional Status during Pregnancy and Lactation. *Part 1, Weight Gain; Part II, Nutrient Supplements.* Washington, DC: National Academy Press; 1990.

Ferris A, Reece A. Nutritional consequences of chronic maternal conditions during pregnancy and lactation: lupus and diabetes. *Am J Clin Nutr.* 1994;59(suppl):465S–473S.

Diet Manual of the Georgia Dietetic Association. Decatur, Ga: Georgia Dietetic Association; 1992.

Luke B. Maternal-fetal nutrition. *Clin Obstet Gynecol.* 1994; 37:93–104.

MacBurney M. Pregnancy. In: Gottschlich MM, Matarese LE, Shronts EP, eds. *Nutrition Support Dietetics Core Curriculum.* 2nd ed. Silver Spring, Md: American Society for Parenteral and Enteral Nutrition; 1993:125–136.

McGanity W, Dawson E, Fogelman A. Embryonic development, pregnancy, and lactation. In: Shils M, Olson JA, Shike M, eds. *Modern Nutrition in Health and Disease.* 8th ed. Philadelphia, Pa: Lea & Febiger; 1994:705–727.

National Academy of Sciences. *Recommended Dietary Allowances.* 10th ed. Washington, DC: National Academy Press; 1989.

Olson C. Promoting positive nutritional practices during pregnancy and lactation. *Am J Clin Nutr.* 1994;59(suppl): 525S–531S.

Roberts-Worthington B. Nutrition during pregnancy and lactation. In: Mahan LK, Arlin M, eds. *Krause's Food, Nutrition, and Diet Therapy.* 1992:151–176.

Robinson C, Weigley E, Mueller D. *Basic Nutrition and Diet Therapy.* 7th ed. New York, NY: Macmillan.

Rush D. Periconceptional folate and neural tube defect. *Am J Clin Nutr.* 1994;59(suppl):511S–516S.

Scholl T, Hediger M. Anemia and iron-deficiency anemia: compilation of data on pregnancy outcome. *Am J Clin Nutr.* 1994;59(suppl):492S–501S.

Stuijvenberg M, Schabort I, Labadarios D, Nel J. The nutritional status and treatment of patients with hyperemesis gravidarum. *Am J Obstet Gynecol.* 1995;172:1585–1591.

Pulmonary Conditions

Denise B. Schwartz

DESCRIPTION

Pulmonary patients are individuals who are at risk of pulmonary failure. This organ failure is the end result of many types of chronic lung disease. The condition can occur as a complication of severe trauma, septicemia, and other acute conditions. Pulmonary failure is when the lungs fail to oxygenate the arterial blood adequately and/or fail to prevent CO_2 retention. $P_{O_2} < 60$ mm Hg or $P_{CO_2} > 50$ mm Hg.

CAUSES

Acute Lung Disease

- Fulminating viral or bacterial pneumonias
- Vascular diseases, including pulmonary embolism
- Exposure to inhaled toxic substances

Neuromuscular Disorders/Conditions

- Drug therapy, ie, barbiturates use
- Encephalitis
- Poliomyelitis
- Guillain-Barre syndrome
- Myasthenia gravis
- Anticholinesterase poisoning
- Progressive muscular dystrophy
- Chest wall trauma

Acute or Chronic Lung Disease

- Chronic bronchitis
- Chronic emphysema
- Asthma
- Cystic fibrosis

Acute Respiratory Distress Syndrome (ARDS)

- Trauma with direct or indirect injury to the lung
- Septicemia

Malnutrition

- Due to inadequate nutrient intake or secondary to metabolic stress

ASSESSMENT

Areas

- Drive mechanism
- Respiratory muscle function
- Gas-exchange process
- Hemoglobin-oxygen affinity
- Arterial blood gases
- Mechanical ventilation
- Ventilatory capacity and mechanics

Instruments

- Spirometer
- Ventilator
- Metabolic cart

PROBLEMS

Motor

- Limitations on food procurement and meal preparation with dyspnea on exertion
- Involuntary weight loss may result in physical weakness and decreased muscle strength
- Easily fatigued and reduced endurance of respiratory muscles

Sensory

- Altered food taste with medications
- Pain with breathing
- Impaired gastric function, limiting appetite and tolerance to tube feeding administration
- Early satiety, caused by flattened diaphragm or air swallowing
- Feeling of fullness
- Abdominal discomfort, caused by bronchodilator drugs or corticosteroids

Cognition

- Limited understanding of the disease process and the role of adequate nutrition to optimize remaining lung function

Intrapersonal

- Depression
- Anxiety due to shortness of breath

Interpersonal

- Focus on breathing and on limiting external responsiveness
- Increased dependency on significant other or caregiver as functional capacity is reduced
- Exhaustion, depression, and dyspnea, preventing alertness and receptive potential for interaction

Self-Care

- Activities of daily living curtailed, as the ability to breathe requires concentration
- Ability to shop for food limited, with shortness of breath restricting going out of the house
- Meal preparation restricted; use of more ready-prepared food items

Productivity

- More time required to do most activities
- Frequent rest periods required with shortness of breath

Leisure

- Individual unable to participate in leisure activities due to shortness of breath and depression with curtailment of normal activities

TREATMENT/MANAGEMENT

Motor

- Increase tolerance to activities with breathing exercises.
- Practice controlled-breathing techniques to slow down expiration and help break the vicious cycle of breathless panic and air trapping.
- Obtain adequate rest to fight off infection.

Cognitive

- Have the individual pace his or her strength with rest periods.
- Teach energy conservation and work simplification.
- Use a calm, confident, reassuring approach; relaxation techniques; positioning; and assisting the individual if it is necessary to reduce energy expenditure.

Intrapersonal

- Provide discussion groups to enhance verbalization of problems, lifestyle changes, ways to

improve eating, balanced diet, and simply prepared, nutritious meals.
- Use guidelines for appropriate meal pattern
and selection of foods:
  1. 5–6 small meals per day
  2. rest before and after meals
  3. use of oxygen during meals
  4. separation of liquid and dry constituents of
  meal to avoid distention
  5. use of soft, easy-to-chew foods to avoid
  overexertion
  6. sodium restriction only if necessary

Interpersonal

- Involve family members to discuss ways to
assist the individual in performing activities of
daily living and becoming more independent.
- Involve the individual in group activities and
discussions with other persons with pulmonary problems.

Self-Care

- Focus on the relation between nutrition and
pulmonary function; the importance of a balanced diet; ways to increase calorie intake;
and management of dyspnea, fatigue, and
early satiety.
- Work with the individual and the family to
determine the need for supplementary nutrition intake if oral intake is inadequate, nightly
tube feeding to supplement nutrition intake,
use of oral supplements, and small, frequent
meals as appropriate.
- Design a nutritional regimen for the individual
with lung disease to provide a diet that will
minimize metabolic demands while maximiz-
ing functional improvements.
- Avoid cooking fumes if these are found to be a
bronchial irritant.
- Take bronchodilators and steroids with food
to avoid gastric irritation.

PRECAUTIONS

- Symptoms of increasing dyspnea, increasing
coughing spells, fatigue, chills, tremors, tachycardia, and nervousness

- Signs of discolored sputum and sudden loss of
appetite (could be related to bronchodilator
toxicity)
- Excessive work of breathing, causing visible
use of neck muscle
- Abdominal tensing on expiration and generally distressed appearance, including pursed-
lip breathing and gasping inspiratory efforts
- Limitation of increase in carbon dioxide production (especially excessive calories when
providing a balanced diet of protein, fat, and
carbohydrate) related to fuel provided either
orally, by tube feeding, or by parenteral feeding—especially important during weaning
from mechanical ventilation or for an individual with declining pulmonary function
who may soon require ventilatory support

PROGNOSIS AND OUTCOME

- The person demonstrates knowledge of the
disease process and its relationship to maintaining good nutrition.
- The person is able to maintain his or her
weight (gradual weight gain if individual is
cachectic and weight loss only as it relates to
overall health if individual is significantly
greater than ideal body weight).
- The person is able to perform activities of
daily living at a maximum level of independence within medical limitations.
- The person understands that the stable ambulatory individual with chronic obstructive pulmonary disease (COPD) has a hypermetabolic
state at rest.

REFERENCES

Colaizzo-Anas T. Assessment and nutrition management of
the patient with compromised pulmonary function. In:
Winkler MF, Lysen LK, eds. *Suggested Guidelines for
Nutrition and Metabolic Management of Adult Patients
Receiving Nutrition Support.* 2nd ed. Chicago, Ill: Ameri-
can Dietetic Association; 1993:80–90.

Grant JP. Nutrition care of patients with acute and chronic
respiratory failure. *Nutr Clin Pract.* 1994;9:4–17.

Grossbach I. The COPD patient in acute respiratory failure. *Crit Care Nurse.* December 1994:32–38.

Hagaman M, Christman JW. Nutritional support in acute respiratory failure. *Contemp Intern Med.* 1994;6:29–41.

Hahn K. Slow-teaching the C.O.P.D. patient. *Nurs.* 1987;17:34–41.

Hugli O, Frascarolo P, Schutz Y, et al. Diet-induced thermogenesis in chronic obstructive pulmonary disease. *Am Rev Respir Dis.* 1993;148:1479–1483.

Jones MA, Hoffman LA, Delgado E. A.R.D.S.: new ways to fight an old enemy revisited. *Nurs.* 1994;94:34–43.

Schwartz DB. Respiratory disease and mechanical ventilation. In: Skipper A, ed. *The Dietitian's Handbook of Enteral and Parenteral Nutrition.* Rockville, Md: Aspen Publishers, Inc; 1989:137–150.

West JB. *Pulmonary Pathophysiology: The Essentials.* 3rd ed. Baltimore, Md: Williams & Wilkins; 1987:3–202.

Renal Conditions

Michelle M. Romano

The main function of the kidney is to serve as a filter that removes substances the body does not need and eliminates them in the urine. In this way they maintain fluid, electrolyte, and acid-base balance and rid the body of metabolic waste products. The kidneys also help maintain blood pressure, produce erythropoetin, and activate vitamin D.

The work of the kidney is done by the nephron. There are over 1 million nephrons in the kidney. Renal failure is due to loss of nephron function. This can occur over time (chronic) or suddenly (acute).

CHRONIC RENAL FAILURE

Description

Slow, irreversible loss of kidney function. The glomerular filtration rate (GFR) decreases, as well as the urine-concentrating ability and urea clearance.

Cause

- Hereditary, biochemical, or metabolic disorders that cause conditions such as polycystic kidney disease and diabetic nephropathy
- Reflux of urine caused by obstructions in the lower urinary tract
- Abnormalities in immune system function or intrarenal vascular coagulation, leading to various conditions such as membranoproliferative glomerulonephritis
- Infection
- Hypertension
- Nephrotoxic substances

Assessment

Diet History

Assess for

- Weight changes
- Adequacy of meals; timing and frequency of meals
- Chewing/swallowing difficulty
- Nausea/vomiting/diarrhea/constipation
- Taste changes
- Poor-fitting dentures
- Adequacy of diet and compliance with recommended intakes of sodium, potassium, phosphorus, calories, protein, and fluids
- Compliance with medications (phosphate binders, vitamins, minerals)

Social History

- Potential risk factors for malnutrition
  1. living alone
  2. inadequate income

3. inability to buy own food
4. inadequate refrigeration or cooking facilities
5. alcohol/drug addiction

Anthropometrics

Determine

- *Height/weight* (without shoes or prosthesis)
  1. *Dry weight:* refers to body weight when the patient is free from edema and fluid retention; weight gain of more than 0.5 to 1 kg/day usually represents fluid retention and not body weight (Metropolitan Life Height/Weight tables, 1983, can be used)
  2. *Adjusted body weight* (adjusted for obesity, or over 120% of recommended body weight):

     adjusted body weight = [(actual body weight – recommended body weight) × 0.25] + recommended body weight

- *Triceps skinfold thickness (TSF):* uses Lange skinfold calipers to estimate body fat; best when used long term, as acute changes in fluid status may skew results
- *Midarm muscle circumference (MAC):* measurement of calorie and protein stores; positive fluid balance may skew results

Physical Exam

Examine for

- Muscle wasting
- Poor skin turgor
- Brittle hair, nails
- Edema
- Ascites
- Decubitus ulcers

Presence of Other Disease States

- Diabetes mellitus
- Cardiovascular disease
- Multiple organ dysfunction syndrome

Laboratory Values

- Glomerular filtration rate (GFR)
  1. Normal values range from 90–120 ml/min.
  2. Moderate failure is approximately 70–25

ml/min; severe is under 25 ml/min. When the rate falls to 4–5 ml/min, dialysis is usually started.
  3. Rate is measured by the clearance of a solute that is filtered but not resorbed into the blood. Creatinine clearance is readily calculated and has been used to approximate GFR.
- Serum albumin
  1. Level may be falsely elevated in dehydration and depressed in overhydration.
  2. Level may be depressed because of chronic losses (nephrotic syndrome) and poor intake.
  3. Level may be elevated after the patient receives whole blood, albumin, or plasma.
  4. Trends in serum albumin levels should be evaluated on a regular basis.
  5. Low serum albumin (< 4.0) has been associated with increased mortality.
- Serum transferrin
  1. Level is probably a more sensitive indicator of acute changes in protein nutrition and albumin, but because transferrin transports iron, it is also affected by iron nutriture.
  2. Level increases in iron deficiency and decreases with iron loading.
  3. Levels of 1.0–1.5 g/dL reflect moderate malnutrition; levels under 1.0 g/dL reflect severe malnutrition.
- Prealbumin, retinol-binding protein
  1. These levels are increased due to impaired degradation by the kidney; thus, they probably are not good indicators of nutrition status.
- Total lymphocyte count (TLC)
  1. TLC is inaccurate with sepsis, infection, immunosuppressives, and corticosteroids.
  2. A level of 800–1200/mm^3 suggests moderate depletion; a level under 800/mm^3 suggests severe depletion.
- Protein catabolic rate (PCR)
  1. PCR is used in urea kinetic modeling (see Appendix W) to assess nitrogen balance in renal disease. It is an index of nitrogen balance in a steady state and does not measure catabolism.

2. In stable patients, dietary protein intake = PCR.

3. The lower limit for adequate PCR is 0.8 g/kg of body weight/day.

- Blood urea nitrogen (BUN)
  1. Levels increase with renal failure, excessive protein intake, and anything that increases body catabolism.
  2. A level >100 mg/dL indicates a need for protein restriction with predialysis patients.
  3. Levels decrease with malnutrition.
- Serum creatinine
  1. Levels increase with renal failure.
  2. Levels are not related to dietary intake of protein or any other nutrient.
  3. Directly proportional to muscle mass.
- Serum sodium
  1. Levels increase with dehydration.
  2. Levels decrease with overhydration.
- Serum potassium
  1. Cardiac arrhythmias can occur with potassium > 7.0.
  2. Catabolism (trauma, injury, surgery, infection, fever, acidosis) can result in the release of potassium from the cells into the blood.
- Serum chloride
  1. Levels are normal or increased with metabolic acidosis.
  2. Levels are increased with dehydration, fever, and renal insufficiency.
- Serum calcium
  1. Levels are decreased in renal failure due to elevated phosphorus levels and impaired vitamin D metabolism.
  2. Levels are increased with hyperparathyroidism.
  3. Sixty percent of calcium is bound to albumin. To determine the ionized calcium concentration, calculate:

     (4.0 g/dL – patient's albumin level × 0.8) + serum calcium

- Serum phosphorus
  1. Levels are elevated with renal failure, as the kidney is unable to excrete.

2. Calcium phosphorus product = serum phosphorus × serum calcium. If > 60–70, there is an increased risk of metastatic calcification.

- Serum glucose
  1. Insulin is degraded by the kidney; therefore, requirements may be decreased in diabetics.
- Hemoglobin/hematocrit
  1. Levels are chronically depressed in renal disease.

Problems

Uremia/Uremic Syndrome

- *Uremia:* toxic waste products in the blood; associated with renal insufficiency
- *Uremic syndrome:* a complex of symptoms caused by uremia; characterized by abnormal energy and protein metabolism and net protein catabolism; symptoms include
  1. fatigue
  2. weakness
  3. decreased mental alertness
  4. muscular twitches
  5. muscle cramps
  6. anorexia
  7. nausea/vomiting
  8. stomatitis
  9. dysgeusia
  10. skin itch
  11. gastrointestinal ulcers and bleeding (common in later stages)
  12. reduced gastrointestinal absorption of many nutrients
  13. reduced inactivation of many hormones, including insulin, parathyroid hormone, and glucagon
  14. reduced synthesis of active vitamin D and erythropoietin

Metabolic acidosis increases catabolism.

Wasting Syndrome

- Protein/calorie malnutrition occurring in predialysis patients but more prevalent in hemodialysis and peritoneal dialysis patients

- Manifested by decreased
  1. body weight
  2. body height (children)
  3. growth (children)
  4. body fat (skinfold thickness)
  5. muscle mass (MAC)
  6. total body potassium
  7. total albumin mass, synthesis, and catabolism
- Caused by
  1. inadequate dietary intake due to anorexia associated with uremic toxicity
  2. debilitating effects of chronic illness
  3. depression
  4. diet prescription that is restrictive and/or unpalatable
  5. high incidence of superimposed catabolic illness
  6. protein-rich blood loss due to frequent blood drawing for laboratory testing or gastrointestinal bleeding

Renal Osteodystrophy

- As phosphorus levels increase with renal disease, calcium levels decline, signaling parathyroid hormone (PTH) to maintain blood levels. Eventually PTH becomes ineffective at reducing phosphorus levels. There is also decreased absorption of calcium from the gut and decreased calcium intake due to protein-restrictive diets.

Diabetic Nephropathy/Glucose Intolerance

- There is peripheral insulin resistance.
- With hyperglycemia, increased thirst and fluid overload are problems.
- Hyperkalemia also occurs with hyperglycemia as potassium shifts from intracellular to extracellular space.
- Other complications of neuropathy, retinopathy, gastroparesis, and amputation all increase malnutrition risk.
- Proteinuria can occur.
- Hyperinsulinemia can occur.

Electrolyte Imbalance

- Hypokalemia can occur with diuretic use.
- Hyperkalemia can occur when urine output decreases to below normal. This should be avoided, as the risk increases for cardiac arrythmia and arrest.
- Hypertension, edema, and heart failure may result from sodium retention.
- Hypermagnesemia occurs secondary to decreased excretion by the kidney; avoid magnesium-containing antacids.

Anemia

- Caused by
  1. uremia, which impairs intestinal absorption of iron
  2. gastrointestinal bleeding
  3. limited production of erythropoietin
  4. shortened red cell survival

Hyperlipidemia

- Problems include
  1. hypertriglyceridemia
  2. increased very low density lipoprotein (VLDL), normal to low low density lipoprotein (LDL), and decreased high-density lipoprotein (HDL)
  3. carnitine deficiency

Vitamin Deficiency

- Supplementation is needed with diets providing less than 50 g protein per day.
- Uremia can affect metabolism of nutrients.

Treatment/Management

Predialysis

The goals of nutrition therapy for the predialysis patient are

- controlling nitrogen intake to minimize the accumulation of nitrogenous waste product
- providing adequate calories and nitrogen to prevent wasting of lean body mass
- slowing the decline of GFR

Therapy should be individualized to the patient's condition.

Some therapy guidelines are listed below. (For specific food exchange lists and a sample meal plan, see Table 3–22.)

- Protein (see Table 3–23)
  1. Two-thirds of protein intake should be of high biologic value (meats, eggs).
  2. Ketoacids and essential amino acids and very low protein diets (20–25 g/day) have been used to promote nitrogen balance and to maintain albumin and transferrin levels. But there is only small benefit with moderate renal insufficiency.
  3. See below, "Nephrotic Syndrome," for protein needs with proteinuria.
- Energy (see Table 3–23)
  1. Adequate energy intake improves protein utilization and reduces net protein catabolism.
  2. Supplements may be indicated that are low in protein [eg, Travasorb Renal (Clintec), Amin-Aid (Kendal-McGaw), Suplena (Ross), and Polycose (Ross)]
  3. If the patient is > 120% of recommended body weight, fewer calories should be provided.
- Diabetic nephropathy
  1. attainment of reasonable body weight, as determined by the health care provider, is recommended through slow weight loss and has been shown to improve glucose tolerance and lipid levels (approximately 0.5–1.0 lb/wk).
  2. Blood sugar should be controlled.
  3. Protein intake of 0.8 g/kg should be sufficiently restricted.
- Phosphorus (see Appendix N)
  1. Phosphate binders (ie, calcium acetate and calcium carbonate) are often needed in addition to a low-phosphorus diet.
  2. Aluminum-containing binders should be limited, as aluminum may deposit in bone and brain.
- Calcium
  1. Provide daily supplementation of 1200–1600 mg of calcium to prevent bone disease.

  2. Vitamin D will improve absorption of calcium (Rocaltrol, Calderol).
  3. The patient should be monitored over time for hypercalcemia.
- Hyperlipidemia
  1. Institute a low-cholesterol/low–saturated-fat diet.
  2. Establish glycemic control in diabetics.
  3. Avoid excessive alcohol intake, smoking, obesity, and hypertension.
  4. Institute a low-triglyceride diet when serum triglycerides increase to 50 to 100 mg/dl above upper limit.
- Vitamins/minerals: see Table 3–23 for guidelines.

Desired outcomes of treatment are

- reduced nitrogenous waste products in the blood
- reduced catabolism of lean body mass
- blood pressure control
- provision of adequate calories
- control of hyperphosphatemia and renal osteodystrophy
- decreased risk for cardiovascular disease

Hemodialysis

Hemodialysis removes wastes from the blood by passing the blood outside the body (via artery) through tubing made of semipermeable membrane back into the body (via vein). Blood is cleared of toxins by diffusion and osmosis through the membrane.

The hemodialysis patient should be assessed on

- Anthropometric measures
  1. height
  2. dry weight
  3. TSF, MAC (on nonaccess arm)
- Laboratory values
  1. BUN and serum creatinine pre and post dialysis
  2. serum albumin
  3. serum transferrin
  4. serum cholesterol and lipid profile
  5. serum calcium

Table 3–22 Food Exchange Lists for Protein, Sodium, and Potassium Control

Summary of Nutrients in One Serving from Each Exchange Group

Exchange Group	kcal*	Protein (g)	Fat (g)	Carbohydrate (g)	Sodium (mEq)	Potassium (mEq)	Phosphorus (mg)
Meat	75	7	5	Trace	1–3–8	2.5	70
Milk	Varies	4	0–2.5–5	6	2.5	4	115
Dessert (made with milk)	150	4	Varies	18	2.5	4	115
Starch	70	2	Trace	15	0.5–8	1.5–4–7–12**	45
Vegetable	25	1	Trace	5	0.5–12	4–7	30
Fruit	60	0.3	Trace	15	Trace	2–4–7	15
Low-protein product	100	0.2	2	20	0.5	Trace	Trace
Fat	45	Trace	5	Trace	0–2	Trace	1
Calorie supplement	100	Trace	Trace	25	Trace	Trace	Trace
Beverage	Varies	Varies	Varies	Varies	Varies	Trace–2–4	Varies

*Average calories per serving noted.

**Potassium content of most starch servings is approximately 1.5 mEq. The higher levels of potassium reflect the potassium content of starchy vegetables within the starch group.

Meat and Meat Substitute

Each exchange contains approximately 7 g of protein and 2.5 mEq of potassium. The sodium content varies. Portion sizes refer to cooked weights.

Unsalted: 1 mEq of Sodium
1 oz	Beef, lamb, pork or veal
1 oz	Poultry
1 oz	Fish; any fresh or frozen
¼ cup	Salmon or tuna, fresh or unsalted, waterpacked
1 oz	Unsalted cheese
2 Tbsp	Unsalted peanut butter* (limit to 1 serving daily)

Salted: 3 mEq of Sodium
1	Egg (no salt added)
¼ cup	Egg substitute (no salt added)
1 oz	Lightly salted meat, fish, poultry (¼ tsp of salt per lb)
1 oz	Liver, heart, kidneys
1 oz	Clams, crab, lobster
2 oz (1 med)	Oysters
1 oz (2 med)	Shrimp
1 oz	Swiss cheese†

High Sodium: 8 mEq of Sodium
¼ cup	Cottage cheese†
1 oz	Cheese†: brick, cheddar, Colby, mozzarella
2 Tbsp	Regular peanut butter* (limit to 1 serving/day)

*These foods contain 6 mEq of potassium and are low biological value protein.
†These foods contain 1 mEq of potassium.

continues

Table 3–22 continued

Milk and Milk Products

Each exchange contains approximately 4 g of protein, 2.5 mEq of sodium, and 4 mEq of potassium.

½ cup	Skim, 2%, or whole milk*
½ cup	Half and half*
¼ cup	Evaporated milk*
2 Tbsp	Nonfat dry milk (before adding liquid)
⅔ cup	Whipping cream, light*
¾ cup	Whipping cream, heavy*
½ cup	Yogurt (plain)

*These foods are to be included in fluid allowance.

Desserts Made with Milk

The following milk products contain additional carbohydrate. Omit one-half serving of carbohydrate supplement in addition to one serving of milk for diabetic patients.

⅓ cup	Bread pudding		¾ cup	Ice cream*
½ cup	Chocolate milk*		⅔ cup	Ice milk*
⅓ cup	Custard		½ cup	Pudding
½ cup	Frozen yogurt dessert*		½ cup	Yogurt (flavored)

*These foods are to be included in fluid allowance.

Starch

Each exchange contains approximately 2 g of protein and 1.5 mEq of potassium unless otherwise specified. Sodium content is indicated. Unsalted cooked cereal, rice, pasta, and starchy vegetables are prepared without salt and contain less than 1 mEq of sodium. Salted cooked cereal, rice, pasta, and starchy vegetables are prepared with ⅛ tsp of salt per serving and contain approximately 10 mEq of sodium per serving.

Unsalted: Less Than 1 mEq of Sodium (Average, 0.5 mEq)

Bread
1 slice	Unsalted bread
1	Tortilla, 6-in diameter

Crackers
6	Saltines, unsalted, 2½-in square

Cereal
½ cup	Barley
½ cup	Cooked cereal (no salt)
¾ cup	Corn flakes, unsalted
¼ cup	Granola
½ cup	Grits (cooked, no salt)
1½ cups	Puffed wheat or rice, unsalted
1 biscuit	Shredded wheat, unsalted
1 Tbsp	Wheat germ (2 mEq of potassium)

continues

Table 3–22 continued

Rice and Pasta
   ⅓ cup   Rice (cooked, no salt)
   ½ cup   Pasta, spaghetti, noodles, macaroni (cooked, no salt)

Starchy Vegetables
   These foods contain more potassium than other foods in this group. If potassium is controlled in the diet, the number of servings of these foods will be limited.
   3 to 5 mEq of Potassium
     ⅓ cup   Corn
     1 small ear Corn on the cob, 3½-in long
     10 (1½ oz) French fried potatoes, 2 to 3½-in long
     ⅓ cup   Lima beans
     ½ small   Sweet potato, baked
     ¼ cup   Sweet potato or yam, canned
   5 to 10 mEq of Potassium
     ½ cup   Mashed potato
     1 small   Potato, peeled, boiled
   10 to 15 mEq of Potassium
     ⅔ cup   Parsnips
     1 small   Potato, baked
     1 cup   Pumpkin
     ¾ cup   Squash: acorn, butternut, or winter

Other Bread Products
   2½ Tbsp Cornmeal, dry
   3 Tbsp   Flour
   1½ cups Popcorn (popped, no salt)

Salted: 5 to 10 mEq of Sodium (Average, 8 mEq)
   Bread: .5 mEq of Potassium
     ½   Bagel
     1 slice   Bread: white (including French or Italian), whole-wheat, rye, raisin
     4   Breadsticks, unsalted tops (4-in long)
     ½   Hamburger bun
     1   Plain roll
   Bread: 3 to 5 mEq of Potassium
     ½   English muffin
     1 slice   Pumpernickel bread
   Cereal: 1.5 mEq of Potassium
     ¾ cup   Cereals, ready to eat
     ½ cup   Cereals (cooked, with ⅛ tsp of salt)
     ½ cup   Barley (cooked, with ⅛ tsp of salt)
     3 Tbsp   Grapenuts
     ½ cut   Grits (cooked, with ⅛ tsp of salt)
   Crackers: 1.5 mEq of Potassium
     10   Animal crackers
     6   Arrowroot
     3   Graham crackers, 2½-in square
     ¾   Matzo, 4-in by 6-in
     5   Melba toast, 2-in by 3¾-in
     3   Rye wafers, 2-in by 3½-in

continues

Table 3–22 continued

6	Round butter or whole-wheat crackers (low sodium)
6	Saltines, unsalted tops, 2½-in square

Rice and Pasta

⅓ cup	Rice (cooked, with ⅛ tsp of salt)
½ cup	Pasta: spaghetti, noodles, macaroni (cooked, with ⅛ tsp of salt)

Starchy Vegetables

These foods contain more potassium than other foods in this group. If potassium is controlled in the diet, the number of servings of these foods will be limited.

3 to 5 mEq of Potassium

⅓ cup	Corn
1 small ear	Corn on the cob, 3½-in long
10 (1½ oz)	French fried potatoes, 2 to 3½-in long
⅓ cup	Lima beans
½ small	Sweet potato, baked
¼ cup	Sweet potato or yam, canned

5 to 10 mEq of Potassium

½ cup	Mashed potato
1 small	Potato, peeled, boiled

10 to 15 mEq of Potassium

⅔ cup	Parsnips
1 small	Potato, baked
1 cup	Pumpkin
¾ cup	Squash: acorn, butternut, or winter

Other Bread Products

½ cup	Chow mein noodles*
1 square	Cornbread, 2-in by 2-in by 1-in*
1 oz	Corn chips, unsalted†
1 small	Croissant†
½ cup	Croutons
¼ cup (4 Tbsp)	Dried bread crumbs
2	Pancakes from mix, 4-in diameter*
1	Pita bread, 6-in diameter
1 small	Plain muffin, biscuit, 2-in diameter*
1 oz	Potato snack chips, unsalted†
¾ oz (25 sticks)	Pretzels, unsalted
2	Taco shells, 6-in diameter*
1	Tortilla, 6-in diameter
1	Waffle, 5-in diameter*

Desserts (Nutrient Content Varies with Recipe)

¹⁄₁₆ of 10-in cake	Angel food cake, plain
1	Cake doughnut, plain
2 small	Cookies, 1¾-in diameter
5	Gingersnaps
2	Ice cream cones (cone only)
2	Shortbread cookies
¹⁄₁₆ of 10-in cake	Sponge cake, plain
5	Vanilla wafers

*These foods contain one additional fat exchange.
†These foods contain two additional fat exchanges.

continues

Table 3–22 continued

Vegetables

Each exchange equals approximately 1 g of protein. Unsalted vegetables are prepared without salt (less than 1 mEq of sodium). Salted vegetables are canned with added salt or prepared with ⅛ tsp of salt per serving (approximately 12 mEq of sodium).

One serving of vegetable equals ½ cup cooked or 1 cup raw unless otherwise specified. There are no "free" vegetables.

Moderate Potassium: 3 to 5 mEq of Potassium (Average, 4 mEq)

Avocado (⅛ med)	Dandelion greens	Peas, green (¼ cup)
Alfalfa sprouts	Eggplant	Pea pods or snow peas
Bean sprouts	Endive	Radishes
Beets	Escarole	Rhubarb
Broccoli	Green pepper	Rutabaga
Cabbage	Green string beans	Summer squash
Carrots	Kale	Turnips
Chard	Lettuce	Water chestnuts
Chinese cabbage	Mustard greens	Watercress
Collards	Onion	Yellow string beans
Cucumbers	Parsley, raw (1 Tbsp)	Zucchini

Higher Potassium: 5 to 10 mEq of Potassium (Average, 7 mEq)

Artichokes	Cauliflower	Mushrooms	Tomatoes
Asparagus	Celery	Okra	Tomato juice (no salt)
Bamboo shoots	Chicory greens	Parsley	Turnip greens
Brussels sprouts	Kohlrabi	Spinach	Vegetable juice cocktail (no salt)

Fruit

Each exchange contains 0.5 g of protein, a trace of sodium, and averages of 2, 4, or 7 mEq of potassium.

Low Potassium: Less Than 3 mEq of Potassium (Average, 2 mEq)

1 small	Apple, fresh, 2-in diameter	1¼ cup	Cranberries
½ cup	Apple juice or cider	⅓ cup	Cranberry juice cocktail
½ cup	Applesauce	1¼ cup	Cranberry juice cocktail
¾ cup	Blueberries		(low calorie)

Moderate Potassium: 3 to 5 mEq of Potassium (Average, 4 mEq)

½ cup	Cherries, canned	½ small	Mango	2 med	Persimmons, native
12	Cherries, fresh	3 med	Passion fruit		
2 large	Dates	½ cup	Peaches, canned	⅓ cup	Pineapple, canned
½ cup	Fruit cocktail	2 halves	Peaches, dried	¾ cup	Pineapple, fresh
½ med	Grapefruit, fresh	1 med	Peach, fresh	½ cup	Pineapple juice
½ cup	Grapefruit juice	½ cup	Peach nectar	3 or ½ cup	Plums, canned
¾ cup	Grapefruit sections	½ cup	Pears, canned	2	Plums, fresh, 2-in
15 small	Grapes, fresh	1 half	Pear, dried	2 Tbsp	Raisins
⅓ cup	Grape juice	1 small	Pear, fresh	1 cup	Raspberries
5 med	Kumquats	½ cup	Pear nectar	1 cup	Rhubarb

continues

Table 3–22 continued

Calorie Supplements

Each exchange contains negligible amounts of protein, sodium, and potassium and 100 kcal.

Sugar and Syrups
2 Tbsp	Sugar
2 Tbsp	Honey
2 Tbsp	Jelly or jam
2 Tbsp	Syrup, pancake or light corn

Candy
3 large	Fondant or sugar mints
5 large	Marshmallows
8 small	Gumdrops
6 pieces	Hard candy, unfilled
10 large, 30 small	Jelly beans
11	Lifesavers™
2 med	Lollipop, unfilled

Fruit Desserts
¼ cup	Cranberry sauce or relish
½ cup	Fruit ice (sherbert made without milk)
1 twin bar	Popsicle™ (2½ oz bar)

Flavored Beverages
1 cup (8 oz)	Carbonated, fruit flavored Kool Aid™, artificially flavored lemonade

Flour Products
¼ cup	Cornstarch or tapioca (may be used to thicken sauces and gravies)

Other Carbohydrate Supplements
¼ cup	Polycose™ powder or liquid (contains 2 mEq of sodium, use as suggested)

Beverages

One cup (8 oz) of the following beverages contains only a trace of protein and sodium. The relative potassium content is noted.

Trace of Potassium

Cola	Orange soda	Gingerale	Postum™
Kool Aid™	Root beer	Lemonade	Seven Up
Limeade	Strawberry soda		

2 mEq of Potassium
Coffee, instant and freeze-dried
Coffee, decaffeinated, instant, and freeze-dried
Decaffeinated coffee, brewed
Tea

4 mEq Potassium
Coffee, brewed

1.5 oz of liqueur contain a trace of sodium and a trace of potassium.
1.5 oz of rum, whiskey, or vodka contain no sodium and a trace of potassium.
12 oz of beer contain 1.5 mEq of sodium and 3 mEq of potassium.
4 oz of wine contain a trace of sodium and 3 mEq of potassium.

continues

Table 3–22 continued

SAMPLE MEAL PLAN

40 g of protein, 2 g of sodium, 2.5 g of potassium, 1000 mg of phosphorus

Morning	Noon	Evening
½ cup oatmeal	¼ cup tuna fish	2 oz. chicken
2 plums	1 slice bread	½ cup broccoli
½ cup pear nectar	2 peach halves	⅓ cup rice
2 tsp margarine	1 Tbsp mayonnaise	½ cup grape juice
½ cup whole milk	½ cup apple pie filling	1 oz angel food cake

Sweetened fruit should be used whenever possible as well as additional fats to starches, vegetables, and meats to increase calories.

Source: Reprinted with permission of Mayo Foundation from CM Pemberton, et al, *Mayo Clinic Diet Manual,* 7th ed, © 1994. Mosby-Year Book, Inc.

---

6. serum phosphorus
7. serum magnesium
8. PCR
- Social history
- Diet history
  1. adequacy of potassium, phosphorus, protein, sodium, fluid, and calorie intake and compliance with dietary recommendations

Attendant problems of hemodialysis treatment include the following:

- Malnutrition, which increases mortality in hemodialysis patients (see Exhibit 3–5)
  1. Enhanced protein breakdown may be caused by the dialysis procedure or factors related to the dialysis treatment.
  2. During one dialysis treatment, approximately 10–13 g of protein can be lost.
  3. Side effects of dialysis treatments include hypotensive episodes, vomiting, and headache; intake may be decreased on these days.
- Anemia from blood loss associated with the dialysis procedure and laboratory testing
- Hyperlipidemia
  1. carnitine deficiency
  2. type IV hyperlipidemia; increased triglycerides, LDL, VLDL, and total cholesterol; decreased HDL
- Renal osteodystrophy

To address these problems and maintain good nutritional status, nutrition counseling should encourage the patient's adherence to protein, potassium, sodium, phosphorus, and fluid allowances as well as meeting of calorie needs (see Table 3–23 for determining nutritional needs). Support from significant others may improve the patient's motivation to comply with the diet. Nutritional supplementation may be needed to meet nutritional needs, eg, Regain (McGaw), Nepro (Ross), or modular carbohydrate, fat, or protein supplements.

The following specific guidelines are suggested:

- Fluids
  1. Dry weight should be checked periodically, as true weight loss can be concealed by chronic overhydration.
  2. Excessive fluid weight gain between treatments should be discouraged (> 1.5 kg between treatments).
  3. Fluid intake should equal urine output plus 500 cc for insensible losses.

Table 3–23 Daily Nutrient Recommendations for Patients with Chronic Renal Failure and for Those Undergoing Hemodialysis and Peritoneal Dialysis

Nutrient	Chronic Renal Failure	Hemodialysis	Peritoneal Dialysis
Protein (based on IBW)	0.6–0.8 g/kg 65% high biologic value 0.8–1.0 g/kg (nephrotic syndrome) 0.28 g/kg (high or low biologic value, supplemented with essential amino acids or keto acids)	1.1–1.4 g/kg	1.2–1.3 g/kg (maintenance) 1.2–1.5 g/kg (repletion/ diabetes)
Calories (based on IBW)	> 35 kcal/kg	30–35 kcal/kg (maintenance)	25–35 g/kg (maintenance; oral + dialysate) 35–50 g/kg (repletion; oral + dialysate) 20–25 g/kg (diabetes; oral + dialysate)
Fat	30%–40% total kcal	30%–40% total kcal	
Sodium	1–3 g if fluid retention present	2–3 g	3–4 g (individualize)
Potassium	< 70 mEq if serum level elevated	1.5–3.0 g	3–4 g (unrestricted unless abnormal)
Calcium	1200–1600 mg (including supplements)	1400–1600 mg	1000–1500 mg
Phosphorus	8–12 mg/kg	12–17 mg/kg	15 mg/g of protein
Iron	100 mg (elemental) if needed	100 mg (elemental)	maintain serum ferritin and transferrin sat. levels
Niacin	20 mg NE	20 mg	RDA
Thiamin (B$_1$)	2 mg	1.5–2.0 mg	RDA
Riboflavin (B$_2$)	2 mg	1.8–2.0 mg	RDA
Pantothenic acid	10 mg	10 mg	RDA
Pyridoxine (B$_6$)	5 mg	10 mg	5–10 mg
Biotin	0.2 mg	0.2–0.3 mg	
Folic acid	0.8–1.0 mg	0.8–1.0 mg	0.4–1.0 mg
Vitamin B$_{12}$	0.003 mg	0.003–0.006 mg	
Vitamin C	60 mg		60–100 mg
Vitamin D			Individualize on the basis of Ca, PTH, alk phos levels
Vitamin A		no additional	
Vitamin E		10 IU	
Zinc		15 mg	10–50 mg if deficient
Fluids		700–1000 ml + urine output	Unrestricted if weight and BP are controlled

Source: Adapted from © 1994, the American Dietetic Association. *A Clinical Guide to Nutrition Care in End-Stage Renal Disease,* 2nd ed. Used by permission.

Exhibit 3–5 Risk Factors for Malnutrition

- Actual body weight less than 80% of ideal body weight
- Unplanned weight loss > 10% of "dry" body weight within a 6-month period
- Decrease of ≥ 15% in anthropometric measurements such as TSF or MAC
- Increased metabolic needs from infection/sepsis, recent surgery, and/or fever
- Nutrient losses secondary to malabsorption
- Persistent nausea, vomiting, and/or diarrhea
- Serum albumin concentration < 3.5 g/dL
- Total serum protein concentration < 6.0 g/dL
- Plasma transferrin concentration < 150 mg/dL
- Protein catabolic rate < 0.8 g/kg of body weight per day
- Cancer and cancer treatment
- Problems with mastication and/or dysphagia

Source: Used with permission of Ross Products Division, Abbott Laboratories, from *Dietetic Currents* (Table 2. Risk Factors for Malnutrition), 1992; 19(3):10.

4. To help with fluid control, advise the patient to
   - avoid high sodium foods
   - take sour hard candies and chewing gum to moisten mouth
   - drink to thirst only
   - rinse with water but not swallow
   - use small cups and glasses for beverages
   - freeze fruit juices and allowed fruit
- Vitamins/minerals (see Table 3–23)
  1. Supplements are needed, as some are lost through dialysis and limited on restrictive diets.
  2. Vitamin C is limited due to oxalate formation.
  3. Dietary phosphate should be restricted (see Table 3–23); phosphate is poorly dialyzed by the artificial kidney.
  4. Supplementation of vitamin A can lead to toxicity in renal failure.
  5. Zinc may be deficient in dialysis patients who complain of anorexia and dysgeusia; supplementation may be indicated.
  6. Iron supplementation of 10–18 mg/day is recommended for losses in dialysis and bleeding.
- Diabetes
  1. Institute a diet appropriate for diabetes.
  2. Supply 1.0–1.2 g of protein/kg/d.
  3. See Table 3–23 for mineral restrictions.
- Hyperlipidemia
  1. Institute a low-cholesterol/low–saturated-fat diet.
  2. Carbohydrates should be complex.
  3. Serum carnitine levels should be evaluated if triglycerides remain elevated despite diet therapy.
- Tube feedings
  1. Formula selection should take restrictions into account.
  2. A calorically dense formula may be needed for fluid control.
  3. Products such as Amin-Aid (McGaw), Nepro (Ross), and Suplena (Ross) are low electrolyte with varying amounts of protein.
- Parenteral nutrition (PN)
  1. PN is indicated with inadequate oral intake and inability to use the gastrointestinal (GI) tract.
  2. Hypophosphatemia is a potential problem.
  3. Monitor intake and output.
  4. Provide a standard amino acid solution.
- Interdialytic parenteral nutrition (IDPN)
  1. IDPN is indicated for treatment of protein-calorie malnutrition that has failed enteral trial. Results have been mixed.
  2. Hypertonic glucose and protein can be administered during dialysis treatment via fistula.
  3. The patient should ingest carbohydrate 15–30 minutes before the infusion is completed to prevent hypoglycemia.

Desired outcomes of treatment are

- improved blood pressure control
- reduced nitrogenous waste products in blood
- achieved or maintained nitrogen balance

Sample IDPN Formula

10% amino acid formula	550 cc	55 g of protein
+ 50% dextrose	250 cc	125 g of carbohydrate
+ 20% lipids	200 cc	40 g of fat
	1050 cc	1005 kcal

1 mg of folic acid, 10 ml of multivitamin, and 1 ml of trace elements can be added.

- decreased risk of renal osteodystrophy
- prevention of hyperkalemia and cardiac arrhythmias
- decreased risk of cardiovascular disease

Peritoneal Dialysis

Peritoneal dialysis is dialysis using the semipermeable membrane of the peritoneum. A catheter is surgically placed into the peritoneal cavity. Highly concentrated dextrose solutions are instilled into the peritoneum. Osmosis and diffusion remove waste products from the blood into the dialysate. The fluid is then removed and discarded. This procedure is usually done four to five times per day with continuous ambulatory peritoneal dialysis (CAPD) or throughout the night, by a machine called a cycler, with continuous cyclic peritoneal dialysis (CCPD) and nocturnal peritoneal dialysis (NPD). With intermittent peritoneal dialysis (IPD), patients are dialyzed by a cycler for 8 to 12 hours, three times per week. IPD is considered less efficient than CCPD or CAPD. Exchanges vary in concentration and volume. The dextrose concentration can be 1.5%, 2.5%, or 4.25% with a volume of 1.0 to 3.0 L per exchange.

Assessment of the Peritoneal Dialysis Patient

- Anthropometric measures
  1. height
  2. dry weight
  3. MAC, TSF
- Laboratory values
  1. serum albumin, total protein
  2. serum transferrin (affected by iron status)
  3. BUN/creatinine
  4. TLC
  5. serum cholesterol, lipid profile
  6. serum calcium
  7. serum potassium
  8. serum phosphorus
  9. PCR; may be an inaccurate measure
- Diet history: adequacy and compliance with protein, calorie, phosphorus, and lipid intake and compliance with dietary recommendations
- Physical exam
- Social history
- Estimated glucose absorption
  1. Initial dialysate solution contains the following amounts of glucose:
     1.5%—15.0 g/L
     2.5%—25.0 g/L
     4.25%—45.5 g/L

See Exhibit 3–6 for calculation examples.

Attendant problems of peritoneal dialysis treatment include the following:

- hyperlipoproteinemia/hyperlipidemia
- malnutrition
  1. loss of 9 g of protein or more through dialysate
  2. peritonitis, increasing protein loss
- renal osteodystrophy
- weight gain/obesity due to 400–700 kcal absorbed daily from dialysate
- hypotension, requiring additional fluid and sodium replacement
- deficiencies in vitamin D, B vitamins, vitamin C, folic acid

Exhibit 3–6 Estimation of Glucose Absorption

Method 1

$y = 11.3 (x) - 10.9$ where

y = glucose absorbed per liter of exchange

x = average initial concentration (g/L) of glucose solution

For example: four 2-L exchanges in 24 hours:
        two exchanges using 2.5% solution
        two exchanges using 4.25% solution

average initial concentration of glucose:

2.5 g/L × 4 L = 10.0 g of glucose

4.25 g/L × 4 L = 17.0 g of glucose

27.0 gm glucose

27.0 g of glucose per 8 L = 3.4 g/L average

$y = 11.3 (3.4) - 10.9$

= 27.5 g of glucose absorbed per liter

27.5 g of glucose per liter × 8 L = 220 g of glucose absorbed/day

220 × 3.4 kcal/g = approximately 749 kcal absorbed/day

Method 2

calories from dialysate = glucose concentration (g/L) × 3.4 (kcal/kg) × 0.8 × volume (L)

For example:

42.5 g/L × 3.4 kcal/g × 0.8 × 4 L = 462 kcal

25.0 g/L × 3.4 kcal/g × 0.8 × 4 L = 272 kcal

approximately 734 kcal absorbed/day

- early satiety
- carnitine deficiency

To address these problems and maintaining good nutritional status, nutrition counseling should include meeting protein needs, maintaining desirable weight or weight control, limiting phosphorus, controlling edema, and controlling hyperlipidemia.

The following specific guidelines are suggested:

- Protein
  1. A dialysate containing 1% amino acids may improve total body nitrogen, serum transferrin, and serum albumin; not all studies show nutritional improvement.
- Energy
  1. Adjusted dietary calorie requirement = dietary calorie requirement – calories from dialysate
- Sodium/fluids
  1. In some patients, a large intake of dietary sodium and water (ie, 6–8 g of sodium, and up to 3 L of water) allows the quantity of fluid removed from the CAPD patient and daily dialysate volume to be increased
  2. Patients with edema, hypertension, and congestive heart failure may require a more restrictive intake of fluids and sodium (see Table 3–23).
- Phosphorus
  1. Eight to 12 mg/kg can decrease the risk of severe hyperparathyroidism.
- Vitamins
  1. Provide water-soluble vitamin supplementation.
  2. Vitamin D supplement may be indicated, as there is a loss through dialysate.
- Minerals/Trace Elements
  1. Calcium
    - The more hypertonic the peritoneal dialysate, the greater the dialysate outflow volume and calcium losses.
    - Supplements may be needed, but no more than 2000 mg of elemental calcium per day.
  2. Iron: for anemia, give iron supplements (10–15 mg/day).
  3. Potassium
    - Restriction is not usually needed, as peritoneal dialysis is a daily procedure.
    - If level is elevated, intake should be restricted to 60–70 mEq/day.
- Early satiety
  1. Drain dialysate prior to mealtime, and reinfuse with fresh exchange at the end of the meal.
  2. Provide small, frequent meals.
- Hyperlipidemia/hyperlipoproteinemia
  1. Provide a low-cholesterol/low–saturated-fat diet.

2. Provide a low-triglyceride diet when triglycerides increase to 50–100 mg/dL above upper limit.
3. If triglycerides are unresponsive to diet therapy, carnitine levels should be measured.
4. Avoid alcohol.

- Diabetes
  1. Follow the diet appropriate for diabetes, adjusted to meet protein and calorie needs.
  2. Control hyperlipidemia and fluid retention.
  3. Institute weight reduction as indicated.
  4. Insulin is added to dialysate rather than being injected subcutaneously. This results in less fluctuation of plasma glucose levels.
  5. There is approximately 15% absorbed glucose. Therefore, 35% of the carbohydrates provided should be low glycemic index and high fiber. Good glycemic control can reduce triglyceride levels.

Desired outcomes of treatment

- achieved or maintained nitrogen balance
- prevention of excessive weight gain
- decreased risk of renal osteodystrophy
- decreased risk of cardiovascular disease

Transplant

A transplant is the surgical implantation of an organ from a living related or cadaveric donor. There are two phases of transplantation. The acute phase occurs immediately post transplant and can last up to 2 months. The chronic phase occurs after the acute phase.

Transplant patients should be assessed on

- Anthropometric measures
  1. height/weight
  2. TSF
  3. MAC
- Laboratory values
  1. serum phosphorus
  2. serum calcium
  3. serum potassium
  4. serum albumin
  5. serum transferrin
  6. TLC
  7. serum cholesterol, lipid profile
  8. PCR (if GFR is < 50 ml/min)
- Diet history
  1. weight changes
  2. nutrient intake
  3. GI symptoms
  4. vitamin supplementation
- Social history
- Physical exam

Attendant problems of transplantation include the following:

- gain of body weight and fat
- corticosteroids, associated with
  1. impaired growth in children
  2. protein wasting
  3. altered serum lipid concentration; increased serum triglycerides, serum cholesterol, VLDL, and LDL
- cardiovascular disease, the major cause of death in transplant patients
- abnormalities in bone metabolism; osteoporosis, inhibition of normal vitamin D, calcium, and phosphorus metabolism
- abnormalities in mineral metabolism
- abnormalities in vitamin metabolism; decreased serum folate
- glucose intolerance
- hypertension and hyperkalemia associated with cyclosporine use
- nutrition deficits, tending to be more severe in diabetics with chronic renal failure
- hyperparathyroidism

To address these problems and maintain good nutritional status, nutrition counseling during the acute and chronic phases should focus on appropriate protein, carbohydrate, and lipid intake; appropriate weight; and calcium, vitamin D, and phosphorus intake.

Nutrition guidelines for the *acute phase* are shown in Table 3–24. In general

- Institute moderate sodium restriction to minimize fluid retention.
- Fluid intake should match urine output.
- A low-carbohydrate diet (1.0 g of carbohydrate per kilogram) can reduce cushingoid

Table 3–24 Posttransplant Nutritional Guidelines

Nutrient	Acute Phase	Long Term
Calories	130% to 150% of BEE, or measure REE	Maintenance: 120% to 130% of BEE, depending on activity level
Protein	1.3 to 2 g/kg/d	1 g/kg/d
Carbohydrate	50% to 70% of total calories (If patient develops steroid-induced diabetes mellitus, limit concentrated sweets)	50% to 70% of total calories (Limit concentrated sweets)
Fat	30% of total calories Up to 50% of total calories with severe hyperglycemia	< 30% of total calories < 10% of calories from saturated fat
Calcium	800 to 1200 mg/d	1000 to 1500 mg/d (consider the need for estrogen or vitamin D supplements)
Sodium	2 to 4 g/d	3 to 4 g/d
Magnesium and phosphorus	Encourage intake of foods high in nutrients Supplement as needed	Encourage intake of foods high in nutrients Supplement as needed
Potassium	Supplement or restrict on basis of serum potassium levels	Supplement or restrict on basis of serum potassium levels
Other vitamins and minerals	Multivitamin/mineral supplement to RDA levels	Multivitamin/mineral supplement to RDA levels

Source: Used with permission of Ross Products Division, Abbott Laboratories, from *Dietetic Currents* (Table 3. Posttransplant Nutritional Guidelines), 1993;20(5):24.

side effects resulting from steroid administration and improve nitrogen balance.
- Diets high in simple carbohydrate can be undesirable, as glucose intolerance frequently occurs due to stress and steroid therapy.
- Hypokalemia can occur due to diuretics and refeeding syndrome.
- Hyperkalemia is associated with cyclosporine use and warrants potassium restriction.
- Hyperphosphatemia should be avoided.

Nutrition guidelines for the *long term* are also shown in Table 3–24. In general

- Sodium
  1. Intake should be individualized.
  2. Limit intake with hypertension and edema.
- Lipids
  1. Institute a low-cholesterol/low–saturated-fat diet.
  2. Limit simple carbohydrates with increased triglyceride levels
  3. Encourage exercise.
  4. Fish oil, 3 g/d, may be given to transplant patients with increased triglyceride levels who are not amenable to traditional diet therapy.

- Appropriate calorie restriction for weight control
- Diabetes/steroid-induced diabetes
  1. Institute a diet appropriate for diabetes.
  2. Control weight.
  3. Encourage exercise.
- Vitamins/minerals
  1. Vitamin A supplements should not be given, as levels are increased in transplant patients.
  2. Provide calcium supplementation to decrease bone wasting.

Desired outcomes of treatment are

- minimized long-term complications (obesity, hypertension, hyperlipidemia, new-onset diabetes, bone disease)
- enhanced quality of life

ACUTE RENAL FAILURE

Description

Acute loss of excretory function can be reversible. There are three phases. During the *oliguric phase*, urine volume is decreased, and azotemia and acidosis develop, with increased potassium and phosphorus levels, high blood pressure, and edema. During the *diuretic phase*, there are large fluid and electrolyte losses. The *recovery phase* is a gradual return of renal function.

Cause

- Shock
- Sepsis
- Trauma
- Multisystem organ failure
- Obstruction
- Toxins
- Medications (most commonly aminoglycoside antibiotics)
- Certain types of glomerulonephritis
- Rhabdomyolysis

Assessment

- Anthropometrics
  1. height/weight (without edema)
  2. TSF/MAC (may be skewed depending on fluid status)
- Diet history
  1. special diet
  2. vitamin/mineral supplement
  3. weight changes
  4. GI symptoms (diarrhea/constipation/nausea/vomiting)
  5. other medications
  6. alcohol or drug abuse
  7. other disease states
  8. chewing/swallowing ability
- Physical exam
  1. edema
  2. cachexia or obesity
  3. decreased muscle mass
  4. decubitus ulcers
  5. skin turgor
  6. ascites
- Laboratory values
  1. GFR
  2. BUN/serum creatinine
  3. serum potassium
  4. serum phosphorus
  5. serum calcium
  6. serum magnesium
  7. intake and output
  8. serum albumin
  9. serum transferrin
  10. serum glucose
- Determination of appropriate feeding route
  1. oral
  2. enteral feeding tube
  3. total parenteral nutrition (TPN)
  4. combination of above

Problems

- Extensive protein catabolism and negative nitrogen balance
  1. Underlying medical condition could be the cause (eg, infection, surgery, trauma).
  2. Treatments of hemodialysis and continuous arteriovenous dialysis (CAVH) increase protein losses.
- Insulin resistance; hyperglycemia
- Metabolic acidosis

1. Affects glucose metabolism by contributing to glucose intolerance
- Altered lipid metabolism
  1. increased VLDL and LDL
  2. decreased cholesterol and HDL
- Electrolyte imbalance
  1. hyperphosphatemia; but hypophosphatemia can occur with nutrition support
  2. hyperkalemia; but may be decreased with nutrition support and volume depletion
  3. hypocalcemia from losses through fistulas and dialysis
- decreased oral intake due to nausea/vomiting and confusion

Treatment/Management

Nutrition therapy should consist of control of protein, sodium, potassium, fluids, and calories according to dialysis and the needs of the individual:

- Energy
  1. Using Harris-Benedict equation, compute basal energy expenditure (BEE) $\times$ 1.3.
  2. Using indirect calorimetry, compute resting energy expenditure $\times$ 1.25.
  3. 30–45 kcal/kg desirable body weight.
- Protein
  1. Provide 0.6–0.8 g/kg/day in unstressed nondialyzed patients or 30–40 g of protein per day.
  2. To avoid or decrease frequency of dialysis, with severely low GFR, 0.3–0.5 g/kg/day of essential amino acids (EAA) can be used; however, more than 40 g/day may cause amino acid imbalance.
  3. Provide 1.0–1.2 g/kg/day with catabolism and dialysis.
  4. Provide 1.2–1.5 g/kg/day with peritoneal dialysis.
  5. Histidine and arginine are conditionally essential.
- Fluids
  1. Supply amount of urine output plus 500 cc for insensible loss.

2. With vomiting and diarrhea, give additional fluid.
3. Provide small volume with oliguric phase.
4. Provide up to 3 L in diuretic stage.
- Sodium
  1. Possibly restrict in oliguric phase (500–1000 mg/day).
- Potassium
  1. Restrict in oliguric phase (< 2 g/day).
  2. Possibly supplement during diuretic phase.
- Vitamins
  1. Vitamin C should be limited to 60–100 mg/day.
  2. Water-soluble vitamins should be supplemented.
  3. Avoid vitamin A, as levels are increased.
  4. Vitamin D requirements not well defined.
  5. Supplement vitamin K if the patient is not eating and is receiving antibiotics.

The following are nutritional guidelines for different feeding routes:

- Oral feedings
  1. High-calorie and, depending on provision of dialysis, high-protein supplements may be necessary to meet nutritional needs.
  2. The patient may need sodium, potassium, fluid, and/or phosphorus restrictions.
  3. Make consistency modifications as indicated.
- Enteral/tube feedings
  1. The enteral route should be used whenever possible, as feedings help to maintain the GI tract and prevent bacterial translocation.
  2. Formulas should be calorically dense.
  3. Take into account nutrient needs and restrictions.
- Parenteral feedings (see Appendix S)
  1. D70 should be infused at approximately 5 g/kg/day; otherwise there is a potential of lipogenesis with fatty infiltrate of the liver, excessive carbon dioxide production, and hypercarbia.
  2. lipid emulsions should be infused over 12–24 hours to prevent impairment of the reticuloendothelial system.

—These should be supplied as 10% and 20% emulsions providing 1.1 and 2.0 kcal/cc, respectively.

—They may provide 40%–50% of total calories but should not exceed 60%.

—They can be given to prevent essential fatty acid deficiency (500 cc of 10% emulsion three times per week).

—Triglycerides should be monitored, and lipids should not be given if levels are over 350 mg/dL.

3. protein

—EAA have value in helping to stabilize BUN and decrease production of urea nitrogen.

—EAA should not be used alone > 7 days, as the small amount of nitrogen provided is usually inadequate to meet requirements if given for a prolonged period. Once the BUN stabilizes or starts to fall below 70 mg/dL, increase the amino acids by adding 250 cc of a standard (8.5%) solution.

4. Serum concentrations of potassium, phosphorus, and magnesium may decrease and need supplementation.

5. Trace mineral requirements have not been defined in uremic patients receiving TPN and are probably not necessary, with the exception of zinc and iron.

6. CAVH and TPN have been combined to provide intravenous nutrition and control fluid and mineral imbalances.

7. IDPN can be beneficial for stable patients who have slightly suboptimal intake of nutrients; it is probably inadequate for stressed uremic patients because their intakes are decreased and their needs are increased.

Desired outcomes for treatment are

- decreased protein catabolism and wasting of lean body mass
- prevented overhydration
- minimized accumulation of nitrogenous wastes in the blood

NEPHROTIC SYNDROME

Description

Nephrotic syndrome is a complex of symptoms caused by increased glomerular permeability, resulting in loss of plasma proteins into the urine. It is characterized by proteinuria (> 3 g/day), lipiuria, hypoalbuminemia, hypercholesterolemia, and edema.

Cause

- Diabetes mellitus
- Glomerulonephritis
- Renal vein thrombosis

Assessment

- Anthropometric measures
  1. height
  2. weight gain or loss
  3. TSF/MAC (without edema)
- Laboratory values
  1. serum albumin
  2. serum cholesterol and lipid profile
  3. serum calcium
  4. serum phosphorus
  5. urinalysis; proteinuria
- Diet history
  1. assessment of calorie, protein, sodium, and lipid intake

Problems

- Hyperlipoproteinemia
- Massive proteinuria, leading to catabolism of lean body mass
- Anorexia
- Urinary losses of vitamins and trace elements that are protein bound
- Edema
- Loss of immunoglobulin, which can increase infection risk
- Loss of transferrin, which can lead to anemia
- Hypocalcemia
- Hypovitaminosis D

Treatment/Management

Nutrition counseling should focus on appropriate protein, calorie, lipid, and sodium intake:

- Protein
  1. Diets high in protein increase renal injury.
  2. Protein-restricted diets decrease progression of renal failure.
  3. Supply 0.8–1.0 g of protein/kg/day.
- Energy
  1. Provide 35 kcal/kg/day for weight maintenance.
  2. Provide 20–25 kcal/kg/day for weight loss.
  3. Provide 40–50 kcal/kg/day for weight gain.
- Lipids
  1. Provide a low-cholesterol/low–saturated-fat diet
- Sodium
  1. Restrict with edema and tendency to retain sodium (60–90 mEq/day).
- Vitamins
  1. Supplement normal daily allowance for fat- and water-soluble vitamins.
- Minerals
  1. Supplement zinc, iron, and copper if there is a large amount of proteinuria.

Desired outcomes of treatment are

- controlled blood pressure
- minimized edema
- decreased urinary albumin loss
- decreased protein malnutrition/prevented muscle catabolism
- slowed progression of renal disease

KIDNEY STONES

Description

Kidney stones are formed when the concentration of components in the urine reaches a level in which crystallization occurs. The stones can be composed of calcium salts, uric acid, cystine, or struvite.

Cause

- A bowel disease causing malabsorption
- Cysteinuria
- Glucocorticoid excess
- Hyperparathyroidism
- Paget's disease
- Recurrent urinary tract infections
- Vitamin D intoxication
- Excessive vitamin C ingestion

Assessment

- Diet history: Assess for excess intake of calcium, oxalate, purines, protein, and vitamin C.

Problems

- Extremely painful when passing through the ureters
- Can block urine flow or cause infection

Treatment/Management

- Ensure a large volume of oral fluid intake, to produce > 2 L of urine per day; the goal is to keep the urine dilute to prevent crystallization.
- Avoid excessive doses of vitamin C, which metabolizes to oxalate.
- There may be benefit in limiting protein intake to Recommended Dietary Allowance (RDA).
- Additional nutrition therapy depends upon stone type:
  1. Calcium stones
     - Patients with absorptive hypercalciuria type II should be limited to the RDA for calcium and should avoid calcium-containing antacids.
     - Vitamin D can increase absorption of calcium.
     - In other forms of hypercalciuria, a low-calcium diet is not indicated.
     - A low-oxalate diet should be followed (see Appendix E)
  2. Calcium oxalate stones
     - Restrict foods high in oxalate (see Appendix E).

−Maintain an adequate calcium intake; provide calcium supplementation as needed.

−Patients with steatorrhea should keep to a low-fat diet.

−A moderate sodium intake (4–5 g/day) may reduce excessive calcium levels in the urine with or without use of thiazide diuretics.

3. Uric acid stones

−Provide a low-purine diet (includes avoidance of organ meats, sweetbreads, brains, anchovies, sardines, meat extracts, gravy broth, and bouillon).

−Alkaline-ash diets (see Appendix A) manipulate urine pH nutritionally to supplement the effects of medical therapy. But the diet can be monotonous and compliance poor. It may be sufficient to avoid excessive amounts of foods.

4. Cystine stones

−An alkaline-ash diet may be followed (see Appendix A)

5. struvite stones

−No nutrition management is indicated.

Desired outcomes are

• reduced intake of stone-forming materials
• decreased recurrence of stones
• maintained dilute urine

REFERENCES

Alfrey AC, Hammond WS. Renal iron handling in the nephrotic syndrome. *Kidney Int.* 1990;37:1409–1413.

Allman A, et al. Energy supplementation and nutritional status of hemodialysis patients. *Am J Clin Nutr.* 1990;51:558–562.

Alvestrand A. Protein metabolism and nutrition in hemodialysis. *Contrib Nephrol.* 1990;78:102–118.

American Dietetic Association. Nutrition recommendations and principles for people with diabetes mellitus. *J Am Diet Assoc.* 1994;94:504–506.

Ames M, Bayne C, et al. Renal disease. In: Pemberton CM, Moxness KE, et al, eds. *Mayo Clinic Diet Manual.* 6th ed. Toronto, Canada: BC Decker, Inc; 1988:212–255.

Askanazi J, Rosenbaum SH, et al. Respiratory changes induced by the large glucose loads of total parenteral nutrition. *JAMA.* 1980;243:1444–1447.

Auwerx J, DeKeyser L, et al. Decreased free 1,25 dihydroxycholecalciferol index in patients with nephrotic syndrome. *Nephron.* 1986;42:231–235.

Bergstrom J. Nutritional requirements of hemodialysis patients. In: Mitch WE, Klahr S, eds. *Nutrition and the Kidney*, 2nd ed. Boston, Mass: Little, Brown and Co; 1993:263–289.

Bilbrey GL, Cohen TL. Identification and treatment of protein calorie malnutrition in chronic hemodialysis patients. *Dial Transplant.* 1989;18:669–700.

Blake PG, Sombolos K, Abraham G, et al. Lack of correlation between urea kinetic indices and clinical outcomes in CAPD patients. *Kidney Int.* 1991;37:700–706.

Blue LS. Nutrition considerations in kidney transplantation. *Top Clin Nutr.* 1992;7:17–23.

Blumenkrantz MJ, et al. Methods for assessing nutritional status of patients with renal failure. *Am J Clin Nutr.* 1980;33:1567–1585.

Blumenkrantz MJ, Gahl GM, et al. Protein losses during peritoneal dialysis. *Kidney Int.* 1981;19:593–602.

Blumenkrantz MJ, Kopple JD, et al. Metabolic balance studies and dietary protein requirements in patients undergoing continuous ambulatory peritoneal dialysis. *Kidney Int.* 1982;21:849–861.

Blumenkrantz MJ, Kopple JD, et al. Nitrogen metabolism and urea kinetics in patients undergoing continuous ambulatory peritoneal dialysis. *Kidney Int.* 1979;16:882.

Bodnar DM. An update on peritoneal dialysis and nutrition. *Support Line.* 1993;15:5–8.

Bosch JP. Continuous arteriovenous hemofiltration: operational characteristics and clinical use. *AKF Nephrol Lett.* 1986;3:15.

Bouffard Y, et al. Energy expenditure in the acute renal failure patient mechanically ventilated. *Intensive Care Med.* 1987;13:401–404.

Brodsky IG, Robbins DC, et al. Effects of low protein diets on protein metabolism in insulin-dependent diabetes mellitus patients with early nephropathy. *J Clin Endocrinol Metab.* 1992;75:351–357.

Brown WW, Wolfson M. Diet as culprit or therapy: stone disease, chronic renal failure, and nephrotic syndrome. *Med Clin North Am.* 1993;77:783–794.

Burrowes JD, Levin NW. Morbidity and mortality in dialysis patients. *Diet Curr.* 1992;19:1–4.

Burton BJ, Hirshman GH. Current concepts of nutritional therapy in renal failure: an update. *J Am Diet Assoc.* 1983;82:359–363.

Carvounis CD, et al. Nutritional status of maintenance hemodialysis patients. *Am J Clin Nutr.* 1986;43:946–954.

Chan MK, et al. Lipid abnormalities in uremia. *Kidney Int.* 1981;19:625–634.

Compher CW. Nutrition assessment in chronic renal failure. *Nutr Support Serv.* 1985;5:18–21.

Curtis JJ, Luke RG, et al. Hypertension in cyclosporine-treated renal transplant recipients is sodium dependent. *Am J Med.* 1988;85:134–138.

D'Amico G, Remuzzi G, et al. Effect of dietary proteins and lipids in patients with membranous nephropathy and nephrotic syndrome. *Clin Nephrol.* 1991;35:237–242.

Davis SP, Reaveley DA, et al. Amino acid clearances and daily losses in patients with acute renal failure treated by continuous arteriovenous hemofiltration. *Crit Care Med.* 1991;19:1510–1515.

Dietch EA, Winterton J, Berg R. The gut as a portal of entry for bacteremia. *Ann Surg.* 1987;205:681–692.

Disler PB, Goldberg LK, et al. The role of diet in the pathogenesis and control of hyperlipidemia after renal transplantation. *Clin Nephrol.* 1981;16:29–34.

Druml W. Nutritional support in acute renal failure. In: Mitch WE, Klahr S, eds. *Nutrition and the Kidney.* 2nd ed. Boston, Mass: Little, Brown and Co; 1993:314–345.

Dwyer J, Kenler SR. Assessment of nutritional status in renal disease. In: Mitch WE, Klahr S, eds. *Nutrition and the Kidney.* 2nd ed. Boston, Mass: Little, Brown and Co; 1993:61–89.

Evanoff G, et al. Prolonged dietary protein restriction in diabetic nephropathy. *Arch Intern Med.* 1989;149:1129–1133.

Feinstein EI, Blumenkrantz MJ, et al. Clinical and metabolic responses to parenteral nutrition in acute renal failure. *Med.* 1981;60:124–137.

Feinstein EI, Kopple JD, et al. Total parenteral nutrition with high or low nitrogen intakes in patients with acute renal failure. *Kidney Int.* 1983;26:S319–S323.

Fleming LW, et al. The effect of oral aluminum therapy on plasma aluminum levels in patients with chronic renal failure in an area with low water aluminum. *Clin Nephrol.* 1982;17:222.

Foulks, CJ. Nutritional evaluation of patients on maintenance dialysis therapy. *ANNA J.* 1988;15:41–47.

Franz MJ, Horton ES, et al. Nutrition principles for the management of diabetes and related complications (technical review). *Diabetes Care.* 1994;17:490–518.

Gammarino M. Renal transplant diet: recommendations for the acute phase. *Dial Transplant.* 1987;16:497–502.

Goldfarb S. Dietary factors in the pathogenesis and prophylaxis of calcium nephrolithiasis. *Kidney Int.* 1988;34:544–555.

Golper TA. Continuous arteriovenous hemofiltration in acute renal failure. *Am J Kidney Dis.* 1985;6:373–386.

Grant A, Dehoog S. History and anthropometry. In: Grant A, Dehoog S, eds. *Nutrition Assessment and Support.* 3rd ed. Seattle, Wash: Anne Grant and Susan Dehoog Publishers; 1985:1–18.

Grodstein GP, Blumenkrantz MJ, et al. Glucose absorption during continuous ambulatory peritoneal dialysis. *Kidney Int.* 1981;19:564–567.

Grodstein GP, Kopple JD. Urea nitrogen appearance: a simple and practical indicator of total nitrogen output. *Kidney Int.* 1979;16:953.

Harum P. Indications for intradialytic parenteral nutrition (IDPN). *Nephrol News Issues.* 1990;7:18–31.

Harvey KB, et al. Nutritional assessment and treatment of chronic renal failure. *Am J Clin Nutr.* 1980;33:1586–1597.

Hasse J. Nutritional management of renal transplant patients. *Diet Curr.* 1993;20:1–4.

Holmes J. Intradialytic parenteral nutrition. *Contemp Dial Nephrol.* 1990;4:50–53.

Hostetter TH, Mitch WE. Protein intake and the prevention of chronic renal disease. In: Schrier RW, Gottschalk CW, eds. *Diseases of the Kidney.* 5th ed. Boston, Mass: Little, Brown and Co; 1993:3131–3149.

Hoy WE, Sargent JA, et al. Protein catabolism during postoperative course after renal transplantation. *Am J Kidney Dis.* 1985;5:786–790.

Joven J, Villabona C, et al. Abnormalities of lipoprotein metabolism in patients with nephrotic syndrome. *N Engl J Med.* 1990;323:579–584.

Kaysen GA. The nephrotic syndrome: nutritional consequences and dietary management. In: Mitch WE, Klahr S, eds. *Nutrition and the Kidney.* 2nd ed. Boston, Mass: Little, Brown and Co; 1993:213–242.

Kaysen GA, Ganbertoglio J, et al. Effect of dietary protein intake on albumin homeostasis in nephrotic patients. *Kidney Int.* 1986;29:572–577.

Klahr S, Levey AS, et al. The effects of dietary protein restriction and blood pressure control on the progression of chronic renal disease. *N Engl J Med.* 1994;330:887–884.

Kluthe R, Luttgen FM, et al. Protein requirements in maintenance hemodialysis. *Am J Clin Nutr.* 1978;31:1812–1820.

Kopple JD. Nutritional status of patients with different levels of chronic renal failure. *Kidney Int.* 1989;27:S184–S194.

Kopple JD. Dietary considerations in patients with advanced chronic renal failure, acute renal failure and transplantation. In: Schrier RW, Gottschalk CW, eds. *Diseases of the Kidney.* 5th ed. Boston, Mass: Little, Brown and Co; 1993:3167–3210.

Kopple JD. Nutrition, diet and the kidney. In: Shils M, Olson J, Shike M, eds. *Modern Nutrition in Health and Disease.* 8th ed. Philadelphia, Pa: Lea & Febiger; 1994:1110–1134.

Kopple JD, Hirschberg R. Nutrition and peritoneal dialysis. In: Mitch WE, Klahr S, eds. *Nutrition and the Kidney.* 2nd ed. Boston, Mass: Little, Brown and Co; 1993:290–311.

Kopple JD, Monteon FJ, Shaib JK. Effect of energy intake on nitrogen metabolism in non-dialyzed patients with chronic renal failure. *Kidney Int.* 1986;29:734.

Kopple JD, Swendseid ME. Evidence that histidine is an essential amino acid in normal and chronically uremic man. *J Clin Invest.* 1975;55:881.

Krumlovsky, FA. Disorders of protein and lipid metabolism associated with chronic renal failure and chronic dialysis. *Ann Clin Lab Sci.* 1981;11:350–360.

Lau YK, Wasserstein AG, et al. Proximal tubular defects in idiopathic hypercalcuria: resistance to phosphate administration. *Mineral Electrolyte Metab.* 1982;7:f237–249.

Legrain M, Rottembourg J. Peritoneal dialysis in diabetics. In: Nolph KD, ed. *Peritoneal Dialysis.* Boston, Mass: M Nijhoff; 1985:506.

Levey AS. Measurement of renal function in chronic renal disease. *Kidney Int.* 1990;38:167–184.

Lowrie EG, Lew NL. Death risk in hemodialysis patients. *Am J Kidney Dis.* 1990;15:458–482.

Madigan KM, Olshan A, Yingling DJ. Effectiveness of intradialytic parenteral nutrition in diabetic patients with end-stage renal disease. *J Am Diet Assoc.* 1990;9:861–863.

Mai ML, Emmett M, et al. Calcium acetate: an effective phosphorus binder in patients with renal failure. *Kidney Int.* 1989;36:690–695.

Mansy H, Goodship THJ, et al. Effect of a high protein diet in patients with nephrotic syndrome. *Clin Sci.* 1989;77:445–451.

Marckmann P. Nutritional status and mortality of patients in regular dialysis therapy. *J Intern Med.* 1989;26:429–432.

Maroni JB. Requirements for protein, calories and fat in the predialysis patient. In: Mitch WE, Klahr S, eds. *Nutrition and the Kidney.* 2nd ed. Boston, Mass: Little, Brown and Co; 1993:185–212.

Massry SG, Kopple JD. Requirements for calcium, phosphorus and vitamin D. In: Mitch WE, Klahr S, eds. *Nutrition and the Kidney.* 2nd ed. Boston, Mass: Little, Brown and Co; 1993:96–110.

Matarese LE. Renal failure. In: Gottschlich MM, Matarese LE, Shronts EP, eds. *Nutrition Support Dietetics Core Curriculum.* 2nd ed. Silver Spring, Md: American Society for Parenteral and Enteral Nutrition; 1993:327–340.

McCann L. Nutrition management of the adult peritoneal dialysis patient. In: Stover J, ed. *A Clinical Guide to Nutrition Care in End-Stage Renal Disease.* 2nd ed. Chicago, Ill: American Dietetic Association; 1994:45–55.

Miller DG, et al. Nutritional status of diabetic and nondiabetic patients after renal transplantation. *Am J Clin Nutr.* 1986;44:66–69.

Mirtallo JM, et al. A comparison of essential amino acid infusions on the nutritional support of patients with compromised renal function. *JPEN.* 1982;6:109.

Mitch WE. Rationale and prospects for nutritional therapy in renal failure. In: *Renal Nutrition: Report of the Eleventh Ross Roundtable on Medical Issues.* Columbus, Ohio: Ross Laboratories; 1991:1–5.

Mitch WE, May RC, et al. Influence of insulin resistance and amino acid supply on muscle protein turnover. *Kidney Int.* 1987;32(suppl 22):104–108.

Moore LW. Nutrition in end-stage renal disease: a life cycle perspective. *Nephrol Nurs Today.* 1991;1:1–8.

Motil KJ, Harmon WE, et al. Complications of essential amino acid hyperalimentation in children with acute renal failure. *JPEN.* 1980;4:32.

Nath KA, Hostetter TH. Nutritional requirements of diabetics with nephropathy. In: Mitch WE, Klahr S, eds. *Nutrition and the Kidney.* 2nd ed. Boston, Mass: Little, Brown and Co; 1993:152–184.

Norwood K. An expanded role for the dietitian in the treatment of renal osteodystrophy and secondary hyperparathyroidism. *Contemp Dial Nephrol.* 1987;8:22–26.

Pagenkamper JJ. Attaining nutritional goals for hyperlipidemic and obese renal patients. In: *Renal Nutrition: Report of the Eleventh Ross Roundtable on Medical Issues.* Columbus, Ohio: Ross Laboratories; 1991:26–33.

Pagenkemper JJ, DiMarco NM, et al. The management of hypertriglyceridemia and hypercholesterolemia by omega-3 fatty acids in renal transplant patients. *CRN Q.* 1989;13:9.

Pak CYC, et al. Ambulatory evaluation of nephrolithiasis: classification, clinical presentation and diagnostic criteria. *Am J Med.* 1980;69:19.

Pak CYC, et al. Evidence justifying a high fluid intake in treatment of nephrolithiasis. *Ann Intern Med.* 1980;93:36–39.

Panzetta G, Maschio G. Dietary problems of the dialysis patient. *Blood Purification.* 1985;3:63–74.

Powers DV. Prolonged experience with intradialytic hyperalimentation in marasmic chronic hemodialysis patients: an overview. *Contemp Dial Nephrol.* 1989;5:22–28.

Pruchno CJ, Hunsicker LG. Nutritional requirements of renal transplant patients. In: Mitch WE, Klahr S, eds. *Nutrition and the Kidney.* 2nd ed. Boston, Mass: Little, Brown and Co; 1993:346–364.

Pruchno CJ, Wilkins KE, Schroeder KW. Nutritional care in renal disease. In: Mahan LK, Arlin MT, eds. *Krause's Food, Nutrition, and Diet Therapy.* Philadelphia, Pa: WB Saunders Co; 1992:592–623.

Salahudeen AK, Hostetter TH. Effects of dietary protein in patients with chronic renal transplant refection. *Kidney Int.* 1992;41:183–190.

Sargent J, Gotch F, et al. Urea kinetics: a guide to nutritional management of renal failure. *Am J Clin Nutr.* 1978;31:1696–1702.

Schneeweiss B, Graininger W, et al. Energy metabolism in acute and chronic renal failure. *Am J Clin Nutr.* 1990;52: 596.

Schmitz O. Insulin-mediated glucose uptake in non-dialyzed and dialyzed uremic insulin-dependent diabetic subjects. *Diabetes.* 1985;34:1152.

Schrier RW. Acute renal failure. *JAMA.* 1982;247:2518–2525.

Seidner DL, Mascioli EA, et al. Effect of long-chain triglyceride emulsions on reticuloendothelial system function in humans. *JPEN.* 1989;6:614–619.

Stec J, Podracka L, et al. Zinc and copper metabolism in nephrotic syndrome. *Nephron.* 1990;56:186–187.

Warwick GL, Caslake MJ, et al. Low-density lipoprotein metabolism in the nephrotic syndrome. *Metab.* 1990;39: 187–192.

Whitney EN, Cataldo CB, Rolfes SR. Disorders of the kidneys. In: *Understanding Normal and Clinical Nutrition.* 2nd ed. St Paul, Minn: West Publishing Co; 1987:812–834.

Whittier FC, Evans DH, et al. Nutrition in renal transplantation. *Am J Kidney Dis.* 1985;6:405–411.

Wolfson M, Jones MR, Kopple JD. Amino acid losses during hemodialysis with infusion of amino acids and glucose. *Kidney Int.* 1981;21:500–506.

Zeller KR. Low protein diets in renal disease. *Diabetes Care.* 1991;14:856–866.

Zeller K, et al. Effect of restricting dietary protein on the progression of renal failure in patients with insulin-dependent diabetes mellitus. *N Engl J Med.* 1991;324:78–84.

Solid Organ Transplantation

Jeanette Hasse

DESCRIPTION

Solid organ transplantation is a viable option for individuals suffering from end-stage organ failure that is refractory to medical or surgical treatment. Living donors can donate kidneys, and sometimes a family member may donate a portion of his or her liver to a pediatric recipient. The majority of donor organs are cadaveric (from a brain-dead donor).

TYPES OF ORGAN TRANSPLANTATION

- heart
- kidney
- liver
- lung
- pancreas
- small bowel

NUTRITIONAL ASSESSMENT

Objective Nutritional Assessment Parameters

Many objective parameters can be affected by symptoms of organ failure (eg, fluid retention) or by organ failure itself (eg, inability of the liver to synthesize serum proteins during failure). Table 3–25 shows factors that must be taken into consideration if objective parameters are used to help determine nutritional status.

Subjective Nutritional Assessment Parameters

Evaluating subjective parameters of nutritional status is vital to assess transplant patients. A patient's nutritional status usually can be determined using the Subjective Global Assessment technique alone. The evaluator should focus especially on persistent or recurring symptoms and the findings of the physical examination. The primary confounding factors for obtaining subjective history are the ability of the patient to recall the information and the ability of the evaluator to do a brief physical assessment. The following areas should be covered:

- weight history (ask about weight changes due to fluid fluctuations)
- appetite history
- dietary history (current and recent dietary intake compared to estimated needs)

Table 3–25 Nutritional Assessment Parameters and Confounding Factors

Parameter	Confounding Factors
Laboratory Measures	
Serum albumin	Hydration; albumin infusion; liver function; administration of corticosteroids; renal insufficiency; zinc deficiency; burn; loss through skin, GI tract, or wound; blood loss
Serum transferrin	Hydration, liver function, iron deficiency or overload, zinc deficiency, increased excretion from burns or nephrotic syndrome
Serum thyroxine-binding prealbumin	Hydration, liver function, renal function, infection
Serum retinol-binding protein	Hydration, renal failure, vitamin A supplementation or deficiency, hyperthyroidism, cystic fibrosis
Total lymphocyte count	Immunosuppressive medication, infection, cancer, liver disease, kidney failure, trauma
Glycosylated hemoglobin	Uremia, aspirin intake, alcoholism, anemia
Anthropometric Measures	
Body weight	Hydration
Triceps skinfolds	Hydration, age, evaluator's technique, insensitive measurement (ie, small changes over a short period of time are difficult to detect)
Midarm circumference	Hydration, evaluator's technique, insensitive measurement (ie, small changes over a short period of time are difficult to detect)
Other Objective Measures	
Skin antigen testing	Immunosuppressive medication
Creatinine-height index	Liver and renal function, aging, protein intake
Nitrogen balance	Renal function, protein intake, other sites of losses (eg, ostomy, chest tubes)
3-methylhistidine excretion	Age, sex, protein intake, renal function, infection
Indirect calorimetry	Measurement will vary with changes in patient's condition

- Gastrointestinal (GI) symptoms (duration and severity of nausea, vomiting, diarrhea, steatorrhea, constipation)
- ability to chew and swallow
- current diet restrictions
- use of dietary and/or vitamin and mineral supplements
- use of tube feeding or parenteral nutrition
- diabetes history
- alcohol usage
- social history
- coexisting diseases
- current medications
- physical exam (muscle, fat, edema, ascites)
- current physical functional capacity

PRETRANSPLANT PROBLEMS AND TREATMENT

See sections on organ failure: "Cardiology," "Gastroenterology," "Pulmonary Conditions," and "Renal Conditions."

POSTTRANSPLANT PROBLEMS

Common nutritional problems over the short-term posttransplant (usually up to 2 months posttransplant)

- depressed appetite
- early satiety
- taste changes

- GI problems (nausea, vomiting, diarrhea, constipation)
- preexisting malnutrition

Common nutritional problems over the long-term posttransplant (usually up to 2 months post-transplant)

- increased appetite
- excessive weight gain
- hyperlipidemia
- hypertension
- diabetes
- osteoporosis

Medical complications following transplantation influence nutrition

- Infection
  1. Nutritional needs can increase.
  2. Treatment with medications can cause anorexia, nausea, vomiting, or diarrhea.
- Rejection
  1. Treatment often involves administering additional corticosteroids, which can cause hyperglycemia and increase nitrogen loss.
  2. Persistent rejection may require the use of monoclonal antibodies (OKT3), which can cause anorexia, nausea, vomiting, or diarrhea.
- Technical problems (eg, bleeding, anastomotic leakages)
  1. If surgery is required to treat the problem, the patient may require a period of NPO status.
  2. If a patient is significantly malnourished, nutrition support should be considered.
- Renal insufficiency
  1. It may be necessary to restrict protein, sodium, fluid, or potassium.
  2. If dialysis is initiated, diet goals need to be adjusted.
- Organ failure
  1. Refer to sections on organ failure for review of nutritional needs during organ dysfunction.

There are special nutritional considerations unique to small-bowel transplant patients:

- Transit time
  1. Transit time can vary from 30 minutes to 5 hours (mean = 2 hours).
  2. A sudden change in transit time may suggest infection or rejection.
  3. Some transplant teams use paregoric, loperamide, immodium, pectin, or somatostatin to increase transit time after rejection is excluded.
- Malabsorption
  1. Lacteals and lymphatics are severed during transplant, resulting in malabsorption.
  2. Some carbohydrate enzymes are deficient in the early posttransplant phase.
  3. A lactose- and fat-restricted diet is better tolerated early posttransplant than a full liquid diet.
- Ostomy output
  1. Output can be as high as > 4 L/day.
  2. Fluid and electrolytes need to be replenished daily.
  3. Metabolic acidosis may occur and may require treatment with sodium bicarbonate.
  4. Zinc supplementation may be required with increased ostomy output.

Transplant recipients must take immunosuppressive medications to prevent rejection of their new organs. These drugs have multiple nutrient side effects (Table 3–26).

TREATMENT/MANAGEMENT

Short-Term Nutrition Management

Tube Feeding

- The feeding tube should be placed in the small bowel; patients are more likely to have delayed emptying from the stomach soon after the transplant.
- Nasointestinal tubes are appropriate when tube feeding is for a short duration.
- Tube feeding can be started within 12 hours after the transplant (except in the case of small-bowel transplant).
- Tube feeding should be initiated at a low rate and increased gradually.

Table 3–26 Drugs Administered to Transplant Recipients and Their Common Side Effects

Drug	Common Nutritional Side Effects
Cyclosporine	Hyperlipidemia Hyperglycemia Hypomagnesemia Hyperkalemia
Glucocorticoids	Catabolism/impaired wound healing Hyperlipidemia Hyperglycemia Sodium retention Hyperphagia Increased calciuria
Azathioprine	Nausea, vomiting, sore throat, anorexia Altered taste acuity
Muromonab CD3	Nausea, vomiting, diarrhea, anorexia
Tacrolimus	Hyperglycemia Hyperkalemia Nausea and vomiting
Mycophenolate mofetil	Diarrhea

- Small-bowel transplant recipients may receive enteral feedings when signs of bowel function are present (output via terminal ileostomy), usually at 1–2 weeks posttransplant.

Total Parenteral Nutrition (TPN)

- TPN is required initially for small-bowel transplant recipients; as enteral feedings are tolerated, TPN can be weaned.
- When rejection or infection is present in small-bowel transplant recipients, gut function tends to be decreased, and TPN may be required.
- For other types of organ transplant, TPN is reserved for malnourished patients without functioning GI tracts who will require nutrition support for at least 5 days.

- TPN may be required in transplant patients who develop pancreatitis.

Oral Feeding

- Small meals with snacks and/or supplements help patients achieve calorie and protein goals.
- Oral feedings may start as early as 12 hours posttransplant (kidney transplant); oral diets usually are allowed when patients are passing flatus and/or having bowel movements.
- Acceptance of oral diets may be poor in small-bowel transplant patients who have been TPN-dependent for a long time.

Suggested Treatments for Nutritional Problems

- Decreased appetite, taste changes, early satiety
  1. Offer small, frequent meals and snacks.
  2. Offer alternative foods.
  3. Consider tube feeding.
- Diarrhea/constipation
  1. Review medications as a cause of GI disturbance.
  2. If possible, change drug.
  3. Adjust fiber and fluid intake.
- Nausea/vomiting
  1. Review medications as a cause of GI disturbance.
  2. Offer small, frequent meals and snacks.
  3. Offer alternative foods.
  4. Consider tube feeding.
- Increased loss of nitrogen secondary to steroids
  1. Offer high-protein snacks and supplements.
  2. Use high-nitrogen tube-feeding formula.
- Renal insufficiency
  1. Adjust protein, sodium, potassium, and fluid intake as needed.

Specific Guidelines for Short-Term Nutrient Goals

- Calories: 1.3–1.5 × basal energy expenditure (BEE)
- Protein: 1.5–2.0 g/kg dry weight

- Carbohydrate: ~ 50% of nonprotein calories
- Fat: ~ 30% of nonprotein calories
- Vitamins: supplement to recommended dietary allowance (RDA); supplement those likely to be depleted due to preexisting disease
- Minerals/electrolytes: magnesium and phosphorus deplete rapidly; consider zinc losses via wounds, drains, or ostomy
- Fluid: monitor intake and output

Long-Term Nutritional Management

Weight Management

- Patients with a previous history of obesity are at highest risk of excessive weight gain.
- Counsel on appropriate calorie intake to achieve/maintain desirable body weight.
- Encourage regular aerobic exercise.
- Consider long-term behavioral and nutritional counseling when excess weight gain is expected to be a problem.

Hyperlipidemia

- Encourage a low-fat diet (20%–30% of calories as fat).
- Stress weight maintenance.
- Limit alcohol and simple sugars when serum triglyceride level is elevated.
- Encourage a high fiber intake (25–30 g of fiber), including sources of soluble fiber.

Hypertension

- Stress weight maintenance.
- Impose moderate salt restriction.
- Encourage calcium intake (1000–1500 mg/day).

Diabetes

- Patient should be instructed on an individualized diabetic diet.
- Stress weight maintenance.
- Encourage regular aerobic exercise.
- Patient should be instructed on self-monitoring of glucose and administration of medication.

Osteoporosis

- Encourage calcium intake of 1000–1500 mg/day; supplement as needed.
- Consider hormone replacement for women past menopause.
- Encourage regular aerobic exercise.

Specific Guidelines for Nutrient Goals

- Calories: $1.2–1.3 \times$ BEE
- Protein: 0.8–1.0 g/kg
- Carbohydrate: 50%–60% of nonprotein calories; limit simple carbohydrates in diabetes
- Fat: $\leq$ 30% of nonprotein calories; $\leq$ 10% of nonprotein calories as saturated fat
- Vitamins: supplement to RDA, with consideration to vitamins that may have been deficient prior to transplantation due to original disease
- Minerals/electrolytes: supplement to RDA, with consideration to calcium, magnesium, and phosphorus; hyperkalemia occurs 15%–30% of the time and may require a potassium-restricted diet
- Fluid: moderate sodium restriction; adjust on the basis of major shifts in fluid output

PRECAUTION

Because all transplant patients are immunosuppressed, they should avoid uncooked or undercooked meats and wash raw fruits and vegetables well.

REFERENCES

Abu-Elmagd K, Fung JJ, Reyes J, et al. Management of intestinal transplantation in humans. *Transplant Proc.* 1992; 24:1243–1244.

Ballantyne CM, Podet EJ, Patsch WP, et al. Effects of cyclosporine therapy on plasma lipoprotein levels. *JAMA.* 1989;262:53–56.

Baron P, Waymack JP. A review of nutrition support for transplant patients. *Nutr Clin Pract.* 1993;8:12–18.

Beaudette T. Nutrition therapy in organ transplantation. *Sem Nutr.* 1990;9:1–18.

Blue LS. Nutrition considerations in kidney transplantation. *Top Clin Nutr.* 1992;7:17–23.

Blue LS, Hasse JM, Levy ML, et al. Effect of obesity on clinical outcomes in liver transplantation. *J Am Diet Assoc.* 1993;93(suppl):A-49. Abstract.

Delafosse B, Faure JL, Bouffard Y, et al. Liver transplantation: energy expenditure, nitrogen loss, and substrate oxidation rate in the first two postoperative days. *Transplant Proc.* 1989;21:2453–2454.

DiCecco SR, Wieners EJ, Wiesner RH, et al. Assessment of nutritional status of patients with end-stage liver disease undergoing liver transplantation. *Mayo Clin Proc.* 1989; 64:95–102.

Eid A, Steffen R, Porayko MK, et al. Beyond one year after liver transplantation. *Mayo Clin Proc.* 1989;64:446–450.

Frazier OH, Van Buren CT, Poindexter SM, Waldenberger F. Nutritional management of the heart transplant recipient. *Heart Transplant.* 1985;4:450–452.

Grady KL, Herold LS. Comparison of nutritional status in patients before and after heart transplantation. *J Heart Transplant.* 1988;7:123–127.

Hasse J. Nutritional implications of perioperative medications used in liver transplantation. *Dietitians Nutr Support.* 1989;11:2,7,11.

Hasse JM. Nutritional implications of liver transplantation. *Henry Ford Hosp Med J.* 1990;38:235–240.

Hasse JM. Role of the dietitian in the nutrition management of adults after liver transplantation. *J Am Diet Assoc.* 1991; 91:473–476.

Hasse JM. Nutrition considerations in liver transplantation. *Top Clin Nutr.* 1992;7:24–33.

Hasse JM, Blue LS, Crippin JS, et al. The effect of nutritional status on length of stay and clinical outcomes following liver transplantation. *J Am Diet Assoc.* 1994;94:A-38. Abstract.

Hasse JM, Blue LS, Liepa GU, et al. Early enteral nutrition support in patients undergoing liver transplantation. *JPEN.* 1995;19:437–443.

Hasse JM, Blue LS, Watkins LA. Solid organ transplantation. In: Gottschlich MM, Matarese LE, Shronts EP, eds. *Nutrition Support Dietetics Core Curriculum.* 2nd ed. Silver Spring, Md: American Society for Parenteral and Enteral Nutrition; 1993:409–421.

Hasse JM, Strong S, Gorman MA, et al. Subjective global assessment: alternative nutritional assessment technique for liver transplant candidates. *Nutr.* 1993;9:339–343.

Hehir DJ, Jenkins RL, Bistrian BR, et al. Nutrition in patients undergoing orthotopic liver transplant. *JPEN.* 1985; 9:695–700.

Hiyama DT. The current role of small-bowel transplantation in intestinal failure. *Nutr Clin Pract.* 1993;8:5–11.

Hoy WE, Sargent JA, Freeman RB, Pabico RC, McKenna BA, Sterling WA. The influence of glucocorticoid dose on protein catabolism after renal transplantation. *Am J Med Sci.* 1986;291:241–247.

Hricik DE, Bartucci MR, Mayes JT, et al. The effects of steroid withdrawal on the lipoprotein profiles of cyclosporine-treated kidney and kidney-pancreas transplant recipients. *Transplant.* 1992;54:868–871.

Katz IA, Epstein S. Posttransplant bone disease. *J Bone Mineral Res.* 1992;7:123–126.

Keeffe EB, Gettys C, Esquivel CO. Liver transplantation in patients with severe obesity. *Transplant.* 1994;57:309–311.

Levy MF, Husberg BS, Goldstein RM, et al. Diabetes mellitus and liver transplantation. *Hepatol.* 1992;16:50A. Abstract.

Mathe D, Adam R, Malmendier C, et al. Prevalence of dyslipidemia in liver transplant recipients. *Transplant.* 1992;54:167–170.

Merion RM, Twork AM, Rosenberg L, et al. Obesity and renal transplantation. *Surg Gynecol Obstet.* 1991;172: 367–376.

Mieles L, Todo S, Fung JJ, et al. Oral glucose tolerance test in liver recipients treated with FK 506. *Transplant Proc.* 1990;22:41–43.

Miller DG, Levine SE, D'Elia JA, Bistrian BR. Nutritional status of diabetic and nondiabetic patients after renal transplantation. *Am J Clin Nutr.* 1986;44:66–69.

Moore RA, Callahan MF, Cody M, et al. The effect of the American Heart Association step-one diet on hyperlipidemia following renal transplantation. *Transplant.* 1990; 49:60–62.

Munoz SJ, Deems RO, Moritz MJ, et al. Hyperlipidemia and obesity after orthotopic liver transplantation. *Transplant Proc.* 1991;21:1480–1483.

Ohara M. Immunosuppression in solid organ transplantation: a nutrition perspective. *Top Clin Nutr.* 1992;7:6–11.

O'Keefe SJ, Williams R, Calne RY. "Catabolic" loss of body protein after human liver transplantation. *Br Med J.* 1980; 280:1107–1108.

Palmer M, Schaffner F, Thung SN. Excessive weight gain after liver transplantation. *Transplant.* 1991;51:797–800.

Perez R. Managing nutrition problems in transplant patients. *Nutr Clin Pract.* 1993;8:28–32.

Pikul J, Sharpe MD, Lowndes R, et al. Degree of preoperative malnutrition is predictive of postoperative morbidity and mortality in liver transplant recipients. *Transplant.* 1994;57:469–472.

Plevak DJ, DiCecco SR, Wiesner RH, et al. Nutritional support for liver transplantation: identifying caloric and protein requirements. *Mayo Clin Proc.* 1994;69:225–230.

Poindexter SM. Nutrition support in cardiac transplantation. *Top Clin Nutr.* 1992;7:12–16.

Porayko MK, DiCecco S, O'Keefe SJD. Impact of malnutrition and its therapy on liver transplantation. *Semin Liver Dis.* 1991;11:305–314.

Porayko MK, Wiesner RH, Hay JE, et al. Bone disease in liver transplant recipients: incidence, timing, and risk factors. *Transplant Proc.* 1991;23:1462–1465.

Ragsdale D. Nutritional program for heart transplantation. *J Heart Transplant.* 1987;6:228–233.

Reilly J, Mehta R, Teperman L, et al. Nutritional support after liver transplantation: a randomized prospective study. *JPEN.* 1990;14:386–391.

Rosenberg NE, Hostetter TH. Nutrition. In: Toledo-Pereyra LH, ed. *Kidney Transplantation.* Philadelphia, Pa: FA Davis Co; 1988:169–186.

Schindler R, Gundlach M, Dorner K, et al. Effect of orthotopic small-bowel transplantation on vitamin A and zinc metabolism. *Transplant Proc.* 1990;22:2453.

Shanbhogue RLK, Bistrian BR, Jenkins RL, et al. Increased protein catabolism without hypermetabolism after human orthotopic liver transplantation. *Surg.* 1987;101:146–149.

Shapiro R, Fung JJ, Jain AB, et al. The side effects of FK 506 in humans. *Transplant Proc.* 1990;22:35–36.

Shronts EP, Teasley KM, Thoele SL, et al. Nutrition support of the adult liver transplant candidate. *J Am Diet Assoc.* 1987;87:441–451.

Todo S, Tzakis AG, Abu-Elmagd K, et al. Cadaveric small bowel and small bowel-liver transplantation in humans. *Transplant.* 1992;53:369–376.

Tzakis AG, Todo S, Reyes J, et al. Clinical intestinal transplantation: focus on complications. *Transplant Proc.* 1992;24:1238–1240.

Whittier FC, Evans DH, Dutton S, et al. Nutrition in renal transplantation. *Am J Kidney Dis.* 1985;6:405–411.

Williams JW. Early postoperative care. In: Williams JW, ed. *Hepatic Transplantation.* Philadelphia, Pa: WB Saunders Co; 1990:137–162.

Bone Marrow and Peripheral Blood Stem Cell Transplantation

Susan R. Roberts

DESCRIPTION

These procedures are used to restore marrow function in patients treated with intensive chemotherapy and total body irradiation (TBI) therapy for malignant and nonmalignant diseases.

The types of bone marrow/peripheral blood stem cell (PBSC) transplants are

- *Autologous:* Patient's own marrow is used.
- *Allogeneic:* Marrow is provided by an HLA-matched donor (usually a sibling or other family member, but can be unrelated too).
- *Syngeneic:* Marrow is provided by an identical twin.
- *Peripheral Blood Stem Cells (PBSC):* Stem cells, collected from the peripheral blood, are given instead of or in addition to marrow. Both autologous and allogeneic PBSC transplants are being performed.

Cause

Marrow and stem cell transplantation are used to treat a variety of diseases, including hematologic disorders, genetically determined diseases, hematologic malignancies, and solid tumors.

Nutritional Assessment

Objective Parameters

Available objective data are often invalid due to the effects of the treatment and medications on organ function, fluid status, and immune function. Table 3–27 shows factors that must be taken into consideration if objective parameters are used to help determine nutritional status.

Subjective Parameters

A complete nutrition/medical history is essential to an accurate nutritional assessment in marrow transplant patients.

Table 3–27 Nutritional Assessment Parameter and Confounding Factors

Parameter	Confounding Factors
Laboratory Measures	
Serum albumin*	Hydration, capillary leak syndrome, skin and GI GVHD, hepatic function, albumin infusion, high-dose corticosteroid use, blood loss, blood component transfusions
Serum prealbumin*	Infection, inflammation, hepatic function, renal function, hydration
Serum transferrin*	Hydration, hepatic function, renal function, iron overload, blood component transfusions, zinc deficiency
Serum retinol-binding protein	Hydration, renal function, hepatic function, hyperthyroidism, Vitamin A supplementation or deficiency
Total lymphocyte count	Immunosuppressed state due to intensive chemotherapy/radiation, infection, cancer, immunosuppressive medications
Anthropometric Measures—more useful if serial measurements are followed	
Body weight	Hydration, capillary leak syndrome, venocclusive disease
Triceps skinfold	Hydration, age, evaluator's technique
Midarm circumference	Hydration, evaluator's technique
Other Objective Measures	
Skin antigen testing	Immunosuppressed state due to intensive chemotherapy/radiation, immunosuppressive medications
Creatinine-height index	Renal function, liver function, aging, protein intake, presence of diarrhea mixed with urine
Nitrogen balance	Renal function, protein intake, diuretic use, presence of diarrhea mixed with urine, significant nitrogen losses with stool as with GI GVHD
3-methylhistidine excretion	Age, sex, protein intake, renal function, infection
Indirect calorimetry	Presence of stomatitis is indication for use of hood system, more useful in critically ill, long-term TPN or GVHD patients

*All three of the above serum proteins follow a trend of dropping significantly after the intensive chemotherapy/radiation and returning toward normal with engraftment (recovery of the bone marrow).

- current and recent appetite
- usual weight/weight changes
- gastrointestinal (GI) complaints affecting oral intake (now and with previous oncologic therapies)
- vitamin/mineral supplementation
- food allergies or intolerances
- special diet
- recent activity level
- nutritional supplement
- diabetes history
- recent or current medications
- previous need for nutrition support
- physical exam (muscle loss, caloric reserves)

Problems

Nutritional complications and their causes are shown in Table 3–28.

Medical Complications

- Hepatic venocclusive disease (VOD)
  1. There is a 20% incidence.
  2. VOD results from damage to the liver by high-dose chemotherapy.
  3. The small intrahepatic veins are obstructed by fibrous material.
  4. Symptoms usually begin 1 to 3 weeks post-transplant.

Table 3–28 Nutritional Complications of Bone Marrow and PBSC Transplant and Their Causes

GI Side Effects	Possible Causes
Nausea and vomiting	Chemotherapy/TBI, medications, dehydration, electrolyte imbalances, mucositis, GI GVHD, GI infections, high serum glucose or amino acid levels
Oral mucositis and esophagitis	Chemotherapy, TBI, infections, GVHD, methotrexate (used for GVHD prophylaxis)
Xerostomia	TBI, antiemetics, chronic GVHD, narcotics
Early satiety	Decreased gastric motility due to prolonged absence of enteral nutrition, narcotics, high-dose chemotherapy
Thick, viscous saliva	TBI, intensive chemotherapy
Dysgeusia	TBI, intensive chemotherapy, antibiotics, narcotics
Diarrhea and steatorrhea	TBI, intensive chemotherapy, antibiotics, GI and liver GVHD, intestinal infections
Anorexia	Disease state, intensive chemotherapy, TBI, drug toxicities, infections, fluid and electrolyte imbalances, psychological and environmental factors
Micronutrient abnormalities	Medications, vomiting, diarrhea, decreased oral intake, altered absorption

5. Symptoms may include increased bilirubin with low to moderate increases in liver function tests, significant weight gain, hepatomegaly, right–upper-quadrant pain, jaundice, ascites, encephalopathy, and sodium and fluid retention.

• Infection
1. Opportunistic infections are common due to profound neutropenia after intensive chemotherapy/TBI and the use of immunosuppressive drugs to prevent GVHD.
2. Multiple antibiotics are employed to prevent/treat infections.

• Acute graft-versus-host disease (GVHD)
1. This major complication of allogeneic transplant occurs within 100 days post transplant.
2. Donor T cells (from the graft) attack the recipient (host).
3. Organs most affected are the skin, GI tract, and liver.
   – Skin: macropapular rash appearing on trunk, palms, soles, and ears; can progress to generalized erythroderma with desquamation and bullae (burnlike injury)
   – GI tract: secretory diarrhea, guaiac-positive stools, abdominal cramping, nausea/vomiting, GI protein losses, hypoalbuminemia, ileus
   – Liver: elevated liver function tests and serum bilirubin, cholestasis, malabsorption, ascites, encephalopathy, decreased synthesis clotting factors

• Chronic GVHD
1. This multisystem autoimmune disease develops after 100 days posttransplant.
2. It may involve the skin, liver, eyes, mouth, esophagus, skeletal muscle, and upper respiratory tract.
3. It is treated with immunosuppressive medications, including corticosteroids.
4. Nutritional problems may include weight/muscle loss, failure to thrive, stomatitis, dysphagia, xerostomia, anorexia, diarrhea, steatorrhea, and dysgeusia.

A variety of medications taken by bone marrow and PBSC transplant patients have nutritional side effects:

• Refer to the section "Solid Organ Transplantation" for side effects of immunosuppressive medications. Most commonly used are cyclosporine, corticosteroids, and FK-506. Occasionally, OKT-3 and ATG are used in steroid-resistant GVHD.

- Methotrexate (used to prevent GVHD) can cause mucositis, nausea, vomiting, diarrhea, and hepatotoxicity.
- Antibiotics, antivirals, and antifungals can cause nausea, vomiting, diarrhea, anorexia, dysgeusia, electrolyte imbalances, and renal toxicity.

Treatment/Management

Nutritional Complications

- Nausea and vomiting
  1. Consider etiology.
  2. Encourage clear liquids, salty foods, and cold, bland foods as tolerated.
  3. Avoid foods with high fat content and strong odors.
  4. Encourage slow drinking and eating.
  5. Monitor fluid status with excessive vomiting.
  6. Use antiemetics—either scheduled doses or prior to meals to control nausea with or without vomiting.
- Oral mucositis and esophagitis
  1. Good mouth care is very important due to absence of antimicrobial effects of saliva.
  2. Saliva substitutes or mouth moisturizers may help.
  3. Increase fluid content of foods with addition of gravy, broth, and sauces.
  4. Drink liquids with meals and throughout the day.
  5. If salivary glands are minimally functional, citric acid (in lemonade or sugarless lemon drops) may stimulate saliva production.
- Early satiety
  1. Encourage small, frequent feedings.
  2. Limit liquids with meals.
  3. Encourage high-carbohydrate liquids as snacks between meals.
  4. Choose nutrient-dense foods.
  5. Consider use of medication (Metaclopromide or Cisipride) to increase gastric motility.

- Thick, viscous saliva
  1. Temporary liquid diet may be helpful.
  2. Club soda, hot tea with lemon, or sour lemon drops may help break up the mucous.
  3. Encourage high fluid intake.
  4. Milk products may be difficult to swallow but have not been proven to increase the mucous thickness.
  5. Rinse frequently with physiologic saline to clear secretions and freshen mouth.
  6. Condition usually resolves with engraftment and healing of oral mucosa. Recurrence after this may be caused by dehydration or medications.
- Dysgeusia
  1. Encourage cold or room-temperature foods and beverages.
  2. Strongly flavored foods, whose taste can better be detected, are recommended in patients with minimal or no mucositis.
  3. Use of plastic utensils may help if foods taste metallic.
  4. Adding sauces and spices to foods may be helpful.
  5. Rinse mouth often with physiologic saline.
  6. Recovery of taste usually occurs 45 to 60 days posttransplant.
- Diarrhea and steatorrhea
  1. Provide adequate fluid intake orally or parenterally.
  2. Avoid high-fiber and high-fat foods.
  3. Lactose intolerance may be present. Use of lactase enzyme replacement may be beneficial.
  4. With documented steatorrhea, use of medium chain triglyceride (MCT) oil may be indicated.
  5. Consider use of antidiarrheal medications.
- Anorexia
  1. Attempt to determine etiology of anorexia; if psychological, intervention by a social worker or psychologist is needed.
  2. Encourage small, frequent high-calorie meals (every 2 hours).
  3. Light exercise may help stimulate the appetite.

4. Drink high-nutrient liquids—avoid liquids with no nutritional value.
- Micronutrient abnormalities
  1. Vitamins
     - Supplement to recommended dietary allowance (RDA).
     - Provide vitamin K weekly to those patients on parenteral nutrition support.
     - The following vitamins may be depleted: thiamine, vitamin B_{12}, vitamin E, and beta carotene.
  2. Minerals
     - Supplement to RDA.
     - The following minerals are likely to be affected by medications and GI side effects: calcium, phosphorous, zinc, magnesium, and potassium.

Nutrition support

Nutrient needs

- *Calories:* 25–35 kcalories per kilogram or 1.3–1.5 × basal energy expenditure (BEE)
- *Protein:* 1.5–2.0 grams per kilogram depending on stress factors (infection, GVHD) and corticosteroid dose
- Oral diet
  1. Oral diet indicated when GI dysfunction is minimal.
  2. Snacks, oral supplements, and encouragement necessary to obtain an acceptable oral intake.
  3. Most centers use low-microbial or modified hospital diet (general diet without raw fruits or vegetables).
  4. Sterile and low-microbial diets most appropriate in laminar-air-flow isolation.
  5. A modified hospital diet appropriate for the patient with < 500 neutrophils.
  6. Patients with > 500 neutrophils who are still on immunosuppressive medications and/or low WBC count should adhere to strict food safety rules (avoid uncooked/undercooked meats and wash raw fruits/vegetables well).
  7. Nutrition support often needed due to presence of nutritional and medical problems.

8. Oral glutamine supplementation under investigation.
- Tube feedings (early—during first 1–3 weeks posttransplant)
  1. Not used extensively due to GI dysfunction, thrombocytopenia, infection risk associated with enteral feeding system.
  2. Some centers are researching use of tube feedings in the early posttransplant period for a more physiologic and cost-effective feeding method.
  3. Continuous feedings via small bowel may be best tolerated.
  4. Combined enteral and parenteral nutrition support may be needed if adequate nutrition cannot be tolerated enterally.
  5. To reduce microbial contamination of the enteral feeding system, use only commercial sterile products, avoid mixing formula, and limit hang time to 8 hours.
  6. If thrombocytopenia is present, provision of platelet transfusion prior to placement of the feeding tube is recommended.
  7. Polymeric formulas may be tolerated. If not, use of an elemental or small peptide formula may be necessary. Other considerations are whether the formula is lactose free, is isotonic, or has a high nitrogen content.
- Tube feeding (late—after 3–4 weeks posttransplant)
  1. Enteral feedings should be used in patients who have marrow engraftment and minimal/controllable GI side effects.
  2. Usually includes patients with GVHD, sepsis, infection, VOD, or Acute Respiratory Distress Syndrome (ARDS) or who require lengthy hospitalization or readmission.
  3. Use of percutaneous endoscopic gastrostomy tube may benefit patients requiring long-term nutrition support.
  4. Polymeric formulas may be tolerated. If not, use of an elemental or small peptide formula may be necessary. Other formula considerations: is lactose free, is isotonic, or has a high nitrogen content.
- Total parenteral nutrition (TPN)

1. Concentrated formulas often needed with volume overload.
2. Dextrose: 50%–60% of total calories; hyperglycemia common due to stress, immunosuppressive medications, and TPN.
3. Amino acids 20%–25% of total calories; this may need to decrease in severe renal or liver dysfunction.
4. Lipids 25%–30% of total calories; hypertriglyceridemia may occur due to immunosuppressive medications. Recent research suggests that provision of lipid emulsion in these amounts will not cause increased infections in marrow transplant patients.
5. Use of glutamine-supplemented TPN is under investigation.

Medical Complications

- VOD
  1. Concentration of nutrition support.
  2. Facilitate diuresis without depletion of intravascular volume.
  3. Fluid and sodium restriction.
  4. Protein restriction may be needed with encephalopathy. Provision of protein should continue with encephalopathy to decrease muscle breakdown and contribution of endogenous protein to urea pool.
  5. Use of liver failure amino acids may be tried with encephalopathy.
  6. Remove copper/manganese from TPN if hyperbilirubinemia is persistent.
  7. Monitor lipid utilization.
- Infection
  1. The nutrition support provided will depend on clinical status of the patient.
  2. Consider metabolic and volume status.
  3. Evaluate type and severity of organ dysfunction.
  4. Consider antibiotic side effects.
  5. Provide at least $1.3–1.5 \times$ BEE.
  6. Provide protein at 1.5 g/kg.
  7. Sodium and fluid restriction may be needed as well as concentrated nutrition support.
- Acute GVHD

1. Severe skin
   - Meet increased calorie and protein needs (possibly up to 50 kcal/kg and 2 g of protein per kg).
   - Provide adequate vitamin C and zinc for healing.
   - Meet increased fluid needs.
2. Gastrointestinal
   - NPO until diarrhea < 500 ml/day
   - Meet increased zinc requirements.
   - Meet increased nutrient needs (same as listed above for severe skin).
   - Maintain serum albumin > 2.0 g/dL.
   - Control GI side effects with antiemetics and H_2 blockers.
   - Antidiarrheals are usually contraindicated.
   - When an oral diet is appropriate, restriction of fat, fiber, lactose, acidic foods, and gastric irritants may be needed.
3. Liver
   - Avoid overfeeding with TPN.
   - Monitor tolerance of IV lipids.
   - Decrease or remove copper and manganese from TPN.
   - Provide adequate vitamin K.
   - Sodium and fluid restrictions may be necessary.
   - Liver failure—amino acids may be beneficial with encephalopathy.
- Chronic GVHD
  1. Nutrition support regimen prescribed should be dependent on severity and type of organ involvement.
  2. Oral supplements and/or enteral feedings should be used with poor oral intake and inappropriate weight loss.
  3. Oral and esophageal involvement
     - Require avoidance of acidic foods and use of bland liquids/soft foods.
  4. Liver involvement
     - Provide calories for weight gain or maintenance, whichever is appropriate.
     - Provide protein at 1.5 g/kg.
     - With steatorrhea, moderate fat restriction (50–70 g/day) may be needed.
     - Water-soluble forms of fat-soluble vita-

mins may be needed with fat malabsorption.

- Monitor potassium, magnesium, and calcium with steatorrhea, corticosteroid treatment, and cyclosporine/FK-506.

5. Pulmonary involvement
   - Meet increased nutrient requirements.
   - Patient is often unable to meet nutrient needs via oral intake.
   - Encourage use of nutritional supplements and small, frequent meals of high-calorie foods.
   - Enteral feedings may be needed.

6. Consider nutritional side effects of corticosteroid therapy.

Medication Side Effects

- Treat GI side effects of medications with antiemetics, antidiarrheals, and nutrition interventions as needed.
- Replace electrolytes as needed.
- Modify nutrition support as needed if organ dysfunction occurs due to medications.

REFERENCES

Aker SN. Bone marrow transplantation: nutrition support and monitoring. In: Block AS, ed. *Nutrition Management of the Cancer Patient.* Rockville, Md: Aspen Publishers Inc; 1990; pp. 199–225.

Cheney CL, Abson KG, Aker SN, et al. Body composition changes in marrow transplant recipients receiving total parenteral nutrition. *Cancer.* 1987;59:1515–1519.

Geibig CB, Ponting-Owens J, Mirtallo JM, et al. Parenteral nutrition for marrow transplant recipients: evaluation of an increased nitrogen dose. *JPEN.* 1991;16:184–188.

Herrmann VM, Petruska PJ. Nutrition support in bone marrow transplant recipients. *Nutr Clin Pract.* 1993;8:19–27.

Lenssen P. Nutrition support in transplantation. Post-graduate course at ASPEN. 17 Clinical Congress. San Diego, Calif, 1993.

Lenssen P, Bruemmer B, Aker S, et al. Relationship between IV lipid dose and incidence of bacteremias and fungemias in 492 marrow transplant (MT) recipients. *JPEN.* 1994; 18:22S.

Lenssen P, Sherry ME, Cheney CL, et al. Prevalence of nutrition-related problems among long-term survivors of allogeneic marrow transplantation. *J Am Diet Assoc.* 1990; 90:835–842.

Mulder POM, Bouman JG, Gietama JA, et al. Hyperalimentation in autologous bone marrow transplantation for solid tumors. *Cancer.* 1989;64:2045–2052.

Peters E, Beck J, LeMaistre C. Changes in resting energy expenditure (REE) during allogeneic bone marrow transplantation. *Am J Clin Nutr.* 1990;51:521.

Roberts SR. Bone marrow transplantation. In: Gottschlich MM, Matarese LE, Shronts EP, eds. *Nutrition Support Dietetics Core Curriculum.* 2nd ed. Silver Spring, Md: American Society for Parenteral and Enteral Nutrition; 1993: 423–432.

Sullivan KM, Forman SJ, Blume KG, Thomas ED, eds. Graft-versus-host disease. In: Forman SJ et al, eds. *Bone Marrow Transplantation.* Boston, Mass: Blackwell Scientific Publications; 1994: 339–362.

Szeluga DJ, Stuart RK, Brookmeyer R, et al. Energy requirements of parenterally fed bone marrow transplant recipients. *JPEN.* 1985;9:139–143.

Szeluga DJ, Stuart RK, Brookmeyer R, et al. Nutritional support of bone marrow transplant recipients: randomized clinical trial comparing total parenteral nutrition to an enteral feeding program. *Cancer Res.* 1987;47:3309–3316.

Weisdorf SA, Lysne J, Wind D, et al. Positive effect of prophylactic total parenteral nutrition on long-term outcome of bone marrow transplantation. *Transplant.* 1987;43: 833–838.

Ziegler TR, Young LS, Benfell K, et al. Clinical and metabolic efficacy of glutamine-supplemented parenteral nutrition after bone marrow transplantation. *Ann Intern Med.* 1992;116:821–828.

Trauma/Sepsis

Deborah Silverman

DESCRIPTION

Trauma is damage from force to the human body that crushes tissue, fractures bone, and/or creates wounds, resulting in disability and an alteration in metabolism. There are three types:

- *Blunt trauma:* Trauma that causes severe damage by crushing of tissue, by fractures, and by shear forces developed by rapid deceleration. Examples are closed head and spinal cord injuries and motor vehicle accident injuries.
- *Penetrating wounds:* Trauma that causes severe damage by the explosive force of a high-velocity missile, resulting in massive destruction of soft tissues and vessels and subjecting the individual to contamination from debris and dirt that can enter the wound in conjunction with the entry of the missile. Examples are gunshot wounds, stab wounds, and cuts from sharp objects.
- *Pressure sores or ulcers:* Also referred to as *decubitus* ulcers. Pressure-induced tissue necrosis.

Trauma is the most serious public health problem in the United States. It is the number one killer of young adults. Approximately 50% of deaths from trauma occur within the first few seconds after the injury. A second peak in deaths occurs within hours of the trauma and is dependent on the available intervention and treatment. A third peak occurs days or even weeks after the injury and is usually caused by sepsis or multiple organ dysfunction.

The cost of trauma exceeds $80 billion each year and causes more disability and lost productivity than heart disease and cancer combined.

CAUSE

Common causes include motor vehicle accidents, gunshot wounds, stab wounds, falls, and sports-related injuries.

METABOLIC RESPONSE TO TRAUMA

The quantitative metabolic response varies with the type and severity of injury, previous health status, and medical care.

- Characteristics of metabolic phases that occur after severe injury are classified in relation to the injury, with the early phase termed the *ebb phase* and the secondary responses referred to as the *flow phase*.
- The flow phase is often divided into *acute response* and *adaptive response* segments.

Ebb Phase Characteristics

- Usually persists for 12–36 hours.
- Cardiovascular instability, impairment of oxygen transport, and heightened autonomic activity.
- Alterations in circulating blood volume, tissue ischemia stimulating release of endotoxins, interleukins, tumor necrosis factor, interferons, and colony-stimulating factors.
- Decrease in metabolic rate, with epinephrine stimulated glycogenolysis, gluconeogenesis, lipolysis, and ketogenesis in the liver. Lipolysis is favored. Hyperglycemia with insulin resistance results.
- Elevated levels of plasma catecholamines, glucagon, growth hormone, and glucocorticoids result in muscle catabolism.
- Provision of exogenous nutrition support has low priority in treatment protocols.

Flow Phase Characteristics: Acute Response Segment (Catabolism Predominates)

- Usually peaks at 3–4 days.
- Increased oxygen consumption and body temperature.
- Production of acute-phase proteins, release of cytokines, with increased excretion of nitrogen.

- Increase in metabolic rate and altered substrate utilization.
- Glucocorticoids, glucagon, and catecholamines remain elevated; may also remain hyperglycemic.
- If prolonged, is often associated with marked morbidity and organ failure.

Flow Phase Characteristics: Adaptive Response Segment (Anabolism Predominates)

- Resolves in 9–14 days but can be reactivated by repeated insults such as pneumonia or bacteremia.
- Hormonal response gradually diminishes and glucose returns to normal.
- Metabolic rate and substrate utilization returns to normal.
- Recovery associated with anabolic processes such as wound healing, medical complications.
- Priority for nutrition support during the flow phase depends on preillness nutritional status.
  1. The more poorly nourished the patient was before the illness, the greater the need for support.
  2. The nature of the illness or injury influences when eating may occur, the route(s) accessible for feeding, and the composition of nutrients to be administered.
- The three major features of the metabolic response to trauma that affect clinical care are the degree of hypermetabolic state, the degree of muscle wasting, and the severity of glucose intolerance.
- Objectives of medical nutrition therapy
  1. Provide adequate nutrients to permit tissue repair and maintain body weight; restore normal patterns of intermediary metabolism, and preserve organ structure and function.
  2. Assist in the optimization of oxygen delivery to tissues by delivery of a nutrient substrate load that does not impair cardiorespiratory function.

  3. Assist in the prevention of sepsis through optimization of normal host defenses.

ASSESSMENT

Trauma victims commonly have injury to more than one body system. Assessment depends on the systems that are injured.

Subjective

Conduct a comprehensive interview with the patient and/or significant other to obtain

- information on usual nutrient intake prior to the traumatic event, including appetite changes, chewing and swallowing ability, adherence to prescribed nutrition regimens, uses of nutritional supplements, food preferences/aversions, and alcohol intake
- detailed history of weight changes
- information on socioeconomic factors, including substance abuse, ethnic/cultural influences, and degree of independence and mobility

Objective

Review the medical management for diagnostic and clinical factors that impact nutrition status. It is important to recognize that the conventional markers used to assess nutritional status of patients are limited in their usefulness until the patient becomes hemodynamically stable. Selection of markers for use in the assessment of nutritional status must take into consideration the degree of organ dysfunction, fluid requirements, metabolic needs, and the patient's ability to communicate, particularly in the description of the functional ability to perform activities of daily living and instrumental activities of daily living prior to admission. Use recognized instruments/questionnaires to determine functional status and severity of illness.

- *General:* Height, weight (consider hydration status), temperature, vital signs.

- *Rationale:* Assessment of initial signs and symptoms for determination of the patient's nutritional status requires the gathering of measured markers that document general nutriture and the body's energy and lean tissue stores. Fever is a consistent finding in trauma patients and is an indicator of infection.
- *Diagnostic:* Hematocrit, hemoglobin, white blood cell (WBC) count with differential, serum sodium, potassium, blood urea nitrogen (BUN), creatinine, glucose, prealbumin (or other appropriate protein/nitrogen status marker following acute phase protein synthesis response), additional biochemical markers as deemed appropriate.
- *Rationale:* Diagnostic factors should focus on the patient's glucose tolerance, fluid and electrolyte balance, visceral protein/lean tissue compartment status, and additional markers that provide valid information as to the patient's metabolic and immunological status; posttraumatic depression of serum albumin levels often correlates with acute blood loss.
- *Cardiopulmonary:* Respiration rate, oxygen consumption/saturation, cardiac output, heart rate, blood pressure, presence of edema, possible requirement for prolonged ventilatory support, peripheral vascular tone, ability to maintain hemodynamic stability. *Rationale:* Hemodynamic and metabolic abnormalities appear to be so closely coupled that the health care practitioner may be able to predict metabolic status and volume limitations on the basis of hemodynamic information and vice versa. Increases in respiratory rate and oxygen consumption are secondary to the rise in resting energy expenditure and the endocrine alterations. Increases in cardiac output and heart rate are mediated by the neuroendocrine response to trauma. If peripheral vascular tone is maintained, adequate oxygen exchange can occur within the capillary beds. Prolonged ventilatory support may necessitate alteration of nutrient substrate/consideration as to the appropriate site for feeding.
- *Gastrointestinal:* Presence of post-traumatic ileus, presence of wound fistula losses, stress ulcerations, prolonged gastric drainage, presence of abdominal trauma that interferes with ability to administer enteral nutrition.
- *Rationale:* Initiation of early enteral nutrition support warrants placement of the feeding site distal to any ileus. Increasing macronutrient and micronutrient needs should be considered on the basis of analysis of fistula losses and other drainage. Stress ulceration may occur in trauma and necessitate the use of prophylactic antacid therapy, which may decrease serum phosphate. Degree of abdominal trauma should be considered in the determination of efficacious use of parenteral nutrition support.
- *Nutrition/Metabolic:* Increased resting energy expenditure, excretion of urinary urea nitrogen; ability to administer nutrition support within 72 hours of trauma; return of acute phase protein synthesis to within normal limits; ability to maintain or achieve preillness weight; signs of general nutriture/muscle strength and tone. *Rationale:* A marked hypermetabolism persists that is proportional to the severity of the trauma. Hepatic glucose utilization rate is normal and allows for 0.4–1.2 g glucose/kg/hr to be metabolized. A persistent hypercatabolism depletes lean body mass as a result of the hormonal changes associated with trauma. A large increase in urinary urea nitrogen occurs with a net negative nitrogen balance. Circulating amino acids also provide a critical substrate for synthesis of acute phase proteins, immunologic components, nutrients for wound healing, and maintenance of functional status of vital organs. Free fatty acids are mobilized as the main energy source for peripheral tissues. The host defense mechanism sequesters zinc and iron, thus decreasing the availability for microorganisms that would proliferate in a high-iron environment. The patient's ability to return to an appropriate level of functional status depends on the ability to maintain body weight/lean body mass.
- *Genitourinary:* May be dehydrated upon admission; monitor specific gravity and ability of patient to maintain urine output.

- *Rationale:* Dehydration is associated with an increase in urinary specific gravity. The urine should also be tested for glucose and protein due to the hormonal milieu associated with trauma and damage to internal tissues. Ability of the patient to excrete metabolic waste products, tolerate fluid loads, and maintain hydration status is dependent upon renal function.

PROBLEMS

Factors That Affect Ability To Deliver Appropriate Nutrition Support

- Current weight should not be less than 10% of pretrauma weight.
- Maintain or achieve pretrauma weight through the early administration of nutrition support.
- Nutrition support prescription and intake should meet estimated needs within ± 10%.
- Protein should be administered at levels to achieve nitrogen equilibrium.
- The functional level of the gastrointestinal tract should permit initiation of enteral feeding.
- Nutrient intake should be adjusted as metabolic stress subsides or as nutrition status changes.

Factors That Affect Formulation of Nutrition Diagnosis

- Nutrition diagnosis should focus both on preventing specific nutrient deficiencies and on providing a substrate appropriate to the existing metabolic state.
- The patient may present with preexisting physiologic impairment or disease state.

Diagnoses and/or Problems That Increase Risk of Multiorgan Failure

- Severe trauma with prolonged shock and direct organ injury
- Penetrating abdominal trauma with peritoneal spillage
- Prolonged intestinal ischemia
- Overwhelming sepsis, especially intra-abdominal
- Hemodynamic instability
- Erosion of lean body protein, associated with diminished immune function, increased infection rates, delayed tissue repair, decreased wound healing, and diminished skeletal muscle function that impairs functional status
- Inability to extubate within a 48–72-hour postoperative period, associated with cellular hypertrophy of the liver and cardiorespiratory muscles; cytogenesis of the gastrointestinal mucosa, lymphocytes, and wounds; and a need to support regeneration of the endothelium
- Inadequate perfusion and delivery of oxygen, glucose, and other essential nutrients that may impair the cellular processes involved in wound healing
- Total body oxygen consumption greater than normal because of the increased oxidation of body fuels needed to provide the energy to drive hypermetabolism

TREATMENT/MANAGEMENT

Metabolic Alterations during Stress

Protein Metabolism

- Mobilized for energy, even if adequate carbohydrate and fat are available.
- Increased protein breakdown in peripheral tissues to mobilize amino acids for conversion to glucose in the liver.
- Decreased uptake of amino acids by muscles.
- Increased urinary excretion of nitrogen.
- Skeletal muscle proteolysis provides fuel for protein synthesis by releasing branched-chain amino acids (leucine, isoleucine, and valine).

Fat Metabolism

- Mobilization from adipose stores to provide energy, glycerol, and fatty acids.
- Administer total fat in diet within an appropriate range of tolerance, generally at 30% of total kilocalories.

- Increase in lipolysis, circulating free fatty acids results from the presence of elevated levels of catecholamines along with a concurrent decrease in the level of insulin.
- Increase in oxidation of triglycerides in the cell.
- Turnover of medium and long chain fatty acids is increased.
- Clearance rate of long chain fatty acid triglycerides becomes reduced, primarily through a reduction in peripheral lipase activity.

Carbohydrate Metabolism

- Mobilization of hepatic glucose production with increased hepatic glucose flow to and uptake in the peripheral tissue.
- Maximum amount of glucose that can be metabolized in most patients ranges between 5 and 7 mg/kg of body weight per minute.
- Increase in glycogenolysis and gluconeogenesis that is not readily suppressible, even with exogenous glucose or insulin administration.
- Use of glycogenic amino acids and glycerol for energy.
- Insulin levels and glucose utilization are actually increased; the hyperglycemia and relative excess in glucose production seem driven, in part, by an elevated glucagon:insulin ratio.
- In the periphery, there is increased lactate release with reconversion to glucose in the liver.
- Exogenous insulin does not seem to increase the oxidative use of glucose.

Hydration/Fluid Status

- Provide 1 ml free water per kilocalorie or 30–35 ml/kg body weight for maintenance.
- Increase for losses secondary to fever, urine output, diarrhea, draining wounds, or diuretic therapy.
- Measure other fluids, such as intravenous solutions and medications, flushes via enteral and parenteral tubing, and oral intake.

Metabolic Aspects in Wound Healing

- All wounds heal by progressing through four distinct but overlapping phases.

- Malnutrition can delay this healing process, causing the wound to heal inadequately or incompletely.
- *Phase I: The Hemostatic Phase.*
- Begins as soon as the wound occurs.
- Blood accumulates in the wound; platelets and leukocytes initiate coagulation and the inflammatory process.
- *Phase II: The Inflammatory Phase.*
- Leukocytes initiate the inflammatory phase by ingesting bacteria and debris.
- Macrophages begin to release growth factors that stimulate capillary synthesis and tissue vascularization necessary to bring nutrients to the wound.
- *Phase III: The Connective Tissue Phase.*
- Wound begins to accumulate fibroblasts that produce collagen to help the wound close.
- Myofibrils begin to help the wound contract, which facilitates epidermal coverage.
- *Phase IV: The Epithelial Phase.*
- Epithelial cells begin to cover the wound.
- Healing is considered complete when tissue strength is normal, when continuity across the wound is reestablished, and when appropriate resurfacing is achieved.

Healing is affected by systemic physiologic changes influenced by

- blood flow
- pulmonary function
- nutrition status

Adequate wound healing is dependent on substrate delivery of oxygen, glucose, and protein.

- Adequate oxygenation is required for protein synthesis, cell replication, hydroxylation of proline and lysine, and resistance to infection.
- Decreased circulation and oxygenation to wound area increases risk of infection.
- A relationship between protein depletion and delayed wound healing has been shown in protein-depleted animals compared to normally nourished control animals.
- Patients with protein-energy malnutrition, when compared with normally nourished patients, have significantly less hydroxyproline

content in experimental wounds.
- Patients who consumed diets < 50% of usual intake for 1 week prior to surgery had poorer wound-healing responses than surgical patients who ate normally.
- Exocrine and metabolic changes promote wound healing at the expense of other tissues, even in the presence of skeletal muscle wasting.
- Obesity may play a role in the development of pressure sores as a result of excessive weight on body prominences, moisture collecting between skinfolds, and the poor vasculation of adipose tissue, making it more vulnerable to breakdown with sustained pressure.
- Wound healing response is less dependent on the degree of tissue loss than on the direction in which the patient is moving metabolically at the time of the wound insult.
- Effective markers of wound healing potential are serum albumin and total lymphocyte count.

Role of Specific Nutrients in Wound Healing

Glucose

- Serves as the primary energy source for all body cells.
- Utilization by leukocytes appears to promote phagocytic activity of lymphocytes prior to fibroplasia.

Fatty Acids

- Important component of cellular membrane, presumed essential for cellular proliferation and prostaglandin synthesis.
- Conserve utilization of protein as a fuel source.

Protein/Amino Acids

- Essential for cellular multiplication, fibroplastic proliferation, and collagen synthesis.
  1. Methionine serves as a precursor for cystine, which is critical for proper alignment and attachment of peptide chains and the formation of the collagen triple helix.
  2. Arginine has a strong stimulatory effect on collagen synthesis.
  3. Glutamine serves as a precursor in the synthesis of purines and pyrimidines.
- Amino acids in general are components of collagen and other structural proteins found in wounds. Enzymes are synthesized for proteins and function in all steps of collagen synthesis.

Vitamins and Minerals

- Vitamin A is needed to maintain normal humoral defense mechanism and to limit the complications associated with wound infections.
- Vitamin C functions as a cofactor in hydroxylation of proline to collagen, an essential step in collagen synthesis. Deficiency alters collagen turnover, resulting in poor healing or the reopening of old wounds.
- The B vitamins serve as cofactors in many enzymatic pathways. Thiamine, in particular, is needed for lysyl oxidase to strengthen collagen.
- Vitamin K is necessary for normal coagulation. Deficiency may result in prolonged bleeding times, hematoma formation, and subsequent wound infection and/or dehiscence.
- Vitamin E deficiency may impair collagen synthesis and retard wound healing.
- Calcium is required as a cofactor in the action of various collagenases during remodeling.
- Magnesium is necessary in all phases of healing, particularly translation and synthesis of polypeptide chains.
- Iron is needed to enhance the enzymatic activity of prolyl hydroxylase and lysyl hydroxylase during the hydroxylation of proline and lysine.
- Copper is required for collagen polymerization and formation of cross-linkages to enhance scar strength.
- Zinc is necessary for synthesis of nucleic acids, essential in a number of enzymatic reactions.

Nutrition Management of Trauma and Wound Healing

- The role of nutrition in maintaining or raising tissue collagen synthesis cannot be minimized.

- The wound has a high priority for available nutrients. Any element contributing to malnutrition will retard healing.
  1. Recent weight loss of > 10% of lean body mass increases wound complications.
  2. The presence of hypermetabolic, catabolic states rapidly depletes tissue protein.
  3. Decreased serum albumin or low serum transferrin levels will delay healing.
- Therapy should maintain a serum albumin level high enough to overcome the patient's hydrostatic pressure, keep the tissue free of edema, and raise the colloid osmotic pressure higher than the hydrostatic pressure to eliminate hypo-oncotic edema.
- Attention should be focused on the nutritional needs of the patient and early identification of those patients at risk for developing nutritional deficits. Prevention is much better than treatment; treatment costs 2.5 times more than prevention.
- Clinical indicators that should be monitored are
  1. *Body weight:* Weight loss of > 10% usual body weight or obesity in presence of prolonged immobility.
  2. *Depressed serum albumin:* Development of pressure sores increases threefold with every gram decrease in serum albumin.
  3. *Impaired intake of nutrients to meet estimated need:* Monitor decreases in appetite/intake that may result from polypharmacy.
- The nutrition prescription should include
  1. Protein intake to promote wound healing and preserve tissue integrity (1.2 to 2.0 g/kg body weight)
     - Also provide sufficient fluid and monitor renal status when considering level of intake and tolerance of metabolic load.
     - Increases in BUN can be expected. Patients have been able to tolerate protein intakes as high as 150 g/day without renal complications.
     - Protein level that is prescribed varies depending on the patient's degree of stress.
  2. Energy intake sufficient to meet metabolic needs
     - Use the Harris-Benedict equation, indirect calorimetry, or 25–35 kcal/kg body weight as determinants.
     - Intake must be sufficient to prevent protein from being utilized as fuel and will vary depending on the patient's degree of stress.
  3. Vitamin and mineral supplementation
     - *Vitamin A* = 20000 to 25000 IU/day for 10 days in patients with suspected poor nutrient stores or malabsorption.
     - *Vitamin C* = 1–2 g/day in patients with vitamin C deficiency, suspected depleted stores, or critically ill patients. Supplementation will not enhance healing in patients with normal vitamin C stores.
     - *Zinc* = 220 mg/day of zinc sulfate should restore low zinc levels and promote wound healing. In patients with normal zinc stores, supplementation has not been shown to accelerate wound healing.
- It is important to individualize nutrition prescription and implementation of nutrition support.
  1. Adjunctive enteral support may be necessary to facilitate wound healing, particularly when oral intake is suboptimal. Parenteral feedings should be administered when enteral access cannot be obtained, when enteral nutrition support fails to meet nutritional needs, or when access to feeding via the gastrointestinal tract is contraindicated. Transitional feedings to enteral/oral should be instituted as gastrointestinal tolerance improves or when enteral access is obtained.
  2. Products that are more nutritionally complete have been found to promote wound healing.
  3. Preoperative and/or early postoperative nutrition support enhances the wound-healing response.
  4. The prescription should focus both on preventing specific nutrient deficiencies and on providing substrate appropriate to the existing metabolic state.

• Monitoring of clinical nutrition/metabolic status is essential to reassess patient needs and enhance patient outcome.

REFERENCES

Bessey PQ. Metabolic response to critical illness. In: American College of Surgeons, ed. *Care of the Surgical Patient.* New York, NY: Scientific American, Inc; 1989.

Border JR. Death from severe trauma: open fractures to multiple organ dysfunction syndrome. *J Trauma.* 1995;39: 12–22.

Champion HR, Sacco WJ, Carnazzo AJ, et al. Trauma score. *Crit Care Med.* 1981;9:672.

Committee on Medical Aspects of Automotive Safety. Rating the severity of tissue damage. I. The abbreviated scale. *J Am Med Assoc.* 1972;220:717.

Daly JM, Vars HM, Dudrick SJ. Effects of protein depletion on the strength of colonic anastomoses. *Surg Gynecol Obstet.* 1972;134:15–21.

Duke University Center for the Study of Aging and Human Development. *Multidimensional Functional Assessment Questionnaire.* 2nd ed. Durham, NC: Duke University; 1978.

Fillenbaum G. Screening the elderly: a brief instrumental activities of daily living measure. *J Am Geriatr Soc.* 1985;33:698.

Hanan K, Schelle L. Albumin vs. weight as a predictor of nutritional status and pressure ulcer development. *Ostomy/Wound Manage.* 1991;33:22–27.

Haydock DA, Hill GL. Impaired wound healing in surgical patients with varying degrees of malnutrition. *JPEN.* 1986;10:550–554.

Hunt TK. *Wound Healing and Wound Infection: Theory and Surgical Practice.* New York, NY: Appleton-Century-Crofts; 1980.

Irvin TT. Effects of malnutrition and hyperalimentation on wound healing. *Surg Gynecol Obstet.* 1978;146:33–37.

Katz S, Downs TD, Cash HR, Grots RC. Progress in the development of the index of the ADL. *Gerontologist.* 1970; 10:20–30.

Kay SP, Moreland JR, Schmitter E. Nutritional status and wound healing in lower extremity amputations. *Clin Orthop.* 1987;217:253–256.

Kobak MW, Benditt EP, Wissler RW, et al. The relation of protein deficiency to experimental wound healing. *Surg Gynecol Obstet.* 1947;85:751–756.

Lawton MP, Brody EM. Assessment of older people: self-monitoring and instrumental activities of daily living. *Gerontologist.* 1969;9:179–186.

Levenson SM, Seifter E, Van Winkle W. *Fundamentals of Wound Management in Surgery: Nutrition.* South Plainfield, NJ: Cirurgecom Inc.

Moore EE, Dunn EL, Moore JB, et al. Penetrating abdominal trauma index. *J Trauma.* 1981;21:439.

Orgill D, Demling RH. Current concepts and approaches to wound healing. *Crit Care Med.* 1988;16:899–907.

Pinchocofsky-Devin G. Hazards of immobility and polypharmacy. *Support Line.* 1992;14:5–7.

Ruberg RL. Role of nutrition in wound healing. *Surg Clin North Am.* 1984;64:705–714.

Stewart AL, Hayes RD, Ware JE. The MOS short-form general hospital survey: reliability and validity in a patient population. *Med Care.* 1988;26:724–735.

Temple WJ, Voitk AJ, Snelling CFT, et al. Effect of nutrition, diet, and suture material on long term wound healing. *Ann Surg.* 1975;182:93–97.

Wilson RF. Trauma. In: Shoemaker WC, Ayres S, Grenvik A, Holbrook PR, Thompson WL, eds. *Textbook of Critical Care.* 2nd ed. Philadelphia, Pa: WB Saunders Co; 1989.

Windsor JA, Knight GS, Hill GL. Wound healing response in surgical patients: recent food intake is more important than nutritional status. *Br J Surg.* 1988;75:135–137.

Young ME. Malnutrition and wound healing. *Heart Lung.* 1988;17:60–67.

Ziegler TR, Gatzen C, Wilmore DW. Strategies for attenuating protein-catabolic responses in the critically ill. *Annu Rev Med.* 1994;45:459–480.

CHAPTER 4

Nutrition Support

- Enteral Nutrition
- Parenteral Nutrition
- Transitional Feeding

Enteral Nutrition

Laura E. Matarese

DESCRIPTION

Enteral nutrition is the delivery of nutrients through the gastrointestinal (GI) tract.

RATIONALE/BENEFITS

- Absorption of nutrients by the portal system with subsequent delivery to the liver may better support visceral, particularly hepatic, protein synthesis; regulation of metabolic processes; and enhancement of immune competence.
- Enteral nutrition prevents intestinal atrophy.
- Delivery of nutrients through the GI tract may protect against the translocation of bacteria into the systemic circulation.
- Although enteral nutrition is not without potential complications, it is generally considered to be safer than parenteral nutrition.
- Enteral nutrition is generally more convenient than parenteral nutrition.
- Enteral nutrition is less expensive than parenteral nutrition.

INDICATIONS

- The GI tract must be functional, accessible, and safe to use, as indicated by
  1. signs of adequate GI function
  2. normal upper-GI and small-bowel X-ray

  3. normal flatus or bowel movement
  4. presence of bowel sounds
  5. hunger
  6. absence of vomiting
  7. no X-ray or clinical evidence of GI obstruction or ileus
  8. no uncontrolled diarrhea
- Inability to take adequate nutrition by mouth
- The presence of malnutrition and/or anticipated prolonged period of nil per os (NPO)

CONTRAINDICATIONS

- Nonfunctioning GI tract
- Mechanical obstruction of the GI tract
- Prolonged ileus
- Intractable diarrhea or vomiting
- Upper-GI tract hemorrhage
- Requirement for bowel rest
- High risk for aspiration
- Adequate oral intake
- Enterocutaneous fistula

ENTERAL ROUTE

- The route of administration is usually determined by the anticipated length of therapy and risk of aspiration.
- Nasoenteric tubes are used for short-term therapy, generally 4–6 weeks.

1. Nasogastric tubes are used for patients with an intact gag reflex.
2. Nasoduodenal or nasojejunal tubes are used for patients at risk for aspiration or with gastroparesis.

- Percutaneous or surgically placed feeding tubes are indicated for long-term therapy since they are more comfortable and inconspicuous. Types are
1. percutaneous endoscopic gastrostomy (PEG)
2. percutaneous endoscopic jejunostomy (PEJ)
3. direct endoscopic jejunostomy (DEJ)
4. surgical gastrostomy
5. surgical jejunostomy
6. needle catheter jejunostomy

ENTERAL FORMULAS

Enteral formulas are generally classified according to their composition and use:

- *Polymeric formulas*, containing intact nutrients
- *Predigested formulas*, containing partially or completely hydrolyzed nutrients
- *Disease-specific formulas*, for use in organ dysfunction or specific metabolic conditions
- *Modular formulas*, for supplemental use or to create a formula for specific use

In selecting a formula, consider

- limiting factors such as digestive or absorptive capabilities
- fluid requirements
- nutrient requirements
- whether a fiber-containing formula is necessary
- whether there are any metabolic abnormalities that would require the use of a specialized or modified formula
- route of administration

ADMINISTRATION TECHNIQUES

- *Bolus:* Rapid delivery by syringe or feeding reservoir; 240–400 ml of formula are generally given every 4–6 hours.

- *Timed intermittent:* 100–400 ml of formula are given over 20–40 minutes every 2–4 hours.
- *Continuous:* Formula is delivered by infusion pump or gravity drip over 16–24 hours.
- *Cyclic:* Formula is infused for 8–16 hours, usually overnight by infusion pump, and then discontinued in the morning.

MANAGEMENT OF COMPLICATIONS

Infectious

Pulmonary Aspiration

- Verify tube tip location with X-ray before initiating enteral feedings.
- Elevate head of bed at least 30 degrees.
- Check residuals; hold feeding for residual of 100 ml or greater.
- Monitor for distention.
- Small-bore feeding tubes probably do not compromise the lower esophageal sphincter as much as large-bore tubes.
- Use transpyloric feeding or transpyloric feeding with simultaneous gastric decompression for patients at high risk for aspiration.

Formula Contamination

- Use commercially prepared sterile formulas whenever possible.
- Use clean technique.
- Hang feedings for no longer than 8 hours unless the feeding is in a prefilled closed container.
- Change administration container and tubing every 24 hours.
- Refrigerate open formula, and use within 24 hours.

Gastrointestinal

Diarrhea

- Consider concurrent drug therapy that may cause diarrhea.
- Evaluate for *Clostridium difficile*.
- Consider composition and osmolality of enteral formula. Formulas should be lactose free. It may be necessary to change to a low-fat,

predigested, or fiber-containing formula. It may also be necessary to dilute the feeding.

- Decrease the rate or extend the infusion time.
- Use clean technique and hang formulas for no longer than 8 hours at a time unless they are in the form of a prefilled closed system in order to minimize bacterial contamination.
- Use antidiarrheal agents.
- If diarrhea persists in spite of all of the above, the cause may be a resolving ileus or impaction.

Nausea and Vomiting

- Nausea and vomiting usually result from gastric retention, rapid infusion of feeding, high-fat formulas, lactose, or the smell of the formula (polymeric formulas generally smell better than the predigested formulas).
- Use isotonic formulas whenever possible. Persistent gastric retention may require the use of prokinetic agents or transpyloric feedings.
- Feedings should be initiated slowly and gradually advanced as tolerated.
- Feeding tube placement may have to be reconfirmed in patients with severe vomiting.

Abdominal Distention, Cramps, Flatulence

- This is generally caused by rapid delivery of cold formulas, delayed gastric emptying, or malabsorption.
- Feedings should be administered slowly and at room temperature.
- The composition of the formula may have to be changed to low fat or predigested if malabsorption is a problem.

Constipation

- Patient may require more free water or fiber.
- Encourage ambulation if possible.
- May be a sign of GI obstruction or fecal impaction.

Metabolic

Refeeding Syndrome

- Hypophosphatemia and fluid and electrolyte shifts may occur if enteral feedings are initi-

ated too rapidly in severely malnourished patients.

- If possible, correct electrolyte abnormalities before initiating enteral nutrition. Start with hypocaloric feedings and gradually increase formula. Monitor phosphorus, potassium, magnesium, glucose, and electrolytes.

Dehydration

- Results from inadequate fluid intake or excessive losses and/or the administration of hypertonic, high-calorie, high-protein formulas.
- Provide adequate free water; monitor daily weights, intake and output records, serum electrolytes, and clinical manifestations of dehydration.

Overhydration

- May result from excessive fluid intake or rapid infusion of enteral feeding, especially for those patients with cardiac, renal, or hepatic insufficiency.
- Administer enteral feedings slowly; monitor daily weights, intake and output records, serum electrolytes, and clinical manifestations of overhydration.
- May be necessary to restrict volume with a calorically dense formula.
- Institute diuretic therapy.

Hypernatremia

- Results from inadequate fluid intake with excessive losses or excessive sodium intake.
- Monitor daily weights, intake and output records, serum electrolytes, and clinical manifestations of dehydration.
- Replace fluid as additional free water to the enteral feeding or as intravenous fluids.

Hyponatremia

- May be caused by excess fluid intake, fluid overload, syndrome of inappropriate secretion of antidiuretic hormone (SIADH), or excessive GI losses.
- Monitor daily weights, intake and output records, serum electrolytes, and clinical manifestations of overhydration.

- Restrict fluid intake; use calorically dense enteral formula; institute diuretic therapy. Sodium is generally restricted in order to decrease fluid retention; supplement sodium intake only if necessary.

Hyperkalemia

- Occurs in metabolic acidosis, cardiac or renal disease, or excessive potassium intake.
- Monitor serum potassium levels; assess potassium intake from diet, enteral formula, intravenous fluids, and medications.
- Decrease potassium intake; may need to use Kayexelate, glucose, and/or insulin therapy.

Hypokalemia

- Generally occurs as a consequence of refeeding syndrome, diuretic or insulin therapy, or metabolic alkalosis.
- Monitor serum potassium levels; supplement potassium enterally or with intravenous fluids. Severe hypokalemia may require intravenous bolus.

Hyperphosphatemia

- Occurs in renal insufficiency or with excessive use of phosphorus-containing antacids.
- Monitor serum phosphorus levels; use phosphate binders; use low-phosphorus formula; change antacids.

Hypophosphatemia

- Occurs in refeeding syndrome, with insulin therapy, or with excessive use of phosphorus-binding antacids.
- Monitor serum phosphorus levels; if possible, correct phosphorus level prior to initiation of feeding; severe hypophosphatemia may require intravenous bolus; change antacids.

Hypercapnia

- May occur with excessive calorie and/or carbohydrate administration, especially in patients with respiratory compromise.
- Estimate caloric requirements carefully or use indirect calorimetry to avoid overfeeding; use an enteral formula with a balanced distribution of carbohydrate, protein, and fat.

Mechanical

Tube Occlusion

- Irrigate feeding tube frequently with water.
- Minimize the use of the feeding tube as a means to administer medications.
- Flush with water before and after aspirating from the tube.
- If occlusion occurs, mix papain (meat tenderizer) and water to lyse the occlusion; never flush with cranberry juice.

Nasopharyngeal/nasolabial irritation

- Results from prolonged use of large-bore feeding tubes, especially those made from vinyl, rubber, or polyvinylchloride.
- Whenever possible, use small-bore tubes made from polyurethane or silicone.
- Tape tubes securely, without putting pressure on nares.

Acute Otitis Media/Acute Sinusitis

- Acute otitis media is an infection of the middle ear that occurs as a result of pressure from a nasoenteric feeding tube at the opening of the eustachian tube.
- Acute sinusitis occurs when a nasoenteric feeding tube occludes the sinus tract.
- Use small-bore feeding tubes made of polyurethane or silicone.

REFERENCES

American Society for Parenteral and Enteral Nutrition, Board of Directors. Guidelines for the use of parenteral and enteral nutrition in adult and pediatric patients. *JPEN.* 1993;17(no 4, suppl):1SA–52SA.

Bell SJ, Apour CS, Burke PA, Forse RA. Enteral formulas: an update. In: Torosian MH, ed. *Nutrition for the Hospitalized Patient.* New York, NY: Marcel Dekker; 1995: 293–306.

Cataldi-Betcher EL, Seltzer MH, Slocum BA, Jones KW. Complications occurring during enteral nutrition support: a prospective study. *JPEN.* 1983;7:546–552.

DeChicco RS, Matarese LE. Selection of nutrition support regimens. *Nutr Clin Pract.* 1992;7:239–245.

Edes TE, Walk BE, Austin JL. Diarrhea in tube-fed patients: feeding formula not necessarily the cause. *Am J Med.* 1990;88:91–93.

Ideno K. Enteral nutrition. In: Gottschlich MM, Matarese LE, Shronts EP, eds. *Nutrition Support Dietetics Core Curriculum.* Silver Spring, Md: American Society for Parenteral and Enteral Nutrition; 1993:71–91.

Lysen LK. Metabolic complications during enteral nutrition. In: Krey SH, Murray RL, eds. *Dynamics of Nutrition Support.* Norwalk, Conn: Appleton-Century-Crofts; 1986: 349–359.

Lysen LK, Winkler MF. Assessment and nutrition management of the patient receiving enteral nutrition support. In: Winkler MF, Lysen LK, eds. *Suggested Guidelines for Nutrition and Metabolic Management of Adult Patients Receiving Nutrition Support.* 2nd ed. Chicago, Ill: American Dietetic Association; 1993:6–19.

Matarese LE. Rationale and efficacy of specialized enteral nutrition. *Nutr Clin Pract.* 1994;9:58–64.

Rombeau JL, Caldwell MD, eds. *Clinical Nutrition: Enteral and Tube Feeding.* 2nd ed. Philadelphia, Pa: WB Saunders Co; 1990.

Parenteral Nutrition

Jo Ann McCrae

DESCRIPTION

Parenteral nutrition (PN) is the intravenous provision of macronutrients and micronutrients to the individual who has a nonfunctional gastrointestinal tract, has an enteral tract that cannot be accessed, or is unable to digest nutrients.

Total Parenteral Nutrition (TPN)

TPN allows a highly concentrated, hypertonic solution to be administered to the patient. The parenteral solution can be tailored to meet the macronutrient and fluid requirements of the patient. It may be used indefinitely, especially if a tunneled vascular access is used.

- Hypertonic solutions (> 900 mOsmol/l) can be used.
- Provides long-term feeding access.

Peripheral Parenteral Nutrition (PPN)

PPN avoids the use of a central vein and the complications that can arise from its use. Because it is administered by a peripheral vein, the osmolarity needs to be < 900 mOsmol/l to prevent vein damage and thrombophlebitis (normal serum osmolarity is 275–295 mOsmol/kg). As a result, the solution will provide fewer calories and less protein per volume. The concentration of electrolytes is also limited. To meet the nutrient requirements of a patient, a large volume of solution is required, and this volume may exceed the fluid requirements of the patient. Vein damage can occur, and peripheral vein access may be exhausted so that central access is then required. PPN is usually limited to < 2 weeks because of potential injury to the peripheral veins and the frequent need to change the infusion site.

INDICATIONS

TPN should be used

- when the patient is unable to absorb nutrients via the gastrointestinal tract because of
  1. massive small-bowel resection
  2. small intestinal disease
  3. radiation enteritis
  4. severe diarrhea
  5. intractable vomiting
- during high-dose chemotherapy or radiation or bone marrow transplant therapy
- in acute pancreatitis
- in severe malnutrition when the gastrointestinal tract is nonfunctional

- in catabolic patients when the gastrointestinal tract will not be usable within 5–7 days

  TPN may be used

- with major surgery, moderate stress, enterocutaneous fistula, inflammatory diseases, intensive chemotherapy, hyperemesis gravidarum, or malnutrition when enteral nutrition cannot be established within a 7- to 10-day period

  TPN may be of limited use

- in well-nourished patients who are undergoing minimal stress when the gastrointestinal tract can be used in 10 days or who are immediately postoperative

  TPN should not be used

- in patients with a functional gastrointestinal tract
- if TPN is needed for less than 5 days
- when an urgent operation would have to be delayed for TPN to be administered
- when TPN is not desired by the patient/guardian and when the patient/guardian's wishes are in accordance with hospital policy and existing law
- when prognosis does not warrant therapy
- when risks exceed potential benefits

CARBOHYDRATE SOLUTIONS

Requirements

- Glucose is the primary energy substrate. Brain and red blood cells require glucose as a fuel. Maximum glucose oxidation is ~ 5–7 mg/kg/min.
- Carbohydrate is provided through dextrose parenteral solutions.
- Dextrose monohydrate provides 3.4 kcal/kg.
- Dextrose concentrations range from 5%–70%.
- Higher concentrations are used to decrease volume in cases of fluid restrictions.
- A quick estimate of osmolarity is 50 times dextrose g/l.
- Dextrose suppresses gluconeogenesis.

Precautions

- Excess glucose can cause lipid synthesis and fatty liver.
- Excess glucose can cause elevations in liver function tests.
- Glucose oxidation causes an increase in carbon dioxide production, which may be clinically significant in chronic obstructive pulmonary disease (COPD). Therefore, it is important to avoid overfeeding to prevent increase in carbon dioxide production.
- High doses may cause hyperglycemia.
- Intolerances may be seen in diabetes mellitus, stress, trauma, pancreatitis, and postoperative stress.
- Sudden glucose intolerance may indicate infection.
- Glucose intolerance can be managed by administering exogenous insulin or by adding insulin to the bag.
- Chromium deficiency can cause glucose intolerance.
- Steroids can cause hyperglycemia.
- With hyperglycemia, advance dextrose infusions slowly, starting with 150–200 g/day.
- With hyperglycemia, use both glucose and fat.

AMINO ACID SOLUTIONS

Requirements

- Amino acids are required for cell structure and skeletal muscle. Amino acid components include enzymes, hormones, cytokines, circulating and transport proteins, and cell messenger components.
- The requirement for healthy adults is 0.8 g/kg/day.
- Protein needs depend on age, nutritional status, physical activity, metabolism and stress, and renal and hepatic function.
  1. Critical illness: 1.2–1.5 g protein/kg/day.
  2. Trauma: > 1.5 g protein/kg/day.
  3. Renal and hepatic disease may require a protein restriction.

Considerations

- Standard solutions contain an essential, semi-essential, and nonessential amino acid profile.
- Amino acid concentrations range from 3.5%–15% amino stock solution.
- A nonstress formula—300 nonprotein calories for optimal utilization of 1 g of nitrogen.
- A stress formula—100–150 nonprotein calories for optimal utilization of 1 g of nitrogen.
- Amino acids provide 4 kcal/g.
- A quick estimate of osmolality is $100 \times \%$.

Precautions

- Parenteral amino acid solutions differ according to concentrations, nitrogen content, osmolality, electrolyte concentrations, and specific amino acids—especially in specialty amino acid products available for stress, hepatic, and renal failure.

LIPID SOLUTIONS

Requirements

- Lipids serve as a concentrated form of energy (9 kcal/g), a structural component of cell membranes, and a precursor of prostaglandin synthesis; they also prevent essential fatty acid deficiency.
- Approximately 4% of calories must be provided as essential fatty acids to prevent a deficiency.
- Should provide 500 cc of lipid infusion 2–3 times per week.

Considerations

- Lipid emulsions are available in 10%, 20%, and 30% concentrations.
- 10% lipid emulsions = 1.1 kcal/cc; 20% = 2 kcal/cc; 30% = 3 kcal/cc.
- Maximal fat dosage should not exceed 60% of calories.
- 30%–50% of calories commonly prescribed.
- < 1.0 g/kg/day of lipid recommended.

- < 30% of calories from lipids reduces the negative effect of suppression of the immune system and dysfunction of the reticuloendothelial system.
- A 24-hour infusion is better tolerated than a 10-hour infusion.
- Lipids are important fuel in glucose-intolerant patients.
- Less carbon dioxide is produced during fat oxidation than with glucose oxidation, which may be helpful in the COPD.
- Lipid emulsions are isotonic.
- Decrease in elevated liver function test values when using glucose and fat versus just a glucose-based parenteral solution.
- Provide a concentrated form of energy.
- Available as soybean oil and soybean/safflower oil long chain triglyceride emulsions.

Precautions

- Linoleic acid has been thought to be immunosuppressive. Limit dosage to < 30% of calories.
- The reticuloendothelial system may be impaired due to accumulation of lipids.
- In hyperlipidemia, restrict lipids, but provide essential fatty acid requirements.
- In the case of the altered lipid metabolism seen in pancreatitis, familial hyperlipidemia, stress, and moderate liver disease—must monitor closely to see if lipid solutions cause increases in blood lipid levels.
- If serum triglyceride concentration exceeds 550 mg/dL, the cause should be investigated.
- Lipid clearance can be evaluated by measuring serum triglyceride concentration pre-infusion and 6 hours postinfusion.
- Lipid-intolerance clearance is indicated by concentrations > 300 mg/dL.
- Hypertriglyceridemia is indicated by concentrations > 250–300 mg/dL.
- To prevent fat overload syndrome, do not exceed 2.5g/kg/day as maximum fat dosage, or 60% of the calories provided as fat.
- Potential adverse reactions include respiratory difficulties, fever, and chills (may be related to infusion rate), and or allergic reaction due

to egg allergy; when egg phosphatides are used as an emulsifying agent.

Structured Lipids

- Not available in the United States—used only in research.
- May have a favorable impact on immunosuppression by lipids.
- Are a mixture of medium chain triglycerides (MCT) and long chain triglycerides (LCT).
- Administration results in decreased bacterial sequestration in the lung and improved reticuloendothelial system (RES) function.

FLUID

Requirements

- Calculation of fluid requirements:
  1. Young healthy adult: 40 cc/kg/day
  2. Adult: 30–35 cc/kg body weight
  3. Elderly patient: < 30 cc/kg body weight
- Needs are increased with renal, gastrointestinal (fistulas, drainage tubes, diarrhea, nasogastric suction, and ostomies), respiratory, and skin losses.
- Needs are decreased with renal, hepatic, or cardiac failure.
- Usual fluid intake is ~ 1 cc/kcal/day.
- Monitoring includes signs and symptoms of dehydration or overhydration; intake and output; and daily weights.

TOTAL NUTRIENT ADMIXTURES (TNA)

TNA is a combination of glucose, amino acids, and lipids in a single container for intravenous administration. TNAs decrease risk of external contamination, decrease nursing and pharmacy time, and improve patient compliance.

Precautions

- TNAs provide increased opportunity for growth of bacteria.
- In-line filters cannot be used.

- The common 0.22-micron filter effectively removes bacteria and fungi but is too small to allow passage of lipid particles. A 1.2-micron filter may be used (1.2-micron filter will remove *Candida*).
- It is difficult to inspect particulate matter.
- If emulsion breaks or cracks, discard formula. Report to pharmacy when oil globules on the surface of a creamed emulsion coalesce.
- The order in which nutrients are combined in a TNA may also affect stability.

VITAMIN SOLUTIONS

Requirements

Appendix G contains guidelines for usual parenteral daily intake of vitamins for adults formulated by the Nutrition Advisory Group of the American Medical Association.

Vitamin Considerations

- Stability is affected by light, temperature, pH, storage time, and solution.
- Should be added on a daily basis unless there is a preexisting condition.
- Should be added prior to infusion.
- Vitamin K is added separately as a daily or weekly dose.

TRACE ELEMENT SOLUTIONS

Considerations

- Deficiencies are usually attributed to the lack of trace element addition/supplementation to the TPN.
- Excess gastrointestinal loss may contribute to a deficiency.
- Urine losses may contribute to a deficiency.
- Assessment of total body stores by serum plasma levels is difficult and controversial. See chart in Appendix F for Guidelines for Usual Parenteral Daily Intake.
- An additional 20 µg/day of chromium is recommended with intestinal losses.

- An additional 12.2 mg of zinc per liter of small-bowel fluid lost and 17.1 mg of zinc/kg of stool or ileostomy output; 2.0 mg/day for acute catabolic stress.

Precautions

- Parenteral iron supplementations have been associated with anaphylaxis and death; test dose required before administration.
- Requirements for specific disease states unknown.

ELECTROLYTE SOLUTIONS

Considerations

- Standard electrolyte doses are used in the majority of patients.
- Additions, reductions, and/or deletions of electrolytes are indicated in disease states and altered metabolic states.
- Increased losses via gastrointestinal tract may be secondary to vomiting, diarrhea, ostomies, fistulas, and nasogastric suctioning.
- Medications may require adjustments in electrolyte doses.
- Renal, liver, and heart dysfunction may decrease electrolyte intake.
- Excess calcium and phosphorus supplementation may cause crystalline precipitation, which can cause catheter occlusion and death; strict adherence to pharmacy guidelines is needed.

Requirements

The usual daily electrolyte requirements are:

- Calcium: 10–15 mEq
- Phosphorus: 20–45 mMol
- Potassium: 60–100 mEq
- Sodium: 60–100 mEq
- Magnesium: 10–20 mEq

Precautions

- Electrolyte disorders secondary to diseases, organ dysfunction, gastrointestinal losses, and medical and drug treatment can be treated not only by attention to their possible causes but also by adjustment of the parenteral solution, followed by careful monitoring (see Table 4–1).

MONITORING

Monitoring should include the following:

- Daily weights
- Daily intake and output
- Diabetic urines
- Nutrient intake record if eating by mouth
- Changing of tubing, bag, and filter according to policy (not to exceed 48 hours)
- Laboratory values including:
  - Blood glucose, blood urea nitrogen/creatinine, and serum electrolytes (potassium, sodium): Monitor daily until stable, then 2–3 times per week.
  - Serum calcium, phosphorus, and magnesium levels: Monitor daily until stable, then weekly.
  - Serum triglyceride levels: Take baseline and pre- and postinfusion values initially.
  - Liver function tests (alkaline phosphatase, bilirubin, AST) levels: Take initially and then weekly.
  - Visceral protein status (albumin, transferrin, prealbumin): Monitor weekly.
  - Zinc level: Take initially.
  - Prothrombin levels: Monitor weekly.
  - Complete blood count (CBC) with differential and platelets: Monitor weekly.
- Changes in clinical status, including acid-base balance, medical therapy, drug-nutrient interactions, gastrointestinal function and losses, major organ function, and fever
- Oral and/or enteral intake
- Continued goals of nutrition therapy

BRANCHED-CHAIN AMINO ACID (BCAA) SOLUTIONS

- BCAAs include essential amino acids: leucine, isoleucine, and valine.

Table 4–1 Electrolyte Disorders: Etiology and Treatment by Parenteral Solution Adjustment

Electrolyte Disorder	Possible Etiology	Treatment
Hypercalcemia	Renal failure Bone cancer Immobilization, stress Excess vitamin D administration	Decreased calcium supplementation Isotonic saline Phosphorus supplementation
Hypocalcemia	Low vitamin D intake Hypoalbuminemia Hypoparathyroidism Hypomagnesemia, hyperphosphatemia Malabsorption, inadequate Ca in TPN	Calcium supplementation if ionized calcium is low Corrected magnesium deficiency
Hyperphosphatemia	Renal failure Excess phosphate administration	Phosphate binders Decreased phosphorus supplementation
Hypophosphatemia	Refeeding syndrome Exogenous insulin Phosphate-binding antacids Alcoholism Diabetic ketoacidosis	Phosphorus supplementation Additional IV supplementation if severely depleted Check on antacids
Hypermagnesemia	Renal failure Excess Mg administration	Decreased Mg supplementation
Hypomagnesemia	Refeeding syndrome Chemotherapy Alcoholism Diuretics Medications (cisplatin, amphotericin B) GI losses	Magnesium supplementation Additional IV supplementation if severely depleted
Hyperkalemia	Renal failure Metabolic acidosis Excess K administration Medications Catabolism	Decreased K supplementation Potassium binders
Hypokalemia	Refeeding syndrome Medications Inadequate potassium intake Excess losses (GI drainage, ostomies, fistulas, diarrhea, diuretics)	Potassium supplementation Additional IV supplementation if severely depleted
Hypernatremia	Dehydration, excess water losses Excess sodium intake Osmotic diuresis secondary to hyperglycemia	Fluid replacement if dehydrated Decreased sodium supplementation
Hyponatremia	Excess water intake Cirrhosis Congestive heart failure SIADH Excessive losses	Decreased fluid intake Increased sodium in TPN if appropriate

- Are oxidized primarily outside the liver, but during stress, oxidized primarily in muscle and a valuable fuel.
- It is theorized that infusion of BCAAs parenterally may prevent catabolism of muscle protein.
- Indications for use are controversial, including use during sepsis, condition of polytrauma, multiple organ system failure, > 10 g of urinary urea nitrogen excreted in 24 hours, ongoing negative nitrogen balance.
- Have no proven efficacy with mortality or morbidity compared to standard solutions.
- Dose of up to 5.0 g/kg/day is acceptable.
- For further information, see the Trauma/Sepsis section in Chapter 3.

HEPATIC FAILURE SOLUTIONS

- The aromatic amino acids (AAAs)—phenylalanine, tyrosine, and tryptophan—function as precursors to neurotransmitters (dopamine, norepinephrine, epinephrine, and serotonin) and may cause hepatic encephalopathy.
- AAAs are metabolized primarily in the liver and accumulate in liver failure, whereas BCAA levels decrease.
- For further information, see the Gastrointestinal Disorders section in Chapter 3.

RENAL FAILURE SOLUTIONS

Considerations

- Contain essential amino acids.
- Controversial—based on urea recycling.
- Use in acute renal failure indicated when dialysis is not possible.
- For further information, see the Renal Conditions section in Chapter 3.

REFERENCES

American Medical Association, Department of Foods and Nutrition. Guidelines for essential trace elements preparations for parenteral use: a statement by an expert panel. *JAMA.* 1979;241:2051–2054.

American Medical Association, Department of Foods and Nutrition. Multivitamin preparations for parenteral use: a statement by the Nutrition Advisory Group. *JPEN.* 1979; 3:258–262.

American Society for Parenteral and Enteral Nutrition, Board of Directors. Guidelines for the use of total parenteral nutrition in the hospitalized adult patient. *JPEN.* 1986;10:441–445.

American Society for Parenteral and Enteral Nutrition, Board of Directors. Guidelines for the use of parenteral and enteral nutrition in adult and pediatric patients. *JPEN.* 1993;17(no 4, suppl):21S–22S.

Baker A, Rosenberg I. Hepatic complications of total parenteral nutrition. *Am J Med.* 1987;82:489–497.

Baptista R, Bistrian B, Blackburn G, Miller D, Champagne C, Buchanan L. Utilizing selenious acid to reverse selenium deficiency in total parenteral nutrition patients. *Am J Clin Nutr.* 1984;39:816–820.

Cleghorn E, Esenberg L, Hack S, Parton P, Meritt R. Observations of vitamin A toxicity in three patients with renal failure receiving parenteral alimentation. *Am J Clin Nutr.* 1986;44:107–112.

Compher C. Nutritional support in renal failure. *Surg Clin North Am.* 1991;71:597–608.

Davey-McCrae J, Udine L, O'Shea R. Parenteral nutrition: hospital to home. *J Am Diet Assoc.* 1993;93:664–670.

Davis A, Franz F, Courtnay D, Ullrey D, Scholten D, Dean R. Plasma vitamin and mineral status in home parenteral nutrition patients. *JPEN.* 1987;11:480–485.

Fischer J. Branched-chain-enriched amino acid solution in patients with liver failure: an early example of nutritional pharmacology. *JPEN.* 1990;14:249S–256S.

Gottschlich M. Selection of optimal lipid sources in enteral and parenteral nutrition. *Nutr Clin Pract.* 1992;7:152–165.

Hahn P, Allardyce D, and Frolich J. Plasma carnitine levels during TPN of adult surgical patients. *Am J Clin Nutr.* 1982;36:569–572.

Klein G, Rivera D. Adverse metabolic consequences of total parenteral nutrition. *Cancer.* 1985;55:305.

Narins R. Diagnostic strategies in disorders of fluid, electrolyte and acid-base homeostasis. *Am J Med.* 1982;72:496–519.

Ott S, Maloney N, Klein GL, Alfrey A, Ament M, Coburn J. Chronic parenteral nutrition. *Ann Intern Med.* 1983;98: 910–914.

Riggle M, Brandt R. Decrease of available vitamin A in parenteral nutrition solutions. *JPEN.* 1986;10:388–392.

Shils M, Baker H, Frank O. 1985. Blood vitamin levels of long-term adult home total parenteral nutrition patients: the efficacy of the AMA-FDA parenteral multivitamin formulation. *JPEN.* 1985;9:179–188.

Veterans Affairs Total Parenteral Nutrition Cooperative Study Group. Perioperative total parenteral nutrition in surgical patients. *N Engl J Med.* 1991;325:525–532.

Transitional Feeding

Marion F. Winkler

DESCRIPTION

Transitional feeding is the period of time during the progression from parenteral nutrition support to enteral tube feeding or oral diet, or from enteral tube feedings to oral diet. The overlapping of one regimen with another is essential for successful transitioning and allows for maintenance of nutrient intake.

CAUSE

Readiness to make the transition from one form of nutrition support to another is related to gastrointestinal function, adequacy of fluid, nutrient, and calorie intake; and availability of an access route. Transitional feeding can occur over a short time period in an acute care setting or over a longer period of time in the home environment. Persons with short-gut syndrome may require a prolonged transitional feeding period as gut adaptation occurs.

ASSESSMENT

- Evaluate gastrointestinal function and ability to tolerate enteral or oral nutrients. Tests for malabsorption and a gastrointestinal workup may be necessary.
- Evaluate potential enteral access sites if the transition is from a parenteral to an enteral route. Feeding-tube placement is related to the patient's overall condition and anticipated duration of nutrition support therapy.
- Note any change in the patient's ability to feed dependently or independently.
- Assess adequacy of intake for fluids, nutrients, and calories during the transitional feeding period.

PROBLEMS

- Inability to tolerate enteral or oral feedings due to impaired digestion or absorption

- Inability to maintain weight, hydrational status, electrolyte balance, and/or nutritional parameters without parenteral nutrition or intravenous fluid support
- Rebound hypoglycemia due to sudden cessation of parenteral nutrition feedings
- Discontinuation of nutrition support despite inadequate oral intake

TREATMENT/MANAGEMENT

- Anticipate long-term needs for nutrition support; recommend placement of percutaneous endoscopic feeding tubes or postpyloric feeding tubes at the time of endoscopy or gastrointestinal workup; recommend placement of gastrostomy or jejunostomy tube at the time of other operative procedures.
- Recommend simultaneous decrease in parenteral nutrition support as enteral tube feeding or oral intake improves, or recommend decrease in enteral nutrition as improvement in oral diet is noted; take into account total calories, nutrients, and fluid intake.
- The selection of enteral tube-feeding product is based on digestive and absorptive capacity, disease state, organ function, and overall clinical status. Progression to oral diet is typically advancement from clear liquids to full liquids to soft or regular diet, with modifications made on the basis of digestive and absorptive function, disease state, overall clinical status, and the ability to chew and swallow. Oral nutritional or between-meal supplements should be used to augment caloric intake if necessary.
- Weaning can occur by decreasing the total volume of formula, changing the concentration or caloric density of the formula, decreasing the number of hours of infusion, or decreasing the number of days/nights of infusion.
- Cyclic infusions of parenteral or enteral nutrition support or intermittent enteral tube feed-

ings are useful during the transition to oral diet and allow the patient the freedom to eat meals during the day while receiving supplemental nutrition overnight. In the case of weaning from enteral tube feeding to oral diet, tube feedings can be temporarily stopped for 1 hour before and after meals.

- Parenteral nutrition should be tapered cautiously to avoid rebound hypoglycemia. Intravenous solutions of 5% or 10% dextrose can be used prior to discontinuation of total parenteral nutrition (TPN) if the patient is not receiving tube feedings or a meal.
- Calorie counts or food diaries should be kept during the period of transitional feeding.
- Document tolerance and achievement of at least 50% of required fluid, nutrient, and calorie goals for 3 consecutive days before completely discontinuing parenteral or enteral nutrition support.
- Document improvement in nutritional status (change in or maintenance of plasma proteins and weight and change in functional ability) and achievement of nutritional goals.

EXAMPLE

A 30-year-old male suffered pancreatic injuries and a transected colon in a motor vehicle accident. He underwent multiple operative procedures for pancreatic debridement, bowel resection, and creation of an ileostomy. His postoperative course was complicated by multiple abdominal abscesses that required drainage. He remained in the surgical intensive care unit, was sedated, and was on mechanical ventilation. TPN was begun on hospital day 2, providing 2500 kcal and 120 g of protein to meet measured energy expenditure and 1.5 g protein/kg. When his condition stabilized and his ileostomy began to function, a nasoduodenal tube was placed under fluoroscopy for enteral feedings. A low-fat, elemental diet was selected because of presumed maldigestion and malabsorption secondary to pancreatic insufficiency. Tube feedings were initiated at 20 ml/hr and were advanced slowly. Parenteral nutrition was simultaneously tapered as tube feedings were increased, as indicated below:

Enteral Intake	Parenteral Intake
0	2500 kcal 120 g protein
1000 kcal 40 g protein	2000 kcal 120 g protein
1500 kcal 60 g protein	1500 kcal 90 g protein
2000 kcal 75 g protein	1000 kcal 60 g protein

The patient tolerated tube feedings for 10 days before a trial with a polymeric diet was attempted in an effort to increase caloric density and achieve adequate protein intake. TPN was maintained until tolerance to the 1.5-kcal/ml formula was demonstrated. The volume, consistency, and color of the ileostomy output were monitored. The patient experienced no increase or change in ileostomy output. Parenteral nutrition was then discontinued, as the patient was tolerating approximately 3000 calories and 120 g of protein via the nasoduodenal feeding.

REFERENCES

Skipper A. Transitional feeding and the dietitian. *Nutr Support Serv.* 1982;2(no 8):45–46.

Wade J. Parenteral and enteral transition techniques. In: Krey SH, Murray RL, eds. *Dynamics of Nutrition Support.* Norwalk, Conn: Appleton-Century-Crofts; 1986:489–496.

Winkler MF. Standards of practice for the nutrition support dietitian: importance and value to practitioners. *J Am Diet Assoc.* 1993;93:1113–1116.

Winkler MF, Lysen LK, eds. *Suggested Guidelines for Nutrition and Metabolic Management of Adult Patients Receiving Nutrition Support.* 2nd ed. Chicago, Ill: American Dietetic Association; 1993.

Winkler MF, Pomp A, Caldwell MD, Albina JE. Transitional feeding: the relationship between nutritional intake and plasma protein concentrations. *J Am Diet Assoc.* 1989;89:969–970.

Winkler MF, Watkins CK, Albina JE. Adequacy of TPN intake: an indicator for quality nutrition care. *J Am Diet Assoc.* 1991;91(suppl):A-50. Abstract.

Zibrida JM, Carlson SJ. 1993. Transitional feeding. In: Gottschlich MM, Matarese LE, Shronts EP, eds. *Nutrition Support Dietetics Core Curriculum.* Silver Spring, Md: American Society for Parenteral and Enteral Nutrition; 1993:459–466.

CHAPTER 5

Hospital Discharge Planning: The Role of the Dietitian

Karen Buzby and Joan R. Ullrich

DESCRIPTION

As the length of hospital stay decreases and as patient care and rehabilitation are increasingly provided in the outpatient setting, it is imperative that the dietitian assess the postacute nutritional needs of the patient and develop a plan to address these needs prior to discharge. Early and effective hospital discharge planning will facilitate the patient's transition between the hospital and the home, skilled nursing facility, or rehabilitation center. Depending on the specialty area of practice, the discharge planning responsibilities of the dietitian may range from nutrition education and counseling to coordinating the resources needed to provide home enteral nutrition support.

To provide a smooth transition from the hospital to the home for patients requiring total enteral nutrition, a multidisciplinary approach to discharge planning is necessary. It is essential for the dietitian to collaborate with other members of the health care team, including the physician, nurse, pharmacist, social worker, hospital case manager, and discharge planner, to ensure that the patient's feeding-related needs, equipment, and supplies will be arranged for prior to discharge. In certain instances, the dietitian may need to interface with home care and nursing agencies to process certification of medical necessity and treatment authorization request forms and to negotiate with the insurance company to guarantee payment for nutritional therapies at home.

ASSESSMENT OF DISCHARGE NEEDS

Medical History

- Review records to identify current medical management, including recent diagnostic tests and procedures.
- Identify clinical variables affecting food intake, digestion, or absorption, and assess for changes in appetite, intake, and food tolerances.

Nutrition History

- Review information previously collected about food habits and eating patterns.
- Evaluate for appetite changes, anorexia, dysphagia, nausea, vomiting, diarrhea, or constipation.
- Estimate oral intake, and analyze food frequency for missing food groups suggestive of dietary inadequacies and food allergies, aversions, or intolerance.
- Document current or previous use of special therapeutic or modified diets, dietary supplements, and vitamin and/or mineral usage.
- Document previous or current use of total enteral nutrition (TEN) or total parenteral nutrition (TPN).

Nutrition Assessment

- Review and update previously collected nutrition assessment information. For a review of important nutrition assessment parameters, see Chapter 1.

- Evaluate current diet order and determine if changes may be indicated.
- Recommend appropriate discharge diet order and dietary instruction if necessary prior to discharge.
- Establish and record goals and objectives of outpatient nutritional therapy.
- Assess the adequacy of the current nutrition support regimens in relation to goals of nutrition therapy; if these are inadequate, make recommendations to achieve the goals of therapy.

DIETARY INSTRUCTION

Nutrition education and diet counseling are provided to patients who require dietary modification to prevent disease or to treat a preexisting disorder. For a complete overview of dietary meal plans and modifications, indications for use of therapeutic diets, and the nutritional adequacy of various diets, refer to Chapter 7.

The following are suggested strategies for patient diet instruction:

- Family members or the primary caregiver should be included in all teaching.
- Encourage the patient to discuss eating problems with the dietitian.
- Review general nutrition information and the link between good nutrition and health.
  1. Discuss rationale for diet and identify exact diet prescription.
  2. State amount of protein (g/day) needed for maintenance of muscle mass, protein repletion, or protein restriction as indicated.
  3. State number of calories (kcal/day) needed for weight maintenance, gain, or loss as indicated.
  4. Specify fluid restrictions or requirements (ml/day) if indicated.
  5. Identify electrolyte or mineral restrictions or requirements if indicated.
  6. Discuss vitamin requirements and need for supplementation if indicated.

- Assist the patient/caregiver in developing a meal plan consistent with the prescribed diet.
  1. Review daily intake (servings per day) from the food groups.
  2. Recommend a meal pattern for the patient to follow.
- Review prescribed or restricted food lists/food groups.
  1. Define acceptable foods and amount/serving.
  2. If restrictions are indicated, the dietitian may need to develop a list of foods to avoid.
  3. Identify appealing foods to substitute for items restricted.
- Offer the following general advice for post-discharge meal preparation and consumption:
  1. Make use of timesavers such as prepared foods.
  2. Find help with the cooking; if you are unable to prepare food, use a home meal delivery program such as "Meals on Wheels" or contact relatives, friends, or neighbors to assist in meal preparation.
  3. Prepare lists for food shopping.
  4. A pleasant mealtime atmosphere encourages consumption.
  5. Avoid food that you find unappealing.
- Take into account the following eating problems prior to developing a diet instruction. Oral supplements may be needed to meet the patient's requirements, and a home health nursing consult or home health aide may be needed.
  1. Anorexia (recommend small, frequent feedings)
  2. Problems with nausea and vomiting
  3. Chewing and swallowing problems (recommend modification of food consistency/texture)

DISCHARGE PLANNING DATA COLLECTION/RECORDKEEPING

Collect the following data for use in coordinating the discharge planning process for patients requiring follow-up at home or enteral nutrition support:

- Patient name, address, and phone number
- Primary caregiver name, address, and phone number
- Referring primary care physician name, address, and phone number
- Home care agency or vendor name, address, phone number, and fax number
- Home care nursing supervisor contact name, phone number, and fax number
- Health benefits: Medicare, Medicaid, or insurance company; coverage; contact person and phone number and authorization number
- Medical and nutrition assessment data
  1. Primary and secondary diagnoses
  2. Operations and dates
  3. Malabsorption problems or existing nutrient deficiencies
  4. Age, date of birth
  5. Height, ideal body weight, usual body weight
  6. Discharge weight and date
  7. Basal energy expenditure (BEE; calculated using the Harris-Benedict equation)
     –Males: BEE (kcal/day) = 66 + 13.8 (weight in kg) + 5 (height in cm) – 6.8 (age in years)
     –Females: BEE (kcal/day) = 655 + 9.6 (weight in kg) = 1.8 (height in cm) – 4.7 (age in years)
  8. Resting energy expenditure (measured by indirect calorimetry); respiratory quotient and date
- Nutrition care plan and goals of therapy
  1. Daily calorie goal (kcal/day, kcal/kg)
  2. Daily protein goal (protein g/day, protein g/kg)
  3. Fluid requirements (ml/day, ml/kg)
  4. Discharge diet order; TEN or TPN orders
  5. Nutrition education materials provided and diet instruction (date)
  6. Average oral intake (kcal/day, nonprotein kcal/day, carbohydrate g/day, fat g/day, protein g/day)
  7. Supplement usage and preferences

8. Medication list
- Pertinent laboratory data—for each of the following, record most recent laboratory values, highlight abnormal values, and determine nutritional significance:
  1. Blood glucose (date)
  2. Blood urea nitrogen/creatinine (date)
  3. Electrolyte abnormalities (date)
  4. Serum albumin (date)
  5. Hemoglobin and hematocrit (date)
- Tube-feeding data
  1. Type of tube: nasoenteric or feeding enterostomy
  2. Insertion date (month/day/year), attending physician
  3. Formula(s), start date and stop date
  4. Method of feeding: syringe, gravity, or pump
  5. Administration technique—bolus, intermittent, cyclic, or continuous—and rate of formula delivery
  6. Feeding schedule: feeding times (number of feedings per day), formula (ml), water (ml) used to flush tube
  7. Equipment required: administration set, feeding containers, feeding pump, syringes

HOME ENTERAL NUTRITION

Evaluate patient eligibility for home enteral nutrition using preestablished criteria for patient selection:

- Gastrointestinal (GI) tract is functional, and nutrient absorption is adequate.
- Patient is unable to meet nutrient needs by oral route alone.
- Patient has stable clinical and hydration status.
- Calorie, protein, and fluid (free water) needs are achievable by tube feeding.
- Patient and family are willing to comply with home feedings.
- Anticipated duration of enteral nutrition is sufficient for insurance reimbursement. (For Medicare reimbursement, tube feeding must be the sole source of nutrition, feeding must be required for a minimum of 3 months, and there

must be a diagnosis of nonfunction of the structures that normally permit food to reach the GI tract.)
- Tolerance to enteral nutrition has been demonstrated.
- Patient and family able to prepare and administer feedings.
- The home environment is safe.
- Financial responsibilities and insurance arrangements have been considered.
- Ongoing monitoring is feasible.
- Home tube feeding is more advantageous than inpatient care.
- Follow-up care for tube and pump problems or non-nutritional problems is available.

Selection of access route, formula, and feeding schedule of home tube feeding:

- Factors to consider when selecting a feeding tube are the nutritional goals of the patient, the patient's ability to tolerate the procedure for tube placement, and the expected duration of therapy.
- Refer to the section in Chapter 4 on Enteral Nutrition for a comprehensive review of feeding tube and placement, formula selection, and feeding progression.

Factors to consider in selecting a home care company are as follows:

- *Staff:* number, credentials, 24-hour availability, continuing education and inservice, dietitian on staff
- *Equipment and supplies:* type available, method and frequency of delivery, inventory and rotation of stock in the home, 24-hour-a-day and 7-days-a-week delivery, maintenance capabilities
- *Services:* evaluation of the home environment prior to discharge, home visit policies, instruction materials, geographic range served, feedback referral, provision of laboratory services, processing and reporting results, ability to dispense medication, 24-hour on-call pharmacy, nursing and physician availability, equipment repair and maintenance, disaster plan

- *Financial policies:* billing systems, verification of payment, Medicare, Medicaid, and private insurance, price list available, allowance for creative payment plans for clients, process of application for medical assistance
- *Quality management procedures:* written protocols and procedures for care, patient assessment (initial, ongoing, and discharge), monitoring of professional services, patient satisfaction surveys, patient grievance resolution plan, outcome analysis, criteria for subcontracting
- *Communications:* provision of written reports on all home visits, written incident reports, and written confirmation of all verbal orders to the primary physician

The following are tips for negotiating with insurance companies and case managers:

- Discuss the reason for placement of tube enterostomy and the need for enteral nutrition support (eg, s/p neck resection, dysphagia, promotion of wound healing).
- Document that the enteral feeding is the patient's sole source of both hydration and nutrition.
- Bill as a prescription for medical nutrition therapy—*not food.*
- Have the prescription signed by the attending Medicare-certified physician.
- Discuss dietitian involvement postdischarge to the home.
  1. Dietitian will see the patient at clinic visits.
  2. There will be frequent telephone conversations with patient, caregiver, and home care nurse.
  3. Dietitian will monitor laboratory data.
  4. Dietitian will document patient's progress with the case manager.
- Agree to accept payment authorization for a shorter period of time, eg, 30 days, and renegotiate with the case manager on that date after following the patient's progress.
- Be flexible when negotiating payment options, per diem, and separate billing for durable medical equipment.

HOME TUBE-FEEDING INSTRUCTION

The following techniques of home enteral feeding must be reviewed with the patient and a family member (or the primary caregiver) prior to discharge. In some institutions, the dietitian and the primary nurse share the responsibility for home tube-feeding education. When more than one health care professional is responsible for home tube-feeding instruction, a teaching plan checklist should be used to ensure that all the necessary information is reviewed prior to discharge.

General Nutrition Information

- Discuss the need for good nutrition while recovering from illness.
- Describe the general content of the tube-feeding formula: calories for energy (carbohydrate and fat), protein for building and maintaining muscle mass and other important cells, vitamins and minerals to help the body use the calories and protein, and water to maintain hydration status.
- If a disease-specific formula is selected, discuss the rationale for its use and the nutrient content in relation to the disease state.
- If the patient is allowed to take food by mouth, review oral dietary requirements and expectations, and review specific modifications if needed.

Feeding Tubes

- Identify tube by name.
- Explain insertion site and tip location.

Formula

- Review each product prescribed by the physician.
- Specify amount needed per day and per week (to identify storage needs).
- Emphasize that substitutions are not permitted without approval from the health care team.
- Review the following precautions concerning formula storage:

1. Unopened cans, bottles, packets, or envelopes are sterile or free from harmful germs.
2. Check expiration dates stamped on the product container.
3. Check expiration dates on each case of formula.
4. Product should not be used after the expiration date.
5. Unopened formula should be stored in a dry place at room temperature.
6. Unused portions of opened or prepared formula should be covered, labeled, and refrigerated.
7. Discard unused formula after 24 hours.

Formula Preparation

- Emphasize that preparation area should be clean.
- Emphasize washing hands with soap prior to handling formula.
- Instruct that ready-to-use formula should be shaken and container top cleaned before opening.
- Instruct on the proper procedure for mixing powder formulas or mixing two products together.
- When the addition of special ingredients to feeding formula is indicated, supply a list of the items or product(s), clearly define amount to be used per feeding, and discuss the rationale for use.
- Emphasize that formula must be administered according to the feeding schedule.
- Prepare special instructions for the preparation and storage of blenderized formula.
- If medications are to be added to feeding formula, identify medication(s), clearly define amount and frequency of use, discuss how medicine is to be delivered, and identify potential complications secondary to mixing medicine with formula or administering it directly by tube into the GI tract.
- Emphasize the importance of accurate measurement during the preparation of feeding formula.

1. Review the procedure for measuring in commonly used household measures or metric measures.
2. Supply a table of commonly used measurements and their metric conversions.

Tube-Feeding Schedule

• Provide an outline of feeding times and amount of formula to be administered per feeding.
• If the feeding schedule needs to be progressed, provide complete instructions on changing feeding times and amounts.

Checking Tube Position

• Explain the importance of maintaining proper tube position.
• Teach how to check the feeding tube position.
• For assessing nasal tube position, measure and record length of tube outside the nose; if tube length changes by 3–5 in, the next feeding should be held and a health care professional contacted.
• For a gastrostomy tube secured by sutures, check sutures during dressing changes; if the tube is held in place by a retention device, check for balloon inflation and the ruler marking position on the retention device; if sutures break or the tube position changes, the dressing should be replaced and the health care professional should be contacted to have tube resutured/repositioned.

Checking for Gastric Residuals (Gastrostomy Tubes Only)

• Prior to feeding, check the amount of residual remaining in the stomach.
• Measure the residual and replace contents into the stomach.
• If the residual exceeds the predetermined amount, hold the next feeding for 1 hour. The residual should be checked again and the feeding administered accordingly. If the residual is still high, the health care professional should be contacted for instructions.

Intermittent Feeding

• Explain use of feeding bag or syringe.

Continuous Feeding

• Explain use of enteral feeding pump.

Care and Maintenance Issues in Tube Feeding

• Nasogastric or nasoenteric tube
  1. care of nostrils
  2. tube care
• Gastrostomy tube
  1. dressing changes
  2. tube care
• Jejunal tube
  1. dressing changes
  2. tube care

Tube-Feeding Equipment and Supply Needs

• Formula
• Feeding bags
• Pump
• 30-ml and 50-ml piston syringe
• Irrigation kit
• Clamp
• Tape
• Feeding pole or wall hook
• Gauze pads
• Scissors
• Measuring cups/measuring spoons
• Blender/sieve
• Other supplies as needed, depending on tube type, method of feeding, or formula used

Vendor or Home Care Company

• Contact vendor to obtain formula, equipment, and supplies.
• Arrange for delivery to home.

Care and Maintenance of Equipment and Supplies

• Store equipment and supplies in a clean, dry place. Do not store in direct sunlight.

- Check each delivery for accuracy.
- Keep utensils used to prepare formula clean.
- Change syringes and enteral feeding bags every 24 hours; rinse bag and tubing with hot water between feedings.

Complications of Enteral Feeding

A physician should be notified if any of the following symptoms occur:

- nausea or vomiting
- fever
- weight gain or loss
- hard breathing or wheezing
- swelling of ankles or hands
- redness or draining from the tube site
- damage to the tube
- diarrhea
- constipation

Unclogging Tubes

- Instruct in method for unclogging feeding tubes.
- Instruct on procedure to follow in case of accidental tube removal.

Home Tube-Feeding Diary

- Distribute a diary for the patient to complete 2–3 days prior to the next scheduled physician visit.

REFERENCES

American Society for Parenteral and Enteral Nutrition. Standards for home nutrition support. *JPEN.* 1992;7:65–69.

American Society for Parenteral and Enteral Nutrition, Board of Directors. Guidelines for the use of parenteral and enteral nutrition in adult and pediatric patients. *JPEN.* 1993;17(no 4, suppl):1SA–52SA.

Davey-McCrae J. Assessment and nutrition management of the patient receiving home nutrition support. In: Winkler MF, Lysen LK, eds. *Suggested Guidelines for Nutrition and Metabolic Management of Adult Patients Receiving Nutrition Support.* 2nd ed. Chicago, Ill: American Dietetic Association; 1993:30–41.

Gorman RC, Nance ML, Morris JB. Enteral feeding techniques. In: Torosian MH, ed. *Nutrition for the Hospitalized Patient: Basic Science and Principles of Practice.* New York, NY: Marcel Dekker, Inc; 1995:329–351.

Lysen L, Masino K. Oral nutrition management. In: Hermann-Zaidins M, Touger-Decker R, eds. *Nutrition Support in Home Health.* Rockville, Md: Aspen Publishers, Inc; 1989:40–57.

Mahan LK, Escott-Stump S. *Krause's Food, Nutrition, and Diet Therapy.* 9th ed. Philadelphia, Pa: WB Saunders Co; 1996.

CHAPTER 6

Nutrition Management of the Patient outside the Hospital Setting

- Clinical Pathways/Home Care
- Long-Term Care
- Private Practice

Clinical Pathways/Home Care

Carol S. Ireton-Jones

CLINICAL PATHWAYS

A clinical pathway (also called *critical pathway*, *care map*, or *care path*) is an optimal sequencing or timing of interventions by physicians, nurses, and other staff members for a particular diagnosis or procedure. It is designed to utilize resources better, maximize quality of care, and minimize delays. Clinical pathways were first used in

- 1970s—construction and engineering fields to manage complex projects.
- 1980s—hospital reimbursement systems to evaluate how patients were treated and how resources were consumed.
- 1990s—hospital and home care patient management systems to organize information related to patient outcomes and to review diagnostic categories that represented high cost, high risk, and high variability in order to provide a quality outcome to a particular patient population.

Clinical pathways are currently used in health care to define processes in disease state management in order to

- reduce length of stay
- reduce costs associated with specific diagnoses and procedures
- eliminate variances in treatment protocols
- enhance patient outcomes

Clinical pathways should be effective for about 80% of patients placed on them. They should have validity, reliability/reproducibility, clinical applicability, clinical flexibility, and clarity. Pathways should be regularly reviewed.

The components of clinical pathways are

- condition identification
- scope
- categories of action
- outcomes
- documentation

Development of clinical pathways involves

- selection of diagnosis
- utilization of the multidisciplinary team
- identification of characteristics
- statement of current versus ideal care process
- clinical validation and revision

Benefits to using clinical pathways are

- a multidisciplinary plan of care
- planning and coordination of care
- standardization of care and reduction of variance
- education and orientation
- cost control and management
- communication tool
- potential reduction in litigation

Dietitians can contribute to clinical pathway processes by

- determining if clinical pathways, whether disease specific (eg, diabetes, cardiovascular disease) or episode specific (hip fracture/replacement), are currently in use or are being developed and requesting to be a committee member or to review current clinical pathways (a committee might include a physician, a nurse, a dietitian, a social worker, an occupational therapist, a physical therapist, a pharmacist, and others)
- providing input as a committee member
- participating in outcome data collection as a part of the formal process or as ancillary assistance through clinical management

NUTRITION CARE PROVIDED BY DIETITIANS IN ALTERNATE SITES

Nutrition Screening

Screening is the first step in the nutritional care of a patient, conducted prior to a nutritional assessment. It is the process of identifying characteristics known to be associated with nutrition problems, and it is an effective method of ensuring early, cost-effective medical nutrition therapy intervention. The purpose of screening is to identify individuals who are at nutritional risk or are malnourished so that further intervention, if needed, can occur.

Nutrition screening is particularly useful for patients in very large care settings, patients receiving various therapies in the home besides nutritional support to identify those at risk for malnutrition, and patients within specific types of disease categories, such as human immunodeficiency virus (HIV) and cancer.

When the nutrition screening parameters indicate the need for further intervention, a nutrition assessment may be warranted.

Nutrition Assessment

Nutrition assessment is a comprehensive approach by a registered dietitian to defining nutritional status. It uses medical, nutrition, and medication histories; physical examination; anthropometric measurements; and laboratory data. Further, it includes the organization and evaluation of information to declare a professional judgment.

Nutritional assessment obtains static measurements of body compartments and examines their alterations as caused by undernutrition. It usually includes anthropometric measurements such as height, weight, body mass index (BMI), skinfold measurements, and body composition measurements (to assess lean and fat mass). It also assesses the structure and function of organ systems, of altered metabolism as it relates to the loss of lean body mass or other body compartments, and of the metabolic response to nutritional interventions.

Biochemical measurements are typically included to assess

- *Serum protein status:* Levels of rapid-turnover proteins—that is, those with a 3-day or less half-life—are not useful in home care or long-term care. Levels of albumin and transferrin, which have half-lives of approximately 3 weeks and 10 days respectively, should be used.
- *Vitamin status:* Selected vitamin and mineral analyses may be useful for patients on long-term total parenteral nutrition (TPN) or tube feeding.
- *Presence of anemia:* This may be assessed by hematological indices.
- *Immunocompetence:* This may be assessed either by total lymphocyte count (TLC) or by

delayed hypersensitivity skin testing (DHST). TLC may be more useful than DHST for home care patients, as DHST requires a return visit by the clinician to read results.

For the patient receiving home care and long-term care, availability of current biochemical measurements to determine nutritional status may be limited.

With this information, and with data obtained from a medical history, a nutrition/diet history, a weight history, and clinical evaluation, a complete evaluation of the nutritional condition of a patient can be performed.

Classification of Nutrition Status

Three categories of malnutrition exist:

- *Kwashiorkor:* characterized by abnormal visceral protein stores with preservation of fat mass
- *Marasmus:* a type of protein-calorie malnutrition with depression of anthropometric measurements
- *Kwashiorkor-marasmus mix:* often seen in malnourished patients who have levels below normal for both lean and fat body mass

Malnutrition may also be categorized by degree:

- *Mild*—normal to 90% of normal standard
- *Moderate*—89%–80% of normal standard
- *Severe*—< 79% of normal standard

Determination of Energy Requirements

Energy requirements must either be determined by indirect calorimetry or be estimated from energy equations. The most widely used equations are those developed by Harris and Benedict for estimating the caloric requirements of normal subjects. The Harris-Benedict equations (HBEs) are adjusted using a mathematical factor to provide an estimation of a hospitalized patient's calorie requirements. This factor ranges from 1.1 to 1.75. Two specific equations developed and validated in the acute care setting

take into account many of the variables of the HBE and also account for diagnosis, ventilatory status, and obesity:

For ventilator-dependent patients:

$$EEE(v) = 1925 - 10(A) + 5(W) + 281(S) + 292(T) + 851(B)$$

For spontaneously breathing patients:

$$EEE(s) = 629 - 11(A) + 25(W) - 609(O)$$

where:

EEE = estimated energy expenditure (kcal/day), (v) = ventilator dependent, (s) = spontaneously breathing, A = age (years), W = body weight (kg), S = sex (male = 1, female = 0), T = diagnosis of trauma (present = 1, absent = 0), B = diagnosis of burn (present = 1, absent = 0), and O = obesity (present = 1, absent = 0).

Measurement of energy expenditure may be accomplished using indirect calorimetry, which involves the measurement of oxygen consumption and carbon dioxide production during respiratory gas exchange. From those values, one can calculate energy expenditure by using the Weir or similar equations.

Determination of Protein Requirements

The amount of protein required by the infant or child is greater than that required by the adolescent or adult. Protein requirements are usually based on the number of grams of protein to be provided per kilogram of ideal body weight. For normal adults, the recommended dietary allowance (RDA) for protein is 0.8 g of protein per kilogram of ideal body weight.

For the ill or stressed patient, the goal of the nutrition support regimen is to supply adequate protein to promote anabolism. The amount of protein required varies according to disease state and the amount of stress that each disease state may cause to physiological functioning. Protein requirements in stress may be estimated as 16% of total energy requirements or calculated using a calorie-to-nitrogen ratio (ie, ratio of total energy requirements provided to amount of nitrogen provided). This ratio varies from 110–150 kcal/g of nitrogen (protein) provided in the diet. Protein requirements are often calculated on the basis of gram per kilogram of ideal body weight, graduated upward to account for degree of stress or malnutrition. A rule of thumb for amount of protein to be given patients with varying degrees of malnutrition or stress is

- Mild: 0.8–1.0 g/kg/day
- Moderate: 1.0–1.5 g/kg/day
- Severe: 1.5–2.0 g/kg/day

Monitoring

Timing and frequency of monitoring a patient who is receiving home nutrition support will depend on the type of nutrition support the patient is receiving (enteral vs parenteral), the disease state and status of the patient, and the management plan developed by the nutrition support/health care team, including the patient's case manager.

- Generally, the patient receiving enteral (tube) feeding is followed at less frequent intervals than the patient receiving TPN.
- For the patient in transition from one feeding technique to another (enteral to parenteral or parenteral to enteral), follow-up and monitoring may be required more often to ensure a smooth and successful therapy transition.
- Patient monitoring may be accomplished by a home visit or by telephone contact. Chart review to monitor weight and laboratory changes may provide the impetus for determining the monitoring regimen.
- The patient receiving long-term therapy should be monitored according to the standards of the Joint Commission for Accreditation of Healthcare Organizations, as well as by internal standards developed by home care clinicians.
- It is important to involve the patient's case manager in the development of a monitoring plan for any patient receiving home nutrition support.

Other Nutrition Services Provided in the Home by Registered Dietitians

- Diet counseling/diet instruction
- Food preparation and safety instructions
- Diabetic teaching and, if the dietitian is a certified diabetes educator (CDE), all aspects of diabetic care
- Metabolic measurements of energy expenditure, using indirect calorimetry
- Body composition determinations, using skin caliper measurements or bioelectrical impedance analysis
- Teaching and evaluation of feeding-tube site status and patient care techniques
- Evaluation of intravenous line site status and care technique
- Dietary recall analysis
- Grocery-shopping educational tours
- Determination of accessibility and availability of community or home feeding programs
- Assistance with communication with other health care professionals
- Coordination of all aspects of home care, including but not limited to nutrition support
- Inservices for health care professionals on nutrition and on enteral and parenteral products and services
- Hospice care
- Coordination of patient care from physician office to home

Getting Started in Home Care

- Determine the services a dietitian can bring to a home care agency.
- Find out what types of services are currently being provided.
- Provide a cost-benefit approach to the marketing of the services to be provided.
- Negotiate a salary or hourly/visit rate that takes into consideration the type of expertise required and the time involved.

- Know the standards and guidelines of the home care, home infusion, and home nutrition support industry.
- Be creative and innovative.
- Be self-motivated and self-sufficient.
- Be knowledgeable and resourceful.
- Have your own diet instruction materials for oral, enteral, and parenteral nutrition if necessary.

REFERENCES

ADA's definitions for nutrition screening and assessment. *J Am Diet Assoc.* 1994;94:838–839.

American Society for Parenteral and Enteral Nutrition. Standards of practice/standards of care for home nutrition support. *Nutr Clin Pract.* 1992;7:65–69.

American Society for Parenteral and Enteral Nutrition, Board of Directors. Guidelines for the use of parenteral and enteral nutrition in adult and pediatric patients. *JPEN.* 1993;17 (no 4, suppl):1SA–52SA.

Anthony PS, Ireton-Jones C. Dietitians in home care: a new challenge. *Support Line.* 1994;16(no 6):1–8.

Bower RH. Home parenteral nutrition. In: Fisher JE, ed. *Total Parenteral Nutrition.* Boston, Mass: Little, Brown and Co; 1991:367–387.

Coffey RJ, Richards JS, Remmert CS, et al. An introduction to clinical paths. *Quality Manage Health Care.* 1992;1: 45–54.

Guenter PA, Moore K, Crosby LO, et al. Body weight measurement of patients receiving nutritional support. *JPEN.* 1982;6:441–443.

Harris JA, Benedict FG. *Biometric Studies of Basal Metabolism in Man.* Washington, DC: Carnegie Institute of Washington; 1919. Pub No. 270.

Hennessy K. Development of clinical pathways for the management of patients on nutrition support. *Proceedings of the 19th Meeting of the American Society for Parenteral and Enteral Nutrition, Clinical Congress Program Book.* Miami, Fl: 1995;584.

Hermann-Zaidins M, Touger-Decker R, eds. *Nutrition Support in Home Health.* Rockville, Md: Aspen Publishers, Inc; 1989.

Hopkins, B. Nutrition assessment. In: Gottschlich MM, Matarese LE, Shronts EP, eds. *Nutrition Support Dietetics Core Curriculum.* Silver Spring, Md: American Society for Parenteral and Enteral Nutrition; 1993.

Ireton-Jones CS, Hasse J. Comprehensive nutritional assessment: the dietitian's contribution to the team effort. *Nutr.* 1992;8:75–81.

Ireton-Jones C, Hennessy K, Howard D, et al. Multidisciplinary clinical care of the home parenteral nutrition patient. *Infusion.* 1995;1(no 8):21–30.

Ireton-Jones CS, Long A, Garritson BK. The use of indirect calorimetry in the assessment of energy expenditure in patients receiving home nutrition support. *J Am Diet Assoc.* 1994;94 (no 9, 1 suppl):A30. Abstract.

Ireton-Jones CS, Turner WW, Liepa GU, et al. Equations for the estimation of energy expenditures in patients with burns with special reference to ventilatory status. *J Burn Care Rehabil.* 1992;13:330–333.

Jacobs DO, Scheltinga MRM. Metabolic assessment. In: Rombeau JL, Caldwell MD, eds. *Clinical Nutrition: Parenteral Nutrition.* Philadelphia, Pa: WB Saunders Co; 1993:245–274.

Klotz RS, Andrusko-Furphy KT. Care paths: an interdisciplinary approach to patient focused care. *Infusion.* 1996; 2(no 5):24–31.

Lykins TC. Nutrition support clinical pathways. *Nutr Clin Prac.* 1996;11:16–20.

Matthews DE, Fong Y. Amino acid and protein metabolism. In: Rombeau JL, Caldwell MD, eds. *Clinical Nutrition: Parenteral Nutrition.* Philadelphia, Pa: WB Saunders Co; 1993:75–112.

Nagel MR. Nutrition screening: identifying patients at risk. *Nutr Clin Pract.* 1993;8:171–175.

Orr ME. Nutritional support in home care. *Nurs Clin North Am.* 1989;24:437–445.

Position of the American Dietetic Association: nutrition monitoring of the home parenteral and enteral patient. *J Am Diet Assoc.* 1994;94:664–666.

Viall CD, Crocker KS, Hennessy KA, et al. High tech home care: surviving and prospering in a changing environment. *Nutr Clin Pract.* 1995;10:32–36.

Williamson J. Physiologic stress: trauma, sepsis, burns and surgery. In: Mahan LK, Arlin M, eds. *Krause's Food, Nutrition, and Diet Therapy.* Philadelphia, Pa: WB Saunders Co; 1992:491–506.

Long-Term Care

Janice Raymond

Long-term care encompasses several types of health care facilities, ranging from facilities catering to minimal-care residents to facilities providing high-tech hospital services.

- *Adult Family/Developmentally Disabled Family Home*—Provides room and board and basic supervision for persons who are unable to care for themselves independently. This care is provided in a homelike setting.
  Opportunity—Home care dietitians may be used when a resident requires tube feeding or oral supplementation.
- *Assisted Living*—This is the fastest-growing portion of the industry. Generally, individual apartments have some food preparation facilities. Residents can choose either to dine in a congregate setting or to cook for themselves. In addition to menus, assisted living centers provide laundry service, housekeeping, planned activities, transportation, and some assistance with activities of daily living.
  Opportunity
  - Nutrition counseling can be included in the monthly services.
  - Menu evaluation of nutrient content.
  - Home care dietitian used for tube-feeding management and oral supplementation management.
- *Skilled Nursing Facility (SNF)*—A facility for the patient requiring round-the-clock supervision and skilled nursing services. Most SNFs have specific beds or a designated unit for Medicare patients. The Medicare program requires specific space allocation, staffing, and documentation to obtain proper insurance reimbursement. Some SNFs now have subacute units for those residents requiring specialized high-tech care such as intravenous fluids and ventilators. Subacute units are taking over the care of some patients who would otherwise require hospitalization.

- *Opportunity*—Specific dietitian services are required by state and federal legislation. Each facility must employ a dietitian as an employee or consultant.

LEGISLATED RESPONSIBILITIES OF DIETITIANS IN SKILLED NURSING FACILITIES

- Approve regular and therapeutic menus that meet the dietary allowances of the Food and Nutrition Board of the National Research Council, National Academy of Sciences.
- Do nutrition assessments.
- Provide inservice training.
- Act as a liaison with medical and nursing staff and administrators.
- Assist with completion of the minimum data set (MDS), which in most states must be completed within 14 days of admission or readmission (see state administrative codes for exceptions by state).

Nutrition Assessment

A comprehensive nutrition assessment should be completed by the dietitian within 14–30 days, depending on state regulation.

The initial nutrition assessment should include

- diagnosis, diet order
- mental status, medical history, psychosocial history
- appetite
- allergies, intolerances, likes/dislikes
- medications and any food/drug interactions
- conditions affecting food intake or nutrient needs
- usual day's intake
- Alcohol (ETOH) intake and history of abuse
- assessment of adequacy of past/present intake

- height, weight, weight history, and any other available anthropometric measurements
- pertinent laboratory data and dates obtained
- summary of resident's nutritional status, evaluation of oral intake, nutrient requirements, and need for eating assistance
- prioritization of problems of the resident relating to nutrition and a plan of action to meet specific goals
- list of specific recommendations
- prescription for frequency of follow-up
- communication with other facility personnel that is needed to meet nutrition goals

Ongoing Nutritional Evaluation

- Residents should be monitored at least quarterly in conjunction with the Certified Dietary Manager.
- The dietitian must document nutrition status annually and after any readmission.
- High-risk residents must be identified and monitored monthly.
- A procedure should exist that alerts the dietitian to any change of condition, particularly in the case of unplanned weight loss or decrease in food intake.
- Residents at high risk for malnutrition are those with the following characteristics:
  1. under 85% of desirable weight for height
  2. unplanned weight loss of 5% of body weight in 1 month, 7.5% of body weight in 3 months, or 10% of body weight in 6 months
  3. serum albumin less than 3.5 mg/dL
  4. serum cholesterol less than 140 mg/dL
  5. eating less than 75% of food served
  6. stage II or greater pressure ulcer
  7. poorly controlled diabetes
  8. acute illness (eg, influenza)
  9. age over 80 years

Inservice Training

The dietitian should participate in the training of nursing, nutrition services, and personnel. Recommended topics are

- nutritional needs of older residents
- nutritional needs of the developmentally disabled
- nutrition and wound healing
- tube-feeding policies and procedures
- infection control procedures for serving food
- disease-specific nutritional needs (eg, renal, liver, pulmonary)
- water requirements/hydration
- methods of preventing and treating weight loss
- nutritional interpretation of laboratory parameters

CONCLUSION

The incidence of malnutrition in the U.S. population over 65 years of age has been reported to be 25%. In long-term care, the published incidence ranges from 34%–85%. This population is clearly at nutritional risk and requires the services of a dietitian familiar with age-specific nutrition needs and with federal and local long-term care regulation.

Dietitians should pay attention to changes in federal and state reimbursement structure, since dietitians are currently mandated only in skilled care. They must create opportunity and seek reimbursement for their services in all forms of long-term care.

REFERENCES

American Dietetic Association, Consultant Dietitian Practice Group. *Pocket Resource for Nutrition Assessment.* Chicago, Ill: American Dietetic Association; 1994.

ASPEN Reference Group. *Long Term Care Administration.* Silver Spring, Md: American Society for Parenteral and Enteral Nutrition; 1995.

Chernoff R. *Geriatric Nutrition.* Gaithersburg, Md: Aspen Publishers, Inc; 1991.

Raymond JL. Assessment and nutrition management of the older adult. In: Winkler MF, Lysen LK, eds. *Suggested Guidelines for Nutrition and Metabolic Management of Adult Patients Receiving Nutrition Support.* Chicago, Ill: American Dietetic Association; 1993:42–52.

Washington Administrative Code. Chapter 97: Nursing Homes. 1994.

Private Practice

Kathy Stone

Many dietetic professionals, either while they are students or in their first professional role, dream of starting their own private practice. Today, for rapidly increasing numbers of dietitians, that dream is becoming a reality and often a necessity due to the drastic changes in the health care industry. The majority of dietitians have been employed as clinical dietitians in hospitals. Because dietetic services are seldom reimbursable and because of other changes affecting hospitals, many clinical dietetics positions have been cut, and these cuts will accelerate as we move away from hospitals and the traditional type of care they have provided.

There is often a certain degree of denial on the part of dietitians in seeing the reality of the work situation that is evolving and that may force them out of their jobs. For this reason, the decision to go into private practice is often rushed when it should involve considerable planning. These trends will ultimately affect the quality of services provided in private practices and may result in a lowering of the reputation of the profession.

In the past, it was said that a practitioner should have at least 5 years of general dietetics experience before considering private practice. This was to ensure a broad base of knowledge and experience in the field, as well as the development of a network of peers needed to avoid the isolated feeling that an independent practice can create. Today, many dietitians are going straight from their educational programs into entrepreneurial dietetics. This trend is likely to continue, since newly graduated dietetics students will not be able to resist attractive opportunities in the nontraditional areas.

There are several considerations in going into private practice. Entrepreneurial practice is certainly not for everyone. The following are personality/work traits to ponder when considering private practice:

- Can you work alone without interacting with other professionals, sometimes for days?
- Are you self-motivated?
- Can you meet deadlines?
- How will you get clients?
- Can you follow through with contacts to obtain business?
- What are the special traits that differentiate you from others?
- What is your practice going to be (eg, patient counseling, writing, food service)?
- Are you up to date in your areas of expertise?
- Are you computer/technology literate?

GETTING STARTED

You have decided to begin your own private practice. Although entrepreneurial dietetics is relatively new compared to dietetics as a profession, there has been a traditional role in private-practice dietetics. Most dietitians who have started their own consulting business have provided patient counseling, either in their own office or in a physician's office. In more recent years, a private-practice dietitian rarely does patient counseling solely, and more and more frequently, entrepreneurial dietitians do not do patient counseling at all. The opportunities in entrepreneurial dietetics are endless, limited only by a person's creativity and persistence. Additionally, the pursuit of a variety of activities beyond patient counseling keeps a practitioner from "burning out" and helps to keep the practice diverse so that income is not dependent on a single entity.

Lisa Stollman, MA, RD, former chair of the Nutrition Entrepreneurs Dietetic Practice Group and a private-practice nutritionist who specializes in assisting other dietitians in selling or buying private practices, offers the following advice on starting a nutrition business:

- If finances are a problem, start your practice on a part-time basis while you are holding a full-time job. As your practice grows, you can work on decreasing your hours at your full-time position. Having a part-time job when starting your practice may give you greater flexibility with scheduling your private business and marketing your services if finances are not a major issue.

- If you do not have a referral base when you start out, consider renting space in a medical office building where you come into contact with other health professionals on a regular basis. If you do have a referral base, a home office (if you have the space and there are no legal codes against this) may be a terrific option.
- Carry your business cards with you and leave them at every opportunity. Make sure your business card has sufficient information to let customers know what you do.
- Introduce yourself to merchants in your office neighborhood who may be potential clients or sources for referrals. These businesses may include health food stores, fitness centers, hair salons, and gourmet stores.
- Send announcements to all the local physicians and other health professionals in your locale who may be potential referral sources.
- Become involved in your local dietetic association and advertise in its publications. Other dietitians are often a great source of referrals.
- Network within your community. Consider joining your local chamber of commerce. Become involved with some of your local health organizations.
- Whenever you accomplish something, write a press release and send it out to your local newspaper. Remember, you are your best promoter!
- Tell people what you do as a nutritionist. Make sure they know you are in private practice.

FINANCES

In addition to these considerations is the important aspect of finances. Even though private-practice dietetics is not thought to be a capital-intensive business, it does require sufficient funds to start and stay in business. You need to determine whether to rent an office privately, share an office with other practitioners, or do work or counseling from your home.

To determine finances, you should consider how much money you will need to

- begin the practice—make downpayments on rental space, malpractice insurance, etc
- purchase equipment—scales, computer, furniture, videos, educational models, etc
- survive at least 6 months through inadequate income
- market and advertise the business
- develop educational or marketing materials

REIMBURSEMENT

It is important to understand reimbursement thoroughly if you are going to provide counseling services to clients. This aspect of insurance coverage affects many potential clients' decisions to use your services and to what extent. The entire arena of service reimbursement is changing dramatically. Managed care already monopolizes insurance coverage in many states; it is gaining ground rapidly and may be extended to Medicare and Medicaid programs as well. Find out, from physicians you network with, some of the major payers and managed-care organizations in your area.

Lucille Beseler, MS, RD, CS, LD, a board-certified specialist in pediatric nutrition and owner of a private practice dedicated to pediatric/adolescent nutrition, recommends the following in negotiating managed-care contracts:

- Check that your fees are "in line" with those of other nutrition practitioners in your area.
- Use CPT codes that reflect the amount of time you spend with the patient.
- Contact the department of provider relations for the health maintenance organization (HMO) or preferred provider organization (PPO) for which you wish to become a provider.
    1. Inquire how to become a provider.
    2. Ask what is customary and usual reimbursement for the CPT code you use before

supplying provider relations with your fee schedule.
3. Follow up with a letter of inquiry.
4. Follow up with a call to the provider relations representative.
- If you are accepted:
  1. Negotiate reimbursement (yes, fees are negotiable).
  2. HMOs/PPOs negotiate contract fees based on Medicare allowables. To find out the Medicare allowable fee schedule in your region, contact the Medicare office.
  3. The contract should include a schedule of your fee reimbursement.

At the 1994 annual meeting of the American Dietetics Association, a session entitled "Private Practice Reimbursement: Tales from the Front" was presented. You may wish to obtain this cassette (#WE02b).

MENTORS

Once you have established the basics of your business, some elements are essential in helping you stay in business and stay profitable. One primary consideration should be obtaining and cultivating a mentor. The presence of a seasoned veteran as a "coach" to help you continue to develop professionally can be a priceless commodity. Most people who have been in business on their own have numerous experiences they can share with you to keep you from making common mistakes. Mentors can help with constructive criticism, suggest contacts and networks, and provide that "outside perspective" that is often difficult to obtain independently.

Because of the importance of mentoring, especially in a predominantly female profession, many of the Dietetic Practice Groups (DPGs) of the American Dietetic Association are offering mentors to assist in various aspects of business. Two DPGs, Nutrition Entrepreneurs (formerly "Consulting Nutritionists") and Dietitians in Business and Communications (formerly "Dietitians in Business and Industry"), offer the services of volunteer mentors in helping entrepreneurs through typical and unusual situations. This is extremely helpful to a struggling business practitioner, particularly since the mentors can relate to your specific circumstances.

NETWORKING

Networking is another important aspect of continuing to develop your business. Dietitians traditionally network with other dietitians because it is comfortable to talk with people of similar backgrounds. If, however, you desire to create a successful practice, you need to be networking with the individuals who are unaware of you and the services you provide. Network in your community with friends, your child's school, a volunteer service organization, citizens' groups, homeowners' associations, and so forth. These are the avenues to contact for your business growth.

Networking in key organizations that represent the professionals who are the target of your business is extremely important. Check the library or your chamber of commerce or city hall for local addresses of trade organizations. If there are none locally, get in touch with the national organizations. For example, if you are going to be providing consultations to the restaurant industry, you want to look into the American Culinary Federation, the National Restaurant Association, and the Food Marketing Institute. You also want to get on the mailing list for government publications and food trend publications that influence decisions in these areas. You can find out about the organizations and publications by asking some key people in the area of business that you are interested in about the meetings they attend and the publications they receive.

MARKETING AND ADVERTISING

Once you have become established and business is good, you will get referrals based on your good work with clients. This "word-of-mouth" advertising is often so good it can lull you into complacency. Don't let this happen to you! Marketing and advertising are an ongoing necessity in any entrepreneurial endeavor. The key to successful business is staying several accounts ahead of where you are today. In other words, be courting today the business you want 6–12 months down the road. Most major contracts you seek will not be converted into income on the first try, if at all. Proposals will need to be modified, additional meetings will need to be held, and then, if all goes well, you will get the business! Keeping your name "out there" is essential.

One of the best assets a dietitian can use for free marketing and advertising is the media. Because of the knowledge and expertise of a dietitian and the timeliness of that information, the media is often clamoring for what you know. The trick is not only to become media savvy but to learn to use the media to help your business. It is fine to respond to a request for an interview on a particular subject, but then ask to be identified as the owner of your business and ask that the piece include information on how to contact you.

SALES AND CONTRACT NEGOTIATION

As important as marketing your business is acquiring superb sales skills. You may think that sales is the same as marketing, but it is very different. Sales involves

- targeting the right person to pitch your business ideas
- promoting the benefits to the company before promoting yourself
- learning to ask for the business and, more important, learning to "close the deal"

Sales skills do not come easily in the dietetics profession. Even an MBA program rarely provides sales skills or skills in contract negotiation, which are equally important. Managing contracts is often best done through someone, such as an attorney, who is skilled in contract negotiation, since this is such a critical aspect of your business. Just make sure that the person you se-

lect understands what you do and what you want in the contract. You will learn from this and eventually be able to handle most contracts on your own.

TYPES OF PRACTICE

As previously emphasized, private practice is seldom client counseling alone. And even if it is, is it group, individual, or both? Is it verbal, with visuals, or via computer on the Internet? Is it general counseling or with certain specialties such as wellness, sports nutrition, pediatrics, diabetes, or cardiovascular? There are numerous decisions even in this single area.

The following is a brief, certainly nonexhaustive list, of other careers you might pursue as an entrepreneur:

- author of books for the public, books for the profession, articles for magazines, professional brochures for corporations
- public relations consultant
- media spokesperson
- research and development consultant
- administrative director of various health programs
- case manager for managed-care organizations
- home health consultant
- recruiter/head hunter
- chef/restaurant consultant
- consultant in schools
- wellness coordinator
- food service consultant

Linda McDonald, MS, RD, LD, a consultant to wellness programs, restaurants, medical facilities, and food companies, including Guiltless Gourmet, Inc, offers the following advice in consulting to food service companies:

- List the services you can provide. Make certain that companies know what you can do for them. Lists may include labeling, nutrient analysis, product development, research, media representation, and presentations. Develop a brochure that tells who you are, what services you can provide, why you are qualified, and the benefits to the company.

- Identify the ideal client. Some services, such as nutrition label consulting, are more applicable for small to medium companies, whereas a fairly large company might need a media representative. Companies with health-related products will be your first choice, but do not forget that almost all food products need nutrition labeling and can be made healthier. A producer of salad dressings may be interested in a line of low-fat salad dressings.
- Look for clients everywhere. Peruse grocery stores, catalogues, health food stores, and so on. Network with professionals in their local organizations.
- Do some research. Find out all you can about a prospective company. Know their products, competitors, and services. What are their plans for the future in terms of their products and services? If you have the opportunity to visit the company, talk to as many people and departments as possible.
- Get your foot in the door. Since most companies do not know you or what you can do for them, you need to start small. Labeling consulting is a great entry, but to go beyond that, you need to be creative. New companies are always interested in exposure for their new food products or feedback on proposed products. Offer to arrange a tasting at a local dietetic association meeting or a consumer presentation. Then build on this success by offering presentations in other locales. This is called "pulling" your product into the marketplace, and it is a lot cheaper than "pushing," which involves food reps, distributors, and even paying for shelf space in a supermarket.

- Create a niche. Your goal should be to negotiate a monthly retainer and a yearly contract, but you will probably need to start with individual proposals for specific projects. Enhance your worth with the company by working with as many departments and employees as possible. Continually document what you have done and how it has benefited the company. Be prepared to write 6-month and yearly work plans and reports. Be visible. Visit the company frequently and respond to requests quickly.

Whatever aspects of entrepreneurial dietetics you decide to engage in, you should be prepared for a great deal of competition. The field of private practice will undoubtedly show greater growth in the next decade than any other area of the profession. To stay ahead of the competition, you must stay current in your area, remain creative, and be committed to lifelong learning. In doing so, you will receive the greatest rewards successful entrepreneurs know: profitability and intense job satisfaction.

REFERENCES

Bhide A. How entrepreneurs craft strategies that work. *Harvard Business Rev.* 1994;72:150–161.

Cross A. Practical and legal considerations of private nutrition practice. *J Am Diet Assoc.* 1995;95:21–29.

Greene G, Strychar I. Participation in a worksite cholesterol education program in a university setting. *J Am Diet Assoc.* 1992;92:1376–1381.

Kaitschuck G. Referral sources for dietitians in private practice. *J Am Diet Assoc.* 1987;87:1685–1687.

Lassen A. Enhancing your networking skills. *Consult Nutritionists Newslett.* 1993;9(no 4).

Moores S. The write stuff. *Consult Nutritionists Newslett.* 1994;10(no 3).

Stollman L. Nutrition counseling: an entrepreneurial asset. *Consult Nutritionists Newslett.* 1995;11(no 3).

CHAPTER 7

Meal Planning

Chris Biesemeier

- Standard Diets
  - Regular Diet
  - High-Protein/High-Calorie Diet
  - Vegetarian Diet
  - Pregnancy and Lactation Diet
  - Diet for Infants and Children
  - Geriatric Diet
- Modified-Consistency Diets
  - Soft Diet
  - Bland Diet
  - Dysphagia Diet
  - Dental Mechanical or Mechanical Soft Diet
  - Pureed Diet
  - Clear Liquid Diet
  - Full Liquid Diet
- Gastrointestinal Disorder Diets
  - Antireflux Diet
  - Fiber-Restricted Diet
  - High-Fiber Diet

- Calorie-Controlled Diets
  - Postgastrectomy Diet
  - Diet for Reactive Hypoglycemia
  - Diet for Diabetes Mellitus
  - Diet for Gestational Diabetes
  - Weight Management Diet
- Protein-, Fluid-, and Electrolyte-Controlled Diets
  - Renal Diet
  - Diet for Liver Disease
  - Calcium-Restricted Diet
  - High-Potassium Diet
- Sodium-Controlled Diets
- Fat-Controlled Diets
  - Diets for Hyperlipidemia
  - Fat-Restricted Diet
- Food Allergy/Intolerance Diets
  - Lactose-Restricted Diet
  - Gluten-Restricted Diet
  - Low-Purine Diet

Standard Diets

REGULAR DIET

Objectives

- To meet nutritional needs for optimal health
- To provide a basis for modified diets

Indications for Use

- Individuals who do not need dietary modification

Nutritional Adequacy

- Diet is nutritionally adequate.
- Meets recommended dietary allowances (RDAs).

Summary of Guidelines

- Refer to the U.S. Department of Agriculture (USDA) Dietary Guidelines for a description of an overall approach to healthy eating.

- Use the Food Pyramid to plan meals and snacks.

HIGH-PROTEIN/HIGH-CALORIE DIET

Objective

- To provide protein- and calorie-rich foods for individuals with increased requirements

Indications for Use

- Individuals with increased requirements due to illness or injury
- Individuals who are malnourished and desire repletion of calorie stores and lean body mass

Nutritional Adequacy

- Diet is nutritionally adequate.
- Meets RDAs.

Summary of Guidelines

- Use the suggested servings in the "moderate" and "higher" categories of the Food Pyramid as a guide for food selection.
- Consider between-meal snacks and use of nutritional supplements.
- Vitamin and mineral supplementation may be indicated.

VEGETARIAN DIET

Objective

- To promote adequate nutrition when foods from animal origin are excluded from the diet

Nutritional Adequacy

- Nutritional adequacy will vary according to the type of vegetarian diet and individual food choices. Most vegetarian diets can be nutritionally adequate.
- Careful planning is needed with the vegetarian diet to ensure intake of adequate amounts of vitamins B_{12} and D.

- Omission of milk products makes it difficult to meet the calcium needs of children, teenagers, and pregnant or lactating women.

Summary of Guidelines

- Determine the type of vegetarian diet being followed, and individualize nutrition recommendations accordingly.
- Pay special attention to adequacy of intake of protein, riboflavin, vitamin B_{12}, vitamin D, calcium, and iron.
- Combine complementary plant proteins over the course of the day to meet protein needs.
- Women in their childbearing years may need to take an iron supplement.
- Assess fat intake, especially when dairy foods are consumed. Intake of high-fat versions of dairy products may result in high intake of saturated fat.

PREGNANCY AND LACTATION DIET

Objective

- To meet the nutritional needs of mother and baby during pregnancy and lactation in order to support optimal growth and development

Nutritional Adequacy

- Diet is nutritionally adequate.
- Meets RDAs.

Summary of Guidelines

- Use the Food Pyramid as a guide to food selection.
- Increase calories by an average of 300 kcal/day for pregnancy and 500 kcal/day for lactation.
- Increase protein by 30 g/day above RDA for age for pregnancy and by 20 g/day above RDA for age for lactation.
- Emphasize iron-rich foods. Supplemental iron (30–60 mg of elemental iron) is needed daily during pregnancy and for 2–3 months after delivery.

- Supplemental folic acid may be needed during pregnancy to meet requirement of RDA plus 400 mg/day. Requirement for lactation is RDA plus 100 mg/day.
- Meet requirements for other vitamins and minerals by selecting a variety of foods.
- Discourage use of caffeine.
- High fluid intake (8–10 cups daily) is needed for lactation.

DIET FOR INFANTS AND CHILDREN

Objective

- To meet nutritional needs, especially during periods of accelerated growth, in a form that is compatible with developmental ability

Indication for Use

- Infants and children who are developing in a normal manner and do not need dietary modifications

Nutritional Adequacy

- Diet is nutritionally adequate.

Summary of Guidelines

- Provide nutrition for infants during the first 4–6 months of life from breast milk or commercial, iron-fortified formula. Breast milk is recommended as the ideal nutrition source due to its ability to meet infants' nutrient requirements and provide antibody protection, sterility, and tolerance. Plain, unmodified cow's milk is not recommended.
- Provide an iron supplement to breastfed infants after 6 months of age.
- Consider a vitamin D supplement for infants not exposed regularly to sunlight. Evaluate need for a fluoride supplement.
- Continue breastfeeding or formula feeding until 1 year of age. Wean to a cup at this time.
- Introduce solid foods after 6 months of age, starting with baby rice cereal. Refer to a diet manual for an infant feeding schedule.
- Slowly introduce table foods to infants beginning at 8–10 months of age. Cut food into small pieces. Add foods with new textures and encourage self-feeding.
- Avoid foods commonly causing allergies, intolerance, or hypersensitivities, such as chocolate and, in young infants, egg whites, wheat cereals, mixed cereals, and citrus juices.
- Avoid foods that may cause choking, such as whole grapes, hotdogs, cocktail sausages, nuts, popcorn, and carrot sticks.
- Do not feed honey to infants under the age of 1 year, due to the risk of botulism.
- Transition older infants to family meals gradually.
- Allow preschoolers to choose food portions and give some latitude with food preferences. Offer a variety of nutritious foods at meals and snacks. Avoid sticky, sugary snacks to promote good dental health.
- Develop regular eating patterns. Use moderation in providing food rewards, especially sweets. Encourage breakfast. Encourage parents to provide a good example in their own food choices.
- Encourage physical activity and activity habits that will foster normal body fatness.

GERIATRIC DIET

Objective

- To provide a variety of nutrient-dense foods that will meet the nutritional needs of older adults

Nutritional Adequacy

- Diet is nutritionally adequate according to individual choices.
- RDAs do not specify nutrient requirements for the elderly. Currently, the elderly are included in the category "51 and older."

Summary of Guidelines

- Requirements for specific nutrients are generally the same as those for younger adults.
- Emphasize nutrient-dense foods to ensure nutritional adequacy.
- Adjust calorie intake according to need.

- Smaller, more frequent meals may be better accepted.
- Emphasize adequate calcium intake to maintain bone structure.

- Encourage roughage, water, and fluids to maintain bowel regularity.
- Evaluate psychosocial factors that may affect eating and food availability.

Modified-Consistency Diets

SOFT DIET

Objective

- To provide foods that are soft in texture, easily digested, moderately low in roughage, and mildly seasoned

Indications for Use

- May be used as a transition diet for individuals who cannot tolerate the texture and seasoning of food on a regular diet.
- Traditionally has been used for patients who are experiencing gas or distention, though the benefit derived may arise more from perception than from actual physiological effect. Symptoms of gas can arise from a change in diet, anesthesia, and the general effect of bed rest.

Nutritional Adequacy

- Diet is nutritionally adequate.
- Meets recommended dietary allowances (RDAs).

Summary of Guidelines

- Include foods that are prepared in a plain manner and are not highly seasoned.
- Do not include highly seasoned, fried, or tough foods; whole-grain breads and cereals; nuts and seeds; most fresh fruits and vegetables; pepper; or strongly flavored condiments.

- The trend in meal planning is to liberalize food choices on the basis of individual tolerance.
- Consider smaller, more frequent meals, which may be helpful in relieving symptoms of gas and distention.

BLAND DIET

Objective

- To reduce intake of known gastric irritants and foods that stimulate gastric acid secretion

Indication for Use

- Individuals who are being treated for chronic gastric or duodenal ulcers

Nutritional Adequacy

- Diet is nutritionally adequate.
- Nutritional adequacy possibly varies with individual food selections, limitation of one or more food groups, or limitation of variety within a food group.

Summary of Guidelines

- Avoid pepper, chili powder, curry powder, cocoa, chocolate, and all foods and beverages that contain these ingredients.
- Avoid all caffeine-containing beverages.
- Avoid both regular and decaffeinated coffee.
- Avoid alcohol.

- Choose foods according to individual tolerance.
- Eat regular meals. Frequent meals are not needed. However, some individuals claim relief of symptoms during acute stages of ulcer with more frequent meals. Late-night snacks may stimulate nocturnal acid secretion and are discouraged.
- Traditional ulcer diets have not been proven to be beneficial. Regimens of hourly milk and cream actually stimulate acid secretion.

DYSPHAGIA DIET

Objective

- To provide foods that can be tolerated by individuals with swallowing disorders

Indications for Use

- Individuals with swallowing disorders, including bulbar palsy, myasthenia gravis, amyotrophic lateral sclerosis, polymyositis, complications of radiation therapy to the head and neck, cerebrovascular accident, head injuries, brain tumors, cerebral palsy, Parkinson's disease, multiple sclerosis, Huntington's chorea, stricture of the esophagus, inflammation of the pharynx, and history of aspiration or aspiration pneumonia

Nutritional Adequacy

- The diet may not meet RDAs.
- Nutritional adequacy will depend on individual tolerance of food and amount consumed.

Summary of Guidelines

- Individualize the diet and foods provided according to ability to swallow. Consult a speech pathologist as needed to define a swallowing therapy program.
- Assess ability to tolerate liquids separately from tolerance of solids. Liquids may be defined as *extra thick* (consistency of pureed food), *medium thick* (consistency of honey or thick milkshake), and *thick* (consistency of nectar, eggnog, or soup).
- Provide thickened foods and liquids according to the directions of the speech pathologist. Foods that hold some shape are the easiest to swallow. Use special thickeners, baby rice cereal, mashed potatoes, or bananas to thicken liquids to the appropriate consistency.
- Taste sensation may be decreased. Enhance flavorings as needed unless tissue irritation is present.
- Avoid thin liquids, which are difficult to swallow, until tolerance is determined.
- Use broths and gravies to moisten foods.
- Avoid foods with mixed textures such as stews and fruited jello.
- Provide nutrition supplements as needed to meet nutrient needs.
- Consider six small meals instead of three large meals. Ensure that staff are available to assist with feedings between scheduled meals.

DENTAL MECHANICAL OR MECHANICAL SOFT DIET

Objective

- To provide foods that can be swallowed with minimal to no chewing

Indications for Use

- Individuals who have difficulty chewing and/or swallowing
- Conditions including absence of teeth, loose dentures, sore gums, cancers of the head and neck, and neurological disorders

Nutritional Adequacy

- Nutritional adequacy depends on the variety of foods chosen.

Summary of Guidelines

- Include foods from a regular diet that have been chopped or ground.

- Omit foods that are difficult to chew and swallow, such as raw fruits, vegetables with tough skins, and nuts.

PUREED DIET

Objective

- To provide foods that require minimal chewing and increase the ease of swallowing

Indication for Use

- Indicated for individuals who have difficulty chewing and/or swallowing

Nutritional Adequacy

- Nutritional adequacy depends on the variety of foods chosen.

Summary of Guidelines

- Include foods permitted on a regular diet that have been blenderized.
- Provide bread, rolls, crackers, dry cereal, pasta, rice, and cottage cheese according to tolerance.
- Do not use raw eggs for protein supplementation.
- Omit foods with seeds, nuts, or dried fruits.
- Give consideration to serving foods in an identifiable form and to the use of special pureed food items and casseroles to enhance variety.

CLEAR LIQUID DIET

Objectives

- To provide fluids and electrolytes in order to prevent dehydration
- To reduce amount of residue present in the intestinal tract and to stimulate minimal digestive activity

Indications for Use

- May be used as a transition from NPO order to a full liquid diet or soft diet

- May be used prior to bowel surgery and gastrointestinal diagnostic procedures

Nutritional Adequacy

- Inadequate in all nutrients without the use of low-residue nutrition supplements. Should be used for short intervals only.

Summary of Guidelines

- Provide liberal amounts of coffee, tea, clear fruit juices and drinks, broth, and gelatin.
- Other foods included on the diet are popsicles, plain hard candy, gumdrops, and fruit ices.
- Patients with diabetes mellitus should receive the same foods provided to patients who do not have diabetes, including sweetened carbonated beverages and gelatin.

FULL LIQUID DIET

Objective

- To provide liquid nourishment when solid foods are not tolerated

Indications for Use

- May be used for patients who have had mandibular fractures or facial, dental, or neck surgery
- May be used for individuals who cannot tolerate solid foods and as a transition step in postoperative dietary regimens

Nutritional Adequacy

- Diet is nutritionally adequate only in vitamin C and calcium.
- Protein requirement may be met if adequate amounts of milk are consumed.
- Nutritional supplements enable nutrition requirements to be met.

Summary of Guidelines

- Provide foods that are liquid or semiliquid at room temperature.

- Include strained cooked cereals, soups containing blended meats and vegetables, custard, plain pudding, and yogurt without pulp, nuts, or seeds.

- Diet is high in lactose content.
- Do not use raw eggs for protein supplementation.

Gastrointestinal Disorder Diets

ANTIREFLUX DIET

Objectives

- To provide foods that reduce cardiac sphincter pressure and gastric acidity
- To avoid irritation of an inflamed esophagus

Indication for Use

- Individuals who have reflux esophagitis and hiatal hernia

Nutritional Adequacy

- Diet is nutritionally adequate.
- Individual food selections and avoidance of groups of food may limit nutritional adequacy.

Summary of Guidelines

- Avoid high-fat foods such as fried foods, gravies, pastries, and high-fat meats.
- Limit use of added fats such as margarine, butter, cream, oil, and salad dressing.
- Avoid coffee (regular and decaffeinated) and foods and beverages containing chocolate, cocoa, caffeine, peppermint oil, and spearmint oil.
- Avoid tomatoes, tomato juice, citrus juices, alcohol, and pepper.
- Choose foods according to individual tolerance.

- Achieve and maintain a healthy weight.
- Avoid large meals. Eat small, frequent meals.
- Avoid bending over after eating and lying down within 2 hours of eating.

FIBER-RESTRICTED DIET

Objectives

- To limit the amount of fiber consumed in order to decrease stool volume
- To prevent distention of the bowel and further aggravation of inflamed tissue

Indications for Use

- Individuals experiencing complications of radiation therapy
- Individuals experiencing acute exacerbations of diverticulosis, Crohn's disease, ulcerative colitis, and other inflammatory bowel diseases
- Used for longer periods of time when inflammatory changes have resulted in stenosis of the lumen of the intestine or esophagus
- Used as a pre-and postoperative regimen for lower bowel surgery

Nutritional Adequacy

- Diet is nutritionally adequate.
- Nutritional adequacy may be limited by individual food selections and avoidance of groups of food.

Summary of Guidelines

- Include beverages and juices without pulp; refined breads and cereals; potatoes without skin; refined pasta; most meats; cheese; canned, cooked, and selected fresh fruits; selected canned and cooked vegetables; selected raw vegetables; plain cakes and cookies; sugar; hard candies; jelly; margarine; plain sauces; gravies; and salad dressings.
- Number and size of food portions on diet are limited. Selections of certain foods will depend on individual tolerance. Consult a diet manual for detailed listing of foods.
- Avoid whole-grain flour, bran, oatmeal, granola, seeds, nuts, coconut, fruit and vegetable pulp, dried fruits, berries, dried beans, peas, lentils, legumes, and popcorn. Consult a diet manual for a more detailed listing of foods to avoid.
- Diet may cause a delay in intestinal transit.
- Terms *fiber* and *residue* are not synonymous. *Residue* refers to the total amount of material in the colon and includes undigested fiber and food, intestinal secretions, bacteria, and sloughed cells. Residue can be reduced by limiting milk on Fiber-Restricted Diet to two cups a day and avoiding prune juice.

HIGH-FIBER DIET

Objectives

- To increase the amount of fiber consumed to 25–35 g/day.

- To reduce intracolonic pressure and promote regular elimination

Indications for Use

- Used in treatment of atonic constipation, diverticulosis, hemorrhoids, and irritable bowel syndrome

Nutritional Adequacy

- Diet is nutritionally adequate.
- No recommended dietary alflowance (RDA) for fiber exists. The National Cancer Institute recommends consumption of 20–30 g of fiber daily.

Summary of Guidelines

- Include whole-grain, bran, and granola-type breads and cereals; oatmeal; fruits and vegetables, especially raw and with skin; and legumes, nuts, and seeds. Consult a diet manual for fiber content of foods and recommended servings.
- Increase fiber intake gradually to avoid abdominal gas and cramping.
- Drink eight or more glasses of fluid daily.
- Diet includes sources of both insoluble and soluble fiber. Insoluble fiber does not dissolve in water and is found in wheat bran, whole grains, and vegetables. Soluble fiber has a high water-holding capacity and turns to a gel during digestion. It is found in oat bran, barley, kidney beans, other dried beans, and some fruits and vegetables.

Calorie-Controlled Diets

POSTGASTRECTOMY DIET

Objectives

- To prevent rapid passage of food from the stomach into the intestine and the creation of a hyperosmolar load in the small intestine
- To maintain optimal nutrition status

Indication for Use

- Individuals who have had a partial gastrectomy or another operation that interferes with the function of the pylorus or the ability of the stomach to serve as a reservoir

Nutritional Adequacy

- Nutritional adequacy will depend on the extent of the individual's surgery, food tolerances, and food selections. Undernutrition and poor intake are common due to the problems that accompany eating and digestion.
- Vitamin and mineral supplementation is recommended.
- Injections of vitamin B_{12} may be required due to a lack of intrinsic factor.

Summary of Guidelines

- Avoid sugars and concentrated sweets.
- Choose high-protein, moderate-fat foods. Suggested protein amount is 1.5–2.0 g of protein per kg of ideal body weight. Suggested level of fat intake is 30%–40% of calories. Use the American Dietetic Association/American Diabetes Association "Exchange Lists for Meal Planning" for carbohydrate control.
- Divide food into six small meals.
- Avoid liquids with meals. Drink low-carbohydrate liquids 30–60 minutes after a meal and up to 30–60 minutes before a meal.
- Choose foods of moderate temperature. Avoid temperature extremes.
- Avoid alcohol.
- Determine lactose tolerance by gradual introduction of milk and milk products into the diet.

DIET FOR REACTIVE HYPOGLYCEMIA

Objective

- To prevent a marked rise in blood sugar after meals, thereby avoiding the stimulation of excessive insulin secretion

Indication for Use

- Individuals with diagnosed reactive hypoglycemia

Nutritional Adequacy

- Diet is nutritionally adequate.

Summary of Guidelines

- Calorie level of diet is based on individual requirements.
- Suggested amount of protein is 15%–20% of total calories.
- Carbohydrate level is limited to 40%–55% of total calories, distributed throughout the day. Use the "Exchange Lists for Meal Planning" for carbohydrate control.
- Avoid sugars and concentrated sweets.
- Divide food into six small meals, including protein and fiber sources at each meal.
- Avoid alcohol.
- Determine tolerance of caffeine by restricting initially and establishing individual tolerance.

DIET FOR DIABETES MELLITUS

Objectives

- To provide a variety of nutrients: carbohydrate, protein, fat, vitamins, and minerals

- To attain and maintain blood sugar levels that are as near normal as possible
- To promote the achievement of normal blood lipid levels
- To attain and maintain a healthy, reasonable weight

Indication for Use

- Individuals with diabetes mellitus

Nutritional Adequacy

- Diet is nutritionally adequate.
- Calorie levels below 1200 kcal/day may not meet the recommended dietary allowances (RDAs) and are generally not recommended.

Summary of Guidelines

- Determine total percentage of carbohydrate calories based on glucose, lipid, and weight goals. For healthy eating, emphasize complex carbohydrates over simple carbohydrates.
- The key to glycemic control is the total amount of carbohydrate consumed at each meal and snack, not the type of carbohydrate. Scientific evidence does not support the elimination of sucrose from the diet.
- Determine the total percentage of fat calories based on glucose, lipid, and weight goals. Provide less than 10% of calories from saturated-fat sources.
- Provide 10%–20% of calories from protein. With nephropathy, limit protein to the RDA, 0.8 g/day.
- Distribute food throughout the day to promote better blood glucose control. Develop an individualized meal plan and choose an approach to meal planning that is suited to the individual's diabetes management goals, diabetes medications, lifestyle, and activity level.
- Available approaches to meal planning include
  1. *Menu approaches*—individualized menus or the use of a food choice plan
  2. *Guideline approaches*—"Dietary Guidelines for Americans," "Guide to Good Eat-

ing," "Food Guide Pyramid," and "Guidelines for Healthy Food Choices"
  3. *Exchange lists*—"Healthy Food Choices," "Exchange Lists for Meal Planning," and high-carbohydrate–high-fiber (HCF) exchange lists
  4. *Counting approaches*—carbohydrate counting, calorie counting, calorie point system, fat counting, and fat/calorie counting
- The role of fiber in glycemic control may not be significant. However, fiber may help lower blood lipid levels. Choose high-fiber foods to achieve a goal of 20–35 g of fiber per day.
- Limit cholesterol to less than 300 mg/day and sodium to 3000 mg/day or below.

DIET FOR GESTATIONAL DIABETES

Objectives

- To promote normal blood glucose levels, an appropriate pattern of weight gain, and optimal nutrition for a healthy pregnancy

Indication for Use

- Pregnant women with the diagnosis of gestational diabetes

Nutritional Adequacy

- Diet is nutritionally adequate.

Summary of Guidelines

- Determine calorie level of diet based on desired pattern of weight gain. Women who are overweight before pregnancy need a lower calorie level; women who are underweight before pregnancy need a higher calorie level.
- Determine percentage of carbohydrate calories based on individual eating habits and blood glucose goals. Consider use of lower carbohydrate level (40%–45% of calories) to achieve blood glucose control. Decide use of

sucrose based on its effect on blood glucose levels.
- Provide 60 g/day protein.
- Determine percentage of fat calories based on goals, limiting saturated fat to less than 10% of calories.
- Choose high-fiber sources to achieve a goal of 20–35 g/day.
- Use aspartame and acesulfame K in moderation. Avoid use of saccharin.
- Distribute food throughout the day in three meals and two to three snacks. Limitation of carbohydrate at breakfast may be beneficial due to increased morning release of cortisol and resulting insulin resistance.
- Develop an individualized meal plan, and choose a meal planning approach that is suited to the woman's management goals, medications, lifestyle, and emotional needs.

WEIGHT MANAGEMENT DIET

Objective

- To limit fat and calories to promote the gradual loss of body fat and weight

Indication for Use

- Overweight and obese individuals desiring to lose weight

Nutritional Adequacy

- Diet should be nutritionally adequate.
- Calorie intake should not be less than 1200/day.

Summary of Guidelines

- Individualize the approach to weight loss. Emphasize improved eating habits, nutritious food choices, and regular exercise and activity.
- Set a reasonable weight goal based on personal and family history rather than on a value from a height/weight table or a calculated ideal body weight. For some individuals, maintenance of weight, without further gain, is a suitable goal.
- Reduce intake of fat, saturated fat, and cholesterol. Refer to a diet manual for specific guidelines on food choices. Encourage regular meals.
- Avoid restricting a food or a group of foods. Restrictive dieting may lead to disordered eating. Encourage eating in response to internal hunger and satiety cues.
- Encourage development of a realistic attitude about weight loss and appearance. Promote self-acceptance and self-esteem.
- Consider referral for individual and family counseling when appropriate.

Protein-, Fluid-, and Electrolyte-Controlled Diets

RENAL DIET

Objectives

- To achieve and maintain optimal nutrition status
- To lessen the work of the kidney by decreasing the amount of waste products produced from protein metabolism
- To replace protein lost in dialysis
- To prevent fluid overload
- To prevent imbalances in phosphorus and calcium

Indication for Use

- Individuals with renal failure or renal insufficiency

Nutritional Adequacy

- A diet that is restricted in protein, sodium, potassium, phosphorus, and fluid does not contain adequate amounts of calcium, iron, and water-soluble vitamins.

Summary of Guidelines

- Limit protein during acute failure, before dialysis, or, when dialysis is not indicated, according to assessed needs.
- Increase protein during dialysis to compensate for losses. Provide 1–1.2 g/day for patients on chronic hemodialysis and 1.2–1.5 g/day for patients undergoing peritoneal dialysis.
- Provide 70%–75% of protein allowance in the form of high–biological value proteins.
- Limit sodium according to symptoms of hypertension, fluid retention, edema, and congestive heart failure. Usual limitation in end-stage renal failure is 2 g/day. In some persons, a high-sodium diet may be indicated to prevent low blood pressure and dehydration.
- The usual potassium restriction is 2 g/day, although this should be individualized. Restriction may not be indicated for persons undergoing continuous ambulatory peritoneal dialysis (CAPD). Food sources of potassium include fruits, vegetables, meat, cheese, milk, and salt substitute.
- Phosphorus is limited in order to minimize bone demineralization, which occurs as a result of a high serum phosphorus and the resulting low serum calcium level. Calcium mobilization from the bones produces weakened bones and can lead to mineralization of soft tissues. The usual range of phosphorus restriction is 600 mg/day to 1200 mg/day. Phosphorus sources in the diet include foods high in protein and potassium, especially dairy products.
- When appropriate, limit daily fluid intake to an amount equal to urine output plus 500 ml for insensible losses.
- Provide adequate calorie intake in order to prevent weight loss and promote positive nitrogen balance. Calorie requirement for per-

sons on peritoneal dialysis should take into account carbohydrate absorption from the dialysate, usually approximately 500 kcal.
- Use a water-soluble vitamin supplement to meet needs and replace losses. Do not use a vitamin A supplement, due to elevated vitamin A levels in uremia. Use a vitamin K supplement only if antibiotics have been prescribed.
- Consider calcium supplements to compensate for dietary inadequacy. Consider zinc supplement to improve taste acuity. Evaluate need for an iron supplement on an individualized basis. Avoid magnesium supplements.
- Limit concentrated sweets and reduce body weight as needed to lower serum triglycerides.
- Initiate cholesterol-lowering measures as needed to control serum levels.
- For persons with renal disease who also have diabetes mellitus, improvement in uremic symptoms takes precedence over tight blood glucose control. The carbohydrate and fat content of the renal diabetic diet will be higher, and simple sugars will be included routinely.
- Consult a diet manual for specific diet guidelines, food choices, and portion sizes.

DIET FOR LIVER DISEASE

Objectives

- To maintain or improve nutrition status
- To prevent or improve the symptoms of hepatic encephalopathy
- To prevent further damage to the liver and promote regeneration of new tissue when possible

Indications for Use

- Individuals with hepatitis, cirrhosis, or hepatic encephalopathy
- Individuals in hepatic coma

Nutritional Adequacy

- Nutritional adequacy will depend on the protein level of the diet. Generally, a 40-gram-of-protein diet is adequate in all nutrients except vitamin B_6, vitamin B_{12}, iron, zinc, calcium, niacin, vitamin D, and vitamin E.

Summary of Guidelines

- Hepatitis
  1. Provide 1–2 g protein/kg desired body weight. One half to three fourths of the protein allowance should come from high–biological value proteins, distributed throughout the day.
  2. Provide 40–50 kcal/kg desired body weight, supplied by liberal amounts of carbohydrate and fat.
  3. Six small meals may be better tolerated than three large ones.
  4. Determine need for fluid and sodium restriction and vitamin/mineral supplementation on an individual basis.
- Cirrhosis
  1. Determine protein level of the diet based on degree of liver damage. Range of protein varies from 0.5–2.0 g protein/kg desired body weight. One half to three fourths of the protein allowance should come from high–biological value proteins, distributed throughout the day.
  2. Provide 35 to 50 kcal/kg desired body weight to spare protein from use as an energy source.
  3. Fat limitation may be needed if steatorrhea occurs.
  4. Restrict sodium and fluid based on symptoms of edema and ascites. Initiate tight restriction with severe symptoms, and liberalize as symptoms improve.
  5. Consider vitamin and mineral supplementation, based on individualized needs.
  6. Six small meals may be better tolerated than three large ones.
- Hepatic Encephalopathy/Coma
  1. Individualize protein level of the diet carefully. Severe limitation (to 30–40 g/day or less) may be warranted with coma or impending coma. Very–low-protein diets should be used only for short time periods, since their use may promote tissue protein

catabolism and a worsening of symptoms.
  2. Include increased proportion of vegetable and milk proteins. Vegetable proteins may be better tolerated than meat proteins, possibly due to their decreased content of ammonia-forming amino acids.
  3. Efficacy of the use of oral or parenteral preparations of branched-chain amino acids has not been proved.
  4. Increase calories to prevent use of endogenous and dietary proteins for energy.
  5. Restrict sodium and fluid as needed to control ascites.
  6. Consider vitamin and mineral supplementation, based on individual needs.
  7. Consult a diet manual for specific diet guidelines, food choices, and portion sizes.

CALCIUM-RESTRICTED DIET

Objective

- To limit dietary calcium to 600 mg/day or less

Indication for Use

- Individuals who are predisposed to calcium oxalate stones due to idiopathic hypercalciuria

Nutritional Adequacy

- Diet is nutritionally adequate, with the exception of calcium and vitamin D.

Summary of Guidelines

- Limit foods that are high in calcium, including milk, dairy products, and green, leafy vegetables. Refer to a diet manual for a listing of the calcium content of foods.
- One cup of milk or the calcium equivalent may be consumed.
- Drink large amounts of fluid daily—3000 ml or more.

HIGH-POTASSIUM DIET

Objectives

- To prevent hypokalemia by providing a high intake of potassium

- To restore, maintain, or prevent the depletion of body potassium due to potassium-wasting medications and physiological disorders

Indications for Use

- Individuals for whom the long-term use of potassium-wasting diuretics has been prescribed
- Possibly individuals with edema associated with certain cardiac or hepatic disorders; corticosteroid therapy; dehydration; excess fluid losses; the diuretic stage of nephritis; and the dilution of extracellular fluid volume

Nutritional Adequacy

- Diet is nutritionally adequate.

Summary of Guidelines

- Plan daily food choices by using a reference list of the potassium content of foods.
- Consume a minimum of 140 mEq (5460 mg) of potassium daily.
- Consider the use of a potassium chloride salt substitute, which can contribute a significant amount of potassium to the diet.

Sodium-Controlled Diets

Objectives

- To restore normal sodium balance
- To control hypertension
- To prevent, treat, and eliminate edema
- To prevent stimulation of thirst in individuals on a fluid-restricted regimen

Indications for Use

- The 4-g Sodium Diet is used for individuals with mild hypertension and mild fluid retention and for individuals who are receiving corticosteroid therapy.
- The 2-g Sodium Diet is used for individuals with congestive heart failure, hypertension, edema, renal disease, and cirrhosis with ascites and for individuals who are receiving corticosteroid therapy.
- The 1-g Sodium Diet is used for individuals with severe cases of hypertension, congestive heart failure, cirrhosis with ascites, pulmonary edema, and renal disease. Use in the home setting is not practical.
- The 500-mg Sodium Diet is used on a short-term basis for patients needing severe sodium restriction.

Nutritional Adequacy

- The 4-g Sodium Diet and the 2-g Sodium Diet are nutritionally adequate.
- The 1-g Sodium Diet is nutritionally adequate with the use of low-sodium products.
- Nutritional adequacy of the 500-mg Sodium Diet is difficult to achieve, due to low palatability and the unavailability of required low-sodium products.

Summary of Guidelines

4-g (174-mEq) Sodium Diet

- Include most foods from a regular diet.
- Omit high-sodium foods. High-sodium foods include convenience foods such as pizza, TV dinners, frozen meat entrees, and canned, boxed, and frozen convenience foods; processed, cured, pickled, and smoked meats such as bacon, bologna, Canadian bacon, corned beef, frankfurters, ham, sausage, and luncheon meats; salted snack foods; regular canned soups and frozen and dried soup mixes; sauerkraut, pickled vegetables, hominy, vegetable juice, and tomato juice; and salt and salt seasonings, barbecue and other meat

sauces, meat tenderizers, soy sauce, olives, pickles, commercial salad dressings, and ketchup.
- Include foods that have been lightly salted in cooking.
- Omit the addition of salt to food at the table.

2-g (87-mEq), 1-g (44-mEq), and 500-mg (22-mEq) Sodium Diets

- Avoid the use of salt during cooking.
- Check the sodium content of water used in food preparation.
- Omit high-sodium foods.
- Consult a diet manual for specific diet guidelines, food choices, and portion sizes.

- Include low-sodium products on the 1-g and 500-mg Sodium Diets to replace the higher sodium versions of these items.
- Assess use of nonfood sources of sodium such as chewing tobacco, snuff, and selected toothpastes and antacids.
- Read labels carefully to determine the sodium content of foods.
- Consider the use of a sodium point system for calculating sodium intake as an alternate to the use of lists of foods that are allowed and not allowed. With this system, in which a point equals 1 mEq (23 mg) of sodium, the individual decides the use of allotted points daily, using a reference list of the sodium point values of different foods.

Fat-Controlled Diets

DIETS FOR HYPERLIPIDEMIA

Objectives

- To reduce elevated blood cholesterol and/or triglyceride levels
- To control intake of saturated fat, total fat, and cholesterol
- To promote achievement of a desirable body weight
- To achieve optimal nutrition status

Indications for Use

- Individuals with hyperlipidemia or coronary heart disease (CHD)
- Individuals at risk for CHD

Nutritional Adequacy

- Diet is nutritionally adequate.

Summary of Guidelines

- Dietary guidelines have been established by an expert panel of the National Cholesterol Education Program.
- The guidelines have been divided into two steps that progressively reduce intake of saturated fat and cholesterol and eliminate excess calories. Refer to a diet manual for food choices for each step.
- Reduce total fat intake on both step 1 and step 2 diets to less than 30% of total calories.
- Reduce saturated fat intake on the step 1 diet to less than 10% of total calories and on the step 2 diet to less than 7% of total calories.
- Provide up to 10% of calories on either diet from polyunsaturated fats and 10%–15% of calories from monounsaturated fats.
- Provide 50%–60% of calories from carbohydrate and 10%–20% of calories from protein.

- Limit cholesterol intake to less than 300 mg/day on the step 1 diet and to less than 200 mg/day on the step 2 diet.
- Modify calorie level of diet as needed to achieve and maintain a desirable weight.
- Follow established protocol for use of the step 1 and step 2 diets and for progressing from the step 1 to the step 2 diet. Assess level of current intake carefully when deciding which diet to choose, taking into account the widespread use of the step 1 diet recommendations in the general population.
- Emphasize weight reduction, increased physical activity, and restriction of alcohol for individuals with hypertriglyceridemia.
- Use a very–low-fat diet (10%–20% of calories as fat) when severe hypertriglyceridemia and chylomicronemia are also present.
- For borderline hypertriglyceridemia with hypercholesterolemia, do not exceed the step 1 diet, since a very–low-fat, high-carbohydrate diet may accentuate the hypertriglyceridemia.
- In persons with diabetes mellitus, control of blood sugar levels is key to control of hyperlipidemia. Recommendations for the carbohydrate level of the diet in persons with diabetes and hyperlipidemia differ. Some authorities believe in use of the same carbohydrate level that is used for persons without diabetes and with hyperlipidemia, 50%–60% of calories. Others advocate limiting carbohydrate to 40%–45% of calories.

FAT-RESTRICTED DIET

Objective

- To limit fat intake to 40–50 g/day

Indications for Use

- Individuals with diseases of the biliary tree, including the liver, gall bladder, and pancreas
- Individuals with impaired digestion and absorption of fat

Nutritional Adequacy

- Diet is nutritionally adequate.

Summary of Guidelines

- Limit fats, including margarine, butter, oils, salad dressings, and cream, to three servings daily.
- Limit lean meat and meat substitutes to a 6-oz cooked portion per day.
- Restrict fat sources in the diet, including whole, 2 percent, and 1 percent milk and dairy products and foods made with these ingredients; breads made with large amounts of fat; high-fat desserts and sweets; avocados; fried foods; high-fat soups and stews; vegetables seasoned with fat, cheese, or cream sauces; and gravies.
- Consult a diet manual for specific guidelines on food choices and daily amounts.

Food Allergy/Intolerance Diets

LACTOSE-RESTRICTED DIET

Objectives

- To restrict foods containing lactose
- To prevent the symptoms associated with lactose ingestion

Indication for Use

- Individuals with lactase deficiency

Nutritional Adequacy

- Diet may be deficient in calcium, vitamin D, and riboflavin, depending on the extent to which dairy products are eliminated from the diet.

- Consider the use of calcium supplements.
- Consider use of a vitamin D supplement if exposure to sunlight is limited. Riboflavin supplements are generally not necessary.

Summary of Guidelines

- Individualize the amount of lactose in the diet on the basis of individual tolerance. Small amounts of milk and dairy products may be tolerated by some individuals.
- Establish tolerance by gradually adding sources of lactose to a lactose-free diet.
- Consult a diet manual for specific diet guidelines, food choices, and portion sizes on a lactose-free diet.
- Encourage use of milk and dairy products at meals, due to slower gastric emptying.
- Consider use of yogurt in place of milk. Yogurt contains bacterial lactase, which substitutes for the lactase that is missing in the individual's intestinal tract.
- Read food labels carefully. Be alert to the presence of lactose when the ingredient list includes milk, milk solids, lactose, whey, or casein.
- Consider use of special commercially prepared lactose-reduced products; the use of LactAid, an enzyme that can be added to milk; or ingestion of an enzyme tablet just prior to meals containing lactose.
- The amount of lactose in products varies from one brand to another, due to differences in production. For example, lactose is an optional ingredient used in the process of creaming cottage cheese.
- Cheese spreads have more lactose than aged cheese or processed cheese, due to the addition of dry milk solids and whey powder.

GLUTEN-RESTRICTED DIET

Objectives

- To eliminate gluten from the diet

- To control or eliminate the malabsorption that results from a sensitivity to gluten in individuals with celiac disease

Indications for Use

- Individuals with celiac disease or secondary gluten-induced enteropathy
- Treatment of the skin lesions associated with dermatitis herpetoformis

Nutritional Adequacy

- Diet is nutritionally adequate as planned.
- Nutritional adequacy will depend on individual tolerance of food and food selections made.
- Nutrient supplementation may be needed when malabsorption is present. This includes supplementation of potassium, folic acid, vitamin B_{12} and other water-soluble vitamins, vitamin D and other fat-soluble vitamins, calcium, iron, and magnesium. Supplements can be discontinued as intake improves.

Summary of Guidelines

- Eliminate foods containing wheat, rye, barley, buckwheat, and oats. Individual tolerance of oats can vary.
- Read food labels carefully. Be alert to the presence of one of the grains not allowed on the diet when the ingredient list includes cereal, cereal additive, cereal product, emulsifier, flavoring, hydrolyzed vegetable or plant protein, malt, malt flavoring, modified food starch, soy sauce, stabilizer, starch, vegetable gum, or vegetable protein.
- Plan diet to be high in protein and carbohydrate in order to correct poor nutritional status.
- Assess tolerance of lactose. Limit milk and dairy products, if necessary, until tolerance improves.
- Determine existence of steatorrhea. When present, limit fat in the diet. Reintroduce gradually, as recovery progresses.
- Consult a diet manual for specific diet guidelines, food choices, and portion sizes.

LOW-PURINE DIET

Objectives

- To limit foods high in purine and fat in order to promote the reduction of hyperuricemia
- To increase fluid intake in order to promote excretion of uric acid and prevent calculi
- To attain and maintain a desirable weight

Indication for Use

- Individuals with gout or uric acid stones, as an adjunct to drug therapy

Nutritional Adequacy

- Diet is nutritionally adequate, with the exception of iron for women in their childbearing years.

Summary of Guidelines

- Omit foods with high purine content from the diet (100–1000 mg of purine nitrogen per 100 g of food). Limit foods with moderate purine content (9–100 mg of purine nitrogen per 100 g of food) to one serving daily. Refer to a diet manual for purine content of foods and specific food guidelines.
- Limit fats due to their slowing of uric acid excretion.
- Provide moderate protein intake, with a large proportion of protein coming from milk, cheese, vegetables, and bread.
- Encourage a minimum of 3 l of fluid daily.
- Encourage gradual weight loss in obese individuals. Rapid weight loss or fasting can precipitate an attack of gout.
- Restrict or eliminate alcohol.

REFERENCES

American Dietetic Association, Diabetes Care and Education Dietetic Practice Group. *Meal Planning Approaches for Diabetes Management.* 2nd ed. Chicago, Ill: American Dietetic Association; 1994.

Krummel DA, Kris-Etherton PM. *Nutrition in Women's Health.* Gaithersburg, Md: Aspen Publishers, Inc; 1996.

Mayo Clinic Diet Manual. 7th ed. St. Louis, Mo: Mosby-Year Book, Inc; 1994.

Powers MA. *Handbook of Diabetes Medical Nutrition Therapy.* Gaithersburg, Md: Aspen Publishers, Inc; 1996.

Charts and Tables

Appendix A

Acid, Alkaline, and Neutral Foods

Food Group	Potentially Acid or Acid-Ash Foods
Meat	Meat, fish, fowl, shellfish, eggs, all types of cheese, peanut butter, peanuts
Fat	Bacon, nuts (Brazil nuts, filberts, walnuts)
Starch	All types of bread (especially whole-wheat), cereal, crackers, macaroni, spaghetti, noodles, rice
Vegetables	Corn, lentils
Fruit	Cranberries, plums, prunes
Desserts	Plain cakes, cookies

Food Group	Potentially Basic or Alkaline-Ash Foods
Milk	Milk and milk products, cream, buttermilk
Fat	Nuts (almonds, chestnuts, coconut)
Vegetables	All types (except corn, lentils), especially beets, beet greens, Swiss chard, dandelion greens, kale, mustard greens, spinach, turnip greens
Fruit	All types (except cranberries, prunes, plums)
Sweets	Molasses

Food Group	Neutral Foods
Fats	Butter, margarine, cooking fats, oils
Sweets	Plain candies, sugar, syrup, honey
Starch	Arrowroot, corn, tapioca
Beverages	Coffee, tea

Source: Reprinted with permission of Mayo Foundation from CM Pemberton, et al, *Mayo Clinic Diet Manual,* 7th ed, pp. 329–330, © 1994. Mosby-Year Book, Inc.

Appendix B

Adult Fluid Requirements*,**

A. Calculations (assuming normal renal and cardiac function and euvolemia [normal hydration status]).
   1. 35 ml/kg body weight
   2. 1 ml/kcal intake (referring to enteral formula)
   3. 1500 ml/m² body surface area
   4. 100 ml/kg for the first 10 kg, plus 0.50 ml/kg for the next 10 kg, plus 0.25 ml/kg for the remaining weight
B. Minimal fluid requirements
   1. 500 ml/day urine output obligatory to excrete daily solute load.
   2. 500–100 ml/day of evaporative water loss.
   3. 300 ml/day of water produced from endogenous metabolism.
   4. 2000–3000 ml/day intake to yield approximately 1000–1500 ml/day of urine output.
   5. Fluid requirements increase 150 ml/day for each degree of body temperature over 37°C.
   6. Increased perspiration, ambient and body temperature, respiratory rate and extra renal fluid losses increase fluid requirements.
   7. As a rule of thumb, one necessary bed change due to perspiration represents approximately 1 l of fluid lost.
C. Calculating fluid deficit
   1. Current total body water (TBW, l) = 0.6 × current body weight (kg).
   2. Desired TBW = $\dfrac{\text{Measured serum NA}^+ \text{(mEq/l)} \times \text{current TBW}}{\text{Normal serum Na}^+ \text{(mEq/l)}}$
   3. Body water deficit = desired TBW − current TBW.

*Kohan DE. Fluid and electrolyte management. In: WC Dunagan, ML Ridner, eds. *Manual of Medical Therapeutics*. 26th ed. Boston, Mass: Little, Brown and Co; 1989:52–71.
**Austin C. Water: guidelines for nutrition support. *Nutr Supp Serv.* 1986:6:27–29.

Appendix C

Anemia

	Hemoglobin	Hematocrit	Mean Corpuscular Volume	Serum Iron	Total Iron-Binding Capacity	Transferrin	Reticulocytes
Fe deficiency	→	→	→ ←	→ ←	← →	← →	↑ ↓
B₁₂, folate deficiency	→	→	↑ ↓	↓ ↑	← →	→ ←	↑ ↓
Fe plus megaloblastic	→	→	↓ ← ←	→	← →	← ←	↑ ↓
Dehydration	←*	←*	↑ ↓ ← ←	↑ ↓	↓ ↑	→	↑ ↓
Malnutrition	→↓	→*	↓ ← ←	→ ←	← →	← →	↑ ↓
Malabsorption	→	→	↑ ↓	↑ ↓	← →	↑↓ ← →	↑ ↓
Liver disease	→↓	→↓*	↑ ↓ ← ←	↑ ← →	← →	↑↓ ← →	↑ ↓→
Kidney disease	→↓	→↓*	→↑ →↓	↓ ←	↓ ↑	→	↑ ↓
Gastrectomy	→	→	→	→	← →	← →	↑ ↓←
Small bowel surgery	→	→	→↑ ↓	→	↓ ↑	↑ →	↑ ↓
Blood loss	→↓ →	→↓ →	↑	→	← →	← →	↑ ↓
Sepsis	→*	→*	↓	→	← →	→	↑ ↓←

*Mild decrease.

Source: © 1993, The American Dietetic Association. "Suggested Guidelines for Nutrition and Metabolic Management of Adult Patients Receiving Nutrition Support." Used by permission.

Appendix D

Anthropometric Measures

- Body Mass Index (BMI) = $\dfrac{\text{Weight (kg)}}{\text{Height}^2 \text{ (m}^2)}$

19–25	Appropriate weight (19–34 years)
21–27	Appropriate weight (> 35 years)
> 27.5	Obesity
27.5–30	Mild obesity
30–40	Moderate obesity
> 40	Severe or morbid obesity

- Stature from knee height (for ages 65–90):

  Men = (2.02 × knee height) − (0.04 × age) + 64.19
  Women = (1.83 × knee height) − (0.24 × age) + 84.88

- Determination of Ideal Body Weight by Hamwi method:

  Females: 100 lb for the first 5 ft plus 5 lb for each additional inch above 5 ft.
  Males: 106 lb for the first 5 ft plus 6 lb for each additional inch above 5 ft. + 10% for large frame;
  − 10% for small frame

- Amputee weight calculations:

  Ideal amputee weight = preamputation ideal body weight (IBW) − (IBW × % amputation)
  Segmental body weights:
  entire arm = 6.5%
  upper arm = 3.5%
  lower arm = 2.3%
  hand = 0.8%
  entire leg = 18.5%
  thigh = 11.5%
  knee, lower leg, and foot = 7.1%
  foot = 1.8%

continues

Appendix D continued

- Evaluation of Body Weight

  - Percentage usual body weight $= \dfrac{\text{Actual weight}}{\text{Usual weight}} \times 100$

85%–90%	Mild malnutrition
75%–84%	Moderate malnutrition
< 74%	Severe malnutrition

  - Percentage IBW $= \dfrac{\text{Actual weight}}{\text{IBW}} \times 100$

≥ 200%	Morbid obesity
≥ 130%	Obesity
110%–120%	Overweight
80%–90%	Mild malnutrition
70%–79%	Moderate malnutrition
< 69%	Severe malnutrition

  - Percentage weight loss $= \dfrac{\text{Usual body weight} - \text{Actual body weight}}{\text{Usual body weight}} \times 100$

Significant weight loss		*Severe weight loss*	
5%	over 1 mo	> 5%	over 1 mo
7.5%	over 3 mo	> 7.5%	over 3 mo
10%	over 6 mo	> 10%	over 6 mo

- Measurement of total body fat (arm fat area)

  $$\text{AFA (cm2)} = \frac{\text{MAC} \times \text{TSF}}{2} - \frac{\pi \times (\text{TSF})^2}{4}$$

  where MAC = midarm circumference.

- Measurement of skeletal protein mass:

  $$\text{MAMC (cm)} = \text{MAC (cm)} - 3.14 \text{ TSF (cm)}$$

  $$\text{AMA (cm}^2) = \frac{[\text{MAC (cm)} - 3.14 \text{ TSF (cm)}]^2}{4 \pi}$$

  Bone Free AMA (cm^2):

  $$\text{women: AMA (cm}^2) = \frac{[\text{MAC (cm)} - 3.14 \text{ TSF (cm)}]^2}{4 \pi} - 6.5 \text{ cm}^2$$

  $$\text{men: AMA (cm}^2) = \frac{[\text{MAC (cm)} - 3.14 \text{ TSF (cm)}]^2}{4 \pi} - 10 \text{ cm}^2$$

  where MAMC = mid–upper-arm muscle circumference and AMA = arm muscle area.

Courtesy of Laura E. Matarese, Cleveland Clinic Foundation, Cleveland, Ohio.

Appendix E

Approximate Oxalate Content of Selected Foods

Little or No Oxalate (< 2 mg per serving)	*Moderate Oxalate* (2–10 mg per Serving)	*High Oxalate* (> 10 mg per Serving)
BEVERAGES		
Beer, bottled (light, mild flavor)	Coffee (limit to 8 oz/d)	Beer, 4 oz/d (dark, robust)
Carbonated cola (limit to 12 oz/d)		Ovaltine and other beverage mixes
Distilled alcohol		Tea
Lemonade or limeade without added vitamin C		Chocolate milk
Wine: red, rosé, white (3–4 oz)		Cocoa
MILK		
Buttermilk		
Whole, low-fat, or skim milk		
Yogurt with allowed fruit		
MEAT AND MEAT SUBSTITUTES		
Eggs	Sardines	Baked beans canned in tomato sauce (1/3 cup)
Cheese		Tofu (1/2 cup)
Beef, lamb, or pork		
Poultry		
Fish and shellfish		
VEGETABLES (1/2 cup cooked, 1 cup raw)		
Avocado	Asparagus	Beans: green, wax, dried
Cauliflower	Broccoli	Beets: root, greens
Cabbage	Brussels sprouts	Celery
Mushrooms	Carrots	Chives
Onions	Corn: sweet white or yellow	Collards
Peas, green (fresh or frozen)	Green peas, canned	Cucumbers
Potatoes, white	Lettuce	Dandelion greens
Radishes	Lima beans	Eggplant
	Parsnips	Escarole
	Tomato, 1 small or juice (4 oz)	Kale
	Turnips	Leeks
		Mustard greens
		Okra
		Parsley
		Peppers, green
		Pokeweed
		Potatoes, sweet
		Rutabagas
		Spinach
		Summer squash
		Swiss chard
		Watercress

continues

Appendix E continued

Little or No Oxalate (< 2 mg per serving)	Moderate Oxalate (2–10 mg per Serving)	High Oxalate (> 10 mg per Serving)
FRUITS/JUICES (1/2 cup canned or juice, 1 medium fruit)		
Apple and apple juice	Apricots	Blackberries
Avocado	Black currants	Blueberries
Banana	Cherries, red sour	Currants, red
Cherries, Bing	Cranberry juice (4 oz)	Dewberries
Grapefruit, fruit and juice	Grape juice (4 oz)	Fruit cocktail
Grapes, green	Orange, fruit and juice (4 oz)	Grapes, purple
Mangoes	Peaches	Gooseberries
Melons: cantaloupe, casaba, honeydew, watermelon	Pears	Lemon peel
	Pineapple	Lime peel
Nectarines	Plums, purple	Orange peel
Pineapple juice	Prunes	Raspberries
Plums, green or yellow		Rhubarb
		Strawberries
		Tangerine
		Juices made from the above fruits
BREAD/STARCHES		
Bread	Cornbread (2″ square)	Amaranth (1/2 cup)
Breakfast cereals	Sponge cake (1″ slice)	Fruit cake
Macaroni	Spaghetti, canned in tomato sauce (1/2 cup)	Grits, white corn
Noodles		Soybean crackers
Rice		Wheat germ and bran (1 cup)
Spaghetti		
FATS/OILS		
Bacon		Nuts: peanuts, almonds, pecans, cashews, walnuts (1/3 cup)
Mayonnaise		
Salad dressing		
Vegetable oils		Nut butters (6 Tbsp)
Butter, margarine		Sesame seeds (1 cup)
MISCELLANEOUS		
Coconut	Chicken noodle soup, dehydrated	Carob or tahini (3/4 cup)
Jelly or preserves (made with allowed fruits)		Chocolate, cocoa (3–4 oz)
		Vegetable soup (1/2 cup)
Lemon, lime juice		Tomato soup (1/2 cup)
Salt, pepper (limit to 1 tsp/d)		Marmalade (5 Tbsp)
Soups with allowed ingredients		
Sugar		

Note: Considerable variation exists in the oxalate content of a single type of food. Factors such as growing conditions, age of the plant, bioavailability, and the patient's gastrointestinal abnormalities all affect individual absorption of oxalate. Therefore, the foods have been categorized into low-, moderate-, and high-oxalate groups rather than giving exact values. The data available on the oxalate content of foods are limited and variable. Many foods have been analyzed for oxalate content, using specific name brands or varieties. Data have been extrapolated to include the broader category of food for which analysis of oxalate content is available. The diet is intended to limit oxalate intake to less than 50 mg/d. Therefore, foods high in oxalate should be restricted, and food with moderate oxalate should be limited. Little or no oxalate-containing foods may be consumed as desired unless a portion size is indicated.

Source: Reprinted with permission of Mayo Foundation from CM Pemberton, et al, *Mayo Clinic Diet Manual,* 7th ed, pp. 253–254, © 1994, Mosby-Year Book, Inc.

Appendix F

Assessment of Mineral and Trace Element Nutriture

Nutrient	Requirement	Recommended Intake	Methods of Evaluation	Deficiency Symptoms	Treatment of Deficiency	Toxicity Symptoms
Calcium	3 mg/kg body weight	Enteral: 800–1200 mg/d* Parenteral: 400–600 mg/d	Urine calcium: Reflects absorption more than intake Serum calcium: Total: affected by albumin levels Ionized: physiologically active form Correction: adjusted calcium = [4.0 − Alb (g/dL)] .8 + present Ca⁺⁺ (mg/dL) Bone biopsy	Osteomalacia Rickets Osteoporosis Tetany	1000–2500 mg/d	Excess bone and soft tissue calcification Kidney stones Suppression of PTH hypophosphatemia GI problems: Pancreatitis Nausea
Phosphorus	Same as calcium	Enteral: 800–1200 mg/d* Parenteral: 15–30 mg/kg/d	Serum phosphorus Urinary excretion Calorimetric analysis	Cardiac failure CNS dysfunction Osteolysis Metabolic addemia RBC dysfunction Respiratory failure	800–1500 mg/d	Hyperphosphatemia Paresthesia Listlessness Mental confusion Hypertension Cardiac arrythmias
Magnesium	200 mg/d	Enteral: 300–360 mg/d Parenteral: 3.65–6.00 mg/kg/d RDA: 280–350 mg/d	Serum magnesium (affected by albumin level) Urinary excretion: Correction: adjusted magnesium (mmol/L)-present Mg (mmol/L) + .005 [40 − Alb (g/L)]	Anorexia Cardiac irritability Hypokelemia Hypocalcemia Vomiting	Oral: 600–2400 mg/d Parenteral: Day 1: 12 mg/kg/d Day 3–5: 6 mg/kg/d Day >5: 2.5 mg/kg/d	Nausea Vomiting Mental changes Decreased respiration

continues

Appendix F continued

Nutrient	Requirement	Recommended Intake	Methods of Evaluation	Deficiency Symptoms	Treatment of Deficiency	Toxicity Symptoms
Iron	0.7–2.3 mg/d	Enteral: 10–15 mg/d* Parenteral: 0.5–1.0 mg/d	Hematologic indices: RBC—red blood cells Hb—hemoglobin MCV—mean corpuscular volume MCHC—mean corpuscular hemoglobin concentration Iron studies: TIBC % saturation Free erythrocyte protoporphyrin Serum iron Serum ferritin Peripheral blood smear	Fatigue Listlessness Microcytic anemia Sore tongue Koilonychia Angular stomatitis	Parenteral: only if unable to tolerate or absorb oral iron dextran; venous blood Hb (g/dL) deficit × body weight + 1000 mg Enteral: 200–240 mg/d	Lethargy Coma Vomiting Abdominal cramps
Zinc	15 mg/d	Enteral: 12–15 mg/d* Parenteral: Normal: 2.5–4.9 mg/d Acute catabolic states: 4.5–6.0 mg/d Excessive losses (GI): 12–17 ml/l output	Blood: Serum RBC WBC Sweat Hair Nails 24-hr urine Functional indices: Isotopic turnover Dark adaptation Taste acuity Nitrogen retention Wound healing	Impaired wound healing Hypogonadism Hypospermia Alopecia Skin rashes Immune deficiencies Night blindness Impaired taste	40 mg/d	25 mg/d dose: Nausea Vomiting Metallic taste 225–450 mg/d dose: Vomiting Abdominal cramps Chills Headache

					5–10 mg dose: Nausea Vomiting Epigastric pain Diarrhea
Copper	2–3 mg/d	Enteral: 30 mg/kg/d Parenteral: Normal: 0.3 mg/d Increased GI fluid loss: 0.5 mg/d No RDA	Serum copper: Not accurate reflection of stores Ceruloplasmin Superoxide dismutase	(Rare) Microcytic anemia Neutropenia Skeletal abnormalities Depigmentation of hair and skin Defective elastin formation: arterial aneurysms Hypotonia Hypothermia	2 mg/d (supplement: cupric sulfate)
Selenium	0.05–0.2 mg/d	Enteral: 0.05–0.20 mg/d Parenteral: Normal: 20–40 µg/d Deficient from long-term TPN: 150 mg/d RDA: 55–70 mg/d	Plasma RBC Glutathione peroxidase activity	Muscle tenderness Myalgia Heart failure	Provide recommended intake	Dental defects Hair loss Dermatitis Peripheral vascular collapse Garlic-odor breath Brittle fingernails

continues

Appendix F continued

Nutrient	Requirement	Recommended Intake	Methods of Evaluation	Deficiency Symptoms	Treatment of Deficiency	Toxicity Symptoms
Chromium	0.05–0.20 mg/d	Enteral: 50–200 mg/d Parenteral: Short-term: none Long-term: 10–15 µg/d Increased GI losses: plus 20 µg/d No RDA	Tissue Serum/plasma: Do not reflect body stores 24-hr urine: Correlates with intakes >40 µg Hair: Unreliable	Glucose intolerance Fasting hyperglycemia Peripheral neuropathy Glycosuria Increased serum cholesterol and triglycerides Insulin resistance	200 µg/d	None known
Manganese	2.5–5.0 mg/d	Enteral: 2.5–5.0 mg/d Parenteral: 0.4–0.8 mg/d (except with cholestatic liver disease)	Serum: Neutron activation Absorption spectrophotometry Whole blood: Absorption spectrophotometry	None reported	Recommended intake	Extrapyramidal symptoms Encephalitislike symptoms
Molybdenum	0.15–0.50 mg/d	Enteral: 150–500 µg/d Parenteral: 25–75 µg/d No RDA	Blood: Neutron activation Atomic absorption Methionine levels Urine: Thiosulfate levels	(Uncommon) Headache Night blindness Irritability Lethargy	Recommended intake	Increased copper excretion: 1500 µg/d intake

*Range same as RDA.

Source: Reprinted with permission from Hopkins, B. Assessment of nutritional status. In: M.M. Gottschlich, L. Matarese, and E.P. Shronts, eds. *Nutrition Support Dietetics*, 2d ed. pp. 15–70, © 1993, American Society for Parenteral and Enteral Nutrition.

continues

Appendix G

Assessment of Vitamin Nutriture

Vitamin	Requirement	Recommended Intake	Methods of Evaluation	Deficiency Symptoms	Treatment of Deficiency	Toxicity Symptoms
Water-Soluble Vitamins						
Thiamin	0.35 mg/1000 kcal	Enteral: 1–1.5 mg/d* Parenteral: 3 mg/d	Urinary excretion: Reflects intake, not stores Decreased with deficient intakes Blood: Whole blood thiamin Erythrocyte transketolase activity: Estimates deficiency of body stores Increased with deficiency	Beriberi: Mental confusion Weakness Peripheral neuropathy Heart disease Edema (wet) Muscle wasting (dry) Wernicki's encephalopathy	Thiamin hydrochloride Wernicki's: 50-mg bolus 50 mg/d until stores repleted Limited intake: 1–2 mg/d	(Rare) Irritability Headache Insomnia Interferes with riboflavin and B_6
Riboflavin	0.4–5.0mg/100 kcal	Enteral: 1.2–1.8 mg/d* Parenteral: 3.6 mg/d	Urinary excretion: Correlates with intake, not stores Decreased with limited intakes Increased with $(-)N^2$ balance Blood: Erythrocyte riboflavin Glutathione reductase + flavin adenine dinucleotide reflects body stores deficiency: increased stimulation	Angular stomatitis Chellosis Glossitis Scrotal or vulval dermatitis	5 times RDA per day	Unknown

Appendix G continued

Vitamin	Requirement	Recommended Intake	Methods of Evaluation	Deficiency Symptoms	Treatment of Deficiency	Toxicity Symptoms
Niacin	8.8–12.3 mg niacin equivalents (NE)/d	Enteral: 12–20 mg/d Parenteral: 40 mg/d RDA: 13–19 mg/d	Urinary excretion: Reflects intake, not stores N^1-methylnicotinamide 2-pyridone/N^1-methylinicotinamide decreased excretion with intake Serum: Represents body stores, usually Body stores: none	Pellagra: Diarrhea Dementia Dermatitis Death Scarlet tongue Tongue fissuring	40–200 mg of nicotinic acid or nicotinamide per day	Liver damage Vascular dilation Flushing Irritation
Vitamin B_6	0.2 mg/g of protein ingested	Enteral: 1.6–2.0 mg/d* Parenteral: 4 mg/d	Urinary excretion: Reflects recent intakes Decreased with limited intakes Aminotransferase activity Stimulated: deficiency Measures body stores Plasma levels Tryptophan load test: Tryptophan to nicotinic acid—B_6 dependent Measure tryptophan metabolites Reflects body stores Methionine load test	(Rare except in presence of B_6 antagonist) Polyneuritis Nasolabial seborrhea Glossitis Microcytic anemia Oxalate stones	Pyridoxine hydrochloride 5 mg/d	None known
Pantothenic acid	4–7 mg/d	Enteral: 5–10 mg/d Parenteral: 15 mg/d No RDA	Body stores: none Serum level: Red blood cell (RBC) content responds to changes in dietary intakes Urinary excretion: Correlates with intake	(Rare) Lethargy Abdominal pain Nausea Flatulence Vomiting	10–100 mg	Diarrhea

		Requirements	Assessment	Deficiency		Toxicity
Biotin	50 µg/1000 kcal	Enteral: 150–300 µg/d Parenteral: Normal: 60 µg/d Repletion: 300 µg/d No RDA	Body stores: none Evaluation of intake: Whole blood RBC Plasma Urinary excretion	Skin rash Alopecia Lethargy Anorexia Paresthesias	10–300 µg/d	None known
Folic acid	100 µg/d	Enteral: 200–400 µg/d Parenteral: 400 µg–10 mg/d RDA: 180–200 µg/d	Urine: Foriminoglutamic acid Histidine load Increased excretion with deficiency Not accurate Blood: Serum folate Reflects dietary change Not a single parameter to assess deficiency Used in conjunction with red cell folate Affected by hypoalbuminemia Red cell folate: Most accurate Evaluated with serum folate	(Folate stores last 3–6 mo after cessation of folate ingestion) Macrocytic anemia Stomatitis Glossitis Lethargy Diarrhea	0.5–1.0 mg/d	Not known

continues

Appendix G continued

Vitamin	Requirement	Recommended Intake	Methods of Evaluation	Deficiency Symptoms	Treatment of Deficiency	Toxicity Symptoms
Vitamin B_{12}	Minimal amount for hematologic response: 0.1 µg/d Maximum response: 0.5–1.0 µg/d	Enteral: 3 µg/d* Parenteral: 5 µg/d RDA: 2 µg/d	Methylmalonic acid: Increased excretion with B_{12} deficiency Not as useful as serum Shilling test: Assesses absorption of B_{12} Part 1 of test Normal: no malabsorption, test ends Abnormal: positive test, complete part 2 Part 2 of test Normal: malabsorption secondary to lack of intrinsic factor Abnormal: malabsorption secondary to ileal disease, decreased absorptive capacity, bacterial overgrowth Does not assess body stores with transcobalamin II deficiency Low in folate deficiency with normal stores	Megaloblastic anemia Neuropathy Stomatitis Glossitis Anorexia Diarrhea	Deficient diet: 1 µg/d Inadequate absorption: 1 µg/d parenterally or 100 µg/mo	None known

| Vitamin C | 10 mg/d prevents scurvy but does not provide for adequate reserves | Enteral: 60 mg/d* maintains body pool of 1500 mg
Parenteral: Normal: 100 mg/d
Catabolic stress: 500 mg/d | Blood:
Plasma: Assesses intake, not deficiency state
Whole blood: Assesses intake, not deficiency state
Buffy coat: Anticoagulated centrifuged whole blood; Accurate; Closely related to stores
Leukocyte ascorbate: Closely related to stores
Radioactive-labeled vitamin C: Most accurate measurement; Closely related to stores | Hemorrhaging:
Skin
Nose
GI tract
Weakness
Irritability
Bleeding gums | 10 mg/d alleviates scurvy
60–100 mg/d replenishes stores | Interferes with tests for glucosuria
May cause osmotic diarrhea and formation of oxalate stones
Interferes with anticoagulation therapy
Inactivates or destroys vitamin B_{12} in presence of heat |

continues

Appendix G continued

Vitamin	Requirement	Recommended Intake	Methods of Evaluation	Deficiency Symptoms	Treatment of Deficiency	Toxicity Symptoms
Fat-Soluble Vitamins						
Vitamin A	500–600 retinol equivalents (RE)/d (1 RE = 1 μg RE)	Enteral: 800–1000 RE/d* Parenteral: 1000 RE/d	Urine: known Blood: Serum vitamin A: Reflects body stores, but only at very low levels Retinyl ester (fasting): Reflects toxicity Serum carotene: Used to assess malabsorption Variable since it reflects intake of carotenoids Does not measure stores	Visual changes: Poor dark adaptation Bitot's spots Xerosis Irreversible corneal ulceration Scarring and softening of cornea Male sterility	37500–45000 RE/d	Acute (200000 RE/d): Nausea Vomiting Headaches Increased cerebrospinal pressure Vertigo Double vision Chronic (10000 RE/d): Desquamation of skin Gingivitis Alopecia Swelling of bone Hepatomegaly Pruritis Anorexia

Vitamin D	Exact amount not established 2.50 µg of cholecalciferol/d prevents rickets, promotes growth, ensures adequate absorption of calcium 10 µg of cholecalciferol/d promotes better absorption of calcium, increases growth rate	Enteral: 5–10 µg/d* Parenteral: 5 µg/d	Urine: none Blood: Serum phosphate: Decreased with deficiency Serum calcium: Decreased with deficiency Serum 25-hydroxyvitamin D: Decreased with deficiency Alkaline phosphatase: Increased with deficiency 1,25-dihydroxyvitamin D: Correlates with function, not intake/stores X-ray of bones	Decreased body stores of calcium and phosphorus Rickets Osteomalacia	Amount varies with cause of deficiency (1250–2500 µg cholecalciferol/d)	Excess bone calcification Stiffness Soft tissue calcification Kidney stones Hypercalcemia
Vitamin K	30 µg/d	Enteral: 50–200 µg/d Parenteral: 150 µg/d RDA: 65–80 µg/d	Prothrombin time Serum prothrombin Serum vitamin K	Primary vitamin-K deficiency is uncommon Excessive bruising Purpura Bleeding	Dependent on cause of deficiency	Jaundice

continues

Appendix G continued

Vitamin	Requirement	Recommended Intake	Methods of Evaluation	Deficiency Symptoms	Treatment of Deficiency	Toxicity Symptoms
Vitamin E	2 mg of α-tocopherol per day	Enteral: 8–10 mg of α-tocopherol* Parenteral: 10 mg of α-tocopherol	Serum vitamin E Erythrocyte peroxide hemolysis: Nonspecific Rules out deficiency if normal Serum tocopherol esters: Chromatography High-performance liquid chromatography	Hemolysis Anemia Retinal degeneration Neuronal axonopathy Myopathy	180 mg of α-tocopherol per day	300 mg of α-tocopherol Prolonged clotting time

*Range same as RDA.

Source: Reprinted with permission from B Hopkins. Assessment of nutritional status. In: M.M. Gottschlich, L. Matarese, and E.P. Shronts, eds. *Nutrition Support Dietetics*, 2d ed. pp. 15–70, © 1993, American Society for Parenteral and Enteral Nutrition.

Appendix H

Body Mass Index
Weigh Your Risk with BMI

		Good Weights								Increasing Risk					
BMI		19	20	21	22	23	24	25	26	27	28	29	30	35	40
HEIGHT							WEIGHT (in pounds)								
4'10"		91	96	100	105	110	115	119	124	129	134	138	143	167	191
4'11"		94	99	104	109	114	119	124	128	133	138	143	148	173	198
5'		97	102	107	112	118	123	128	133	138	143	148	153	179	204
5'1"		100	106	111	116	122	127	132	137	143	148	153	158	185	211
5'2"		104	109	115	120	126	131	136	142	147	153	158	164	191	218
5'3"		107	113	118	124	130	135	141	146	152	158	163	169	197	225
5'4"		110	116	122	128	134	140	145	151	157	163	169	174	204	232
5'5"		114	120	126	132	138	144	150	156	162	168	174	180	210	240
5'6"		118	124	130	136	142	148	155	161	167	173	179	186	216	247
5'7"		121	127	134	140	146	153	159	166	172	178	185	191	223	255
5'8"		125	131	138	144	151	158	164	171	177	184	190	197	230	262
5'9"		128	135	142	149	155	162	169	176	182	189	196	203	236	270
5'10"		132	139	146	153	160	167	174	181	188	195	202	209	243	278
5'11"		136	143	150	157	165	172	179	186	193	200	208	215	250	286
6'		140	147	154	162	169	177	184	191	199	206	213	221	258	294
6'1"		144	151	159	166	174	182	189	197	204	212	219	227	265	302
6'2"		148	155	163	171	179	186	194	202	210	218	225	233	272	311
6'3"		152	160	168	176	184	192	200	208	216	224	232	240	279	319
6'4"		156	164	172	180	189	197	205	213	221	230	238	246	287	328

The health risk from any level of BMI is increased if you have gained more than 11 pounds since age 25 or if you have a waist circumference above 40 in (100 cm) due to central fatness.

Courtesy of Pennington Biomedical Research Center, Baton Rouge, Louisiana.

Appendix I

Determine Your Nutritional Health Checklist

The Warning Signs of poor nutritional health are often overlooked. Use this checklist to find out if you or someone you know is at nutritional risk.

Read the statements below. Circle the number in the yes column for those that apply to you or someone you know. For each yes answer, score the number in the box. Total your nutritional score.

DETERMINE YOUR NUTRITIONAL HEALTH

	YES
I have an illness or condition that made me change the kind and/or amount of food I eat.	2
I eat fewer than 2 meals per day.	3
I eat few fruits or vegetables, or milk products.	2
I have 3 or more drinks of beer, liquor or wine almost every day.	2
I have tooth or mouth problems that make it hard for me to eat.	2
I don't always have enough money to buy the food I need.	4
I eat alone most of the time.	1
I take 3 or more different prescribed or over-the-counter drugs a day.	1
Without wanting to, I have lost or gained 10 pounds in the last 6 months.	2
I am not always physically able to shop, cook and/or feed myself.	2
TOTAL	

Total Your Nutritional Score. If it's —

0-2   **Good!** Recheck your nutritional score in 6 months.

3-5   **You are at moderate nutritional risk.** See what can be done to improve your eating habits and lifestyle. Your office on aging, senior nutrition program, senior citizens center or health department can help. Recheck your nutritional score in 3 months.

6 or more **You are at high nutritional risk.** Bring this checklist the next time you see your doctor, dietitian or other qualified health or social service professional. Talk with them about any problems you may have. Ask for help to improve your nutritional health.

Remember that warning signs suggest risk, but do not represent diagnosis of any condition. Turn the page to learn more about the Warnings Signs of poor nutritional health.

These materials developed and distributed by the Nutrition Screening Initiative, a project of:

 AMERICAN ACADEMY OF FAMILY PHYSICIANS

 THE AMERICAN DIETETIC ASSOCIATION

NCOA NATIONAL COUNCIL ON THE AGING, INC.

The Nutrition Checklist is based on the Warning Signs described below. Use the word DETERMINE to remind you of the Warning Signs.

DISEASE

Any disease, illness or chronic condition which causes you to change the way you eat, or makes it hard for you to eat, puts your nutritional health at risk. Four out of five adults have chronic diseases that are affected by diet. Confusion or memory loss that keeps getting worse is estimated to affect one out of five or more of older adults. This can make it hard to remember what, when or if you've eaten. Feeling sad or depressed, which happens to about one in eight older adults, can cause big changes in appetite, digestion, energy level, weight and well-being.

EATING POORLY

Eating too little and eating too much both lead to poor health. Eating the same foods day after day or not eating fruit, vegetables, and milk products daily will also cause poor nutritional health. One in five adults skip meals daily. Only 13% of adults eat the minimum amount of fruit and vegetables needed. One in four older adults drink too much alcohol. Many health problems become worse if you drink more than one or two alcoholic beverages per day.

TOOTH LOSS/ MOUTH PAIN

A healthy mouth, teeth and gums are needed to eat. Missing, loose or rotten teeth or dentures which don't fit well or cause mouth sores make it hard to eat.

ECONOMIC HARDSHIP

As many as 40% of older Americans have incomes of less than $6,000 per year. Having less--or choosing to spend less--than $25-30 per week for food makes it very hard to get the foods you need to stay healthy.

REDUCED SOCIAL CONTACT

One-third of all older people live alone. Being with people daily has a positive effect on morale, well-being and eating.

MULTIPLE MEDICINES

Many older Americans must take medicines for health problems. Almost half of older Americans take multiple medicines daily. Growing old may change the way we respond to drugs. The more medicines you take, the greater the chance for side effects such as increased or decreased appetite, change in taste, constipation, weakness, drowsiness, diarrhea, nausea, and others. Vitamins or minerals when taken in large doses act like drugs and can cause harm. Alert your doctor to everything you take.

INVOLUNTARY WEIGHT LOSS/GAIN

Losing or gaining a lot of weight when you are not trying to do so is an important warning sign that must not be ignored. Being overweight or underweight also increases your chance of poor health.

NEEDS ASSISTANCE IN SELF CARE

Although most older people are able to eat, one of every five have trouble walking, shopping, buying and cooking food, especially as they get older.

ELDER YEARS ABOVE AGE 80

Most older people lead full and productive lives. But as age increases, risk of frailty and health problems increase. Checking your nutritional health regularly makes good sense.

 The Nutrition Screening Initiative • 1010 Wisconsin Avenue, NW • Suite 800 • Washington, DC 20007
The Nutrition Screening Initiative is funded in part by a grant from Ross Laboratories, a division of Abbott Laboratories.

Reprinted with permission by the Nutrition Screening Initiative, a project of the American Academy of Family Physicians, the American Dietetic Association and the National Council on the Aging, Inc., and funded in part by a grant from Ross Products Division, Abbott Laboratories.

Appendix J
Electrolyte Disorders

Electrolyte Disorder	Diagnosis/Etiology

1. Hyponatremia (must evaluate serum osmolality and extracellular fluid volume)

Check serum osmolality
A. Pseudohyponatremia (normal osmolality)
   1. Hypertriglyceridemia (multiply triglyceride value in g/dL by 0.002 to yield the mEq/l reduction in serum Na).
   2. Hypoproteinemia (multiply total protein by 0.25 to yield the mEq reduction in serum Na).
B. Hypertonic hyponatremia (> 290 mOsm)
   1. Hyperglycemia and infusion of hypertonic solutions (glucose, mannitol) causing Na-free water to move from cells to the extracellular fluid space, diluting serum Na.
   2. Hyperglycemia (serum Na falls 1.6 mEq/l for each 100 mg/dL rise in blood sugar above normal).
Evaluate extracellular volume
C. Hypotonic hyponatremia (evaluate extracellular volume)
   1. Hypovolemic hyponatremia: loss of Na-containing fluid (gastrointestinal [GI] tract, skin, lungs, kidneys, sequestration of plasma volume) and replacement with Na-free fluid.
   2. Hypervolemic hyponatremia: reduced effective arterial blood volume (ie, congestive heart failure [CHF], severe hypoalbuminemia limits the excretion of ingested water) causing Na and water retention with a disproportionately greater water retention.
   3. Isovolemic hyponatremia: due to altered mechanism, antidiuretic hormone (ADH) secretion and defective renal diluting mechanisms, syndrome of inappropriate secretion of ADH (SIADH), excessive water intake with loss of salt-containing body fluids.

2. Hypernatremia (osmolality is always elevated)

Extracellular fluid volume
   1. Hypovolemic hypernatremia: loss of hypotonic body fluids without replacement or replacement of hypotonic body fluids with hypertonic solutions, diuresis (urea- or diuretic-induced or glycosuria).
   2. Hypervolemic hypernatremia: infusion of large amounts of hypertonic solutions.
   3. Isovolemic hypernatremia: inappropriate replacement of daily isotonic and hypotonic body fluid loss (ie, skin and respiratory loss) with normal saline; diabetes insipidus.

3. Hypokalemia

A. Potassium depletion: due to cation loss from skin, GI tract, renal potassium wasting (drug-induced or renal tubular acidosis [RTA]).
B. Redistribution hypokalemia: secondary to movement of potassium intracellularly as in alkalosis (K^+ falls 0.6 mEq/0.1 pH unit rise), insulin administration, B_{12} therapy, and stimulation of glycolysis and the Krebs cycle by feeding.

Electrolyte Disorder	Diagnosis/Etiology
4. Hyperkalemia	A. Pseudohyperkalemia: secondary to test-tube hemolysis, ischemic blood drawing, leukocytosis, and thrombocytosis. B. Redistribution: from hyperglycemia, acidosis, tissue necrosis. C. Excessive K^+ ingestion; renal failure.
5. Hypercalcemia	A. Malignancies and hyperparathyroidism are responsible for 70%–80% of all cases. B. Acute tubular necrosis (ATN) recovery after myoglobinuria-induced disease.
6. Hypocalcemia	A. Hypoalbuminemia: (4.0 – actual serum albumin level) × 0.8 yields the amount of hypocalcemia due to protein depletion. B. Hypomagnesemia: impairs parathyroid hormone (PTH) secretion and its peripheral action on the bone. C. Vitamin D deficiency: causes decreased bone responsiveness to PTH or decreased intestinal Ca absorption. D. Hyperphosphatemia: causes decreased conversion of vitamin D to its active form, reduced bone absorption. E. Pancreatitis: mechanism unclear.
7. Hypomagnesemia	A. Renal magnesium wasting. B. Stimulation of glycolysis by feeding enhances magnesium uptake in the cell.
8. Hypermagnesemia	A. Renal failure.
9. Hypophosphatemia	A. Stimulation of glycolysis by feeding enhances phosphorus uptake in the cell. B. Phosphorus binding by albumin- or magnesium-containing antacids. C. Renal phosphate binding.
10. Hyperphosphatemia	A. Renal failure.
11. Hypobicarbonatemia	A. Overproduction of acid (ie, lactic acid). B. Diarrheal loss of sodium bicarbonate with renal retention of sodium chloride. C. Renal failure or ATN, causing retention of acid or urinary wastage of alkali. D. Total parenteral nutrition (TPN), which causes a mild metabolic acidosis. E. Addition of 15 to the serum bicarbonate estimates the last two digits of the pH.
12. Hyperbicarbonatemia	A. Caused by a source of a new alkali and reduced bicarbonaturia. B. Contraction alkalosis as seen in diuresis (bicarbonate concentration in interstitial fluid is similar to that in blood). C. Excessive GI loss of acid (nasogastric suction and vomiting), which leaves unneutralized bicarbonate behind.

Source: Reprinted with permission from JP Grant. Administration of parenteral nutrition solutions. In: JP Grant, ed. *Handbook of Total Parenteral Nutrition.* p. 94, © 1980, WB Saunders Co.

Appendix K

Guidelines To Determine Metabolic Stress

	Level 0 Nonstressed Starvation	Level 1 Elective General Surgery	Level 2 Polytrauma	Level 3 Sepsis
Total nitrogen (g/dL)	5	5–10	10–15	> 15
Glucose (mg/dL)*	100 ± 20	150 ± 25	158 ± 25	250 ± 50
O_2 consumption index (ml/m²)	90 ± 10	130 ± 6	140 ± 6	160 ± 100
Lactate (mmol/L)	100 ± 5	1200 ± 20	1200 ± 200	2500 ± 500
Insulin resistance	No	No	Yes/no	Yes
Amino acids (g/kg/d)	1.0	1.5	2.0**	2.0–2.5**
Nonprotein calories (kcal/kg/d)	25	25	***	***

*In the absence of diabetes, pancreatitis, or steroid therapy.
**Should be evaluated by 24-hour nitrogen balance studies.
***Should be evaluated via indirect calorimetry.
Source: Reprinted with permission from FB Cerra. A Pocket Manual of Surgical Nutrition. p. 43, © 1984, CV Mosby Publishers.

Appendix L

Malabsorption Tests

Target	Test	Normal Values
Fat malabsorption	Sudan stain	< 10 globules of 20-μmol/l diameter
	Labeled carbon	> 3.43% dose
	Fecal fat	< 5% of intake
Small-bowel function	D-xylose	> 35–40 mg/dL, serum; > 4–6.5 g, urine
	Schilling	> 7% labeled dose, urine
Disaccharidase activity	Lactose tolerance	< 20 ppm breath hydrogen
	Stool pH	> 6 bacterial
Overgrowth	Bile acid breath	< 5%–20% labeled dose

Source: Reprinted with permission from MG Hermann-Zaidins. Malabsorption. In: A Skipper, ed. *Dietitian's Handbook of Enteral and Parenteral Nutrition.* p. 42, © 1989, Aspen Publishers.

Appendix M

Nutrient Absorption

Site	Vitamins/Minerals/Electrolytes	Macronutrients
Duodenum	A, thiamin, iron, calcium	Monosaccharides and disaccharides, amino acids and dipeptides, glycerol, fatty acids, and monoglycerides
Jejunum (most nutrient absorption occurs in proximal jejunum)	Entire: C, folate, biotin, copper, zinc, potassium, pantothenic acid, D, E, K, B_1, B_2, B_3, B_6, iodine, calcium, magnesium, phosphorus Proximal: A, folic acid, iron	Entire: Glucose, galactose, amino acids, glycerol and fatty acids, monoglycerides Proximal: Disaccharides (lactose) Distal: Disaccharides (sucrose, maltose), dipeptides
Ileum (site of bile salt absorption)	B_{12}, chloride, sodium, potassium	
Colon	Sodium	Water

Note: The exact sites for absorption of manganese, cobalt, selenium, chromium, molybdenum, and cadmium are unknown.
Source: Reprinted with permission from MD Caldwell, C Kennedy-Caldwell. Normal nutritional requirements. *Surg Clin North Am.* 61:3, p. 491, © 1981, WB Saunders.

Appendix N

Nutrition Support Algorithm

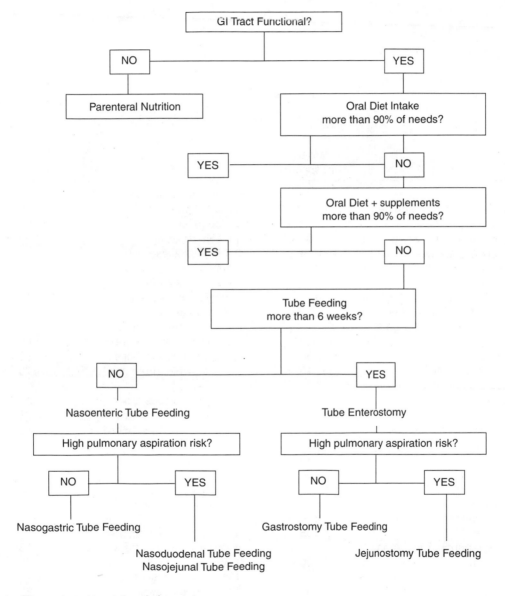

1. Demonstrated by daily caloric counts

Source: Reprinted with permission from KT Ideno. Enteral nutrition, *Nutrition Support Dietetics Curriculum.* p. 83, © 1993, American Society for Parenteral and Enteral Nutrition.

Appendix O

Phosphorus Content of Common Foods

Food	Mg of Phosphorus
Milk Group	
⅓ cup custard, homemade	103
½ cup half and half	112
¾ cup ice cream, vanilla	100
½ cup milk, whole	114
½ cup pudding (vanilla, homemade)	116
½ cup yogurt (plain, whole milk)	108
Meat and Meat Substitutes	
⅓ cup beans, cooked, great northern	98
1 oz beef	65
1 oz cheese, cheddar	145
¼ cup cheese, cottage, creamed	70
1 oz cheese, processed American	211
1 oz cheese, Swiss	171
1 oz chicken (average)	55
1 egg	90
1 oz fish, haddock, cooked by dry heat	68
⅓ cup lentils, cooked	119
1 oz liver	105
2 tbsp peanut butter, creamy/ smooth	120
1 oz pork, lean, roasted	70
1 oz turkey (average)	60
Starch	
½ cup cereal (100% Bran)	344

Food	Mg of Phosphorus
⅓ cup cereal (All Bran, Bran Buds, granola-type)	246
½ cup cereal (Bran Flakes)	108
1 waffle (frozen)	130
2 4-in pancakes, prepared with mix	251
1 biscuit, from mix	128
⅓ cup brown rice	47
1 tbsp wheat germ	81
½ cup oatmeal, cooked	89
1 slice whole-wheat bread	65
⅓ cup lima beans, boiled	69
1/12 cake, white (from mix)	170
Vegetables	
½ cup green peas, boiled	94
½ cup mushrooms, raw pieces	36
½ cup mushrooms, boiled	68
Fruit	
1 oz coconut, dried	59
Fats and Oils	
1 oz peanuts, dry-roasted	100
1 oz sunflower seeds, dry roasted	328
Carbohydrate Supplements	
8 oz carbonated colas	35
1 oz caramels	35
1 oz chocolate, semisweet	43
1 tbsp cocoa powder	35
1 tbsp molasses, blackstrap	17
12 fl oz beer	44

Source: Reprinted with permission from CM Pemberton, et al, *Mayo Clinic Diet Manual,* 7th ed, © 1994, Mayo Foundation.

Appendix P

Physical Markers of Hydration Status*

Volume deficit
- Decreased moisture in oral cavity
- Decreased skin and tongue turgor (elasticity); skin may remain slightly elevated after being pinched
- Flattened neck and peripheral veins in supine position
- Decreased urinary output (< 30 mL/h without renal failure)
- Postural hypotension (severe deficit)
- Tachycardia
- Acute weight loss (≥ 1 lb/d)

Volume excess
- Clinically apparent edema is usually not present until 12–15 L of fluid has accumulated
- 1 L fluid = 1 kg weight
- Acute weight gain (≥ 1 lb/d)
- Pitting edema (especially in dependent parts of the body, ie, feet, ankles, and sacrum)
- Distended peripheral and neck veins
- Symptoms of congestive heart failure (CHF) or pulmonary edema
- Central venous pressure (CVP) > 11 cm H_2O

*Methany NM. Fundamental concepts and definitions. In: Methany NM, ed. *Fluid and Electrolyte Balance: Nursing Considerations*. Philadelphia, Pa: JB Lippincott; 1987:29–34.

Appendix Q

Physical Signs Related to Nutrient Deficiency or Excess*

Nutrient	Deficiency	Excess
PART 1 VITAMINS—FAT SOLUBLE		
Vitamin A	Night blindness Keratomalacia Bitot's spots Xerosis: skin, cornea and/or conjunctiva Follicular hyperkeratosis Crazy paving dermatitis Taste changes	Pruritis Hyperkeratosis Alopedia Painful swelling of bones Syndrome of headache, dizziness, irritability, and drowsiness Hepatomegaly staining of skin (palms and soles) orange, anorexia and vomiting
Vitamin D	Painless costochondral beading Decreased muscle strength Osteomalacia Kyphosis (over lifetime) Bowed legs Pigeon chest and Harrison salcus Prone to fractures Rickets in children Adult osteomalacia	Acute hypercalcemia Nausea Anorexia Abdominal pain Diarrhea
Vitamin E	Sensory loss (R) Decreased vibration sense (R) Impaired position sense (R) Gait sensory ataxia (R) Impaired reflexes (R)	Coagulopathy (vitamin E increases vitamin K requirements) Nausea, flatulence, and diarrhea have been reported
Vitamin K	Ecchymosis Petechia Purpura	
PART 2 VITAMINS—WATER SOLUBLE		
Vitamin C	Petechiae and purpura Perifolliculitis Delayed wound healing Decubitus ulcers Conjunctival hemorrhage Bleeding gums Painful costochondral beading Perifollicular hemorrhages Impaired wound healing	Oxalate stones (R) Gastric irritation Flatulence Diarrhea

Nutrient	Deficiency	Excess
PART 2 VITAMINS—WATER SOLUBLE (continued)		
Vitamin B$_1$ Thiamine	Edema Muscle wasting Muscle tenderness and cramps Confusion Wernicke-Korsakoff syndrome Decreased vibration sense (#) Paresthesia (#) Ptosis (#) Photophobia (#) Angular blepharo-conjunctivitis (#) Amblyopia (#) Dyssebacia (#) Beriberi (wet and dry)	None documented
Vitamin B$_2$ Riboflavin	Flaking, scaly dermatitis Angular blepharo-conjunctivitis Magenta tongue Naso-labial seborrheic dermatitis Corneal vascularization Angular stomatitis Cheilosis Filiform papillary atrophy or hypertrophy Glossitis	None documented

Niacin	Pellegra: dermatitis, diarrhea, dementia
	Red/brown scaly dermatitis
	Erythema and swelling on light exposed
	   areas (Casal's necklace, glove and
	   stocking distribution)
	Beefy red/scarlet tongue
	Confusion
	Depression/irritability
	Atrophy of sublingual papillae
	Fissuring edema of the tongue
	Nasal-labial seborrheic dermatitis
	Corneal vascularization
	Angular stomatitis
	Cheilosis
	Filiform papillary atrophy or hypertrophy
	Glossitis
		For high doses used to treat
		   hyperlipidemia, side effects
		   include cutaneous flushing, and
		   gastric irritation. Elevated liver
		   enzymes hyperglycemia and
		   gout are less common

Vitamin B6 Pyridoxine	Nasal-labial seborrheic dermatitis Angular stomatitis Glossitis Depression Paresthesia Peripheral neuropathy	Sensory neuropathy

continues

Appendix Q continued

Nutrient	Deficiency	Excess
	PART 2 VITAMINS—WATER SOLUBLE (continued)	
Vitamin B$_{12}$ Cobalamine	Megaloblastic anemia Lemon-yellow skin pallor Vertiligo Hyperpigmentation Early greying (associated with pernicious anemia only) Vincent's stomatitis (gums) Angular blepharo-conjunctivitis Scarlet tongue Pale ventral tongue surface Filiform papillary atrophy or hypertrophy Atrophy of sublingual papillae Glossitis Confusion Dementia Sensory loss; paresthesia and vibration sense Decreased or loss of positive sense Gait sensory ataxia	None documented
Folate	Megaloblastic anemia Skin pallor Pallor of everted lower eyelids Vincent's stomatitis (gums) Filiform papillary atrophy Scarlet tongue Apthous-like lesions (R) Atrophy of sublingual papillae Glossitis Sensory loss (R)	None documented
Biotin	Flaking, scaly dermatitis Bands of hypo-pigmentation of the hair shaft Alopecia Coarse hair Pale ventral tongue surface Sensory Loss	None documented
	PART 3 MINERALS	
Calcium	Trousseau's sign Chvostek's sign Kyphosis (over lifetime) Bowed legs Fractures	Rare: Hypercalcemia may result in mineralization of soft tissue. Hypotonia Proximal myopathy

Nutrient	Deficiency	Excess
PART 3 MINERALS (continued)		
Magnesium	Chvostek's sign Trousseau's sign Tetany Decreased level of consciousness Weakness, muscle cramps Vertigo	Decreased level of consciousness
Phosphorus	Osteomalacia Muscle weakness Malaise	Hyperphosphatemia may result in decreased level of consciousness. In renal insufficiency, secondary hyperparathyroidism can occur.
Sodium	Hyponatremia Convulsions Diarrhea Anxiety	Sodium and water retention resulting in edema
Potassium	Hypokalemia Motor function weakness Atonia Cardiac arrhythmia	Anxiety
PART 4 TRACE MINERALS		
Copper	Skin pallor Decreased pigmentation of hair shaft (may be banded)	Wilson's disease Blue lunula Kayser-Fleisher rings
Iron	Skin pallor Koilonychia Pallor of everted lower eyelids Angular stomatitis Filiform papillary atrophy Ventral surface of tongue—pale Glossitis	Hemochromatosis Gray-Tan, bronze, blue-grey skin colour
Zinc	Diffuse erythema Xerosis Flaking, scaly dermatitis Delayed wound healing Decubitus ulcers Alopedia Night blindness Taste change	

continues

Appendix Q continued

Nutrient	Deficiency	Excess
	PART 4 TRACE MINERALS (continued)	
Chromium	Koilonychia	
Iodine	Outer third eyebrow missing Goiter	
Fluoride	Carious teeth Possibly osteomalacia	Fluorosis Paralysis Convulsions GI irritation
		None documented
	MACRONUTRIENTS	
Protein	Kwashiorkor Fullness, moon-shaped face Brittle, pluckable hair Fine, silky hair Alopecia Decreased pigmentation (hair) Muehrcke's lines (nails) Edema Hyperpigmentation (Sun-exposed skin) Flaky paint or crazy paving dermatitis Delayed wound healing Decubitis ulcers Muscle weakness and wasting	
		None documented
Essential fatty acids	Xerosis Flaking, scaly, dermatitis Follicular hyperkeratosis Dry dull hair	
		Accumulation of adipose tissue
Protein/energy	Marasmus Dry dull hair Drawn in cheeks Carious teeth Yellow-brown stained teeth Ascites Impaired grip strength Muscle weakness and wasting Loss of position sense	

(#) Signs associated with B-complex deficiency
(R) = Rare
*Prepared by: Walters, Eleanor, personal communication, 1993. Reference: *Atlas of nutritional support techniques*, 1989. Edited by Rombeau et al., Little, Brown and Company, Boston/Toronto.

Appendix R

Routine Urinalysis* in Nutritional Assessment

Test	Normal Findings	Abnormalities/Deviations
Color	Straw to light amber	Discolor caused by biliary disease (urobilin), hematuria, hemoglobinuria, porphyria, drugs, foods (beets can cause a red color)
Clarity	Clear	Cloudy urine may be due to presence of blood, pus, phosphate, bacteria, fat, vitamin C
pH	4.6–8.0 (average 6.0)	Urine pH (acidic): diabetic ketoacidosis, starvation, uremia, renal acidosis, high-protein or high-fat diet, acidic drugs, intracellular acidosis
		Urine pH (alkaline): metabolic alkalosis, hyperventilation, vomiting, alkali administration, UTI secondary to *Proteus*
Protein	None to slight trace	Proteinuria: glomerulonephritis, nephrotic syndrome, nephrotoxicity from drugs or chemicals, pregnancy/prostatitis
Glucose	None	Glucosuria: diabetes or low renal threshold for glucose reabsorption (if blood glucose within normal limits)
Ketones	Negative	Ketonuria: diabetic ketoacidosis, starvation, prolonged vomiting, toxemia, Gierke's disease, increased fat or decreased carbohydrate diet, fever, thyrotoxicosis
Sediment (RBCs, WBCs, casts, crystals)	None to little (kidney membranes are effective filters)	RBCs: calculi, tumors, hematuria, hemorrhagic cystitis WBCs: infection, pyelonephritis Casts: infection or damage to renal tubules Crystals: calcium oxalate, hypercalcemia
Specific gravity	1.008–1.030	Value increased: fever, acute glomerulonephritis, nephrosis, toxemia, congestive heart failure (CHF), fluid intake
		Value decreased: chronic glomerulonephritis, or pyelonephritis, systemic lupus erythematosus (SLE), parenteral nutrition, fluid intake, hypothermia, diabetes insipidus

*Strasinger SK. Chemical examination of the urine. In: Strasinger SK, ed. *Urinalysis and Body Fluids*. Philadelphia, Pa: FA Davis Co; 1985:54–86.

Appendix S

Sample Nutrition Assessment Form for Long-Term Care

Resident Name _____ Admit Date _____

DOB _____ Age at admit _____yrs. Assessment Date _____

Current Diet Order _____

Diagnoses _____

Medications _____ ETOH use ☐ yes ☐ no

Mental Status _____ Ambulatory ☐ yes ☐ no

Diet History

Obtained from _____

Appetite ☐ Good ☐ Fair ☐ Poor

Intake as percent of food served ☐ 75%–100% ☐ 50%–75% ☐ less than 50%

Check those that apply: ☐ Nausea ☐ Constipation ☐ Diarrhea ☐ Difficulty swallowing

☐ Difficulty chewing ☐ Difficulty self-feeding Explain_____

Allergies/Intolerances _____

Typical Intake:

Breakfast	Lunch	Dinner

Snacks

Adequacy of intake

If Tube Fed: Product _____ Frequency/Feeding Method _____

Total water given _____ ml Protein _____ gms Calories _____ 100% RDA's ☐ yes ☐ no

If no, is resident on a vitamin/mineral supplement ☐ yes ☐ no

Adequacy _____

Anthropometric Data

Height _____ ft. _____ in. Weight _____ lbs Usual weight _____ lbs

% Desirable weight _____ lbs % Usual weight _____ lbs

Other measurements _____

Laboratory Assessment

Date	Albumin	T.Pro	Cholesterol	Bun	Creatinine
_____	_____	_____	_____	_____	_____
	_____	_____	_____	_____	_____
	glucose	Hgb	Hct		

Physical Assessment

Dehydrated ☐ yes ☐ no   *Muscle wasting* ☐ yes ☐ no   *Edema* ☐ yes ☐ no

Pressure ulcers ☐ yes stage _____ ☐ no   *Skin turgor* ☐ good ☐ poor

Evaluation Summary _____

_____

_____

_____

Plan of Action _____

_____

_____

_____

Recommendations

1. Change diet order: ☐ yes ☐ no to: _____

2. Add snack or supplement: ☐ yes ☐ no to: _____

3. Parameters to be obtained: _____

4. Other: _____

Signature _____ Title _____ Date _____

Source: Courtesy of Raymond J, Northwest Pharmaceutical Services, Port Orchard, Washington.

Appendix T

Sample Parenteral Nutrition Formulations for Patients with Renal Failure

Formula	Volume (ml)	Total (kcal/L)	Protein (g/L)	Nonprotein kcal:N_2	% kcal	Possible Indications
1. D_{70}* RF AA	500 250	1640	13.3	744:1	97% CHO 3% PRO	For use in ARF or predialysis: for limited periods (< 7 days)
2. D_{50}* RF AA	500 250	1187	13.3	531:1	96% CHO 4% PRO	For use in ARF or predialysis and glucose intolerance; for limited periods (< 7 days)
3. D_{70}* SAA 8.5% RF AA	500 250 250	1315	31.3	230:1	90% CHO 10% PRO	For use in ARF or predialysis; as BUN stabilizes or begins to decrease, add standard AA
4. D_{50}* SAA 8.5% RF AA	500 250 250	975	31.3	164:1	87% CHO 13% PRO	For use in ARF or predialysis; glucose intolerance; as BUN stabilizes or begins to decrease, add standard AA
5. D_{70}* SAA 8.5% RF AA Fat emulsion 20%	250 250 250 250	1220	31.3	212:1	49% CHO 10% PRO 41% FAT	For use in ARF or predialysis; glucose intolerance; CO_2 retention; as BUN stabilizes or begins to decrease, add standard AA
6. D_{50}* SAA 8.5% RF AA 5.4% Fat emulsion 20%	250 250 250 250	1050	31.3	179:1	40% CHO 12% PRO 48% FAT	For use in ARF or predialysis; glucose intolerance; CO_2 retention; as BUN stabilizes or begins to decrease, add standard AA

Formula	Volume (ml)	Total (kcal/L)	Protein (g/L)	Nonprotein kcal:N$_2$	% kcal	Possible Indications
7. D$_{70}$ SAA 8.5%	500 500	1360	42.5	166:1	87% CHO 13% PRO	Dialysis initiated; fluid restriction
8. D$_{70}$ SAA 10%	500 500	1390	50.0	144:1	85% CHO 14% PRO	Dialysis initiated; fluid restriction; increased protein needs
9. D$_{50}$ SAA 8.5%	500 500	1020	42.5	119:1	83% CHO 17% PRO	Dialysis initiated; no fluid restriction
10. D$_{50}$ SAA 10%	500 500	1050	50.0	103:1	81% CHO 14% PRO	Dialysis initiated; no fluid restriction; increased protein needs
11. D$_{70}$ SAA 8.5% Fat emulsion 20%	250 500 250	1265	42.5	153:1	47% CHO 13% PRO 40% FAT	Dialysis initiated; fluid restriction; glucose intolerance; CO$_2$ retention
12. D$_{70}$ SAA 10% Fat emulsion 20%	250 500 250	1295	50.0	133:1	46% CHO 15% PRO 39% FAT	Dialysis initiated; fluid restriction; glucose intolerance; CO$_2$ retention; increased protein needs
13. D$_{50}$ SAA 8.5% Fat emulsion 20%	250 500 250	1095	42.5	129:1	39% CHO 15% PRO 46% FAT	Dialysis initiated; no fluid restriction; glucose intolerance; CO$_2$ retention
14. D$_{50}$ SAA 10% Fat emulsion 20%	250 500 250	1125	50.0	112:1	38% CHO 18% PRO 44% FAT	Dialysis initiated; no fluid restriction; glucose intolerance; CO$_2$ retention; increased protein needs

Note: D, dextrose; SAA, standard amino acids; RF AA, renal failure amino acids; CHO, carbohydrate; PRO, protein; ARF, acute renal failure; BUN, blood urea nitrogen.

*Alternatively, standard amino acid solutions could be used but may lead to earlier need for dialysis.

Source: LE Matarese, *Nutrition Support Dietetics Core Curriculum*, 2nd ed, © 1993, American Society for Parenteral and Enteral Nutrition.

Appendix U

Selected Laboratory Measures Used in Nutrition Assessment

Test	Biosynthesis Site	Normal Value	Half-life (d)	Function	Increase	Decrease
Blood tests						
Albumin	Hepatocyte	> 3.5 g/100 ml	14–20	Maintains plasma oncotic pressure; transports small molecules (ie, FFA); 40% located in intravascular space and 60% in extravascular space	Dehydration IV albumin administration	Overhydration severe hepatic disease; renal and GI loss; acute catabolic status; inadequate protein intake
Transferrin	Hepatocyte	200–400 mg/100 ml	8–9	Binds Fe^{++} in plasma and transports to bone; approximately a third is bound to Fe; located almost completely in intravascular space; can be estimated from total iron-binding capacity (TIBC)	Dehydration; Fe-deficiency anemia	Severe liver disease; acute catabolic status, overhydration
Prealbumin (thyroxine-binding prealbumin, transthyretin)	Hepatocyte	20–50 mg/100 ml	2–3	Transport protein for thyroxine; forms complex with retinol-binding protein for the transport of vitamin A	Renal failure; dehydration	Acute catabolic states; hyperthyroidism; inadequate protein intake; severe liver disease, overhydration
Retinol-binding protein	Hepatocyte	0.0372 ± 0.0073 g/L	0.5	Transports vitamin A when complexed with prealbumin	Renal disease	Vitamin A deficiency; acute catabolic states; hyperthyroidism; zinc deficiency; severe liver disease

Fibronectin	Synthesized by many cells, especially hepatocytes, endothelial cells, and fibroblasts	Reference ranges not well studied	0.5–1.0	A glycoprotein found in many tissues; important role in cell matrix interactions, cell adhesions, wound healing macrophage function	—	Acute catabolic states; disseminated intravascular coagulation (DIC)
Somatomedin C	Hepatocytes and other tissues	0.55–1.4 g/L	0.1–0.3	Growth-promoting peptides	Hypothyroidism; renal failure; cirrhosis	Protein-energy malnutrition; growth hormone deficiency.
Total lymphocyte count (TLC)*	—	20%–40% total WBC or > 2750 cells per mm^3	—	—	—	Acute catabolic state; infection neoplasia; steroids
Skin test Delayed* cutaneous hypersensitivity (DCH)	—	Healthy persons reexposed to antigens intradermally will have T-cell proliferation and release of mediators causing inflammation at the injection site; skin inflammation is often reduced in malnutrition	—	—	—	Infection, uremia, liver disease, inflammatory bowel disease (IBD), malignant disease, steroids, immunosuppressants, warfarin, cimetidine

continues

Appendix U continued

Urine tests

Test	Purpose	Calculation	Normal Range	Factors Influencing Test
Creatinine height index (CHI)	Reasonable assessment of lean body mass in healthy adults; derived from catabolism of creatinine phosphate, a metabolite found mainly in muscle	See equation in footnote**	Protein depletion: < 40% = severe 40%–50% = moderate 60%–80% = mild	Test requires: • Normal renal function • Normal hydration • Normal urine output (no diuretics) • No prolonged bed rest or strenuous exercise • No recent intake of creatine or creatinine (meat) • No extremes of age (ie, < 2 mo) • No acute catabolic illness • Diet and renal function can significantly alter results • Eliminate exogenous sources (ie, meat) • Any event that increases muscle turnover (ie, sepsis, trauma, starvation) invalidates this test as a predictor of skeletal muscle • Effects of age, sex, nutrition, exercise, hormonal status, and injury on test results have not been quantified
Methyl histidine (an amino acid)	Measure of skeletal protein stores and turnover as it is mainly derived from the breakdown of skeletal muscle proteins (actin and myosin) and is excreted without being further metabolized	24-h urine collection		Incomplete collection (< 24 h) or urine collection > 24 h. It is simple to check and ensure a 24-h urine collection is complete; usual creatinine excretion is 10–25 mg creatinine per kg
Nitrogen balance (NB)	Determine net protein breakdown over a 24-h period	See equation in footnote***	+2 to –2 = balance > +2 = positive < –2 = negative	
Catabolic index (CI)	Estimate degree of stress or catabolism	See equation in footnote****	≤ 0 = no stress 0–5 = moderate stress ≥ 5 = severe stress	

*Low specificity for diagnosing protein-energy malnutrition.

$$**CHI(\%) = \frac{\text{24-h urine creatinine (mg)}}{\text{Normal 24-h urine creatinine excretion for height}} \times 100$$

$$***NB = \frac{\text{Protein intake (g/24h)}}{6.25} - \text{nitrogen output (g/24h)}$$

Where nitrogen output equals: urine urea nitrogen (UUN), insensible losses (4 g), estimate insensible losses at 6g.

study period. If UUN > 30, estimate insensible losses at 6g.

****CI = [UUN (g) + change in BUN (g) – 3] – [0.5 × N intake (g)]

Source: Bistrian BR. A simple technique to estimate severity of stress. *Surg Gynecol Obstet.* 1979;148:675–678.

Appendix V

Subjective Nutritional Global Assessment for Adult Liver Transplant Candidates

Patient name _____ I.D. number _____

Age _____ Diagnosis(es) _____

Duration of disease _____ Referring physician _____

I. **HISTORY**

    A. *Weight*

        Height _____ Current wt. _____ Preillness wt. _____ Ideal wt. _____

        Weight in past 6 months: High _____ Low _____

        Overall change in past 6 months: _____% [(High wt − low wt)/low wt] × 100%

        _____ 1%–5% change _____ 6%–10% change _____ > 10% change

        _____ Weight loss _____ Weight gain _____ Fluctuation

        *Weight change is significant when due to weight loss or ascites/edema

    B. *Appetite*

        1. Dietary intake change—relative to normal

            Appetite in past two weeks

            _____ Good _____ Fair _____ Poor

        2. Early satiety

            _____ None _____ 1–2 weeks _____ > 2 weeks

        3. Taste changes

            _____ None _____ 1–2 weeks _____ > 2 weeks

    C. *Current intake per recall*

        Calories _____ Grams protein _____ Grams sodium _____

        BEE _____ REE _____ Based on weight of _____

        Calorie needs _____ Protein needs _____

    D. *Gastrointestinal symptoms*

        1. Nausea

            _____ None _____ 1–2 weeks _____ > 2 weeks

        2. Vomiting

            _____ None _____ 1 week _____ > 1 week

        3. Diarrhea (loose stools, > 3 per day)

            Number stools day _____ Consistency _____

            _____ None _____ 1 week _____ > 1 week

        4. Constipation

            _____ None _____ 1–2 weeks _____ > 2 weeks

continues

Appendix V continued

> 5. Difficulty chewing
>
>   _____ None   _____ 1–2 weeks   _____ > 2 weeks
>
> 6. Difficulty swallowing
>
>   _____ None   _____ 1–2 weeks   _____ > 2 weeks

E. *Functional capacity*

Occupation _____ # hours still working _____

Increase in fatigue? _____ Type of activities/exercise _____

> No dysfunction _____   Dysfunction _____
>
> _____ weeks
>
> _____ working suboptimally
>
> _____ ambulatory
>
> _____ bedridden

II. PHYSICAL

A. *Status of subcutaneous fat (triceps, chest)*

_____ good stores   _____ fair stores   _____ poor stores

B. *Muscle wasting (quadriceps, deltoids, shoulders)*

_____ none   _____ mild to moderate   _____ severe

C. *Edema and ascites*

_____ none   _____ mild to moderate   _____ severe

III. EXISTING CONDITIONS

A. *Encephalopathy*

_____ none _____ Stage I–II _____ Stage III _____ Stage IV

B. *Other conditions affecting nutritional status*

_____

_____

IV. SUBJECTIVE NUTRITIONAL ASSESSMENT RATING (based on sections I, II, III)

A. _____ *Well nourished*

B. _____ *Moderately (or suspected of being malnourished)*

C. _____ *Severely malnourished*

V. ADDITIONAL INFORMATION

A. *History of Diabetes Mellitus* _____

B. *Vitamin/Mineral supplements* _____

C. *Other dietary supplements* _____

D. *ETOH* _____

E. *Current diet* _____

F. *Compliance to diet based on hx* _____

G. *Food intolerances/allergies* _____

H. *Medications* _____

Source: Courtesy of Baylor University Medical Center, Dallas, Texas.

Appendix W

Summary of Digestive Processes

Source of and Stimulus for Secretion	Enzyme	Method of Activation and Optimal Conditions for Activity	Substrate	End Products or Action
Salivary glands Secrete saliva in reflex response to presence of food in oral cavity	Salivary amylase	Chloride ion necessary; pH 6.6–6.8	Starch Glycogen	Maltose plus 1:6 glucosides (oligosaccharides) plus maltotriose
Lingual glands	Lingual lipase	pH range 2.0–7.5; optimal, 4.0–4.5	Short-chain primary ester link at ω-3	Fatty acids plus 1,2-diacylglycerols
Stomach glands Chief cells and parietal cells secrete gastric juice in response to reflex stimulation and action of gastrin	Pepsin A (fundus) Pepsin B (pylorus)	Pepsinogen converted to active pepsin by HCl; pH 1.0–2.0	Protein	Peptides
	Rennin	Calcium necessary for activity; pH 4.0	Casein of milk	Coagulates milk
Pancreas Presence of acid chyme from stomach activates duodenum to produce (1) secretin, which hormonally stimulates flow of pancreatic juice; (2) cholecystokinin, which stimulates the production of enzymes	Trypsin	Trypsinogen converted to active trypsin by enterokinase of intestine at pH 5.2–6.0, autocatalytic at pH 7.9	Protein Peptides	Polypeptides Dipeptides
	Chymotrypsin	Secreted as chymotrypsinogen and converted to active form by trypsin, pH 8.0	Protein Peptides	Same as trypsin; more coagulating power for milk
	Carboxypeptidase	Secreted as procarboxypeptidase, activated by trypsin	Polypeptides at the free carboxyl end of the chain	Lower peptides; free amino acids
	Pancreatic amylase	pH 7.1	Starch Glycogen	Maltose plus 1:6 glucosides (oligosaccharides) plus maltotriose
	Lipase	Activated by bile salts, phospholipids, colipase; pH 8.0	Primary ester linkages of triacylglycerol	Fatty acids, monoacylglycerols, diacylglycerols, glycerol

continues

Appendix W continued

Source of and Stimulus for Secretion	Enzyme	Method of Activation and Optimal Conditions for Activity	Substrate	End Products or Action
	Ribonuclease Deoxyribonuclease		Ribonucleic acid Deoxyribonucleic acids	Nucleotides Neucleotides
	Cholesteryl ester hydrolase	Activated by bile salts	Cholesteryl esters	Free cholesterol plus fatty acids
	Phospholipase A_2	Secreted as proenzyme, activated by trypsin and Ca^{2+}	Phospholipids	Fatty acids, lysophospholipids
Liver and gallbladder Cholecystokinin, a hormone from the intestinal mucosa—and possibly also gastrin and secretin—stimulates the gallbladder and secretion of bile by the liver	Bile salts and alkali		Fats—also neutralize acid chyme	Fatty acid-bile salt conjugates and finely emulsified neutral fat-bile salt micelles and liposomes
Small intestine Secretions of Brunner's glands of the duodenum and glands of Lieberkühn	Aminopeptidase		Polypeptides at the free amino end of the chain	Lower peptides; free amino acids
	Dipeptidases		Dipeptides	Amino acids
	Sucrase	pH 5.0–7.0	Sucrose	Fructose, glucose
	Maltase	pH 5.8–6.2	Maltose	Glucose
	Lactase	pH 5.4–6.0	Lactose	Glucose, galactose
	Phosphatase	pH 8.6	Organic phosphates	Free phosphate
	Isomaltase or 1:6 glucosidase		1:6 glucosides	Glucose
	Polynucleotidase		Nucleic acid	Nucleotides
	Nucleosidases (nucleoside phosphorylases)		Purine or pyrimidine nucleosides	Purine or pyrimidine bases, pentose phosphate

Source: Reprinted with permission from RK Murray, DK Granner, PA Mayes, VW Rodwell, *Harper's Biochemistry,* 21st ed., pp. 584–585, © 1986 Appleton & Lange.

Appendix X

Urea Kinetic Modeling

Urea kinetic modeling is based on the assumption that the rate of urea generation (GUN) is directly proportional to the protein catabolic rate (PCR).

Abbreviation Key

GUN   Urea generation rate
PCR   Protein catabolic rate
KrUN   Residual urea clearance by kidney (ml/min)
UUN   Urine urea nitrogen (mg/ml)
BUN   Blood urea nitrogen (mg/ml)
Uv   Volume of urine collection (ml)

t   Time interval of urine collection (min)
Vu   Estimated volume of body water in which the urea is distributed (ml)
BUN_1 Postdialysis BUN (mg/ml)
BUN_2 Predialysis BUN (mg/ml)
Vu_1 Urea volume of dry body weight (ml)
Vu_2 Vu_1 + interdialytic weight gain (ml)
$\overline{BUN}$ Mean BUN = $\dfrac{BUN_1 + BUN_2 \ (mg/ml)}{2}$

Equations

1. Stable patient; no dialysis
   Need 12-hour or 24-hour urine collection, BUN, UUN.

   $$KrUN = \frac{UUN}{\overline{BUN}} \times \frac{Uv}{t}$$

   $$GUN = BUN \times KrUN$$

   $$PCR = (GUN + 1.2) \times 9.35$$

2. Catabolic patient; no dialysis
   Need 12- or 24-hour urine collection, BUN before and after urine collection (BUN_2, BUN_1), UUN.

   $$KrUN = \frac{UUN}{\overline{BUN}} \times \frac{Uv}{t}$$

   $$GUN = \frac{(BUN_2 - BUN_1) \times Vu}{\text{time interval between blood samples (min)}} + (KrUN \times \overline{BUN})$$

   $$PCR = (GUN + 1.2) \times 9.35$$

3. Patient on dialysis; no urine output
   Need BUN predialysis and postdialysis.

   $$GUN = \frac{(Vu_2 \times BUN_2) - Vu_1 \times BUN_1)}{\text{time interval between blood samples (min)}}$$

   $$PCR = (GUN + 1.2) \times 9.35$$

4. On dialysis; urine output
   Need total urine volume during dialysis, predialysis, and postdialysis, BUN, UUN.

   $$KrUN = \frac{UUN}{\overline{BUN}} \times \frac{Uv}{t}$$

   $$GUN = \frac{(Vu_2 \times BUN_2) - (Vu_1 \times BUN_1)}{\text{time interval between blood samples (min)}} + (KrUN \times \overline{BUN})$$

   $$PCR = (GUN + 1.2) \times 9.35$$

Source: Reprinted with permission from RL Murray, *Dynamics of Nutrition Support*, © 1986, Appleton-Century-Croft.

Appendix Y

Vitamins in Parenteral Solutions[†]

Vitamin	AMA Guidelines[††]	Jeejeebhoy[†††]
A	3300 IU	2500 IU
D	200 IU	250 IU
E	10 IU	30–50 IU
K	*	10 mg/wk
B₁ (thiamin)	6 mg**	5 mg
B₂ (riboflavin)	3.6 mg	5 mg
Niacin	40 mg	50 mg
Pantothenic acid	15 mg	15 mg
B₆ (pyridoxine)	6 mg**	5 mg
Folic acid	600 µg**	600 µg
B₁₂ (cyanocobalamin)	5 µg	12 µg
C (ascorbic acid)	200 mg**	300–500 mg
Biotin	60 µg	300 µg

[†]AMA Department of Food and Nutrition. Multivitamin preparations for parenteral use: a statement by the Nutrition Advisory Group. *JPEN J Parenter Enteral Nutr.* 1979;3:258–262.

[††]Jeejeebhoy KN. *Total Parenteral Nutrition in the Hospital and Home.* Boca Raton, Fla: CRC Press; 1983.

[†††]Federal Drug Commission. *The Pink Sheet.* August 25, 1985:47T, G7.

*Addition of vitamin K to parenteral solution is under consideration by the AMA.

**1985 revision by AMA recommended increases in these vitamins.

Appendix Z

Trace Elements in Parenteral Solutions†

Trace Element	Stable Adult	AMA Guidelines††	
		Adult in Catabolic State	*Stable Adult with Intestinal Losses*
Zinc	2.5–4 mg	Additional 2 mg	Add 12.2 mg/L of small-bowel fluid lost; 17.1 mg/kg of stool or ileostomy output
Copper*	0.3–0.5 mg	—	—
Chromium	10–20 mg	—	—
Manganese*	0.15–0.8 mg	—	—
Selenium	40–80 mg	—	—

† Levander OA, Burk RF. Report on the 1986 ASPEN research workshop on selenium in clinical nutrition. *JPEN J Parenter Enteral Nutr.* 1986;10:545–549.

††Schlichtig R, Ayres SM. Nutrient requirements of critically ill patients. In: Schlichtig R, Ayres SM, eds. *Nutritional Support of the Critically Ill.* Chicago, Ill: Year Book Medical Publishers, Inc; 1988;66:129–142.

*Excreted via the biliary tract; dose should be modified in states of biliary obstruction.

Index

Page numbers in *italics* denote exhibits and figures; those followed by "t" denote tables.